HELEN TAYLOR has written extensively on women's writing and popular culture, including the first Virago co-authored book on women's studies, *Half the Sky* (1979), a study of Kate Chopin and other American southern writers, *Gender, Race and Region* (LSU Press, 1989), and *Scarlett's Women:* Gone With the Wind *and its Female Fans* (Virago, 1989). She has also published the co-edited *Dixie Debates* (1996) and *Circling Dixie: Contemporary Southern Culture through a Transatlantic Lens* (2001), and is currently writing a book about the transatlantic cultural legacy of prostitution in New Orleans. An active participant in the Daphne du Maurier Festival, Fowey, and on the Board of Bath Festivals, she is currently Professor of English and American Literature, University of Exeter.

THE
DAPHNE
DU MAURIER
COMPANION

Edited by Helen Taylor

virago

VIRAGO

First published in Great Britain in 2007 by Virago Press

Reprinted 2007

A CIP catalogue record for this book
is available from the British Library.

ISBN 978-1-84408-235-3

Papers used by Virago are natural, recyclable products made from wood grown in sustainable forests and certified in accordance with the rules of the Forest Stewardship Council

Typeset in Bembo by Palimpsest Book Production Limited,
Grangemouth, Stirlingshire
Printed and bound in Great Britain by Clays Ltd, St Ives plc
Paper supplied by Hellefoss AS, Norway

Virago Press
An imprint of
Little, Brown Book Group
Brettenham House
Lancaster Place
London WC2E 7EN

A Member of the Hachette Livre Group of Companies

www.virago.co.uk

Contents

Contents

PART 3
Daphne du Maurier's Writing

Novels

Contents

Contents

PART 4
Daphne du Maurier in Adaptation

PART 5
A Rediscovered Short Story

Preface

Sir Christopher Frayling

I first encountered Daphne du Maurier's fiction through film adaptations: first on the big screen, *The Scapegoat*, starring Alec Guinness, then Hitchcock's *Rebecca*, *The Birds* and Nicolas Roeg's *Don't Look Now*, then on television *Jamaica Inn* and *Hungry Hill*. I read the Truffaut/Hitchcock interview book to learn more about the background to *Rebecca* and *The Birds* and discovered that the old rogue considered Daphne du Maurier to be a 'novelette' sort of person who belonged to 'a whole school of feminine literature' and whom he already deemed to be 'old fashioned' and lightweight as early as 1940. On delving deeper, I discovered that literary critics tended on the whole to say similar things. Daphne du Maurier's novels and short stories were filed away under 'romantic fiction' and sometimes 'Gothic fiction', which meant that the author did not begin to qualify for entry into English literature's almost all-male county cricket eleven. Great for train journeys and rainy days by the seaside but that was about it.

I don't know why, maybe because I grew up in a house full of popular fiction, but I have always felt queasy about the critical reflex which tends to patronise a writer just because she/he is popular. It is as if, in the eyes of some parts of academe and the literary establishment, a wide readership automatically confers pulp status. At least that was the orthodoxy then. In the case of Daphne du Maurier, the verdict was particularly unjust – as I discovered when I began seriously to read her books in the

1970s, starting with *Rebecca* (who doesn't?), then most of her other novels, then writings on the Cornish landscape, the biographies and autobiographies. This coincided with my researches into Gothic literature, another genre of fiction that was despised in those days. Since then, there has been an ever increasing critical focus on both categories – 'romantic fiction' and 'Gothic fiction' – what they mean and what they don't mean, as well as deep reappraisals of their most substantial authors. In the United States, the most dramatic reappraisal has been of the work of Mary Shelley. In Britain, of Daphne du Maurier. It has been a spectacular transformation scene.

Criticism of purple prose about crashing waves on the Cornish coast has made way for careful and scholarly readings that stress just how gently subversive she could be – challenging, among other things, her own family legacy 'bequeathed to me by people long since dead', idealised images of the family, conventional sexuality, the point of view of the narrator, the fantasy worlds of childhood, and the clichés of landscape and heritage. Indeed, *Rebecca* no longer seems to be seen as a 'romance' at all. Her work looks increasingly rich and dark. In 1996, after completing my *Nightmare* series for BBC television, I proposed a fifty-minute documentary on Daphne du Maurier, to coincide with the first transmission of the two-part Portman productions/Carlton version of *Rebecca*, starring Faye Dunaway, Charles Dance and Diana Rigg. The programme would explore her changing reputation, and would include her hand-written notes for *The Progress of Julius* (Julius was to be presented as a kind of Citizen Kane before his time), family photographs, and a rare piece of film directed by her son, Christian Browning, of Daphne du Maurier at the age of seventy.

The programme was never commissioned, perhaps because it was not at all what ITV expected. Not a smuggler in sight, and it was absolutely not a travelogue. All the more reason, then, to welcome this timely and exhilarating centenary collection, *The*

Daphne du Maurier Companion, which sensitively examines, from a wide variety of perspectives, the person, her places, her writings, the adaptations of her work, and finishes with a short story that has never been published before. Alfred Hitchcock did concede that the dark, open-ended and uncharacteristic final sequence of *The Birds* owed much to Daphne du Maurier, and that she wasn't, after all, a writer of happy endings. He was right. The story of this remarkable, still underrated writer is far from over.

Sir Christopher Frayling is Rector of the Royal College of Art and Chair of Arts Council England

Introduction

Helen Taylor

Daphne du Maurier's writing deserves a fresh look. She has long enjoyed national and international fame, primarily for her best-selling *Rebecca* (1938), and remains one of Britain's most popular novelists, her books translated into many languages and read all over the world. The renowned film versions of her stories, including Alfred Hitchcock's *Rebecca* (1940) and *The Birds* (1963), and Nicolas Roeg's *Don't Look Now* (1973), have brought her a global reputation, which is continually enhanced by television, radio and theatre adaptations.

However, her status as a household name has sometimes led to patronising commentary, the tag of 'romantic novelist' repeated relentlessly. She deployed – indeed transformed – the romance genre, but the term has been used to diminish her achievement. Aware it was used demeaningly, implying a form of writing for women readers of limited intelligence, she fiercely repudiated it. Without doubt, the extraordinary success of *Rebecca*, mistakenly classified as a 'romance', led to the neglect of her generically varied and thematically wide-ranging body of fiction and non-fiction writing. Happily, in recent decades, distinguished international critics and biographers have paid serious attention to, and offered challenging perspectives on, a complex writer and her work.

While best known for *Rebecca*, du Maurier produced an impressive range of work during a writing life that spanned six decades. Her biographer, Margaret Forster, wrote that at least

three of her novels deserved a place in any literary canon: *Rebecca,
The Scapegoat* (1957) and *The House on the Strand* (1969).[1] While
there is general agreement about the first and last, others admire
different works, including the short stories, demonstrating the
broad scope of her considerable output. Her appeal to readers
lies in her strong narrative drive, superb use of suspense and
horror, a psychologically astute gothic and romantic sensibility,
and the creation of an array of unforgettably luminous and
haunting characters. 'Last night I dreamt I went to Manderley
again' is one of literature's most quoted first lines.

Born in 1907, the granddaughter of George du Maurier,
renowned artist, *Punch* cartoonist and author of three novels
(including the celebrated *Trilby*) and daughter of famous actor-
manager Gerald du Maurier, Daphne seemed destined – and was
urged on strongly by her father – for a brilliant career. Following
the immediate critical and popular success of *The Loving Spirit*
(1931), her first novel published when she was just twenty-three,
she went on to produce a varied body of writing, including
eighteen novels, two plays, two family biographies and an edited
collection of letters by her grandfather, three literary biographies,
an autobiography and a collection of autobiographical essays, an
illustrated study of Cornwall, and dozens of short stories and
articles. As part of a well-known bohemian theatrical London-
based family, the fledgling writer received considerable attention
and found first publication relatively easy. After three novels with
Heinemann, she was contracted by respected publisher and New
Left Books founder, Victor Gollancz, whose editorial and personal
support offered the writer a lifetime's worth of advice and help,
and with whose company the books were successfully published
until after her death. In 1969, she was made a Dame of the
British Empire.

Her family owned a holiday home in Fowey, Cornwall, where
the young Daphne discovered her earliest literary subjects and
began to write novels. It was also in Fowey that she met and

married Major Tommy Browning, with whom she had three children. Although Tommy's Army career involved international travel and a London home, Cornwall was where Daphne settled and took out long leases on two houses, first Menabilly, then Kilmarth, where she died in 1989. It is often suggested that the writer went to live in deepest Cornwall to escape from a contemporary world she dubbed as one of 'meagre mediocrity',[2] immersing herself in wild scenery, seascapes and large houses. To a certain extent she colluded with this, engaging in projects such as *Vanishing Cornwall* and *Enchanted Cornwall*. The narrow perspectives of such a life seem borne out by her autobiography, *Myself When Young* – a personal and intimate account, making only passing reference to events beyond her immediate circle. It is worth remembering, however, that she lived in Britain during an eventful and often traumatic century, including two world wars: in the first, she had to leave London to escape Zeppelin raids, while in the second, her husband was a key figure in the Battle of Arnhem. After the war, Tommy assumed a public role, working for the royal family, and she herself travelled widely in Europe, living for significant periods abroad and in London. Long residence in a small Cornish town, perceived to be peripheral to the nation's heart, did not isolate her from those complex political and social changes, which appear allusively or metaphorically in her writings. Furthermore, her correspondence, especially with publisher Victor Gollancz and writer Oriel Malet, reveals a lively interest in a wide range of matters, an eclectic reading programme, and engagement with matters of the day. Inter alia, there are lively discussions about the death in 1963 of John F. Kennedy, the rise of Cornish Nationalism, Zionism, spirituality and gender politics.[3] And, despite being continually identified as a very 'English' – indeed a specifically 'regional English' – writer, du Maurier had a broadly European sensibility that is manifest in her fiction's many European settings and characters.

As is clear from her name – maintained as nom de plume,

despite the married name, Browning – du Maurier's family tree may be traced back to eighteenth-century Anglo-French alliances. Sent by her parents in 1925 to finishing school in Camposena, near Paris, the eighteen-year-old got to know the city she continued throughout her life to adore – enjoying everything from the cobbled streets and lights of Place de la Concorde to the cultural delights of the Opera, the Louvre and Versailles. Daphne du Maurier was enchanted by the sensual and cosmopolitan atmosphere of the city, and she felt a new affinity with her grandfather, George, and part of a truly European legacy – all of which she mined throughout her writing career. She developed a passion for French writers, such as Guy de Maupassant, whose influence may be felt within her work. In Paris, too, she enjoyed her first 'Venetian' (her term for lesbian) feelings which would recur later; at that time, they were for her sophisticated older teacher, Mlle Fernande Yvon, who became a long-term close friend and guide to the impressionable and restless young woman. As the years went by, she became absorbed in her French roots and made several research trips (also requesting friends and paid researchers to investigate) in order to prepare her fiction and biographies focused on that French history. Apart from her ancestral life story, *The Du Mauriers* (1937), many novels and stories included French settings and characters, while *Mary Anne* (1954) and *The Glass-Blowers* (1963) are fictional accounts of her ancestors' lives, expressions of her passions for that country and her own genealogy.

Tessa, her oldest child, recounts being taken to Paris at the age of sixteen, fêted there by a young American Doubleday editor, who took them to 'the best restaurants, the Ritz Bar, even nightclubs'. She describes being 'enchanted' and claims, '[I] had never seen my mother in such good spirits. She seemed to shed her years and we became girls together.'[4] Du Maurier described her grandfather George's attitude towards his family as 'deep and strong and very French',[5] and joked to her friend Oriel about a special feeling for her son, Kits ('my French blood, I expect'). Indeed, when Kits married in 1964, she was pleased by his growing maturity, commenting that 'all that French family thing will come out in him, when they have children'.[6]

Her grandfather's example, and the artistic milieu of Paris, charmed her. She told Victor Gollancz how much she enjoyed visiting galleries, and imagined herself painting, whenever in London or other European cities. Du Maurier's powers of observation are formidable; her ability to capture the essence of particular places may be seen in more than one creative art form. During the 1950s, she tried her hand at oils, secretly working on canvas while ostensibly writing in her hut in the grounds of Menabilly. She claimed painting as a displacement or therapeutic activity for a disturbed mind: at the time, her husband was drinking heavily and their marriage was troubled, while she was also empathising with the depressions and breakdowns of her biographical subject, painter and writer Branwell Brontë. 'Therapy for schizophrenics!' was how she described painting to her writer friend Oriel Malet, relishing the joy of 'slap[ping] onto canvas what my mind sees, especially the deep, ruddy earth!' and 'getting smothered in oil . . . covering these boards with great smears!' She claimed her paintings 'have a sort of power, like paintings done by madmen. (Perhaps I am!)' but later dismissed them in a television interview as sharing the qualities of American folk artist, beloved of Hallmark cards, Grandma Moses.[7]

In the eight oil paintings that survive from this period, there is evidence of a competent amateur, creating atmosphere through shape and colour (albeit with an unsophisticated use of perspective) – very far from the 'mad' scenario she suggests: one of the glass-blowers' cottages later featuring in her novel of that name, one a French château for *The Scapegoat*, others depicting rural and watery landscapes. Significantly, none of these is a recognisably *English* setting.

By all accounts, Daphne du Maurier was a voracious reader who welcomed recommendations from friends, editors and family. In her autobiography and correspondence, she alluded to Katherine Mansfield as a great favourite; by delightful coincidence, as she discovered in adulthood, the window of her childhood Hampstead home nursery overlooked Mansfield's Acacia Road house bedroom.[8] In 1964, she took the trouble to find the writer's grave in the cemetery at Fontainebleau. Other women writers also feature in her letters. Provocatively, she urged Victor Gollancz to include in an anthology Sappho's famously erotic poem to Aphrodite. Her contemporaries, such as Rosamond Lehmann, Mary Webb and Agatha Christie, feature briefly in correspondence, sometimes suggesting an uneasy rivalry. She did not mingle with these writers, and referred fairly rudely to those who spoke at literary events and who reviewed her books (though she was very encouraging to younger women such as Oriel Malet and Julie Myerson). She followed her own sales and those of others, perhaps seeing women as more direct competition than male writers. In 1965, she confided to Malet that there was 'a new person who has rather taken over from me called Mary Stewart, who sells a lot. I don't now.'[9] When feverishly writing *Hungry Hill* in 1942, she predicted it would be her longest book, 'probably longer than *Gone With the Wind*', and in her last years, with failing memory, she asked Malet, 'Do tell me, did I write *Gone With the Wind*, or was it someone else?'[10]

As many critics have observed, the Brontës were extremely important to du Maurier and, from the first novel, *The Loving Spirit*, with its title and five epigraphs taken from poems by Emily Brontë, she transformed and adapted their work into her own. She was delighted to be invited to write an introduction for the 1954 Macdonalds Classics edition of *Wuthering Heights*, and increasingly felt proprietorial about the Brontë sisters and their brother Branwell. In 1973, repeating her earlier criticism of Brontë biographer Margot Peters, she berated Margaret Drabble's television documentary of the Brontës for its silence about the childhood legendary land of Gondal that constituted their first literary landscape. For du Maurier, this was a magical, secret world of the imagination that spoke powerfully to her own creative impulse; the word 'Gondal' itself became a code for a welcome escape from reality into make-believe and pretence.[11] Its profound influence on her may help explain the many code words and names used by the family: as a girl, du Maurier adopted the persona of a schoolboy, 'Eric Avon', and in adulthood referred to herself variously as 'Bing', 'Tray', 'Track', 'Scroop of Masham', while all the family had nicknames ('Moper' for Tommy, 'Kicky' for George du Maurier, 'Piffy' for her sister Angela). This play on names was also characteristic of her ancestors – not least the master glass-blower, Robert Mathurin Busson, who fled France for England, adding 'du Maurier' to his name to create a fictional aristocratic history. The Brontës' world of make-believe suited Busson's fellow fantasist, his great-great-granddaughter, very well indeed.

Du Maurier has been the subject of several biographical and autobiographical accounts. But it was only when Margaret Forster was commissioned that the writer found her ideal biographer. Forster's previous studies were of long-dead figures (Charles Edward Stuart, William Thackeray and Elizabeth Barrett Browning) and she was seeking a new subject. One day in 1989, idling through her bookshelves, she accidentally knocked down *Rebecca*, a novel she had not read since early teenage. Rereading it with fascination, she wrote to her editor, Carmen Callil, suggesting that, if no one else had done it, she should write the life of Daphne du Maurier. Callil replied by return with a postcard that briefly said no such book existed and it was a brilliant idea. The very day she received the postcard, BBC Radio 4's arts programme, *Kaleidoscope*, and the *Sunday Times* newspaper, rang to ask – since Daphne du Maurier had just died – would she provide obituaries? Daphne's children were impressed by the

Sunday Times obituary, so when Callil talked to agents and executors, they were receptive to the idea. In due course, Callil commissioned the biography. Margaret Forster jokes that her decision to write this biography was finally confirmed when she bought a new red jacket at the London store, Fenwick's, to promote *Daphne du Maurier* during a book tour. On the label listing its price, she found the garment's individual maker's name listed: Rebecca.

Forster has said that writing the biography was 'wildly exciting' – so much so, she has accepted no subsequent biographical commission.[12] Daphne du Maurier's children and editor considerably admire the book, though all share a regret that it focuses on the writer's 'dark' side rather than her 'life-enhancing' lightness, wicked sense of humour and fun. Forster acknowledges this, saying that it was the brooding, secretive elements of the writer that most attracted her, and that she may well have contributed to a more serious and sombre portrait than that of the woman they all knew. However, she shares with scholars the view that a further biography – probably outlining the true nature of du Maurier's relationship with her father, children and (particularly) women friends and employees – will need to be written when du Maurier's early diaries, embargoed until 2029, are released for public scrutiny, and when more letters and other materials are openly available.

Literary and cultural critics are increasingly engaging with Daphne du Maurier's work and its screen versions from new theoretical perspectives, analysing a wide range of her fiction and biography in terms of psychoanalytic, feminist, Gothic and cultural materialist studies. Since the 1980s, critics such as Roger Bromley, Alison Light, Richard Kelly, Avril Horner and Sue Zlosnik, and Nina Auerbach have offered significant insights into du Maurier's recurrent themes of incestuous desire, doppelgänger figures, dynastic and dysfunctional families, polymorphous or multiple sexualities, and fractured notions of appropriate class and gender roles, as well as drawing attention to her literary experimentation with narrative voices and inconclusive endings.[13] These have helped transform a writer pigeon-holed as romantic and parochially regional into a significant literary figure. Nevertheless, it must be remembered that – for many readers – the du Maurier who has brought alive an idyllic pastoral Cornwall through her atmospheric settings and precise descriptions is infinitely precious. One reader, Sue Miller, speaks for others when she relates the experience of reading du Maurier while living abroad: 'I needed to live a fantasy life of wet green hedges and cool stone corridors and read read read about Englishness. I loved *Rebecca* and *The House on the Strand* because they enhanced my fantasy of living in a cool damp climate amongst ghosts from English history.' Several enthusiasts have told me they can 'smell the hedgerows' when reading her work.[14] An enhanced sense of place is one of this writer's great qualities, to which her readers – yearning for the 'otherness' of a Celtic Eden – respond with great enthusiasm.

As you drive down into the Fowey area, a sign greets you: 'Du Maurier Country'. In Fowey, the town she adopted as her own, there is a postcard on sale, 'Daphne du Maurier in Cornwall', depicting a map of the county, annotated with references to the writer's personal associations and works: Pendennis Castle featured in *The King's General*; Frenchman's Creek, where Lady Dona St Columb fell for her French pirate; Bodmin Moor's Jamaica Inn, inspiring the eponymous novel and now a themed inn incorporating a Dame Daphne du Maurier memorial room; Kilmarth, setting for *The House on the Strand*; and of course Menabilly, transmuted into *Rebecca*'s Manderley. This phenomenon is not unique to du Maurier's neck of the woods – there are also 'Shakespeare', 'Catherine Cookson', even '*Pride and Prejudice*' countries/counties, together with themed tea towels and coffee mugs linking particular areas of the nation with writers who lived and set their works there. Literary tourism has a long

history. Tennyson visited Lyme Regis because Jane Austen had
set an incident in *Persuasion* there, and the seaside resort Westward
Ho! was named after Charles Kingsley's 1854 eponymous novel.[15]
Cornwall has had famed literary associations since the early twentieth century, from the *Troytown* tales of Arthur Quiller-Couch
(also based in Fowey) to Winston Graham and the Poldark sagas,
Susan Howatch's *Penmarric* and Rosamunde Pilcher's novels – all
designed to 'provide a text for the glove compartment of the
tourist's car'.[16]

The Daphne du Maurier Festival of Arts and Literature was
established in 1996, and quickly became an established part of
the Fowey tourist calendar. According to Festival Coordinator,
Jonathan Aberdeen, its eponymous name 'opened a lot of doors
for us because everybody knew Daphne du Maurier – everybody recognised the name, so we didn't have to explain what
the Festival was about.'[17] This naming a Festival after a writer
rather than place is increasingly in tune with the branding of
tourist sites; in the early years of this century, for example, neigh-
bouring county Devon's holiday town Torquay participated in
an annual 'Agatha Christie Week'.

Fowey is an exquisite small town built into a steep cliff, and
the majority of events at the Festival take place in marquees
erected on the Fowey Community College cricket pitch. Perched
high above the main streets, exposed to the vagaries of wind,
weather and shrieking rooks, the Festival site seems to chime
perfectly with du Maurier's own anarchic land- and weather-
scapes. The fact that you must sometimes strain to hear a talk
in the town hall because a band starts playing a little too soon
on the quay suggests to Festival-goers that they are an intrusion
(albeit welcome) into a compact Cornish coastal town. Reminders
in local shops and publicity material that London-born Daphne
du Maurier embraced this rather inaccessible part of Cornwall
as her home lure visitors to steep themselves in the du Maurier
'spirit'. Particularly popular during the Festival are guided walks

('*Rebecca* and the du Maurier Coastline', 'Daphne du Maurier's Fowey', 'Castle Dor', etc.). As Jonathan Aberdeen says, 'Daphne du Maurier used to walk the coastal footpath and aficionados love the fact that they can literally follow in her footsteps and see the sights that inspired her. That gives them a great buzz and it's a point of contact. The fans of du Maurier do get a real sense of her being here in this area.'

This Companion is published in the centenary year of Daphne du Maurier's birth. Between 2003 and 2007, Virago reissued almost all of du Maurier's works, commissioning new introductions, mostly by well-known contemporary women writers. It seemed a fitting commemoration to combine these very personal, original introductions into a single volume. They are complemented by new chapters and interviews; the Companion is thus a tribute to a much-loved but often critically underestimated writer, offered by members of her family, her editor at Gollancz, literary critics and established writers from different backgrounds. It focuses on both the most familiar and also lesser-known and neglected novels, stories and biographical writing. Its aim is to demonstrate the scope of her concerns and achievements – hopefully to quell for ever the myth of a humourless, Cornish cliff-walking upper-middle-class recluse who wrote only one good novel.

The Companion closes with a forgotten short story by Daphne du Maurier, discovered by Fowey-based bookseller, Ann Willmore, in the American journal, *Cosmopolitan*. 'And His Letters Grew Colder' is one of du Maurier's earliest publications and contains the elements that were characteristic of the young writer's work, and came to permeate all her fiction: an edgy, cynical tone; grim humour and a shocking conclusion; an account of unreliable and ruthless male desire. It is an example of her youthful stories that are startling for a woman of fairly limited experience – in Margaret Forster's phrase, 'bleak, bitter and sad', revealing a profound disillusionment with male-female relationships.[18] It serves to warn us that this is no writer of idealistic and optimistic romance; from her earliest years, with acute observation and irony, Daphne du Maurier plumbed the depths of human betrayal, exploitation and despair, while at the same time evoking life's unpredictable moments of intense pleasure and desire, often with a wry wit. It also reminds us that, when we curl up to read anything written by this chameleon and versatile writer, we are often in for a disconcerting, subversive, as well as hugely enjoyable, surprise.

Part 1

Daphne du Maurier, by the People Who Knew Her

Daphne du Maurier's Children
Talk About Their Mother

Daphne du Maurier's daughters, Tessa Montgomery and Flavia
Leng, and her son and daughter-in-law, Christian (Kits) and
Olive (Hacker) Browning, in conversation with
Helen Taylor, 2004 and 2006.

On du Maurier's writing:
KITS: My favourite novel is *Julius* and also *The House on
the Strand*. *Julius* seems to be the least well known. I don't
think I read it until I was in my thirties – funnily enough, it
was Tessa's first husband, Peter's, favourite. It's unlike anything
else she wrote – a fascinating story, with an awful lot based
on her father, which I find fascinating. It's a totally ruthless
story and the characters are so different. You don't have this
weak central character, which goes through all her other
books. Her men are always weak, but Julius is utterly ruthless, and has a magnetism and charm. My children love *Rule
Britannia*, which was very much based on our three sons
rushing around the woods at Kilmarth with bows and arrows;
they adored that house and every summer my mother would
watch them playing cricket. I like *The House on the Strand*
because of being in the house [Kilmarth] and seeing how it
all happened. I remember she told us quite a lot about it
before she finished, and going down to the basement and
seeing these awful bottles . . . From my point of view, I think
it would make wonderful television, as would *Julius*.

3

TESSA: I've always liked *Frenchman's Creek* because I remember her writing it at Langley End, Hertfordshire, and she used to come and tell us children how far she'd got – the only time I remember her telling us about a book's progress. I don't like *Julius*, though I think it's quite a clever book, but rather sinister. I like the short stories, but some are rather macabre and frightening.

FLAVIA: I love *Rebecca* and *The Parasites*. I love rereading bits of *Rebecca* – I pick it up and get absolutely enthralled, mainly because of Manderley, which I'm fascinated by. I think Mrs Danvers is absolutely riveting, and both Rebecca and the second Mrs de Winter are based on my mother: the dark side is Rebecca and Mrs de Winter is the timidity and social awkwardness – as when she didn't get up in the morning when the Duke of Edinburgh was staying at Menabilly. She was terrified to go down to breakfast. Also, when she and my father stayed at Sandringham and Balmoral, and my father would go out shooting with all the men, and she wouldn't know when to come down out of her room. She'd tiptoe on to the landing and hover around, then the maid would come along and say, 'Would you like to come down?' It was the same staying with Ellen Doubleday out on Long Island in this wonderful great big house where they used to have about twenty people staying, and she wouldn't know when to come down. Her clothes – it was always her clothes. She'd never have the right things. In agony, she used to be, about what to wear – something grand or smart . . . hence, don't go to anything that's grand or smart.

The most disturbing is *The Progress of Julius*, now known as *Julius*; it's not a nice book. Some readers find it very anti-Semitic, though she wasn't anti-Semitic at all – she was rather pro-Zionist. In the thirties there was an awful lot of anti-Semitism. But it's an unpleasant book with no nice characters. Her men are sometimes rather wishy-washy – complicated and tortured. I think in a funny way she slightly despised men, just slightly, or she picked up very easily on their weak points and found them pathetic. She used to write and say, 'Oh, I do think so-and-so's pathetic,' and it always seemed to be a man she was talking about.

HELEN: The University of Exeter has on loan most of your family papers. When will we be able to read Daphne's early diaries?

KITS: Well, she put a fifty-year embargo on the diaries. I think I'm the only person living who's read them, since my co-executor died. They stop when she gets married, so they're only about her early life up to *The Loving Spirit* or there-abouts. There are some wonderful bits about the difficulty she had actually starting to write, and they are revealing about her relationship with Gerald, her sexuality, lovers and family. There are a lot of mundane things like, 'Had hair wash', and poignant things like, 'Dog's dying'. They'll be of interest to scholars because she talks about the early stages of her writing career, but I don't think there's any big secret that isn't now known about.

Personality:

TESSA: She had a great sense of humour and I think that comes across in her letters to Oriel Malet. In fact, she had a tremendously giggly sense of humour, which the three of us have rather, and my father did too. That comes out a bit from Flavia's biography – what fun she was. She could be very amusing: she'd pick something out and we'd sit there howling with laughter – that's what she and my father had in common. I can see him sitting there shrieking with laughter, tears running down his face.

5

HACKER: Yes, she was always funny, and I have a particular memory of her playing football with her dogs. I also loved being on holiday with her, enjoying her observations of people, giving them code names – this turned into a game that was great at dinner each evening.

Sexuality:

FLAVIA: I think she was rather torn about her sexuality. I mean, this always wanting to be a boy, and her father wanting to have a boy. In *Growing Pains* [now published as *Myself When Young*] she talks about the boy in a box – so I think she was frightfully muddled about her sexuality, sometimes. Actually, she did put it on to me for a bit – never Tessa. She'd say, 'I wish you'd be more boyish. I wish you'd have your hair cut short,' that sort of thing, and then we all used to wear trousers and things like that. She liked anything as a rule she called 'slightly boyish' but she was incredibly feminine-looking herself.

TESSA: Margaret Forster's biography was fine until she discovered about Gertrude Lawrence. I think she'd almost finished the book when all these letters came to the fore [relating to du Maurier's affair with Lawrence and unrequited desire for Ellen Doubleday]. If that hadn't been in it, I'd have really enjoyed her book, but that slightly tainted the whole thing for me because she made such a song and dance about Gertrude. My mother did act a lot herself. There was an awful lot of play-acting in her life; she rather used people and she did get crushes on them.

KITS: The Gertrude Lawrence revelations were a surprise, I think, because we didn't know anything about it and we'd always discussed those sort of things. I mean, I'd certainly discuss somebody who was gay, or what not, because she always used to be amused by people in restaurants. She would say, 'Oh, d'you think those two are . . . ?' Things like that. It was always a sort of banter, whereas nowadays nobody takes any notice, but it certainly was not a hidden thing. I think she would fiercely deny, to this day, if she were sitting here, that she was a 'lesbian'.

I think it goes back to her father – the way he brought up those girls as three sons he wished he'd had, so he could bung cricket balls and play football and make them box. She became besotted and acted out this idea and invented 'Eric Avon', who was this sort of alter ego at school, the captain of cricket and things like that, and she always wanted to wear trousers. Then she was obviously besotted with the French schoolmistress, Ferdy. She had a tremendous crush on Ferdy, and I think Ferdy did on her. Later, I think Daphne became very emotionally involved with Gertrude.

But, you see, there was obviously something there because her sisters were fairly unorthodox in their sexual lives. So I think this is probably why – with me especially, from what I gather through letters and conversations with people – she thought I was going to be gay from the time I left school and was surprised when I wasn't!

Appearance:

HELEN: You talk about your mother's preference for a boyish look but, like most women of her generation, she regularly wore cosmetics, didn't she?

FLAVIA: Oh yes. Before going to something at the Palace with my father she used to have her face done and, after the facial, she was made up beautifully. She looked absolutely stunning.

TESSA: I don't think that Daphne was very bothered about

clothes, although she made a special effort for big occasions and always looked elegant. She had good taste and went to a dressmaker who made her smart outfits. She always wore make-up and lipstick and had her face done in London. When my father died, she wore only black and white for a year.

HACKER: Daphne had a great feel for clothes. I remember she particularly liked shirts by Donald Davis, which were a kind of tweed, and her other great passion was for belts. When coming to visit her, I was always asked to bring her a belt from Dunhill, Hermès and so on.

A daughter's memoir:
HELEN: Flavia, you have written a biography of your mother from the perspective of yourself as a child.
FLAVIA: I wrote my memoir for two years before my mother died and finished it just before her death. I didn't think I wanted to publish it – it was just going to stay in the bottom drawer, in longhand. I was meeting with Margaret Forster so I lent it her to add a bit of information to her biography. She said, 'But you must publish this,' so it was through her and her husband that I was introduced to main-stream publishers. If she hadn't come on the scene, I don't think I'd have published.

When I began to write, suddenly I had this total recall of childhood – I just couldn't stop writing it down. On reflec-tion, I think I might have talked more about my mother's work and conversations we had about her books and her plan-ning, and more about our relationship as I was getting older, in my thirties and forties, not as a child – which was completely different, really.

Her final years:

FLAVIA: Her illness was a terrible shock to all of us –
especially her memory loss, because she became a
completely different person. I think that in the form of
senility she got, all the basic instincts came out that had
gone into her writing hitherto. She lost the power of being
able to write, and one saw the darker side of her, which
was actually rather scary. I've never really decided if that's
how she really thought, about us and everything. She sometimes said cruel things, which she would never have done
years ago when we were children, and I've often wondered
which was the truth . . . was she pretending as a mother?
Because she was never really unkind and – as I said in my
book – I never saw her lose her temper or get cross or irritated at all before her illness. But as the woman with this
rather nasty memory loss, she could be very querulous and
very bitchy, which we'd never seen as young children, ever.
I witnessed it with the nurses – very unkind remarks to
them – but she would never have been unkind about people
when she was younger, when all her faculties were there.
But there was an occasional remark, and I remember
thinking, 'Ah, so that is what you think,' but one must
remember again that it was her illness.

Menabilly:

HELEN: Ever since your mother first discovered Menabilly,
nearly seventeen years before she came to occupy it, she
yearned to live there. Why was she so taken with it?

TESSA: I don't know. Probably because it was empty and
it said something to her imagination. She and Angela
[Daphne's older sister, Angela du Maurier] went there one
day – they'd gone up through the woods. I can remember
when we moved in, and she tried to enthuse us. I well

remember going there for the first time, across the park, and the excitement. We were thinking, 'Ah, well, it's rather large . . . what will it be like?' When my children, aged eight or nine, used to stay there, they were terrified at night. Years later they told me that rather than go down the corridor with the long red carpet to the loo, they would pee on that carpet because they were so frightened. It's amazing how a house can change. When we lived there, it was light and airy – she had very good taste and the main rooms were charming, although the heating (Aladdin paraffin stoves) was pretty minimal. I went there some years later and it seemed very dark and dreary, full of gloomy Rashleigh family portraits.

Film adaptations:
FLAVIA: I think she liked *Rebecca* [Hitchcock, 1940] – it was excellent and Hitchcock did her proud. I can't think of anything that's been done badly on TV or film, actually. *Don't Look Now* [Roeg, 1973] is completely different, the beginning and the sex scene, but the film was very atmospheric. I fainted at the premiere – I've never been so embarrassed. It was long before all the blood at the end – it was when that strange woman got something in her eye in the loo and Julie Christie went in to see her . . . I had to be carried out.
TESSA: She's been done quite a good service by film makers, I think. *Don't Look Now* was very clever. You know, she was taken to see the American version without the sex scene. She wrote books where sex didn't have to come into it – you imagined it – and she used to get frightfully cross at television: 'Always these naked shoulders,' she used to call it. She'd have been *furious* if she'd seen the sex in *Don't Look Now*: 'I never wrote that!'

KITS: I think the original version of *Rebecca* was very good. It's somewhat dated now but I guess will always be the definitive film unless some genius remakes it. *Jamaica Inn* [Hitchcock, 1939] was a great disappointment and my mother hated it – we always thought it should be done like a Western as it's a very violent story and would be great for today's audiences. The same with *The Birds* [Hitchcock, 1963]. With digital effects, it could be horrifying! I thought Nick Roeg's *Don't Look Now* was brilliant and my mother loved it. She wrote to him, wishing he would do another of her macabre stories. Of the recent TV versions, *Rebecca* [Carlton, 1997] and *Frenchman's Creek* [Carlton, 1998] were good, I thought, and got high ratings. I do hope some of the other short stories will be done some time.

HELEN: Kits, your background in film enabled you to develop a working relationship with your mother. How did that come about?

KITS: Well, it all started in 1965 with the Du Maurier Productions film, television and theatre company. She had formed a company initially with Alec Guinness to make *The Scapegoat*, but they then went their separate ways. I was still working in documentary and film, and so we decided – basically for tax reasons to start with – that it would be good if some of the books that hadn't been made into TV versions were put into a company, so we formed Du Maurier Productions. It was just she and myself, and I had quite a lot of film equipment and stuff that had been bought through war savings, so she put the books in that weren't sold and I put the equipment in. That's how we started, with a documentary about W. B. Yeats – it was his centenary in 1965 – which was shown on Irish television and then distributed round the world by CBS.

Then Du Maurier Productions did *Vanishing Cornwall*,

book and film. So I had a professional, working relationship with her, which was wonderful because she came round all the places when I was doing photographs, and also when we were filming at different locations. Now, I had nothing at all to do with the books, and she ran that until she died, though in latter years she didn't really play an active part. I think that's why the books didn't sell very well, since people thought she was dead and I fear Pan, or whoever were publishing the paperbacks, rather lost interest. So it was really after her death and after Margaret Forster's biography that a whole new interest was generated – the books were republished by Arrow and I had to become involved. Now, of course, the books have really taken off with Virago.

One of the things that brings my sisters and myself together is discussions over the estate. With Tessa living in London, she and her husband David attend meetings with publishers there; I concentrate on festival matters down here and run Du Maurier Productions. We get some strange enquiries. Someone wanted permission to write a book about Mrs Danvers emigrating to New Zealand, then having an illegitimate son who grows up there and eventually returns to England to claim he is the son of Max de Winter and wants to rebuild Manderley and turn it into a hotel!

On living at Ferryside, Fowey, which was bought as a holiday home by Daphne's parents:
HACKER: When I first met Aunt Angela at Ferryside, I thought the house had terrific warmth and such good vibes. Perhaps it had something to do with the roaring fire and the wonderful music that Angela played, and, of course, Angela herself – I was very fond of her.
KITS: Daphne's sister, my aunt Angela, was living here and

had been unwell for a long time. She needed proper medical nursing at that stage, so we wanted to move her into a private nursing home – where she lived another ten years, dying just short of her ninety-eighth birthday. Aunt Angela had left the house to the three of us, and Tessa and Flavia didn't want to live here. Hacker had always adored the house and often talked about 'my house across the water', although she never thought we'd come to own it. In the early 1970s, when my mother asked her, 'Could you see yourself in Kilmarth if it was ever available to be sold?', Hacker said, 'No, the only place I ever want is Ferryside.' It took some doing, because at fifty-four or whatever, I didn't see myself cutting off from friends and everything else and coming down. It was a big decision and it was in such an awful state – it was falling into the river – but we thought long and hard and thought we ought to do it, because it's never going to happen again and otherwise it would have to be sold. And at least Angela knew the house was remaining in the family. It's been a positive experience.

FLAVIA: I love this house. I say to Kits and Hacker, 'It still smells of grandmother.' There is a certain scent she had, 'Narcissus Noir', and I can still smell it – it's in the walls, even though they've been painted endless times. I wouldn't want to live here as it's slightly enclosed and depressing, but they've kept it lovely and it's got great atmosphere.

I sometimes think it's strange that she was so famous. Yesterday I walked into the little Du Maurier Festival tourist office in Fowey. I couldn't live with it like Kits does, rammed down one's throat all the time, being, 'Oh, that's Daphne du Maurier's . . .'. That's why, funnily enough, I stopped doing talks for a bit, because I thought, 'I don't want any more of this.'

KITS: Well, you can't afford to mind it, actually. I think you have to say how extremely lucky and privileged you are to be able to live here. If you don't like it, you can hide, and walk away when the boats go past. I don't think tourists expect one to stand on the balcony and wave – and it would be presumptuous to do so! I think if my mother could beam down and see that we were here, she'd be thrilled because when she first came here she adored it. You know, people think she lived here, but she never did – it was her mother's home. But it had special meaning for Daphne since it's where she wrote her first novel, *The Loving Spirit*, as well as *The Progress of Julius*.

Hacker and I had always had an idea of possibly having a literary centre or something down here, but we hadn't gone beyond the idea of 'it might be nice one day', together with informal conversations about commemorative events with the academic, Ella Westland, and writer, Judith Cook. Suddenly we read in the paper that there was to be a Du Maurier Festival in Fowey, and that's the first we heard! Two days later, Restormel Council's Brian Arthur, whose inspiration the Festival was, got in touch and said, 'I'm terribly sorry, it shouldn't have gone into the paper,' and he came and was terribly nice about the whole thing. It was the answer to what we'd been thinking about when we moved here. The Festival has been a great success in bringing people to Fowey who probably hadn't heard of her, and at least now they become interested and tell friends, and books sell far more than they did in the last ten years of her life.

FLAVIA: I think she would have loved the Festival, in a funny sort of way. I don't know what the average Cornishman thinks, but I think it's good. The thing she would have loved – nothing to do with her – is the Eden Project; she always said, 'These china clay pits – something's going to happen one day.' She loved the china clay, the great big deep, dark pits – like something from outer space, she used to think. She would have loved the Lost Gardens of Heligan, all these things resurrecting Cornwall. Except there would have been more people around; she wouldn't have liked that!

On following in their mother's footsteps:

TESSA: I have not inherited any of Daphne's creativity, although I have always been able to write reasonably good English. Regarding any ambitions I might have had, I can't say she was very encouraging, although when I was keen on acting, she came to watch me in the school play and arranged for me to have an interview with the Director of RADA – this came to nothing as I went off the idea. I learned to play the piano at Menabilly, which I much enjoyed, but again she did not try to enthuse me and I always stopped playing when she came into the room. When I learned to cook and became quite good at it, she was pleased; no doubt she thought it a useful accomplishment! Of course, I married very young, only twenty for the first time, and I have often felt that if both my parents had not been going through a bad patch themselves, they would have been much more questioning about my choice of husband, who turned out to be an alcoholic. Sadly, my father had died before I met and subsequently married David [Viscount Montgomery of Alamein], but I always felt he would have been delighted at my choice. My father had served under Monty [Field Marshal Montgomery], who had helped to further his army career. Daphne and Monty had never met, but he was a great admirer of her books and they had corresponded. David, too, was a fan and when they met he bombarded her with questions about them.

FLAVIA: I am influenced by my mother's spirit but I am still

15

frustrated that she was not very supportive of any of our ambitions or ideas. I have given several talks about my mother, mostly to Women's Institutes, etc., taken mostly from my memoir, though latterly I spoke more about my mother's childhood and youth. I gave up recently, though I could have continued since requests from book clubs were unending. I got fed up with the subject matter!

I have artistic talent which she didn't really encourage – though she would like me to have gone to the same Paris school as her grandfather, George du Maurier. I designed two of the original hardback book jackets – *Not After Midnight* and *The House on the Strand*, and I have an unfinished novel which is about twins (all novels seem to be on this theme at the moment). Boys, one an actor, one a priest – that's all I can say, except that the working title is 'Waiting in the Wings'.

HACKER: All our children are talented in their own ways, following in her footsteps – from song writing and writing children's stories to sharing a terrific interest in the arts.

KITS: I think my mother was immensely talented and creative, as were her father and his father before him. Unfortunately, I haven't inherited the du Maurier genius. All I can now do is try to preserve her memory as a famous writer and hope that young people will discover her and be enthralled by her writing, just as previous generations have been. I don't think I've fulfilled my own creative ambitions. Maybe, looking back, I was overcautious and didn't take enough risks. I was very lucky to inherit money from my mother and so was perhaps not as hungry as the next man. I did get bored being an assistant director and wanted to direct, myself, even if it meant doing endless films for industry about forklift trucks and men in white coats holding clipboards. But for me, Hacker and the kids were everything and I loved my home and them. If I'd never married and had the children, who knows, I might have achieved great heights. But I've been very happy and certainly have no regrets.

Vanishing Cornwall

Christian Browning

It was early spring, 1965, and the winds of March blew bitter and black. On Sunday 14th my father died and our family was grief-stricken. Although he had been ill for some time and had been in hospital in London, it was a relief and comfort to my mother that it happened in his own home at their beloved Menabilly.

It was a great pity that my dear father did not live to see the birth of his first Browning grandson, Freddie, who was born in June. Summer was upon us, our sorrow turned to joy and a new life began. My mother, known to us all as Track, was delighted, and the birth of her grandson helped to ease the pain of losing a much-loved husband. Nevertheless, it was her writing that meant more to her than anything and she longed for the inspiration that would lift her from her depression and start her brewing on a new book.

The Swinging Sixties was, of course, the age of new inventions and ideas. In the world of publishing the latest fashion was the coffee-table book. It became a status symbol, the bigger the better. The subject matter was not important as long as the pictures were in glorious colour and the publication looked expensive. It was usually about five pounds (a lot of money then) and, along with the latest Beatles and Rolling Stones albums, adorned the coffee tables of the affluent. Track thought them irritating and suspected that no one actually read them, although she did have quite a few herself, mostly sent by her

American publisher, Doubleday. It was John Sargent, President of Doubleday, who initially suggested a book on her beloved Cornwall.

At first, Track was reluctant. She'd travelled to Venice in the autumn with her sister, Jeanne, and had hoped the trip would spark off an idea for a story. Unfortunately, it would be another few years before that spark ignited into 'Don't Look Now' and so she faced the winter without a project. As a result, John's suggestion began to appeal to her and during the Christmas holidays she decided it might be the answer, so of course we encouraged her. There would have to be a lot of research, something she loved doing, and the book would be fully illustrated with photographs. We had worked together during the previous year on a documentary film to celebrate the centenary of the poet W. B. Yeats. Track had written the script and I directed. It was a wonderful experience and she was very keen to continue the working relationship, so suggested to Doubleday that I should be the photographer. I sent them samples of stills from our Yeats film and they enthusiastically gave us the go-ahead. We were thrilled.

From its first conception, Track had very firm ideas as to how this book would be produced. She loathed the title 'Romantic Cornwall', suggested by Doubleday. She did not want it to be a coffee-table book; the words were all-important and the pictures would complement them. It wouldn't be a tourist guide to encourage visitors. What she was interested in, and what she wanted to write about, was the spirit and history of Cornwall, together with the strange legends, stories and superstitions of the Cornish people. The more she delved into her research, the more fascinated she became by Cornwall's past and how change was taking place, with the old customs and industries disappearing – indeed, vanishing.

In early March, 1966, I drove to Cornwall, cameras at the ready, and so our plan of campaign began. Track had a rough

19

idea of the locations we needed to visit and had made lots of notes from her research. We spent the first few days poring over maps, checking on the best routes and marking the places to be photographed. We divided Cornwall up into regions and prepared a schedule. Although I'd been brought up at Menabilly from the age of three, I'd never seen much of the country apart from the immediate region around Fowey. School holidays were always taken up with cricket and football, trips to the cinema, picnics at the beach and going on the boat, so my knowledge of the rest of Cornwall was very limited. The next three weeks were magical for me. In the evenings we would sit by a roaring fire, Track with her whisky and me with my Worthington beer, and she would brief me about the next day's expedition, the places to be visited, and the various strange characters that had inhabited them. We loved chatting about the day's events, and she would tell me what she was going to write. We would get endless giggles at some of the more eccentric happenings and it was wonderful to see her beautiful blue eyes filled with tears of laughter as opposed to sorrow.

At the end of our shoot, I rushed to London to get all the pictures developed and printed on contact sheets. I would then select what I thought were the best shots, have them blown up and sent to Track. She would agree or disagree and we would usually end up with three prints of each subject. The final decision of what to use was left to the picture editor at Doubleday. By the middle of August, Track finished writing the book. It was to be called 'Vanishing Cornwall'.

John Sargent was delighted, telling us it inspired him to walk every inch of Cornwall – which Track thought hilarious as he was never known to leave his Lincoln Continental! Doubleday published the book in America and sublet the UK rights to Gollancz, who planned to bring it out the following year. This annoyed Track, who couldn't understand the delay – once she had finished a book, she wanted it out and away.

This postponement, however, was a blessing in disguise. After reading the proof copy, I longed to turn the book into a film and, after our collaboration on the W. B. Yeats documentary, we thought it might work. John Sargent came to the rescue once more. Doubleday would put up half the money and we would use the book advance as our share. In February 1966 we filmed for six weeks throughout Cornwall and by the middle of June, a month before the book was due, the film was finished. Track was overjoyed; she saw it at a private showing in the Fowey cinema. Later it was to run at the Curzon cinema in London for six weeks before being shown on BBC2.

Some forty years have passed and now I find myself living in Cornwall. Most of the places we visited in the book remain much as they were. Some of the ruined engine houses of the old tin mines have been restored but they retain their magical beauty. In winter the moors can be as wild as ever, and legends still abound. For those with enquiring minds, who are keen on exploring, and for those who just appreciate the beauty of the landscape, I hope *Vanishing Cornwall* brings as much pleasure as my mother and I had in producing it.

Interview With Sheila Hodges,
Daphne du Maurier's Editor, 1943–1981

HELEN TAYLOR [HT]: How did you come to edit Daphne du Maurier?

SHEILA HODGES [SH]: Quite fortuitously, because this was wartime. After Norman Collins edited *Rebecca* and another novel, he left Gollancz, and the chief reader, J. R. Evans, who edited the next two books, was a conscientious objector. He was called up to do whatever conscientious objectors did, and one day Victor Gollancz gave me this huge manuscript and said, 'Go off and edit it.' I knew nothing at all about editing, so I learned as I went. Anyway, presumably it worked, because I then did all the others.

HT: Norman Collins edited *Rebecca* – did he have to do much editorial work on it?

SH: Norman told me he cut about thirty thousand words from the manuscript – and invented the brilliant first sentence. I doubt the latter as Daphne was extremely good at opening sentences.

HT: Many readers, yourself included, were distressed by *The Progress of Julius*, one of the novels published by Heinemann before Daphne was taken on by Gollancz. It is widely regarded as anti-Semitic.

SH: Victor Gollancz (who was Jewish) didn't read all of Daphne's works by any means. Had he read *Julius*, I don't believe he would ever have taken her on as one of his authors, because he hated the stock picture of rich Jews with fat cigars. However, she was very young when she wrote the book and didn't understand the implications of what she was writing. I believe she was always very sympathetic towards Jews.[1]

HT: Why did she stay with Gollancz all her life (following a short period with Heinemann), even though she was sometimes critical of the way the firm treated her?

SH: She and Victor hit it off in a big way on a personal level. He loved and respected her very much, and if she'd decided to take her books elsewhere, it would have been a big blow personally, as well as the loss of a valuable author. I think she was still quite unsure of herself as a writer when she came to Gollancz with *Gerald*. She was very fond of him, too, regarding him as a kind of father figure. She immensely respected his judgement of her books, but as time went on I think she sometimes found this paternal approach irritating, and I know she was extremely annoyed by his interference in *Mary Anne*. I can't remember why he got involved in the editing of this – he may have been impatient with me about something, because he had this habit of putting you in the doghouse from time to time. I remember being hauled over the coals when he decided I had used the expression 'coup de grâce' incorrectly (in *Mary Anne*)!

Over paperback rights, Curtis Brown – Daphne's literary agent – approached Victor to ask him to release the paperback rights of her novels. Gollancz had always issued their own hardback editions (awful books on cheap paper, with terrible typographical jackets) and Victor regarded them as an important financial asset. So he dug his heels in, about which – very reasonably – Daphne was extremely cross. It really was a bad bit of dog-in-the-mangering on Victor's part. Eventually he had to give way, because on this issue I believe Daphne might have left him. But she was loyal to him and to me. She also didn't like change, and, since she and A. J. Cronin were very important money-spinners on the Gollancz list, Victor

always looked after her very well. She also had an unprece-
dentedly high royalty (twenty-five per cent in early years).

HT: What was it like, editing Daphne's work?

SH: I had total freedom so far as minor issues were concerned.
Daphne wasn't in the slightest bit interested and she knew
she could trust me – even if she did sometimes complain to
others about my chops and changes! There was generally some
cutting that needed to be done – her writing was often quite
tautological – and I always asked her before cutting any passage
that I thought she might cherish. But I was a bit Machiavellian;
I tended to give way on minor details because I knew then
she would be more likely to accept the big changes. As you
know, she never read the edited typescripts that I had retyped
and which then went straight to press from me, via Gollancz.
Luckily for me, she tended to forget what she had written.

HT: Did you go down to visit her in Cornwall?

SH: My husband and I had tea with her once, on the way
home from visiting a Cornish friend. It was Easter bank
holiday, and Tommy Browning was there, too. Daphne was
never interested in food, but as it was Easter she had some
rock-hard hot cross buns that tasted as though they were relics
from the ark. I certainly wish I'd gone down more frequently.
The visit I remember most vividly – and shall never forget
as long as I live – was to Kilmarth after she had written *The
House on the Strand*. The house was elegant and cared for, but
I don't imagine Daphne ever did a spot of housework in her
life. Nor was she much interested in the garden. She'd recently
moved to Kilmarth and had lost some plants running along
the wall in front; they'd all been eaten by slugs. She wanted
some more planted, and I volunteered to put them in. So I
did the planting for her while she filled watering cans. It
suddenly struck me as so funny, that this world-famous author
should be bringing me, a lowly editor, cans of water for her
plants.

Editing Daphne du Maurier

Sheila Hodges

One of the most interesting of the sixteen novels that Daphne du Maurier wrote is *The Parasites*. Published in 1949, when she was forty-two, it is not often mentioned amongst her oeuvre. It was, she said, the only book of hers she ever reread, and even twenty years afterwards it still made her laugh. Dedicated to 'For whom the Caps Fit' (not, significantly, 'For whom the Cap Fits'), it tells the story of three siblings who, one wet Sunday afternoon, discuss their relationships with one another and with their parents. Apart from its qualities as a novel, it is fascinating for the light it throws on Daphne herself, and on the many facets of her very complex personality. In later years she said how much of herself she had put into the portraits of the siblings, and there are striking parallels between episodes in this book and passages both in her biography of her father (*Gerald*, 1934) and in the account of her early life that she wrote over forty years later (*Growing Pains*, 1977).

The most revealing passage in *The Parasites* comes with the admission of the oldest of the three, an actress, that she is always 'being someone else'. 'I'm still acting,' she thinks. 'I'm looking at myself, I'm seeing a person called Maria lying on a sofa . . . but me, the real me, is making faces in the corner.'[1] This was true of Daphne herself: the face she presented to the world was courteous and unruffled (she never lost her temper, and whenever possible avoided confrontation), but behind this calm exterior was a dark, often perturbed mind. She lived on two levels: on the one level was the seemingly serene person, who married, bore three children, walked her beloved West Highland terriers and kept a close eye on the household finances, which she ran firmly and sensibly, at the same time showing great generosity towards her family and friends. On the other level was the woman who wrote nearly thirty highly successful books, and who existed in and through the characters she created. And it was the latter who was much the more real to her. 'Daphne could walk into a bloody lamp-post,' her husband used to say, 'and not notice because she was so wrapped up in her writing.'

As her editor for nearly forty years, from 1943 until 1981, when she published her last book, there was one anomaly about *The Parasites* that particularly intrigued me. When she wrote severally about the three siblings, she referred to them in the third person, but when she wrote of them collectively, she used the pronoun 'we'. Was this unconscious or deliberate? I have no idea, for we never discussed the matter. It seemed to me so ingenious, as emphasising the autobiographical nature of the story, that I felt it would be a pity to suggest any change. Nor do I know whether the critics noticed it – so far as I am aware, not a single reviewer took up the point.

The first book by Daphne that I edited, published in 1943, was *Hungry Hill*. By then she had written six novels, as well as two biographies. *Rebecca*, written five years earlier, had made her name world-famous, but in a way its popularity did her a disservice, for everything she subsequently wrote tended to be measured against it; and the critics, having given it a rapturous welcome, then set themselves – as they tend to do – to write disparagingly of its successors. She became labelled as a romantic novelist, which she certainly was not: the only book of hers which can be put in this category is *Frenchman's Creek* (1941). She herself, quite rightly, greatly disliked being pigeon-holed in this way.

Hungry Hill (which she wrote on an old typewriter), heavily corrected and sometimes quite difficult to decipher, was given to me by Victor Gollancz, her publisher, for whom I was then working. I knew little about editing in those days and was entrusted with one of Gollancz's star authors because it was wartime and her previous editor had been called up. Moreover, this was Gollancz's way; he preferred the devil he knew to the devil he didn't, even if they had few qualifications for the job.

Each of her books was a challenge, and invariably a very fascinating one. The imagination, the narrative power, were there in abundance. But her writing tended to be tautological, and sometimes considerable cutting was necessary. She was touchingly humble and uncertain when she sent in her typescripts, anxious for reassurance that Gollancz liked them, or, after he died, that I did, and worried that the editing would be a nuisance. Over the years we established a warm, trusting relationship; she was always appreciative, and nearly always approving, of the work I did. To other people she might complain, as she did in the case of *Mary Anne* (1954), in the editing of which Gollancz (disastrously) took a hand. This caused her to write, 'Victor did this thing of ringing up and wanting to alter words . . . stupid things . . . who cares . . . it was just like a master teaching grammar on the end of a telephone and showing up one's work to be corrected.'[2] Later she said to me how agonising the succession of phone calls from Gollancz had been, but, typically, at the time she revealed nothing of her feelings.

Over the years our modus vivendi became firmly established in a way that suited us both. Having received the typescript, I would read it and discuss with her any major points that seemed to need attention. I would then go ahead with the editing, ringing her up from time to time to discuss details which didn't 'gel', or cuts that I thought should be made but felt she might not be happy about. After any further modifications the book would be retyped, for it has always seemed to me disconcerting and hurtful to let an author see his or her pages covered with corrections. The pristine script would then go back to her and we would have more – often very long – discussions on the phone if there were alterations she didn't like. Once we had got all the details sorted out, the finished typescript would go straight to the printer, with no intermediary involved. No one could have been more cooperative, or less prima-donna-like, than she was on these occasions. I think she enjoyed our phone conversations – certainly I did, the bonus being that she had a beautiful voice, musical, lilting, which was a pleasure to listen to. There was also a lot of laughter, for she had a lively sense of fun and of the ridiculous.

I know now that there were occasions when she was not happy with my changes, or felt I was 'too factual', but not a breath of this came through; to me she never expressed anything but gratitude for the editing. Only once did she object to my cuts – and with absolute justification. The book in question was her biography of Francis Bacon's brother Anthony, *The Golden Lads* (1975), which had been in her mind for years. She was fascinated by the possible connection between Francis Bacon and Shakespeare, and made several rather cryptic allusions to this in her book about Anthony. Since the references seemed tenuous and lacking in point in the form in which they were included, and since I had no idea how important they were to her, I cut them, which was a big mistake. The result was an extremely polite, but very firm, request that they should be restored:

> My only criticism, and I'm afraid I feel strongly about this, is that you have cut out nearly every reference to my Shakespeare clues, as I call them. And I want them back! The point being – you may not agree, no one may agree or even see them – but I first noticed these things, my clues, *years* ago, when I waded through the life of Francis Bacon by Spedding and checked some of Lady Bacon's

letters, which he had transcribed without a thought of any allusions ... From then on I have been hooked on clue-searching, frail though they may be ... I probably would not have tackled the brothers Bacon at all if I were not *convinced* there is something in the Bacon connection, which, I may say, many people have firmly believed long before I was born! I have been careful throughout *Golden Lads* not to push this, but I do want to keep my slight allusions, which will probably pass most people by, and if it annoys others, I just don't care![3]

Much can be learned from her books about her thoughts and inner life. Some of the most significant of the references concern her father, with whom she had a very close relationship. One passage in *Growing Pains* describes her panic, as a small girl, when he declared his intention of going up on the roof of their London house during an air raid. 'In an agony of fear for him,' she wrote, 'never experienced before or since, I stretched out my arms and cried, "Don't go ... don't go ... don't ever leave me!".'[4] This is repeated almost word for word in a short story called 'A Borderline Case'. 'Don't go, don't ever leave me!'[5] the protagonist cries to the man with whom she has been making love (and significantly, though she doesn't realise it, this man is her father). And again, in slightly different words, in *The Parasites*, when the youngest of the siblings, as a small child, finds that she has been left alone on the beach and believes that her father has deserted her. Terrified, she pants under her breath, 'Pappy ... Pappy ... Truda ... Niall, don't ever leave me. No one must ever leave me' (p.67). Her first book, *The Loving Spirit* (1931), also echoes this theme, when the six-year-old Jennifer screams to her father, who is doomed to die in a storm at sea, 'Daddy – don't go from me, don't go from me.'[6]

These passages raise two interesting points that throw light on another aspect of Daphne – her attitude towards incest and the family. She was fascinated by the phenomenon of incest, which is a recurring thread in her books – not from the sexual aspect, but as a manifestation of the urge that she believed exists in all of us to get back to our families. She was convinced that the family matters more than anything else in life, which perhaps accounts, in some of her early books, for the fact that the stories run through several generations.

Many other examples can be found of the way in which her books reveal aspects of Daphne herself, and of events in her early life which imprinted themselves on her memory, or her subconscious, with such force that they became part of the fabric of her thought. Recollections of bugle sounds first thing in the morning occur in her autobiographical *Growing Pains* as well as in *The Loving Spirit*. On a deeper level, the heroine of *Frenchman's Creek* voices so much of what Daphne herself felt: her longing to be a boy, her love for the Cornish coast and countryside, and above all her abiding passion for freedom. In *The King's General* (1946) the protagonist describes herself as being 'coldly critical as I always am towards the people I love',[7] and this was true of Daphne herself: she loved her family and friends, but she did not spare her criticism of them to other people. Especially telling is a comment in *Mary Anne*, her fictional account of her great-great-grandmother, the mistress of the Duke of York (George III's son), who augmented her allowance from him, which was often not paid, by selling promotions to various position-seekers. Mary Anne, who is the sole supporter of her family, bursts out, 'My God, a woman can be lonely when she's the one to earn the daily bread!'[8] This was Daphne's own position, for her husband earned very little as Comptroller of Princess Elizabeth's household and later as Prince Philip's Treasurer.

In *The House on the Strand* (1969) there is another vignette which shows how thin, sometimes, was the dividing line between fact and fiction. One morning the housekeeper brings the central character his breakfast in bed, and when he apologises for not having got up replies, 'You're on holiday. There's nothing to get up for, is there?'[9] Was Daphne thinking back to her first novel, *The Loving Spirit*, when she was staying in a cottage in Fowey, totally absorbed in writing, heedless of rain, sleet, hail and snow? On one occasion her smiling landlady, bearing a can of hot water, knocked on her bedroom door with the words, 'Why not stay where you are, Miss Daphne? After all, there is nothing for you to get up for, is there?'[10]

How fascinating it would be to know if Daphne realised that she was plagiarising herself, and if she was aware of these links between her real life and the fictitious life that went on so urgently in her mind, and of the way in which events that had imprinted themselves on her subconscious memory emerged years later in her writing.

The change in her reputation over the years has been startling, and if she were alive today she would, I think, be at once pleased and sardonically amused that her work is being studied at universities all over the world, and scrutinised from every literary and psychological angle. Her greatest gift lay in the strength of her imagination. 'She trafficked in dreams,' one of her obituarists said. 'The roots of her success lay in the almost universal appeal of fairy tales.'[11] She herself believed that one reason why she had the power to carry the reader with her was the fact that she so often wrote in the first person; by so doing she was able to identify with her protagonist and bring all the characters vividly alive.

This identification was a trait she shared with her father, who became in turn every character he was acting. But there the similarity ended. He could not free himself from whatever role he was playing; in a happy play he was happy at home, in a sad one he was sad. Daphne, by contrast, somehow managed to keep this identification within bounds, at least outwardly. When she was writing she worked to a strict schedule, for routine (or 'routes', as she called it) was very important to her. But she could spend the morning at her typewriter, come into lunch or take the dogs for their walk, and talk throughout without seeming to be distracted by whatever book she was engaged on.

When she wrote *Growing Pains* I asked her if she could say something about this process of identification. Understandably, she found it difficult to do so:

> The thing is, the process is largely unconscious. I can't say precisely at what given moment I am identifying, or with which character, but of course it is always easier when writing in the first person and when that person can be identified with a house . . . I'm not sure that the older I get the more I don't identify. Certainly I did with *The House on the Strand* and *Scapegoat*, but I simply *don't* know why![12]

Perhaps part of the answer can be found in a letter that she wrote to a friend:

> It is always helpful to trace the 'pegs' in a novel. When I say 'pegs' it is my expression for characters – fictitious – in a tale who now and again become pegs on whom we hang remembrances of real people. And then you project on to those 'pegs' attributes that are imaginary, so that the living person, when encountered, is no longer the character he or she once was, but becomes invested with the fictitious attributes of the story. This can be vexing and sometimes frightening![13]

Generally her fiction was sparked off by some chance experience or someone casually glimpsed: an old woman in a church porch, a man in a French town who resembled someone she knew at home, a letter from a great-great-aunt unexpectedly found at the back of a bureau drawer, the glimpse of a dwarf in Venice. The story would then 'brew', as she put it, for several months, or even years, until she felt ready to write it. Often a holiday abroad would spark off an idea:

> I have just had my 'fortnight in the year'. I felt like a factory worker going off on a spree. I flew to Rome, entirely alone, and then after a night there I had three nights in Assisi, a heavenly place, which I had to myself without any other tourists, and then went on to Florence for the rest of the time, where I had been ten years before and which had started the germ of *Rachel*. It was a lovely break, and bears out my theory that women workers like ourselves do need to get away from home chores and home responsibilities at least once a year. It was really glorious to meditate on St Francis's stigmata for a change![14]

Another expedition provided the inspiration for 'Monte Verità', which appeared in her first collection of short stories, *The Apple Tree* (1952):

> One of the best holidays I've ever had. I had a *heavenly* time. I wasn't sure how I would get on, you know, with a rucksack on my back, and tramping the road, and sleeping at different places each night, but I adored every moment. My companion was an easy-going old Cornish friend who has done an immense amount of walking in out-of-the-way countries, so we lived like two tramps, iron rations of cheese and chocolate mid-day, and a shaving-mug of glacier water to make Nescafé over a camp fire!
>
> The Rhone is quite beautiful, when it is still a mountain torrent, and the strange thing is I found a village up a side valley so much like the valley village in the story, and a great rocky mountain that could have been Monte Verità. I tried to get up it but it defeated me.[15]

There is a fascinating passage in *Growing Pains* that illumin-ates the process through which her books came into being:

> I sat by the open window at Neuilly, and gave my thoughts up to complete negation of active thinking, which is what I subconsciously call working. Some weeks hence the ideas that come into my head without my knowledge today will begin to open and unfold, like the leaves on the tree here that have begun too early. Creation is the same in every way.[16]

She was a very careful craftsman, and took immense pains not to let the suspense sag. This can be seen in her opening sentences, which plunge the reader headlong into the narrative: 'It was Charles who called us parasites'; 'On December the third the wind changed overnight and it was winter'; 'His first instinct was to stretch out his arms to the sky'; 'I left the car by the side of the cathedral, and then walked down the steps into the Place des Jacobins'; 'Years later, when she had gone and was no longer part of their lives, the thing they remembered about her was her smile'; 'They told me afterwards they had found nothing. No trace of anyone, living or dead'; 'The first thing I noticed was the clarity of the air, and then the sharp green colour of the land'.[17] The most famous, of course, is the beginning of *Rebecca* – 'Last night I dreamt I went to Manderley again' – surely one of the best-known first sentences in English fiction.

It was also important to her that each chapter should end on as tantalising a note as possible, so that the reader would be compelled to carry on with the next one. She is not sufficiently credited with the skill and thought that went into this aspect of her writing, and this she found frustrating. When *Mary Anne* was published she wrote to Gollancz that she had spent two morn-ings on the last line (which reads '. . . and watching a million starlings span the sky'), 'and then people think I "dash off" my novels!'[18]

Nor is she often given credit for the many beautiful descriptions of nature, especially in the early books. She loved the countryside and going for long walks with the dogs who were such an important part of the household – her 'boys', as she called them – and was extremely observant of the seasonal changes and of the countryside creatures. 'Conversing with beast and bird is my way of giving thanks,' she wrote in *The Rebecca Notebook*. 'And if anything deepens belief in a Creator, it is by watching wildlife in the countryside, a constant miracle, and noting the changes in their routine through the four seasons . . . They all obey natural law, which is surely God's law.'[19] So she writes vividly and nostalgically of the landscape in winter or in the last days of summer, of oystercatchers, starlings, curlews, wheeling and soaring above the sodden fields, and, as a teenager imprisoned in London, of her longing for primroses and violets, bluebells, wood pigeons and robins. 'Why doesn't someone write an ode to a blackbird?'[20] Here is the central character of *The King's General*, reflecting on the countryside she knows so well (which was Daphne's own countryside):

I have seen the white sea-mists of early summer turn the hill to fantasy, so that it becomes, in a single second, a ghost land of enchantment, with no sound coming but the wash of breakers on the hidden beach, where, at high noon, the children gather cowrie shells. Dark moods too of bleak November, when the rain sweeps in a curtain from the south-west. But, quietest of all, the evenings of late summer, when the sun has set, and the moon has not yet risen, but the dew is heavy in the long grass. The sea is very white and still, without a breath upon it, and only a single thread of wash upon the covered Cannis rock. The jackdaws fly homeward to their nests in the warren. The sheep crop the short turf before they rub together beneath the stone wall by the winnowing place. Dusk comes slowly to the Gribben hill, the woods turn black, and suddenly, with stealthy pad, a fox creeps from the trees in the thistle park, and stands watching me, his ears pricked . . . Then his brush twitches and he is gone.[21]

As her writer friend A. L. Rowse observed, she had a 'remarkably varied body of work'.[22] In addition to her novels she wrote five biographies, a travel book, four volumes of short stories, an autobiography, two plays, and a number of articles. She also completed a novel, *Castle Dor*, which Sir Arthur Quiller-Couch had begun but not finished before his death. (I was not involved in the editing of this, since it was not published by Gollancz. In the copy, which she sent me, she wrote, 'Spot the "take-over" – towards the end of a chapter, but which??' When I got it wrong she wrote 'Hurrah!' on a postcard.)

She started off by writing short stories, and did so at intervals throughout her life, for she enjoyed the genre and the challenge it presented. Many of these stories are very dark, macabre, even sadistic, with little of the charm of her full-length books, and some of her habitual readers dislike them intensely. But she never worried about such things, declaring that she liked to shock. She was incapable of 'writing to order': she wrote what her guiding spirit compelled her to, and nothing would persuade her to write about something that did not interest her simply for the sake of the money. It is totally untrue, as some critics maintained, that she wrote with one eye on the commercial market, though naturally it was important to her, as the family wage-earner, that the books should be profitable.

Early in her writing career she sent a copy of her third book, *The Progress of Julius* (1933), to a friend, Leo Walmsley, a novelist and marine biologist who lived close by and whose opinion she valued. He was horrified by the book, and told her so. Daphne replied, 'Yes, of course it's overwritten, but then in a sense that was deliberately done. I wanted to ooze blood and diarrhoea all over it . . . Yes, I suppose romantic stuff is happier to write and to read, but perhaps it's the old French blood (!) that makes me always want to dig under the surface to find the creepy crawly slugs, and cut out the sentiment!'[23]

Some of the short stories she described as being symbolic of situations in her own life. As she pointed out, each of them 'requires its own mood, and in a way they are trickier than going flat out on a novel'.[24] They are extremely varied in situation and treatment, and it is remarkable how her style changes to fit the subject matter. Like her novels, many are written in the first person, and no doubt it was the compulsion to identify with her characters that gave her a chameleon-like skill in adapting her style to suit their way of thinking and talking, and in endowing the tales with such an authentic ring.

The stories, like the rest of her fiction, were often based on some scene, person or episode that had struck her imagination and had been stored at the back of her mind until she was ready to write it down. 'The Blue Lenses', which was published in 1959 in the collection called *The Breaking Point*, goes back in origin to 1933, when she told Leo Walmsley that she wanted to write about an imaginary nursing home, describing all the odd characters who might be met in such a place. Here, twenty-six years later, they all are. *The Breaking Point* was written at a time of crisis in her own life, and each of these stories reflects her inner turmoil. 'In a sense,' she wrote to her friend Foy Quiller-Couch, 'they are all a protest at the cruelty and misunderstanding which abound in the world – beneath the surface lurk evils we do not understand, things in ourselves.'[25] It was by writing about the things that disturbed, or even tormented, her that Daphne sought to exorcise them.

The amount of editing that was necessary varied from book to book, but there were three occasions when Daphne's imagination rushed her forward to the detriment of the plot. The first occurred in *My Cousin Rachel* (1951). The heroine dies when she falls from a weak plank that has been placed across a sunken garden. What made it difficult to suspend disbelief was the extreme implausibility that such a minor fall would prove fatal, and that a weak plank would have been used in the first place. Despite much discussion, we never did find a watertight solution to this one; the only remedy seemed to be to make the garden deeper, which we did.

The second, with some rewording, was easier to resolve. One of her short stories, 'The Breakthrough', concerns a scientist who is trying to develop a machine that, he hopes, will make it possible to trap the energy released by people when they die. Daphne was always fascinated by questions of life and death; she believed in an afterlife, and, although she did not pretend to have any idea what it consisted of, she often posed the question. The scientist in her story believed that, if somehow he succeeded in his experiment, he would be able to find 'the answer at last to the intolerable futility of death'.[26] Her narrative powers were great enough to carry her – very skilfully – through the complicated and improbable plot until the denouement, which passed the limit of what even she could make believable, for it gave the wild impression that the dying man on whom the experiment was being performed exhaled his last breath, his spirit, into some sort of bag, which was then conveyed to the machine. This was a teaser, but it got sorted out in the end, with a little help from a friend who suggested an alternative way of capturing the released energy.

The third occurred in her penultimate novel, which is also one of her best – *The House on the Strand*.[27] This is very close to my heart, because it led to an extraordinary experience, and gave me the closest understanding of Daphne's exceptional imaginative powers that I was ever lucky enough to have. It was written when she had to leave Menabilly (the Manderley of *Rebecca*), where she had lived for twenty-five years, and which she had loved for even longer. She moved a short distance away to Kilmarth, the dower house, which had fourteenth-century foundations. The previous tenants had been a professor and his wife, who were interested in alchemy. They had stored in the cellar rows of bottles containing the embryos of animals, of a two-headed calf, and of such-like curiosities.

Set in and about the house itself, the plot revolves round a scientist who persuades a rather naive friend to stay there on his own and try out a drug that the scientist has developed. Dick, the friend, has no idea what effect the drug will have, but discovers that it catapults him back to the fourteenth century in a series of 'trips', during which he becomes more and more involved in the life of the original occupants of Kylmerth, as the house was then called. The story was particularly fascinating for Daphne. As A. L. Rowse remarks, she had 'an acute sense of time . . . Time Present leading to Time Future and back into Time Past.[28] Could it be 'all-dimensional' – Dick asked himself – 'yesterday, today, tomorrow running concurrently in ceaseless repetition?'[29]. And, later in the book, 'There [is] no past, no present, no future. Everything living is part of the whole. We are all bound, one to the other, through time and eternity . . . This would be the ultimate meaning of the experiment, surely, that by moving about in time death was destroyed.'[30]

So far so good, but the trouble was that in describing Dick's journeys between past and present Daphne used phraseology which made it sound as if a series of snapshots had been taken in the fourteenth century and developed in the twentieth. This caused me a couple of sleepless nights, but a physicist friend cleverly amended the wording so that it became a question of time running backwards and forwards. Daphne was extremely pleased with his suggestions. 'Let us incorporate them without question,' she wrote. 'After all, my own sentences were fairly difficult to follow for the ordinary reader, and his are not exactly more difficult, but give such an authentic ring. What flatters me is that he has not really changed the basic sense of what I meant to say, but it is now in the proper jargon.'[31]

This book has for me a very special insight into the way in which Daphne lived in and through her characters. The topographical details were confusing to anyone who did not know that part of the world, and it was arranged that I would spend a few days with her so that we could sort them out. Each morning the two of us – Daphne dressed, as usual, in her elegant but well-worn trousers and sweater, a stout walking stick in her hand – would tramp every inch of the terrain that Dick, under the influence of the drug, had covered six centuries before. It was a fascinating and revelatory experience, and one which I shall never forget. Daphne *became* Dick; I ceased to exist for her. Through her eyes I saw a fourteenth-century otter hunt in a spinney at the foot of a hill (the memory is with me to this day), and together we scrambled across the railway line just as Dick had done in his journeys between the past and the present, when, lost in the fourteenth century, he all but plunged beneath the wheels of a twentieth-century train.

So powerful is the atmosphere, so compelling the writing of this book, that it can be quite disturbing, as the reader is drawn more and more deeply into Dick's haunted and perplexed world. The final paragraph, which is typical of the enigmatic ending of several of Daphne's novels, is masterly.

Daphne rarely read her reviews, as she found the patronising dismissal with which the critics tended to consign her books to the dustbin of romantic fiction irritating and depressing. 'I *crave* a notice,' she wrote when *Mary Anne* was published, 'that says "Miss du Maurier has succeeded in writing a dull, heavy book all about a forgotten investigation in the House of Commons"; it might then attract the attention of a new class of reader.'[32] By the time *The House on the Strand* came out, critical opinion of her work had begun to change (one is tempted to say that it had become 'respectable' to praise her), and the reviewers recognised what a brilliant book it was. I sent her some of the reviews, and she commented:

> The only one that irritated me was the *Sunday Times*, and the critic who said something about 'Palm Court genre of writing', or whatever it was. Well, maybe with *Frenchman's Creek*, but you could not say that about the *Strand*, or indeed any of the later books, from *Scapegoat* onwards! So it just proves they don't read the books, or even glance at them to check, but assume that an author continues through the years in exactly the same vein as when they first became at all successful![33]

She was sometimes frustrated, too, because readers did not grasp the underlying symbolism of her novels and the extent to which they expressed her philosophy of life. Of *The Scapegoat* (1957), for instance, she wrote that she had wanted to show, 'How close hunger is to greed, how difficult to tell the difference, how hard not to be confused, how close one's better nature to one's worst, and finally, how the self must be stripped of everything, and give up everything, before it can understand love.'[34] My own feeling about *The Scapegoat* is that it is about compassion – the compassion that the protagonist feels for the dysfunctional family into which he has been catapulted. Daphne herself, who recognised and loved goodness in people, later came to believe that compassion is the one quality worth praising, and cruelty the only sin.

Between 1972 (when she published her last novel, *Rule Britannia*) and 1978 she wrote three non-fiction books – the biographies of Francis and Anthony Bacon and *Growing Pains*. Two volumes of short stories and articles were also published, but they contained no new material. She realised that she was coming to the end of her working days, and the prospect made her desperately unhappy. All the more so since she was not well, and could no longer embark on the journeys abroad which had so often provided the inspiration for her books. Typically, she never whinged about her declining health, but bore it with the courage that had characterised the rest of her life. Writing had been everything to her, even after she had married and had children. 'I wish I could report I am working,' she wrote, 'but I just peg away slowly at the research on the poet John Harington, hoping something will emerge to inspire me, but though I am interested in him as a person the material on his life is very scanty.'[35] So nothing came of the project, and though she lived for another eleven years they were completely fallow so far as any new writing was concerned.

A close friend of Daphne's told me that she had become a writer because she never liked herself, and as a writer she could lose herself in her characters. But that, of course, is only part of the story. Since the world in which she passed her outward, seemingly uneventful, life was far less real to her than her inner one, crowded with the tumultuous creatures of her imagination, she had to find release from inner tension by making them come alive through her books. If she had been unable to do so, life would have been intolerable to her. But it was by no means a case of 'tossing them off': they involved much thought, research and attention to detail. She was an avid reader all her life, interested in an eclectic range of subjects, including philosophy and psychology, and was fascinated by ethics and what makes people tick. So her novels and short stories tend to reflect different aspects of human behaviour, and of the moral problems that interested her.

They also, I believe, to a greater extent than is generally realised, reflect Daphne's inner dialogues about her own life. Since she spent a large part of her days alone, within the space and solitude that were essential to her, she had much time for reading and reflection. In the context within which we worked together, these matters did not arise: it was only to one or two of her most intimate friends that she revealed the dichotomy between her personal life and her life as an author. To me she was a writer to whom I felt very close because of our professional relationship – as I believe she felt close to me – and whom I deeply respected and admired, for her craftsmanship, for her extraordinarily powerful imagination, and for her patience and willingness in coping with my endless questions and suggestions. Much as I enjoyed working with her during her lifetime, it is only since her death that I have realised what a privilege it was to be allowed to do so.

Part 2

The Lasting Reputation and Cultural Legacy of *Rebecca*

Rebecca

Sally Beauman

Rebecca, first published in 1938, was Daphne du Maurier's fifth novel. It was to become the most famous of her many books; over sixty years later, it continues to haunt, fascinate and perplex a new generation of readers. Yet its enduring popularity has not been matched by critical acclaim: *Rebecca*, from the time of first publication, has been woefully and wilfully underestimated. It has been dismissed as a Gothic romance, as 'women's fiction' – with such prejudicial terms, of course, giving clues as to why the novel has been so unthinkingly misinterpreted. Re-examination of this strange, angry and prescient novel is long overdue. A re-appraisal of it should begin, perhaps, with the circumstances under which it was written.

Du Maurier began planning it at a difficult point in her life: only a few years had passed since the death of her adored but dominating father, the actor-manager Gerald du Maurier. She was pregnant with her second child when at the planning stage of the book, and, by the time she actually began writing, at the age of thirty, she was in Egypt, where her husband, Frederick Browning, an officer in the Grenadier Guards, had been posted with his battalion. What many would regard as the quintessential Cornish novel was therefore begun, and much of it written, not in Cornwall, not even in England, but in the fierce heat of an Egyptian summer, in a city du Maurier came to loathe: Alexandria.

Du Maurier was desperately homesick; her longing for her

home by the sea in Cornwall was, she wrote, 'like a pain under the heart continually'. She was also unhappy: this was the first time she had ever accompanied her husband on a posting, and she hated the role forced upon her in Egypt by her marriage.

Shy, and socially reclusive, she detested the small talk and the endless receptions she was expected to attend and give, in her capacity of commanding officer's wife. This homesickness and her resentment of wifely duties, together with a guilty sense of her own ineptitude when performing them, were to surface in *Rebecca*: they cluster around the two female antagonists of the novel, the living and obedient second wife, Mrs de Winter, and the dead, rebellious and indestructible first wife, Rebecca. Both women reflect aspects of du Maurier's own complex personality: she divided herself between them, and the splitting, doubling and mirroring devices she uses throughout the text destabilise it but give it resonance. With *Rebecca* we enter a world of dreams and daydreams, but they always threaten to tip over into nightmare.

At first, du Maurier struggled with her material. The novel had a false start, which she described as a 'literary miscarriage' – a revealing metaphor, given the centrality of pregnancy and childbirth to the plot and themes of *Rebecca*, and given the fact that du Maurier's second child, another daughter – she had hoped for a son – was born during the time she worked on it. She tore up the initial (fifteen-thousand-word-long) attempt at the book, the first time she had ever done this, and an indication, perhaps, of the difficulties she sensed in this material. She began again while still in Egypt, and finally completed it on her return to England.

She sent it off to her publisher, Victor Gollancz, in April 1938. He knew little about the novel at that stage: du Maurier had briefly described it to him as 'a sinister tale about a woman who marries a widower . . . Psychological and rather macabre'. Gollancz must have been somewhat nervous as he awaited that manuscript. Du Maurier's previous novel, *Jamaica Inn*, had sold more copies than any of her previous books, bringing her to the brink of bestsellerdom; but she was an unpredictable author, and difficult to categorise. Two of her earlier novels, *I'll Never Be Young Again* and *The Progress of Julius*, had sold much less well, and the sexual frankness of both books – especially the latter, which dealt with father-daughter incest – had been met with distaste from critics.

Gollancz's reaction to *Rebecca* was relief, and jubilation. A 'rollicking success' was forecast by him, by his senior editor, and by everyone to whom advance copies were sent. Prior to publication, du Maurier's was the lone dissenting voice in this chorus of approbation. She feared her novel was 'too gloomy' to be popular, and she believed the ending was 'too grim' to appeal to readers. Gollancz ignored such pessimism: *Rebecca* was touted to booksellers as an 'exquisite love story' with a 'brilliantly created atmosphere of suspense'. It was promoted and sold, in short, as a gothic romance.

On publication, some critics acknowledged the book's haunting power and its vice-like narrative grip, but – perhaps misled by the book's presentation, or prejudiced by the gender of the author – they delved no deeper. Most reviews dismissed the novel with that belittling diminutive only ever used for novels by women: it was just a 'novelette'. Readers ignored them: *Rebecca* became an immediate and overwhelming commercial success.

The novel went through twenty-eight printings in four years in Britain alone. It became a bestseller in America, and it sold in vast numbers throughout Europe. It continues to sell well to this day: in the sixty-four years since first publication, it has never been out of print. Its readership was swelled by the Oscar-winning success of Hitchcock's memorable expressionistic film version, and has been increased since by countless theatre, radio and television dramatisations. Like Margaret Mitchell's *Gone With the Wind* (1936, and another novel that concerns women and property), *Rebecca* has made a transition rare in popular fiction: it has passed from bestseller, to cult novel, to cultural classic status. Why is that? What is it about this novel that has *always* spoken to readers, if not to critics?

Rebecca is the story of two women, one man, and a house. Of the four, as Hitchcock once observed, the house, Manderley, is the dominant presence. Although never precisely located (the word 'Cornwall' is never actually used in the novel), its minutely detailed setting is clearly that of an actual house, Menabilly. Du Maurier discovered Menabilly, on its isolated headland near Fowey, as a young woman, when she first went to live in Cornwall; she wrote a magical account of the first time she saw it. Eventually, after the war, and after *Rebecca*, she was able to lease the house. She lived there for over twenty years, using it as the location for several other novels; it lit her imagination, and obsessed her, for much of her life. Du Maurier's own term for Menabilly was the 'House of Secrets', and when she placed it at the heart of *Rebecca*, she created an elliptical, shifting, and deeply secretive book. The plot hinges upon secrets; the novel's milieu is that of an era and social class that, in the name of good manners, rarely allowed the truth to be expressed; and suppression coupled with a fearful secretiveness are its female narrator's most marked characteristics.

By the time du Maurier wrote *Rebecca*, she had mastered the techniques of popular fiction. Her novel came well disguised as bestseller material: an intriguing story of love and murder – a 'page-turner' in modern parlance. But examine the subtext of *Rebecca* and you find a perturbing, darker construct, part Grimm's fairytale, part Freudian family romance. You also find a very interesting literary mirroring, of course, an early example of intertextuality – and that is rare in a 'popular' novel, certainly one this early. *Rebecca* reflects *Jane Eyre*, but the reflection is imperfect, and deliberately so, forcing us to re-examine our assumptions about both novels, and in particular, their treatment of insanity and women.

None of these aspects of *Rebecca* was noticed by critics at the time of publication – and few have paused to examine them since. Instead, Charlotte Brontë's gifts were used as a stick with which to beat an impious, hubristic du Maurier over the head: she was Brontë's inferior, how could she dare to annex a classic novel? The critics moved swiftly on, not pausing for thought, and shunted du Maurier into the category of 'romance' writer – a category she detested and resented, but from which she was never able to escape. Thus was du Maurier 'named' as a writer. The question of how we name and identify – and the ironies and inexactitudes inherent in that process – is, of course, of central importance in *Rebecca*. Both female characters – one dead, one alive – derive their surname, as they do their status, from their husband. The first wife, Rebecca, is vivid and vengeful and, though dead, indestructible: her name lives on in the book's title. The second wife, the drab shadowy creature who narrates this story, remains nameless. We learn that she has a 'lovely and unusual' name, and that it was her father who gave it her. The only other identity she has, was also bestowed by a man – she is a *wife*, she is Mrs de Winter.

That a narrator perceived as a heroine should be *nameless* was a source of continuing fascination to du Maurier's readers. It also fascinated other writers – Agatha Christie corresponded with du Maurier on the subject – and throughout her life, du Maurier was plagued with letters seeking an explanation. Her stock reply was that she found the device technically interesting. The question is not a trivial one, for it takes us straight to the core of *Rebecca* – and that may well be the reason why du Maurier, a secretive woman and a secretive artist, avoided answering it.

The unnamed narrator of *Rebecca* begins her story with a dream, with a first sentence that has become famous: *Last night I dreamt*

Sally Beauman

I went to Manderley again. Almost all the brief first chapter is devoted to that dream, describing her progress up the long winding drive, by moonlight, to Manderley itself. The imagery, of entwined trees and encroaching undergrowth that have 'mated', is sexual; the style is slightly scented and overwritten, that of a schoolgirl, trying to speak poetically, and struggling to impress. Moving forward, with a sense of anticipation and revulsion, the dream narrator first sees Manderley as intact; then, coming closer, she realises her mistake: she is looking at a ruin, at the shell of a once-great house. With this realisation – one of key importance to the novel – the dreamer wakes. She confirms that Manderley has indeed been destroyed, and that the dream was a true one. ('Dreaming true' was a term invented by du Maurier's grandfather, George du Maurier, author of *Trilby*; it was a concept that fascinated her all her life. Daphne was aware of Freud and Jung: George was not.)

Du Maurier's narrator can now begin to tell her story – and she does so in cyclic way; she begins at the end, with herself and her husband Maxim de Winter living in exile in Europe, for reasons that as yet are unclear. Their activities, as they move from hotel to hotel, sound like those of two elderly ex-pats. They follow the cricket, take afternoon tea; the wife selects dull newspaper articles to read to her husband, since – again for reasons unexplained – both find dullness reassuring and safe. The narrator describes a routine of stifling monotony, but does so in terms that are relentlessly optimistic and trite. This may be a marriage but it is one carefully devoid of passion, and apparently without sex.

It therefore comes as a considerable shock to the reader to discover, as the story loops back to this couple's first meeting, that this narrator is *young*. The lapse of time between this present and the past she will now describe is unspecified, but it is clearly only a few years. This makes de Winter a man of about fifty, and his childless friendless wife around twenty-five. Their life in

52

Europe is never mentioned again, but *this* is the 'grim ending' to which du Maurier referred. It is easy to forget, as the drama unfolds, that the aftermath for the de Winters will be exile, ennui, and putting a brave face on a living death.

The plot of *Rebecca* thereafter will be familiar: it has echoes of *Cinderella* and *Bluebeard* as well as *Jane Eyre*. The narrator, working as a paid companion to a monstrous and tyrannical American, and staying with her in a palatial hotel in Monte Carlo, meets Maxim de Winter, a widower twice her age, who is the owner of a legendary house, Manderley. She marries him after a few weeks' acquaintanceship, returns with him to Manderley, and there becomes obsessed with Rebecca, his first wife. Patching together a portrait of Rebecca in her mind, she creates a chimera – and an icon of womanhood. Rebecca, she comes to believe, was everything she herself is not: she was a perfect hostess, a perfect sexual partner, a perfect chatelaine and a perfect wife. This image she later understands is false, but before she can grasp the truth about Rebecca's life, she has first to be told the truth about her death. Rebecca did not drown in a yachting accident, as everyone believes: she was killed by de Winter, who from the days of his honeymoon (also in Monte Carlo) loathed his wife.

Mrs de Winter, once enlightened, accepts without question her husband's version of her predecessor as a promiscuous (possibly bisexual) woman, who was pregnant with another man's child when he killed her, and who taunted him that she would pass off this child as his. De Winter's confession – and a very hollow melodramatic confession it is – is accompanied by a declaration of love – the first he has made, despite months of marriage. There is also the suggestion – very subtle but it is there – that their marriage is consummated, and for the first time, after this confession (note the references to single beds in the novel, and the heroine's embarrassment when there is specula- tion as to whether she is yet pregnant – something that recurs frequently. Modesty may explain that embarrassment, but in a du Maurier novel, it may well not).

Without hesitation, Mrs de Winter then gives her husband her full support – her one concern from then onwards is to conceal the truth and protect her husband. Thus, she becomes, in legal terms, an accessory after the fact: more importantly, she makes a moral choice. This is the crux of du Maurier's novel: de Winter has confessed, after all, to a *double* murder. He believes he has killed not only Rebecca, but also the child she was carrying – a heinous crime, by any standards. Here, du Maurier was taking a huge risk, particularly in a novel aimed at a popular market. To have an apparent 'hero' revealed as a double murderer, one prepared to perjure himself, moreover, to save his neck, could have shocked and alienated readers in their thousands. Hitchcock, when he came to film the novel two years later, ran a mile from this scenario, which he knew would be unacceptable. In his version, there *is* no murder, and Maxim's crime is at worst manslaughter since, during a quarrel, Rebecca falls, and (conveniently and mortally) injures herself.

How does du Maurier occlude this issue? She does it with immense cleverness: so involved have we, the readers, become in Mrs de Winter's predicament, and so sympathetic to her, that we conjoin with her. Because she loves her guilty husband, and he appears to love her, we too begin to hope that he will escape justice. If Mrs de Winter is culpable, therefore, so is the reader who endorses her actions – and that issue ticks away like a time bomb under the remaining chapters of the book.

This final section of the novel, which is brilliantly plotted, concerns de Winter's attempts to suppress the truth, and – with his loyal wife's assistance – escape the hangman. And so he does, but not without cost. Returning to Manderley from London, with information that gives Rebecca a motive for suicide and thus saves him, both partners are uneasy. De Winter senses impending disaster; in the back of the car, his wife is asleep, dreaming that she and Rebecca have become one, and that their hair, long and black, as Rebecca's was, is winding about de Winter's neck, like a noose.

Mrs de Winter dreams vividly twice in the novel, once at the beginning and once at the end: each time, the dream conveys a truth to her that her conscious mind cannot, or will not, accept. She prefers the sketchy and cliché-ridden visions she summons up when she daydreams – and she daydreams incessantly. The vision she has just had, of Rebecca and herself united, of first and second wives merged into one dangerous female avatar, she instantly rejects. Her husband halts the car on a crest near their home; the night sky beyond is lit with a red glow. (The colour red is linked with Rebecca throughout the novel.) His wife assumes it is the dawn, but de Winter understands at once: Manderley, his ancestral home, is burning. This destruction was prefigured in the dream with which the novel opened, and the literal agent of the destruction (possibly Mrs Danvers) is far less important than the poetic agent, which is Rebecca. Like some avenging angel, Rebecca has marshalled the elements: she has risen from the sea to wreak revenge by fire – thus echoing, and not for the first time, her literary ancestress, that madwoman in the attic, the first Mrs Rochester.

In this way, and very abruptly, the novel ends; it has come full circle. It is melodramatic in places, of course (even *Jane Eyre* cannot entirely escape that criticism). But it is remarkable, given the plot, how consistently and skilfully du Maurier skirts melodrama. What interested her as a novelist can be summarised by the distinction that Charlotte Brontë drew between writing that was 'real' and writing that was 'true'. There *is* realism in *Rebecca*; the mores, snobberies and speech patterns of the class and era du Maurier is describing are, for instance, sharply observed. The elements that give *Rebecca* its force, however, owe nothing to realism: its power lies in its imagery, its symmetry, its poetry – and that poetry is intensely female. The plot of *Rebecca* may be as unlikely as the plot of a fairytale, but that does not alter the novel's mythic resonance and psychological truth.

One way of reading *Rebecca* is as a convention-ridden love story, in which the good woman triumphs over the bad by winning a man's love: this version is the one our nameless narrator would have us accept, and it is undoubtedly the reading that made *Rebecca* a bestseller. Another approach is to see the novel's imaginative links, not just with the work of earlier female novelists, such as Charlotte Brontë, but also with later work, in particular Sylvia Plath's late poems. *Rebecca* is narrated by a masochistic woman, who is desperate for the validation provided by a man's love – a woman seeking an authoritarian father surrogate, or, as Plath expressed it, a 'man in black with a Meinkampf look'. Her search for this man involves both self-effacement and abnegation, as it does for any woman who 'adores a Fascist'. She duly finds her ideal in de Winter, whose last name indicates sterility, coldness, an unfruitful season, and whose Christian name – Maxim, as she always abbreviates it – is a synonym for a rule of conduct. It is also the name of a weapon – a machine gun.

This woman, not surprisingly, views Rebecca as a rival; what she refuses to perceive is that Rebecca is also her twin, and ultimately her alter ego. The two wives have actually suffered very similar fates. Both were taken as brides to Manderley – a male preserve, as the first syllable of its name (like Menabilly's) suggests. Both were marginalised within the confines of the house – Rebecca in the west wing with its view of her symbol, the sea, and the second wife in the east wing, overlooking the confines of a rose garden. The difference between them lies in their reactions: the second wife gladly submits, allowing her identity to be determined by her husband, and by the class attitudes and value systems he embraces. Rebecca has dared to be an unchaste wife; she has broken the 'rules of conduct' Maxim lives by. Her ultimate sin is to threaten the system of primogeniture. That sin,

Rebecca

undermining the entire patriarchal edifice that is Manderley, cannot be forgiven – and Rebecca dies for it.

The response of Mrs de Winter to Rebecca's rebellion is deeply ambivalent, and it is this ambivalence that fuels the novel. Her apparent reaction is that of a conventional woman of her time: abhorrence. Yet there are indications throughout the text that the second Mrs de Winter would like to emulate Rebecca, even to be her – and these continue, even when she knows Rebecca has broken every male-determined rule as to a woman's behaviour. Although Rebecca is dead, is never seen, and has in theory been forever silenced, Mrs de Winter's obsession with her insures that Rebecca will triumph over anonymity and efface-ment. Even a bullet through the heart, and burial at sea cannot quench her vampiric power. Again, one is reminded of Plath's embodiment of amoral, anarchic female force – *I rise with my red hair / And I eat men like air.* Within the conventions of a story, Rebecca's pallid successor is able to do what she dare not do in life: celebrate her predecessor.

She does so with cunning and with power (du Maurier, of course, is pulling the strings here). Long after the book has been closed, which character reverberates in the memory? Rebecca. And which of the two women are readers drawn to, which of these polar opposites fascinates and attracts? Rebecca, again, I would say – certainly for modern readers. But I think that was probably true for readers in 1938 too: thanks to the cunning of du Maurier's narrative structure, they were able to condemn Rebecca (a promiscuous woman – what other option did they have?); but secretly respond to the anger, rebellion and venge-fulness she embodies.

There is a final twist to *Rebecca* and it is a covert one. Maxim de Winter kills not one wife, but *two.* He murders the first with a gun, and the second by slower, more insidious methods. The second Mrs de Winter's fate, for which she prepares herself throughout the novel, is to be subsumed by her husband.

57

Following him into that hellish exile glimpsed in the opening chapters, she becomes again what she was when she first met him – the paid companion to a petty tyrant. For humouring his whims, and obeying his every behest, her recompense is not money, but 'love' – and the cost is her identity. This is the final bitter irony of this novel, and the last of its many reversals. A story that ostensibly attempts to bury Rebecca, in fact resurrects her, and renders her unforgettable, whereas Mrs de Winter, our pale, ghostly and timid narrator, fades from our view; it is *she* who is the dying woman in this novel. By extension – and this is daring on du Maurier's part – her obedient beliefs, her unquestioning subservience to the male, are dying with her.

The themes of *Rebecca* – identity, doubling, the intimate linkage between love and murder – recur again and again in du Maurier's work. That the circumstances of her own life were the source of many of those themes is, I think, unquestionable. That she often chose to explore those themes within the confines of a story about love and marriage is perhaps not accidental either; there had always been duality in her life – her bisexuality ensured that; after her marriage, that sense of a dual identity deepened, and was to feed all her fiction.

Du Maurier had been born into a rich, privileged but unconventional and bohemian family. Her father, Gerald, was notorious for his affairs – and for running back to his wife after them. She and her sisters grew up surrounded by the writers, actors and artists who were their parents' close friends. Before du Maurier was twenty-one, she had had several affairs with men and at least one with a woman. Yet she chose to marry a career soldier in one of England's most elite regiments, a man who was a traditionalist to his fingertips, a stickler for correct dress and behaviour, a man who was deeply shocked when – prior to their marriage – she suggested they should sleep together. After a long and distinguished military career, 'Boy' Browning, as he was nicknamed, was to go on to become a courtier, spending much of his time in London, while his wife remained at Menabilly. There can be no question of their love and loyalty for each other: long after he died, du Maurier remained fiercely defensive of her husband. But the differences between them were marked, and their expectations of marriage perhaps very different. Eventually that caused problems: there were infidelities on both sides, and later in life, Browning began to drink heavily. Meanwhile, du Maurier had two identities: she was a Lieutenant General's wife, and later, Lady Browning: she was also an internationally celebrated writer, and finally a Dame of the British Empire. That she found it difficult to reconcile the demands of two *personae* is apparent in her fiction, above all in *Rebecca*, but also in her often bitter, and shocking, short stories.

Throughout her life, she was torn between the need to be a wife and the necessity of being a writer – and she seems to have regarded those roles as irreconcilable. Half accepting society's (and her husband's) interpretation of ideal womanhood, yet rebelling against it and rejecting it, she came to regard herself as a 'half-breed' who was 'unnatural'. To her, both her lesbianism and her art were a form of aberrance: they both sprang, she believed, from a force inside her that she referred to as the 'boy in the box'. Sometimes she fought against this incubus – and sometimes she gloried in him.

Given those beliefs, the dualism, the gender-blurring and the *splitting* that are so apparent in *Rebecca* become more understandable. Du Maurier was wrestling with her own demons here, and when she gave aspects of herself to the two women who are the pillars of her narrative she was entering into an area of deeply personal psychological struggle. She gave her own shyness and social awkwardness to Mrs de Winter. She gave her independence, her love of the sea, her expertise as a sailor, her sexual fearlessness, and even her bisexuality (strongly hinted at in the novel, if not spelled out) to Rebecca. It is for readers to decide where their own sympathies lie – and du Maurier's.

I would say that ultimately it is with Rebecca, with the angry voice of female dissent, that du Maurier's instinctive sympathy lies. But it is possible to argue the opposite view – one of the factors that makes *Rebecca* such a rewarding novel to reread and re-examine. One thing is certain: *Rebecca* is a deeply subversive work, one that undermines the very genre to which critics consigned it. Far from being an 'exquisite' love story, *Rebecca* raises questions about women's acquiescence to male values that are as pertinent today as they were sixty-four years ago. We may have moved on from the subservience of Mrs de Winter, but our enfranchisement is scarcely complete. A glance at the current bestseller lists will only confirm that the sly suggestion underlying *Rebecca* remains valid after sixty-four years: both in life and in bookstores, women continue to buy romance.

The Rebecca Notebook
and Other Memories

Alison Light

In the late 1920s a young woman from London falls in love with
a deserted mansion hidden in the Cornish woods in the far west
of England. Her family has bought a holiday place nearby and
so she goes back whenever she can, revisiting the abandoned
property, and harbouring the fantasy of one day living there.
Eventually she pesters the absent landlord and gets permission to
walk in the grounds, but nothing is done to save the house which
falls gently into disrepair. The house lives on in her imagination
and then, miraculously, many years later, her wish comes true –
she acquires the lease, restores the mansion to its former glory,
and makes it her home. By now it is wartime and the girl has
become a wife and mother but she is also Daphne du Maurier,
whose bestseller, *Rebecca*, has recently been a Hollywood success.
Celebrating her arrival at 'Menabilly', du Maurier writes proudly
'the house belongs to me' and yet the author of 'The House of
Secrets' (one of the essays included in *The Rebecca Notebook and
Other Memories*) ends her account on a characteristic note of
suspense. Du Maurier is only a tenant and her happiness, like her
home, is surely temporary. 'It cannot last,' she writes, 'it cannot
endure'. Fans of du Maurier's fiction know that in her world
disenchantment is the price we pay for the magic: 'it is the very
insecurity of the love that makes the passion strong'.

When she peered through the windows into Menabilly's
forlorn and damp rooms, du Maurier wondered 'Where was the

laughter gone? Where were the voices that had called along the passages?' *The Rebecca Notebook and Other Memories*, a volume of short pieces about her family, her life and beliefs, is prompted, like so many of her stories, by the desire to reanimate the past. Daphne du Maurier's was a Romantic temperament, not because she penned exotic tales or swashbuckling costume dramas, and certainly not because she believed in fairytale endings for men and women ('there is no such thing as romantic love', she declares provocatively in one of the essays); rather, she was moved by what the poet Shelley called 'mutability', the inevitable change-fulness of things. For du Maurier change was always ominous. The spirit of a place haunted her, its ghosts were an eerie conso-lation that human loves and attachments were never wholly lost.

In 'The Rebecca Notebook', du Maurier lays out her origi-nal plans for her most famous novel. Du Maurier began *Rebecca* when she was an itinerant army-wife stationed with her husband in Egypt and homesickness seeps into the descriptions of Cornwall (her longed-for Menabilly became 'Manderley' in the novel, another house of secrets where the shy heroine feels like a guilty trespasser). Typically she wrote the disillusioned epilogue first. Mr and Mrs de Winter are introduced as a middle-aged couple of dull English 'expats' living humdrum lives in hotels abroad, a sad pair longing for news of the cricket and pining for the English countryside. The final published version made it less parochial, changing the stodgy-sounding 'Henry' to the more glamorous and international 'Maxim'. Du Maurier also wisely cut those lengthy passages where her narrator snobbishly dispar-ages the *nouveaux riches* who have turned Manderley into a country club with a golf course and cocktail lounge. The melo-dramatic ending was dropped and eventually the epilogue became a prologue, tightening the psychological screws, as if the heroine were compulsively retelling the crime-story at the heart of her marriage. 'We can never go back', she says at the beginning of the novel, launching into retrospect.

Rebecca was published in 1938. Apart from the Notebook, the 'memories' gathered in the volume date from du Maurier's later life when most of her bestsellers were behind her. She begins with accounts of her family, a memoir of her French grand-father, George du Maurier, whose novel of Bohemian Paris, *Trilby*, was the smash-hit of the 1890s (though his fame is now as faded as the drawings he produced for *Punch*), and of her father, Gerald, the leading actor and theatre-manager of his day. Daphne had boldly written his biography not long after his death in 1934. 'The Matinee Idol', nearly forty years later, is a generous portrait of this childlike, affectionate, demanding man, for whom life was always a matter of 'pretending to be someone else'. Nostalgic vignettes, these memoirs are tinged like sepia photographs with a faded charm, and with du Maurier's bittersweet feeling for the transient – the ephemeral nature of an actor's performances or the dying fall of her grandfather's tenor floating out into the Victorian twilight. They are also a disgruntled lament for the disappearance of 'Victorian values', lost, she maintains, 'through our own fault'. Temperamentally at odds with a more egalitarian postwar Britain, du Maurier distances herself here as she does in 'My Name in Lights' from the current 'age of meagre mediocrity' with its meretricious notions of instant celebrity. The enjoyment of success, she believed, should be very private – 'like saying one's prayers or making love'.

Growing up in the 1900s, Daphne du Maurier was of that generation of Edwardian girls who envied and adored their male peers (in her autobiography she made no bones about wanting to be a boy). 'Sylvia's Boys' is her tribute to her cousins, the Llewelyn-Davieses, who were fostered by J. M. Barrie and were the inspiration for his *Peter Pan* (the play in which Gerald took the parts of both the paterfamilias and of the sinister Captain Hook). Like her father's brother, Guy, killed in the 'Great War', they seemed to her straightforwardly and delightfully male (Gerald, on the other hand, in his stage make-up was never quite a proper man). Daphne's models of independence were always masculine and once she had discovered Cornwall, she abandoned the bright lights of London to learn to sail a boat, wear trousers, go fishing and exploring, shocking her neighbours and her family. In imagination at least, Daphne identified with the artists and adventurers amongst the du Mauriers. Nevertheless she held old-fashioned views of men and women and longed for a settled home life. 'This I Believe', presumably written for this volume, upholds 'the law of the family unit' as the strongest in life and is ambivalent about women's emancipation. Not surprisingly, perhaps, when she fell in love, it was with a man in uniform, the young Major Frederick Browning, 'Boy' or 'Tommy', as Daphne called him.

In du Maurier's novels the men are often cheats and bullies, the women fools for love (*Rebecca* is a story about murderous husbands as well as jealous and vicious wives). Psychological violence (though there is actual violence too) seemed inevitable given what was seen as a 'sex war', a battle for power or dominance which must at best end in stalemate. Margaret Forster's biography of du Maurier tells us that her marriage was often turbulent, that her husband was unfaithful, and that she fell in love with women as well as men (how she would have hated these 'revelations'!). Du Maurier's autobiography, *Growing Pains: The Shaping of a Writer* (reprinted as *Myself When Young*) is far more reticent, focusing on her escape from her parents' milieu and her intense and sometimes stifling relationship with her father. Her own marriage in 1932 closes the volume and a sequel was never written. All the more moving, therefore, is her memoir 'Death and Widowhood'. She writes unflinchingly about the pain of losing a relationship of thirty-three years – 'the greater half' of her existence, identifying with her dead husband by wearing his shirts, sitting at his desk and using his pen. Du Maurier is uncompromising, insisting that remarriage is unthinkable; that loneliness and suffering must be embraced. She believed

she could no longer produce fiction, though there were other
novels, and the morbid horrors of her story 'Don't Look Now'
derived from her own mourning. If in her sixties and seventies
du Maurier turned more to autobiography, however veiled, that
too, like this memoir, was a response to loss, a way of reinventing
herself.

The Rebecca Notebook and Other Memories was Daphne du
Maurier's last book, published in 1981 when she was seventy-
four (she died in 1989). The original bookjacket warns the reader
that her views might be 'surprising'. Perhaps only a fear of going
out of circulation (a species of authorial death) could have
persuaded her to write so personally, especially given her avowed
loathing of publicity. There are *longueurs*, but du Maurier can be
the best of company in her memoirs precisely because she refuses
to curry favour (her patrician dismissal of her fans as 'the mob'
might make any publisher nervous). She never patronises the
reader and she never stays long on her high horse. If the picture
emerges of a woman who grew more conservative with age, she
also remained an individualist, as unmoved by fashion as she was
in her girlhood. And she was able to laugh at herself.

The final trio of pieces offer a robust, unsentimental vision
of growing old. After twenty-six years du Maurier had to leave
her beloved Menabilly for Kilmarth, one of the estate's former
dower houses (she describes the upheaval in 'Moving House').
Du Maurier's Cornwall is always stormy and unpeopled (like
the moors of her favourite authors, the Brontë sisters); its beauties harsh yet vulnerable (*Vanishing Cornwall* was the title of the
book she wrote in her last years about her cherished, adopted
county). 'A Winter's Afternoon in Kilmarth' gives short shrift
to the Tourist Board fantasy of a sunny Cornish 'Riviera' (an
image now replaced by that of surfing and gourmet fish restaurants). Battling against wind and rain, in what was almost her
uniform of military jersey and cap, a soldierly figure with her
dog, du Maurier enjoyed the sensation of splendid isolation on

a teemingly wet hillside – upright and formidable, taking life
on the chin. The fantasy of going it utterly alone could be the
compensation for those times which were also deeply lonely
and bereft.

All writers lead double lives. As Lady Browning, wife of a
General who became a royal aide to the Duke of Edinburgh, as
well as a worldwide bestselling author for nearly fifty years,
Daphne du Maurier was often in the public eye. Yet being anonymous and unobserved was crucial to her. Du Maurier's Cornwall
was her home but it was also a country of the mind, the place
where she could be a restless spirit and a writer in retreat. She
needed to be reclusive in order to enjoy 'the secret nourish-
ment' of writing; limelight, she believed, was a bad light to work
in. Her poem of 1926, 'The Writer', composed before she had
begun her first novel, projects a future for herself. It paints a
picture of the solitary, self-sufficient life of a writer, the woman
whose room of her own gives her the psychic and emotional
room she craves. There is menace here too. Being a writer is
imagined as a life without secure ties, involving an obliteration
of the self, 'the thread of the spider who spins on the wall /
Who is lost, who is dead, who is nothing at all'.

Why do writers write? What compels them to this strange
self-absorbed, self-effacing life? Du Maurier's stories take us
into the shuttered places in human psychology where hidden
or repressed feelings – jealousy, rage, lust, terror – threaten to
overwhelm us, or like love and desire, to transport us into
another dimension. Like a medium at a seance, du Maurier felt
taken over by writing, 'possessed' by her plot and her characters. That activity, leaving the world, as she calls it, meant losing
one's boundaries and yet somehow retaining control. We all
fantasise and we all live in our fantasies, imagining we are the
authors of our lives, but the novelist makes something lasting
and shared of her daydreams. A writer's memoirs or biography
will always fascinate us because it offers tantalising glimpses of

this mysterious process. Yet however much we learn, the writing life remains a house of secrets. We press our faces to the glass, frustrated and intrigued, seeing only shadows and our own reflection.

Spectres of Authorship:
Daphne du Maurier's Gothic Legacy

Rebecca Munford

> We can never go back again, that much is certain. The past is
> still too close to us. The things we have tried to forget and
> put behind us would stir again, and that sense of fear, of
> furtive unrest, struggling at length to blind unreasoning panic
> – now mercifully stilled, thank God – might in some manner
> unforeseen become a living companion, as it had been before.
> Daphne du Maurier, *Rebecca*, 1938

The suggestion that *Rebecca* (1938) is indebted to Charlotte
Brontë's *Jane Eyre* (1847) has become a commonplace of critical discussions of Daphne du Maurier's work. This, combined
with its commercial success and unabashed deployment of
Gothic trappings (a forbidding mansion, a brooding villain, a
swooning heroine and the spectral presence of an enigmatic
'other' woman) has led to the novel's recurrent positioning as
a 'Gothic Romance' – an inferior and derivative version of
Brontë's masterwork. Even Angela Carter, whose own fictions
thrive on a dizzying use of citation, appropriation and literary
resonance, claims that du Maurier's *Rebecca* 'shamelessly redu-
plicated the plot of *Jane Eyre*'.[1] The various ways in which the
work of Charlotte and Emily Brontë provides a point of identification and engagement for du Maurier's imaginative proce-
dures has been well documented by critics – from Alison Light's

seminal discussion of romance fiction, sexuality and class to Avril Horner and Sue Zlosnik's more recent exploration of the relationship between the narrative power of the Brontës and the allure of the Cornish landscape.[2] Nevertheless, as Nina Auerbach warns in her vital account of du Maurier's literary career as haunted (as well as *haunting*) heiress, these narrative resemblances need to be drawn watchfully. 'The Brontës,' Auerbach writes, 'if there ever was such an entity, do inhabit Daphne du Maurier's romances, but in twisted, diminished shape.'[3] Similarly interested in themes of haunting and influence, this essay is not only concerned with revisiting the relationship between *Rebecca* and *Jane Eyre*, but also with recontextualising du Maurier's intertextual relationship with contemporary women writers, and mapping her Gothic legacy.

In their pioneering study, *Daphne du Maurier: Writing, Identity and the Gothic Imagination* (1998), Horner and Zlosnik provide a compelling framework for considering du Maurier's relationship to the Gothic. Offering a subtle and sustained reading of her engagements with the genre, they argue that both her novels and short stories, from *Jamaica Inn* (1936) to 'Don't Look Now' (1971), 'offer particularly interesting examples of how Gothic writing is inflected by both personal and broader cultural values and anxieties.'[4] Locating du Maurier's writing within and against the conventions of the 'female Gothic' – a tradition which has a long lineage in the work of eighteenth- and nineteenth-century women writers, including Ann Radcliffe, Jane Austen and Mary Shelley – they provide a space in which to consider du Maurier's Gothic ancestry beyond the axiomatic Brontë influence.[5] Although this study enables a more complex understanding of du Maurier in relation to her Gothic foremothers, discussions of her literary legacy continue to consign her contribution to the development of Gothic forms to the realms of the pulp romance and the 'drugstore Gothic'.[6] It is vital, however, to move beyond this straightforward positioning of *Rebecca* as bequeathing only 'the paperback boom in the female formula during the 1960s'.[7] We must, then, 'go back' to du Maurier's novel in order to reanimate it – to make of it once again 'a living companion' – in relation to a more complex history of literary hauntings and Gothic occupations.

As Sally Beauman suggests in her introduction to the Virago edition of *Rebecca*, it is an exploration of the novel's imaginative links with the work of novelists that both preceded and followed her, that opens up alternative interpretative avenues by which to approach du Maurier's work. In addition to Beauman's example of Sylvia Plath's later poetry (the search for 'an authoritarian father surrogate, or, as Plath expressed it in "Daddy", a "man in black with a Meinkampf look"'), such imaginative links can be traced in a range of post-war Gothic prose texts. For example, in its self-conscious deployment of Gothic trappings and its protagonist's reading of them, du Maurier's novel prefigures the anxieties surrounding the reading/writing of Gothic conventions and the relationship between gender and writerly identities in Margaret Atwood's *Lady Oracle* (1976), an early subtitle for which was 'A Gothic Romance'.[8] Written during the boom in popular Gothics, Atwood's novel at once engages and undercuts Gothic conventions. Its self-conscious treatment of Gothic narration and Joan Foster's precarious position as both Gothic writer *and* Gothic heroine ('The heroines of my books were mere stand-ins')[9] might be read in relation to the 'duality in Rebecca's script' and the question of 'gothic signatures' highlighted by Horner and Zlosnik in their reading of du Maurier's novel.[10] With its heightened evocation of the haunted house, *Rebecca* also looks forward to the representation of domestic interiors and shadowy occupations in such novels as Alice Munro's *Lives of Girls and Women* (1971) and Emma Tennant's *Wild Nights* (1979). In its powerful evocation of landscape, its concern with ghostly presences (such as Aunt Zita in *Wild Nights*) and identification and engagement with the work of the Brontës – for example, *Adèle: Jane Eyre's*

Hidden Story (2000) and *Heathcliff's Tale* (2005) – Tennant's work offers compelling imaginative links with du Maurier.

Perhaps most significant, however, in terms of du Maurier's contribution to the development of the Gothic forms of women's writing in the twentieth century, is her reimagining of the Gothic heroine. In her study *Literary Women* (1976), Ellen Moers set out a definition of the 'female Gothic' that continues to circulate (albeit in more unstable form) in contemporary Gothic scholarship. Here she proposes that '[a]s early as the 1790s, Ann Radcliffe firmly set the Gothic in one of the ways it would go ever after: a novel in which the central figure is a young woman who is simultaneously persecuted victim and courageous heroine.'[11] Although one of the most frequent charges levelled at *Rebecca* is its erasure of the feisty candour and resourcefulness of Brontë's protagonist in *Jane Eyre*, I would argue that the figure of the nameless narrator in du Maurier's novel provides a space for reconsidering the position of the Gothic heroine in relation to the limits and limitations of the female Gothic tradition. Indeed – in spite of the acerbic jibe directed at *Rebecca* in her introduction to the Virago edition of *Jane Eyre*, cited above – it is the device of the nameless narrator that facilitates Angela Carter's own exercise in feminist rewriting in 'The Bloody Chamber' (1979). A reworking of both the fairy tale *Bluebeard* and the female Gothic 'plot' represented by *Jane Eyre*, Carter's short story examines the connections between domination and desire in relation to 'the unguessable country of marriage'.[12] However, if, as Elaine Showalter proposes, Carter's 'The Bloody Chamber' is 'a postmodern reimagining' of Brontë's *Jane Eyre*, then it is a reimagining shaped by the textual and thematic contours of du Maurier's *Rebecca*.[13]

Like *Rebecca*, Carter's short story begins where *Jane Eyre* ends, with the recent marriage of its timid, young and innocent narrator to an alluring yet, it turns out, murderous husband.

And, like du Maurier's narrator, who feels 'rather like someone peering through the keyhole of a locked door',[14] Carter's protagonist occupies the position of both the classic Gothic heroine and Bluebeard's wife in the 'lovely prison of which [she] was both inmate and the mistress'.[15] 'Aghast to feel [herself] stirring' upon her sadistic husband's 'formal disrobing of the bride'[16], the protagonist of 'The Bloody Chamber' reflects a masochistic complicity with patriarchal power and authority. In this respect, she has more in common with the victimised (and collusive) Mrs de Winter than she does with the tough-minded Jane Eyre. Moreover, while the limp hair and uneasy posture of du Maurier's narrator are echoed in the 'mouse-coloured hair . . . bony hips' and 'nervous pianist's fingers'[17] of Carter's protagonist, Maxim de Winter (who 'belonged to . . . a past where men walked cloaked at night, and stood in the shadow of old doorways, a past of narrow stairways and dim dungeons, a past of whispers in the dark, of shimmering rapier blades, of silent, exquisite courtesy'[18]) finds his mirror image in the wealthy Sadeian Marquis, with his 'perfume of spiced leather' and 'strange, heavy, almost waxen face'.[19] Perhaps most significantly, though, Carter's Marquis is also recently bereaved, his previous wife a glamorous Romanian countess of 'high fashion' and 'such potent and bizarre charm . . . a dark, bright, wild yet worldly thing'. This previous wife, too, the narrator tells us, died in a 'boating accident, at his home'; and her body was never found.[20]

Nevertheless, it is not only their narrative resemblances that indicate the imaginative links between du Maurier's *Rebecca* and Carter's 'The Bloody Chamber'. On the surface, both texts represent the journey of self-discovery that has become recognised as a mark of the female Gothic tradition. However, their narrators' identities remain overwritten by the violence of a patriarchal plot. Whether it is the 'splash of blood' that marks the inky sky at the end of *Rebecca*, or the bloody imprint on the forehead of

Carter's narrator, these Gothic heroines remain haunted by the stirrings of those things they 'have tried to forget'. Thus *Rebecca* and 'The Bloody Chamber' are connected also by their re-instatement of the contradictions between romantic ideology and subjective independence that *Jane Eyre* seeks to resolve through its reformation of the heterosexual romance and 'taming' of the vicious patriarch. Carter's narrative inflection of the female Gothic, then, gives material form to the fantasy of dim dungeons and shimmering rapier blades only imagined in *Rebecca*: as her narrator recalls, '"There is a striking resemblance between the act of love and ministrations of a torturer," opined my husband's favourite poet; I had learned something of the nature of that similarity on my marriage bed.'[21] Thus, if *Rebecca* can be read as a 'twisted' reinscription of Brontë's novel in its refusal of the self-affirming narration of the Gothic heroine and its exposition of the proximity of love and murder in the Gothic 'plot', then it is precisely this 'twistedness' upon which Carter draws in her own Gothic reimaginings.

It is, paradoxically, the vitality of *Rebecca*'s 'after-life' that has too often limited discussions of du Maurier's contribution to the development of Gothic forms. Just as the *idea* of Rebecca de Winter casts its inescapable shadow over Manderley, so too does the category of the 'Gothic romance' loom over serious critical considerations of du Maurier's 'bestseller'. As Susanne Becker notes, Gothic writing by women is traditionally marked by an intricate web of interdependencies and influences. Arguing for the importance of Gothic intertextuality throughout two centuries of modern female literary culture, Becker proposes that 'there has been a vigorous exchange of allusions and re-visions, and even of provocations and answers, a dynamic – and self-conscious – writing and rewriting of feminine texts haunting one another'.[22] Rather than a shadowy, yet secure, reiteration of Brontë's *Jane Eyre*, Daphne du Maurier's novel needs to be recontextualised in relation to the spirited and unstable Gothic intertextuality described by Becker. A vital engagement with the Gothic tradition, *Rebecca* is as troubling in its answers to its literary forebears as it is powerful in its provocations to its literary descendants.

Rebecca's Afterlife:
Sequels and Other Echoes

Helen Taylor

A waggish critic once suggested that, without textual intercourse, there could be no literature. However true that may be, the whole business of literary influence is fraught and – in these litigious times of intellectual property rights – even dangerous. Plagiarism charges have escalated against writers accused of stealing from one another. Daphne du Maurier herself faced accusations in 1940 when *Rebecca* was translated into Portuguese, and Brazilian and American critics claimed she had borrowed wholesale from Carolina Nabuco's *A Sucessora* (1934). More serious was an American court case in 1947 when the literary executors of Edwina L. Macdonald unsuccessfully sued du Maurier on the grounds that *Rebecca* plagiarised her story, 'I Planned to Murder my Husband' – later the novel, *Blind Windows* (1927). Critics have whispered about the many parallels between *Rebecca* and Elizabeth von Arnim's novel, *Vera* (1921).[1]

Graham Swift, winner of the 1996 Booker Prize for *Last Orders*, was accused by an Australian critic of plagiarising Faulkner's *As I Lay Dying* (1930). Supported by many other critics who admired a subtle reworking, Swift referred to Faulkner's 'ghostly presence' in his writing. 'Ghostly presence' is one way of alluding to intertextual influence; it is certainly quite a fruitful way of understanding the way writers' works enjoy new life by informing their successors' writings. But that said, there is a fine line between influence and borrowing – as in the serious accusations of literary theft in Alex Haley's *Roots* or Dan Brown's *The Da Vinci Code*. And borrowing a story to take it further is also seen as rather suspect. Sequel writers such as Emma Tennant have found their literary reputations suffering; originality is still at a critical premium. Following the commercially successful explosion of film sequels in recent years, writers – it is assumed – are only doing it for the money.

Writers have always drawn on one another's stories, themes and characters, but in recent decades the creative rewriting of major works has become a cottage industry. Indeed, postmodernism gave a new lift to the business of borrowing – with pastiche and parody, a mingling of high and popular culture, mixed genres and media, and 'serious' novelists engaged in popular sequel or continuation writing. As well as Graham Swift's Faulkner, there is the 'ghostly presence' of Dickens in Sue Roe's creative reworking of *Great Expectations*, *Estella: Her Expectations*, and the many Jane Austen sequels by Rachel Billington and Emma Tennant, with Tennant credited as having created a new sub-genre, the 'classic progression'. There is a growing fashion for finishing the incomplete fragment. In 1980 Charlotte Brontë's unfinished story, 'Emma', was completed and published by 'Another Lady'; this was followed by the critically acclaimed version by Clare Boylan, *Emma Brown* (2003). And Jill Paton Walsh solved Dorothy L. Sayers's 1930s unfinished Lord Peter Wimsey mystery, *Thrones, Dominations* (1998). Du Maurier herself had led the way by completing Arthur Quiller-Couch's fragment, *Castle Dor* (1962).

This chapter is concerned with the afterlife of *Rebecca*, specifically in its sequels and other literary echoes. The sequel helps give new life, dignity, indeed a classic status to a popular text. Like a novel almost contemporary with it, Margaret Mitchell's *Gone With the Wind* (1936), *Rebecca* has achieved the status of 'masterpiece' or classic text largely because of the cumulative impact of acclaimed film version, stage and opera version, critical, commercial, tourist office and biographical attention, and sequel publication. *Rebecca* shares with *Gone With the Wind* a popular reputation as archetypal romantic woman's classic, with its resonant, strong female characters, intense focus on home and family relationships and strong sense of place and roots.

The parallels between the two texts are legion. Since 1936 *Gone With the Wind* has enjoyed many of the same kinds of reproduction as *Rebecca*. It shared David Selznick as its film producer and spawned similar speculation over its ambiguous ending as well as a number of sequels. Both became iconic texts, in each case representing a particular kind of nationalism: in the case of *Gone With the Wind*, neo-Confederate chauvinism, in *Rebecca*'s an almost Rupert Brooke/John Betjeman-like honey-for-tea Englishness. Each text has been misidentified as a 'romance'; both work across genres and produce female protagonists whose excessive energy, and thus meanings, create problems for a satisfying closure. Both Margaret Mitchell and Daphne du Maurier received an avalanche of letters after publication asking about their novels: in Mitchell's case, 'Did Scarlett ever get Rhett back?', in du Maurier's, 'Why is the heroine nameless?'. Neither writer ever wrote a sequel to her novel, despite requests. Mitchell explicitly forebade any such version in her will, a proscription broken only recently by her nephews. Du Maurier contributed a witty epilogue to Antonia Fraser's short story, 'Rebecca's Story',[2] but wrote to her agent that this could all go too far and they would 'need to watch out'.[3] Significantly, both texts are recalled through a haze of mingled film and literary memories; the Hitchcock film inspired at least two writers to pick up their pens.

There is another interesting parallel. From my discussions with women reader-viewers of *Gone With the Wind*, I know that Scarlett's costumes – from her earliest party dresses to the green velvet gown she made out of curtains – were much admired and emulated. Sue Zlosnik recalls a Spanish student telling her that the cardigan worn by Joan Fontaine in the film of *Rebecca* became very fashionable among her mother's generation, where it was referred to as a 'Rebecca'.

On first publication, *Rebecca* was called by *The Times* a 'novel-ette', a term its film director Alfred Hitchcock also used of it dismissively, referring to that good old anti-feminist charge that the story lacked humour. Like *Gone With the Wind, Rebecca* has been perceived as a woman's novel and film, and thus it is hardly surprising so many women writers have been drawn into its orbit. This gender imbalance has also meant it is described repeatedly as 'a great love story', a 'classic romance'.

Rebecca – Romance or Gothic?

The trouble with this simple line is that it is hard to see *Rebecca* in these terms, especially since the very notion of what consti-tutes literary romance has been closely interrogated by feminist critics. *Rebecca* fits most uncomfortably into the romance cate-gory.[4] Daphne du Maurier herself called it 'a study in jealousy', seeing it as 'rather grim' and 'unpleasant'; Alison Light asks, '[W]hat sense does it make to call *Rebecca*, as one Mills and Boon author has, "the archetypal romantic novel" when it ends not with conjugal bliss but middle-aged resignation and exile?' Critics have placed it within the genre of female Gothic, understanding it as a psychological study of personal insecurity, class and national instability, and female Oedipal crisis.[5] The Gothic is a kind of hybrid, contradictory text, somewhere between horror and romance, one that exposes and plays on contradictions (espe-cially the safety/danger of domestic space for women) and also purges the home of its associations with the terrifying and the evil – the burning house as symbolic purgation. Because so often focused on a male/female relationship in a domestic setting, it shares many elements with the romantic novel. It is perhaps du Maurier's refusal of simple, banal solutions and her play on genre that have interested readers and critics. Following *Jane Eyre*, it offers a model for modern Gothic novels, which often advertise themselves 'in the du Maurier tradition', sharing as they do what Joanna Russ summarises as: 'the House, the Heroine, the Super-Male, the Other Woman, the Ominous Dialogue, the Secret and the Untangling'.[6]

There are common factors in all the novels that have been reworked and sequelised in recent years. They end with extremely unsatisfying and incomplete closures. The critic Kari J. Winter wrote of female Gothic novels as expressing women's longing for freedom and triumph over subjugation, thus 'conclud[ing] tensely, refusing to affirm either hope or despair'.[7] But it is not only Gothics of which this is true. The tense conclusion is character-istic of women's fiction that engages seriously with issues of love, marriage, family and home – all fraught areas for women readers. This 'concluding tensely' may suggest the pleasure involved for modern writers in turning again to Austen's *Emma*, Brontë's *Jane Eyre, Gone With the Wind* and *Rebecca* itself. Recognising their predecessors' narrative compromises with the sexual and gender mores of the day, these writers tend to be suspicious of harmo-nious conclusions to disturbing narratives. The literary challenge lies in satisfying readers who are teased and unsatisfied by tense closures, and who share a scepticism about the union of Elizabeth and stuffed-shirt Mr Darcy or Jane and the semi-disabled Mr Rochester, as well as Scarlett O'Hara's unlikely hope of winning back true love Rhett Butler.

The *Jane Eyre* 'happy ending', with Jane and a maimed Rochester united in modest Ferndean following the symbolic burning of Thornfield Hall, has troubled generations of women readers: testimony to this is the host of reworkings of the text, from Elizabeth Barrett Browning's *Aurora Leigh* (1847) and George Eliot's *The Mill on the Floss* (1860) to Jean Rhys's *Wide Sargasso Sea* (1966) and Margaret Drabble's *The Waterfall* (1969).[8] *Jane Eyre* is, according to Patsy Stoneman, 'a modern myth', so familiar to the reading public that when *Rebecca* first appeared in 1938, *Jane Eyre* was the novel most associated with it, especially (curiously enough) by US critics. Du Maurier began her publishing career with a tribute to Emily Brontë (*The Loving Spirit*), and published on the sisters and their brother Branwell; as for other women writers, echoes of their writings recur throughout her work. As Rebecca Munford makes clear in the previous chapter, *Rebecca* forms part of the continuum of Brontë's mythic text, a literary reworking itself focusing on those troubled patriarchal and class relations and issues of Englishness that were as much in flux in 1938 as they had been in Brontë's 1848.

Rebecca is a work that is so widely known, it can be referenced easily throughout popular culture. Bestselling male writers such as Ken Follett and Stephen King have drawn on the novel's iconic qualities in their own books – the former with his Second-World-War spy thriller, *The Key to Rebecca* (1980) and the latter his horror fiction, *Bag of Bones* (1998), both of them haunted by that magical first line, 'Last night I dreamt I went to Manderley again.'[9] In a third male response to the novel, *Jeanne de Winter at the Wars*, David Roach Pierson set out to write a sequel to *Rebecca* – like Follett's book, set during the Second World War – resulting in a rumbustious John Buchan-like romp across wartime Europe.[10] He took a decision that, significantly, no woman writer has dared, to give a name – Jeanne – to the second Mrs de Winter.

While men have acknowledged the power of this novel, it is women writers who have reinterpreted it for subsequent generations of (predominantly female) readers. Two established writers – Susan Hill (1993) and Sally Beauman (2001) – were commissioned by the du Maurier Estate to write sequel or companion versions. Another, Antonia Fraser (1976), produced a short-story 'prequel', while American novelists Mary Wings (1992) and Maureen Freely (1996) rewrote the novel in contemporary terms.

In *My Lover's Lover* (2002), British writer Maggie O'Farrell made *Rebecca* a thematic reference point, the male protagonist playing the Hitchcock film on TV to signal the emotional threat posed by his mysteriously missing former partner.[11]

The Sequel to *Rebecca*

Susan Hill's *Mrs de Winter* follows the original most closely of all these works. The sequel never returns to Manderley, but Manderley remains a powerful lost dream. Rather like Alexandra Ripley's sequel to *Gone With the Wind* (*Scarlett*, 1991), it begins with the death of a significant figure: in Ripley's case, Mammy, in Hill's, Max's sister Bea, who would have had to take up awkward moral positions within any progressed story. Like the original, it is a curiously sexless story. But Manderley and England/Englishness are the centre of the book and provide the main objects of desire throughout. Despite a necessary return trip to the funeral, the narrator (as in *Rebecca*, the second Mrs de Winter) and Max spend much of the novel abroad, wandering from one watering hole to another, leading dull and predictable lives away from the stares of the public who have seen their faces in the papers. The novel provides a moral refrain – 'We make our own destiny' – but with a strong subtext of the pursuing fates (the ominous Mrs Danvers, with a bloated and blackmailing Jack Favell in tow) and a satisfying closure: Max's death by suicide.

The novel is an elegiac tribute to the meanings of home, English houses and landscapes, and the tragedy of exile, displacement and loss. It provides lush and romantic images of a pastoral domestic Englishness, the geography of which represents the moral and emotional innocence the narrator wishes might erase the guilty past she sees each time she looks at Maxim. As in *Rebecca*, the groaning tea table and simplest domestic daily routines embody that elusive English perfection which Mrs de Winter has lost through her husband's crime. Cobbett's Brake,

81

her new home, is the architectural opposite of the romantic Manderley. The latter, all grey stone and mullioned windows, is in sight and sound of the sea, surrounded by woods, high rhododendrons and fat hydrangeas. Cobbett's Brake, with its sturdy English name, and position as far from the sea as could be, is a rose-red Elizabethan manor house with barley-sugar chimneys, pink walls, lawns, rose-beds, pergolas and small ornamental ponds. Of course this is an ironic contrast; Mrs de Winter lives here and holds a large party, echoing the Manderley ball. But she never has the children she dreams of, and the cosy assumption that a new domestic space can offer a fresh start is cruelly dashed. There is no single site of darkness; darkness is in the soul. Cobbett's Brake, too, becomes the Gothic house, the mansion of fear, guilt and retribution.

What is puzzling about this sequel is that, given the decisive closure Hill provides (thus ending any further speculation over Max's fate, though not his widow's . . .), it denies us the vengeance the reader yearns to come from the repressed, innocent narrator herself. Though expressing doubts and a rising rage about her husband (she keeps seeing his hands as those of a murderer) she is never allowed active intervention in his fate. He still makes all the crucial decisions, and her character never develops. As with the original, we are left with a relatively untainted, unnamed Mrs de Winter, who is released from her murderer husband by his own hand. This satisfies Jack Favell and Mrs Danvers, but not – it seems – the forgiving narrator. Indeed, the novel ends with a tragic-romantic flourish – her solitary boat floating in the sea opposite Manderley, while she scatters Max's ashes in the direction of the ruins. Hill tells us no more about Mrs de Winter than we knew before.

Sequels tend to be restricted by the terms of the original. However they may wish to carry the narrative and characters into new areas, they will be judged in terms of the light cast on the original, and the reader's conservative desire for more of the same almost inevitably prevents too radical a departure from original characterisation and narrative. The sequel must offer a narrative of continuity rather than disruption, a labour of love rather than a subversion or parody – a second helping of a favourite dish, not an entirely new course. Its restrictions suggest, therefore, a conservative form that has little creative leeway; *Mrs de Winter* feels constrained by its more brilliant original. More challenging are the freer interpretations and literary game-playing by subsequent writers who have produced provocative, readerly versions of the Urtext.

Renewing the Story

Antonia Fraser's 'Rebecca's Story', published in *Harpers & Queen* in 1976 and reprinted in this collection, was written as a response to another female revisionary writer. Fraser introduces the story with a foreword, describing her fascination with du Maurier's novel and her naming of her eldest child after the eponymous heroine; her inspiration was Jean Rhys's prequel to *Jane Eyre*, *Wide Sargasso Sea* (1966). Drawing a parallel between the characters of the two novels' unknown, and possibly unreliably narrated first wives – Bertha Mason and Rebecca de Winter – Fraser wished to explore the nature of the two most vilified characters in the original, Rebecca and her cousin, Jack Favell. The brief story, a tantalising outline of what might have been a wonderful prequel novel, is Rebecca's first-person account of her marriage to Maxim, one she is completing, and planning to hide, before she tells Max of her terminal illness and intention to leave him for Jack (and, as we know from the original, before Max murders her). Focusing on the narrative of the Bertha Mason figure, defined by du Maurier (following Charlotte Brontë) as nymphomaniac, heartless and uncontrolled, Fraser gives Rebecca's side of the marriage. Here, Rebecca is a wronged innocent, her cousin and housekeeper the figures who recognise her for what she is; the second wife is the childlike icon of Maxim's diseased sexual imagination. Although only a sketch, this proposes a sympathetic version of Rebecca that is impossible for the paranoid, self-demeaning second wife to imagine; and – like *Jane Eyre* and *Wide Sargasso Sea* – it sets the narrative within the patriarchal Bluebeard's Castle that is at the heart of female Gothic.

This is the only literary reworking to which the author responded. Daphne du Maurier provided a witty epilogue that was published with the story, praising Fraser for an 'ingenious and delightful' piece that made her rethink the work she had virtually forgotten, and sardonically reconsidering her resistance to a sequel:

> Fans have always suggested I should write a sequel and now is the time. Frank and the second Mrs de Winter – who never revealed her true name because it was Jemima Piddlequick – shall install an aquarium in Rebecca's cottage on the beach, in which they will house an enormous killer shark, a relative of the one in *Jaws*, so enabling me, an authoress rapidly approaching her dotage, to leap on to the prevailing bandwagon of popular taste, buy myself an island in the Pacific, and thumb my nose at the tax-collector.

Uncharacteristically, du Maurier seemed to enjoy being drawn into the business of sequel writing, suggesting it opened up many new interpretations of her own story. The tone of her response suggests a mild flattery at being reread so elegantly. It would have been fascinating to read her response to two novels that pay homage to *Rebecca*, paradoxically by departing radically from the original.

Mary Wings's *Divine Victim* does so by providing *two* dead Rebeccas. One is the Rebecca whose life is researched by the novel's feminist academic narrator, and whose remote Montana

Gothic house becomes the temporary home for her and new lover, Marya. The second is glamorous, but cruelly destructive, Ilona, the cause of whose death emerges in the course of the novel. Both Rebeccas are talented, beautiful and seductive; both are placed within communities of women that share rivalry, creative tensions and sexual pleasure. The first Rebecca is a nun whose sexual deviance and sacrilegious deeds wreak havoc in the convent and lead to the narrator's terrifying experiences in her spooky house (including near murder by the Mrs Danvers figure dressed in black – the black of a nun's habit). The second Rebecca is a sexy lesbian jet-setter scholar who seems to invite her fate but who keeps returning in memory and in the narrator's unsatisfied emotional and sexual desires. For much of the novel Wings plays on our assumption of the narrator's innocence and victimhood, but the narrative finally reveals her 'complicit[y] in a victim/abuser relationship',[12] as well as her own crime.

The narrator reflects on the kinds of female communities women like herself, Ilona and Marya would have belonged to a hundred years ago, and where they would have 'fulfilled our love of scholarship, our organizational skills, our need for charity, safety, challenge, pleasure in the company of other women', women who were 'All in collusion. Or in competition. Or in love' (pp.169–170). The dynamics of such communities, and particularly the rivalries and betrayals involved in them, all enter into the narrator's researched history of Rebecca's unorthodox past and her own bitter fight with rival art historian Ilona.

Mary Wings described her initial inspiration for writing a 'lesbian gothic' as that iconic moment in Hitchcock's film, *Rebecca*, when the young bride stares at the 'R'-embroidered pillow – in her novel, a letter 'embroidered with lesbian love in every stitch by Rebecca's maid, Danny' (p.11). This 'sapphic tapestry' gave her the idea of updating the absent Rebecca figure as 'every woman's symbol of forbidden sexuality. Uncontrollable, renegade sexuality. Sexuality which feels distinctly lesbian' (p.17), in line with one reading of du Maurier's original as a 'lesbian witch hunt' (p.24). She was struck by the intensely erotic tone of Mrs Danvers's presentation of Rebecca, and indeed the obsession the second Mrs de Winter has with Mrs Danvers herself and the physical beauty of her predecessor. Wings follows biographers, especially Margaret Forster, in spelling out the history and implications of du Maurier's own 'Venetian tendencies' (as she referred to lesbianism), as well as those verbal clues within the novel: allusions to Rebecca's 'shame', 'degradation', 'shadow life', 'abnormality' and 'unspeakable days' which were familiar fictional euphemisms for homosexuality.

Maureen Freely's novel, *The Other Rebecca*, carries a knowing title, suggesting 'the other woman' as well as 'the other novel', and is playfully allusive throughout. Freely claims to have followed her customary fictional track by drawing on several genres – Gothic, satire, romantic thriller and family romance.[13] Unlike Mary Wings, she found inspiration for the novel in a literary rather than film source. As for many girls, *Rebecca* was a resonant text in her teenage years. Calling the original novel 'a departure . . . a shadow', she used the well-known story to explore issues around women's fear of their own power, and their terror that using it would only destroy. The second Mrs de Winter is nameless like du Maurier's, though Freely thinks her name is also Rebecca, and she is a heroine who, though in some ways innocent, ought to have known better. In du Maurier's novel the reader is never given emotional space to ask why the narrator stays with Maxim, but in *The Other Rebecca* one asks the question all the time, in the context of internecine strife between writers within close, incestuous communities. The Gothic house exists, but only as a symbolic site of literary/familial community; the house Mrs de Winter inhabits is a modest cottage nearby. Max is significantly displaced economically, a salaried editor rather than landowner.

While Mary Wings elaborates on the lesbian subtext of the

original, Freely plays with the incestuous overtones of Mrs de Winter's relationships with her first husband (also her cousin), with Max and the dead Rebecca, even to the point of bringing back to life the 'dead' wife to reassert her position as mother and senior wife, an act precipitated by Mrs de Winter's review of Rebecca's novel. Maureen Freely abandons the childlessness in the original in favour of Max's two children by Rebecca, and the second Mrs de Winter's pregnancy, thus further complicating the family romance. Englishness is considered obliquely through the outsider status of both Mrs de Winters, who are married to a very English literary figure, but who (like Maureen Freely herself) are American writers, yearning to be absorbed within English literary and social culture but also having an ironic distance on it. Most obviously they bring to mind the figure of Sylvia Plath, as represented in Anne Stevenson's biography, *Bitter Fame*, though Freely claims her models are also upper-class, clannish groups of British families that intersect with one another in game-playing ways that often exclude and damage outsiders. With its references to writers from William Blake and Mary Wollstonecraft to Sylvia Plath and Ted Hughes, the novel addresses issues of interpretation, literary originality and influence, class, sexual and social alienation and betrayal, and the dissemination and ultimate fate of works of art. The second Mrs de Winter talks to a fire sculptor about his ephemeral artworks, expressing scepticism about art that does not last. He responds with a pithy comment on the whole business of artistic legacy: 'Art might start out as a controlled experiment, but the interesting part was seeing what happened after it was beyond the power of the creator to stop it.' (p.267)

The meanings of the house are very different from those in Hill and Wings: because this Manderley, called Beckfield, is not the only site of Mrs de Winter's narrative, the novel releases the reader from that claustrophobic atmosphere of Gothic domestic space. This version of the *Rebecca* story comments obliquely on women's emotional inertia, as well as women's power, both to destroy and also to bring to life. Mrs de Winter literally gives new life to two very destructive figures, Max and Rebecca, though she herself survives, pregnant, to tell the tale and invite reader response: 'So, reader, it's for you to decide. Why am I still picking through the ashes? Why can't I get that picture out of my head?' (p.279) The writerly narrative open-endedness opens a space for readerly reinterpretation.

A 'Companion Novel'

Maureen Freely and Sally Beauman share a post-modern and post-feminist knowingness about genre, women's writing and creativity. Beauman has long signified on earlier women's writing – *Rebecca's Tale* is no different. Like Freely, she crosses genre, from romance to detective novel, self-consciously alluding to Shakespearian themes of transformation/delusion, drawn from her own profound knowledge of Shakespearian theatre. She also recasts a stock of women writers' characters and concerns, returning, like du Maurier, to Charlotte and Emily Brontë, and to later writers such as Margaret Mitchell, du Maurier herself and Sylvia Plath. Like her female predecessors, she draws on Grimm's tales, uses familiar female Gothic tropes, such as Bluebeard and the wild garden and secret hideaway, and alludes to the problem of women being spoken for rather than finding their own voices. Beauman's *Rebecca's Tale* – like Antonia Fraser's – is a notebook written secretly by the most enigmatic and endangered character, read later by a gay man who is investigating his own past and identity through a forensic dig into hers.

Beauman's 'companion' novel came about because she was complaining to du Maurier's son, Kits Browning, that Rebecca's voice had been utterly silenced. He challenged her, 'Why not give her a voice?'. She approached the key questions – Who was

Rebecca? Why was she murdered? What was the impact of her death? – by narrating the story from different perspectives, including Rebecca's own, and creating characters and situations not in the original novel. *Rebecca's Tale* is in four parts, two narrated by men, two by women. One male narrator, Terence Grey, was invented by Beauman; the other, Colonel Julyan, a minor figure in the original novel, is nevertheless crucial since he knows Max is the murderer. The women are Rebecca herself and Colonel Julyan's daughter Ellie, who becomes the latter-day living spirit of Rebecca. As with all the versions of *Rebecca*, Manderley is a brooding, dominating presence and Gothic prison. Here, too, it is the site of class, gender and sexual corruption and atrophy: the 'mausoleum, the wax house' of Sylvia Plath's poem 'Stings', which is one of the novel's epigraphs (recalling Freely's Plath subtext). There is a pun about the house being both 'heirless' and 'airless', the problems of inheritance and succession being crucial to a study of problematic and mysterious kinship networks.

Permeating the novel are familiar Shakespearian and Gothic themes of power and complicity, metamorphosis and rebirth, gender confusion and performativity through superficial appearance, and different kinds of love. Alluding indirectly to the du Maurier family theatrical lineage, Beauman has identified theatricality as a key element of Rebecca herself and Manderley as a site of various kinds of female masquerade. Beauman invents for Rebecca a dramaturgical history that explains her own destructive relationship with Max and his family home. Rebecca has the most original and haunting voice in the novel, one that poetically addresses an unborn, beloved child in an intimate tone that – like other women writers' first person narratives – engages the woman reader and takes her into the heart of the mysteries.

Talking of learning Shakespeare's lines to speak on stage, Rebecca describes:

Learning those winged words. I hear the meanings behind the meanings under the meanings – what an echo chamber! Max always wanted words to be shackled, so 'love' means this and 'hate' means that: lock them up in a poor prison of sense and slam the door on them ... I don't agree: words should take you on journeys. (p.307)

Those meanings behind meanings, words taking readers on journeys, continue to resonate in the echo chamber of *Rebecca* sequels and revisions, not to mention in multiple other ways through the constantly reprinted novel, Hitchcock's great film, TV and radio versions, play and opera productions, and tourist literature and trails. It seems no coincidence that all these women writers choose to leave her nameless, somewhat undefined and boundaryless, a decentred subject, an enigmatic Everywoman/no woman. In Susan Hill's sequel, she is refused a truly active and powerful afterlife. But for Antonia Fraser, Mary Wings, Maureen Freely and Sally Beauman, her complicity with Max is transformed into different kinds of collaboration and power. Both creative and destructive, their Mrs de Winters are the agents of transformation and apocalyptic change. The Jane Eyre story, deriving as it did from earlier Gothic models, and influencing generations of women writers and readers, is given new relevance in the contemporary world by Daphne du Maurier's version and women writers' various responses to Rebecca's story. This narrative of haunting, uncertainty about one's class and gender identity, and the mutual attraction and hostility that exist between men and women, and indeed between women, continues to tantalise. Indeed, in recent times, it has truly come to life: the potent myth of Mrs de Winter, betrayed innocent in the large mansion amidst an introverted and mendacious family she does not understand, has new resonance since the tragic rise and fall of Diana, Princess of Wales, and her (now triumphant) Rebecca nemesis, the feared/desired Other Woman, Camilla.

Publishers, agents and literary estates have recognised the continuing appeal of this irresistible story. Through *Jane Eyre/Rebecca* 'ghostly presence', sequel, literary reworking and companion, the discerning and lucrative female book-buying public is being well served with the second helpings *and* new courses it craves.

Rebecca's Story

Antonia Fraser

FOREWORD

I have always been fascinated by Daphne du Maurier's famous best-seller, Rebecca. *In fact I called my eldest child after the book: she would have been called Max if she had been a boy. But it was another, more recent, favourite book,* Wide Sargasso Sea *by Jean Rhys, which provided the inspiration for 'Rebecca's Story'. Jean Rhys took the character of Rochester's Creole first wife — mad and destructive by the time we meet her in* Jane Eyre — *and told for the first time her side of the story. It occurred to me one day, rereading* Rebecca *for the umpteenth time, that we know nothing positive about Rebecca's 'vicious' past except as related by Max de Winter to his second wife, and retold by her to us. On the other hand there is a great deal of positive evidence on the other side to her charm, graciousness, sweetness to tenants, old people, etc., etc. The narrator of* Rebecca, *the second Mrs de Winter, is of course madly in love with Max (who is much older than her) and naturally accepts everything he says. Her other marked attribute is her pathological jealousy of the dead Rebecca: she is for this reason not a particularly reliable witness to the character — as opposed to the words and deeds — of Mrs Danvers and Rebecca's cousin Jack. Now read on . . .*

I am waiting now for Max. Here in the boathouse cottage which is so much dearer to me than all the state of Manderley. I have to tell Max the final news from the doctor. He suspects already.

There is a new coldness about him, a new distaste. Last night I dreamt I ran away from Manderley. Down the long drive, away from the great house and the hungry roar of the sea. I ran, away from the chill and silence of our lives, to warmth and safety – I stretched out my arms, I fell – and then I woke up. It doesn't do to tell Max these dreams.

Besides, he no longer comes near me. I don't mean in private, nor in my bedroom which Danny tends with such care. When did he ever do that? Except for that first terrible night of our honeymoon in the South of France . . . Even now I can hardly write about that scene or think about it.

'You know that I do not like disease,' was all he said when I told him of the doctor's suspicions. 'You must inform me of the progress of your condition.'

'Max' – I began desperately. Then I stopped.

'You will be taken care of. I shall arrange for you to leave Manderley, of course.' He looked round the dining room. It was as though the prospect of nurses, sickness, humanity itself was inconceivable in this beautiful room.

I fled to Danny, who, without knowing what it was all about, comforted me. Dear dear Danny, who has always instinctively known the truth between Max and me – Danny, so warm and loving, the only mother I have ever known. It was Danny who warned me, that ominous day when Max first came to our house. I should have listened. 'A cold man, a secret man,' she said. But I didn't heed her. It never occurred to me that such a man could hold my fate in his hands.

Until I was seventeen I had never known a properly unhappy moment. My mother was dead, it was true, but she has always been a shadowy figure to me. My cousin Jack and I were allowed to grow up quite wild together, quarrelling, laughing, quarrelling again. And I suppose even then we loved each other. But of course we didn't realise that. And if we had?

'What a lovely young couple. He so fair and she so dark,'

they used to say. But we were also first cousins. And we were also very poor. We were not encouraged to think that we might love each other. All of that came later . . . tragically later.

And there would always have been my father's financial difficulties and debts. That was how Max first came to the house. We knew my father was desperately worried. Words like banks, and foreclosures, and mortgages penetrated even the enchanted world of our youth. Then one day Danny begged me to keep clear of the house, or if I came in, to be tidy, to be polite, to remember that I was now seventeen years old.

I forgot. I came dancing in. Some silly argument with Jack, as we were riding together, had led to one of our more high-spirited quarrels, and then a sweet reconciliation. I stopped, bewildered. A strange man was at the fireplace. As I entered, I heard my father say in a desperate voice: 'This house is the only thing left . . .' Then he stopped and introduced me.

'This is Mr de Winter, of Manderley, Rebecca. Do you remember I once took you to tea there when you were a little girl?'

I did remember. A beautiful but starchy and pompous house, to my child's eye cold and unwelcoming. Jack and I went off to the woods and played about and got lost and had to be found.

Max's curious eyes fixed me. I can remember nothing more he said, except that as I left the room I did hear him remark in a slightly warmer voice: 'Your house is not quite the only thing you have left, my dear fellow. You also have a very lovely young daughter.'

I don't know how it was fixed and I shall never know what the details were. I am aware that my father stayed in his beloved house and there was some money at last, till he died. I know that I was taken from my home, my world, from Jack, and I was married, still bewildered and lost, to Max de Winter. I became, in theory at least, the mistress of Manderley.

But before that came the honeymoon. I was quite ignorant. No one had even kissed me except Jack, and that – then – in the most brotherly or cousinly way. Danny did try to tell me the facts of marriage, but I didn't understand her.

'My darling wants to give so much,' she said in the end, but still doubtfully. 'So perhaps it will be all right. You've always wanted to give, since the day you were born.'

She was right to be doubtful. I wanted to give – what, I didn't know. Max did not want to receive. And he was quite certain what he did not want to receive.

It was the first night of our honeymoon in our grand suite in the hotel in Menton. I put on my bridal nightdress, part of my new rich trousseau, heavy oyster silk clinging to the body, cut low.

'At last I'm a woman, a married woman,' I thought proudly.

'What is that disgusting garment?' It was Max's voice, a tone I had never heard before. I still smiled, not really understanding, and held out the soft skirt to him. The bodice fell open. I clutched it nervously to me. The silk slipped.

'Stop it,' he said coldly. 'Stop behaving like a whore!' He came closer. 'It's not for that I married you. Don't you understand? Where is it now, that funny young lost look you had when I first saw you in your father's house? I married a child. See that you remain that way. Get something different to wear tomorrow.' He turned on his heel and left the room.

I cried myself to sleep alone in the great bed. I suppose Max spent the night in the dressing room. It was the first of many such nights.

It was the next day, sitting on that high spot on the coast, my hair blowing in the wind, that Max told me things about himself which I never wish even now to repeat to a living person. How he had no use or desire for me as a woman, and never

Antonia Fraser

would have. And that he would never even touch me. But he might sometimes wish to gaze upon me . . .

I turned from him in horror, looking over the bright sea and the precipice. I could have thrown myself over. He knew that. I did not speak but there was no need. He knew that my whole being turned away from what he said. Silently, I was repeating to myself: 'Never. Never. Never.'

I don't know what it was in his childhood or youth which turned him towards those perverse desires – which at the same time he could never gratify. It was all in his diseased mind, the things he outlined to me that day. Later I used to speculate. I used to love his grandmother: she had much warmth in her, and his mother I never knew. I suspected that Max's father might have treated his mother with some coldness, too, from his portrait.

Or was it rooted in his childhood with Bea? Beatrice was a comfortable woman when I became her sister-in-law, and it was difficult to imagine her as a passive child, a little girl. But from the start she disliked me, so perhaps that dislike was rooted in jealousy. And once when Giles was in a drunken fit, he decided to make advances to me. He leered: 'I've got a bloody cold wife, and from what she tells me, you've got a bloody cold husband, if not something worse. So why don't we console each other?'

It seemed to fit.

Certainly Frank knew of Max's tastes: from the first he was always uncomfortable in my presence. I think he felt sorry for me. I tried to make a friend of him once, in desperation. I thought we might discuss Max and see if we could help him, he could help him, anyone could help him. But he was frozen in his loyalty, his embarrassment. The effort failed. After that Frank avoided me.

So we went back to Manderley. And as we drove up the long sweep of the drive, I looked at the house as at an enemy. I vowed that I would conquer it. It should be not only beautiful – but it would also come alive. There would be parties, people, life. No matter what the sham of our private life, Max and I, in public it would be perfection.

For a long time I think I succeeded not only in fooling the world but even in a way Max himself that I was happy in our curious existence. I had Danny to help me. I was allowed Danny to help me run Manderley. In his odd way Max was quite tolerant of her, even fond of her. The fact that Danny too regarded me as a child meant that we all dealt quite easily together on the surface.

It was several years before I even indulged in the slightest flirtation, despite the attentions of such as Giles, and even then my flirtations were quite innocent. I used to tell Danny about them and we used to laugh together lightly and then drop the subject. I don't think Danny understood the precise nature of the gulf between Max and me, though she could not help knowing that he never shared the lovely bedroom looking over the sea, where she kept all my belongings so beautifully and so protectively.

In the same way, I don't think Danny understood how deeply I fell in love with Jack, when the inevitable happened: suddenly I discovered, from the depths of my barren marriage, all the heights of physical passion with him. How could all that warmth have gone forever frustrated? The wonder is that it went so long dammed. Or perhaps, as I like to think, Jack and I were always meant for each other. His wildness, his recklessness, his tenderness, I loved all these things about Jack. Jack would give his last penny to a beggar and not look back: where Max would ask Frank to note the penny as a loan in the Manderley account books. As a result Jack never had any money. But he didn't care. He brought me presents – expensive when a bet came off, cheap when it didn't, but always so full of thought for me, myself, not the adornment of Manderley. He would arrive out of the blue and kiss Danny. There was laughter and joy when Jack was at Manderley.

We discovered our proper adult love in the boathouse cottage which I did up down at the beach. I loved to sail. It consoled me and I was free. And the cottage was something of my own. I used to chat to poor mad Ben on the beach and try to help him. I thought maybe he should see a doctor . . . And then one day Ben shrank away from me. It was Danny who discovered via Robert the footman that Max had told him I was a witch who would have him put in the asylum. It was the same with anyone on the estate with whom I tried to form a friendship. Max wanted me to be isolated, a public person only. So I was left with Danny – and Jack.

At first I didn't tell Jack about Max. We were too caught up in our own love, in London, in the cottage, not caring. But later I wanted him to know. Not the full details of course. Those I have never told to a living soul and never will. But how we had never been man and wife to each other. How our wonderful marriage, our whole life at Manderley, was a mockery.

'Leave him. Come away with me,' said Jack. He said it directly, instantly, as he said everything. 'Even if he won't divorce you, it doesn't matter. We'll have a proper life together, Rebecca. We were always meant for each other. You know that. We'll be poor. But we never minded about that before. We'll go away – to Australia, or Africa, or America. We'll go away. Away from Manderley and Max de Winter.'

I hesitated. Not because I didn't love him. But because it was just recently I had felt the first symptoms of the disease, not like Max's a disease of the mind, but a disease of the body.

I wanted Jack to know everything about me before he decided. I had to see a doctor first.

So now I sit waiting for Max to tell him, and after that in the dawn Jack himself will arrive from London, and we'll be together . . . Max will no longer want me, a sick woman, he has made that quite clear. He has a horror of sickness, because it means age, not childhood, age and death. He'll let me go. He must. I know he will. And I will go to Jack. And for the last months of my life I'll know love and warmth and companionship with Jack. For as long as I can, as we both can.

After that the pain will come. But Danny will care for me then as she always has. Danny will see to it that I don't suffer too long.

At least Max must let me have these last months of my life with Jack. After I've gone he'll find some other wife for Manderley, some other victim. Perhaps she will be a willing victim: perhaps he will find a secret child, where I was always proud to be a woman. Perhaps he will even find happiness, in his own strange way, with another different woman, when I am gone.

I can hear his footsteps now. I put this away and let Max – for the last time – decide my fate.

Epilogue: An Afternote by Daphne du Maurier to Antonia Fraser's 'Rebecca's Story'

I must begin by saying that I have not read Wide Sargasso Sea *by Jean Rhys, although I understand it was widely reviewed and praised, and the idea ingenious. There are many characters in fiction about whose past we know little – coming upon them, as it were, midway through their life story. My own Rebecca was certainly an enigma and intended to be such, although I must confess that after nearly forty years – the book was begun in the autumn of 1937 and finished in 1938 – I have forgotten almost everything but the bare bones of the story. I watched the film repeated on television a few years ago, but have not reread, or even glanced at the novel for very much longer than that, possibly a couple of decades.*

So, I was able to read 'Rebecca's Story' with the awakened interest of a newcomer to the theme, although my memory was jogged now and again by certain puzzled bewilderment that the people I thought I had known I had evidently misjudged.

Poor Rebecca . . . As naïve and unsophisticated as the second wife who supplanted her, and Maxim the real villain of the piece; cold, cruel and perverted into the bargain. Yes, it might well be. I had got everything wrong. Mrs Danvers not the sinister black-robed housekeeper I had once glimpsed on the steps of somebody's house, firing dormant imagination at the time, but a dear, kindly foster-mother to a charming girl whose mother had died, with the cousin Jack Favell a cheerful, faithful playfellow to the end. Oh dear, oh dear, what a shocking judge of character I must have been.

And now I began to doubt the veracity of the second wife. Could she have known the truth from the beginning, and lied throughout her narrative? Did she set her cap at Max from the start, determined to 'get her man' and then break him down, finally setting fire to a Manderley she had detested; realising that a few years abroad would finish him off, upon which she would return to the site, rebuild a vast Country Club from the ashes, and with the agent Frank – who had been her lover – stage pornographic festivals in the minstrels' gallery and thus coin millions from delighted tourists?

Yes, this must have been it. Fans have always suggested I should write a sequel and now is the time. Frank and the second Mrs de Winter – who never revealed her true name because it was Jemima Piddlequick – shall install an aquarium in Rebecca's cottage on the beach, in which they will house an enormous killer shark, a relative of the one in Jaws, *so enabling me, an authoress rapidly approaching her dotage, to leap on to the prevailing bandwagon of popular taste, buy myself an island in the Pacific, and thumb my nose at the tax-collector.*

To end on a more serious note. I thought 'Rebecca's Story' ingenious and delightful, and congratulate Antonia Fraser. But she had better watch out. I have just discovered documents – secreted by King Charles

I when he and his army were in Cornwall – admitting that he and Oliver Cromwell were homosexual. He threatened to tell all. Hence his execution, from which the Lord Protector never fully recovered.

Part 3

Daphne du Maurier's Writing

Who I Am: Adventures in the du Maurier Family Archive

Charlotte Berry and Jessica Gardner

For archivists, the voyeuristic pleasure of sorting through other people's personal papers has professional legitimacy, but it would be dishonest to deny that there is a furtive gratification in opening the boxes, unwrapping parcels, untying bundles of letters and unfolding their secrets as if for the first time. With your white gloves on and magnifying glass in hand, it is easy to give yourself over to the fiction that no one has been here before, and in the archive of the du Maurier family,[1] with documents reaching back five generations and representing the shadowy lives of people such as Mary Anne Clarke (mistress of the Duke of York) and writers of the calibre of George and Daphne du Maurier, the illicit pleasure of the archive is especially sweet. Yet only a little digging in the boxes reveals we are not the first: Daphne du Maurier has left her mark all over the papers as researcher and archivist before us, preserving and exploring her family history, and turning what she found into published memoir and fiction.

Her first instalment of family saga, *The Du Mauriers* (1937), begins with Mary Anne Clarke (1776–1852), whose own fortune, ironically, rested not on the *survival* of documentary evidence but on its *destruction*, for Clarke secured an annuity (later passing to her daughter, Ellen) and an army commission for her son, George, on condition that she did not make public inflammatory letters about her relationship with the Duke of York, second son of George III and brother to George IV and William IV.

These letters, sadly, do not survive. In 1809, Clarke agreed to deliver them up, as failure to do so would forfeit the contract and thus her annuity; evidence in the archive suggests they were burned by their custodian in 1863.[2] The contemporary evidence about Clarke that Daphne du Maurier drew on was relatively scant,[3] but she was captivated by the story and went on to expand on her portrait of Mary Anne in *The Du Mauriers* with a full fictionalised biography, *Mary Anne* (1954).

Daphne du Maurier was equally struck by the family legend of the Busson du Mauriers, into whose family Mary Anne Clarke's daughter Ellen (1797–1870) married in 1831. Her husband, Louis-Mathurin Busson du Maurier (1797–1856), was the son of a French émigré master glass-maker who fled France to escape the revolution – and possibly a charge of fraud. The Busson du Mauriers, like the Clarkes, were in receipt of an annuity or pension, in their case from the French royal family, in compensation for their losses during the Terror (the earliest document in the archive, dated 1816, is the grant of annuity to Louis-Mathurin's sister, Louise Wallace, née Busson du Maurier).[4] Like the Clarkes, the Busson du Mauriers were proud of their royal connections; tradition spoke of an ancestral Château du Maurier with a large glass-works attached, whose Busson master and gentleman glass-workers produced glass of the highest quality, fit for the royal table. Little documentary evidence for this period has survived within the du Maurier family archive, but it was a story that held great charm for Daphne du Maurier. The collection includes an unpublished draft typescript introduction to *The Glass-Blowers* (1963), in which she describes her own pleasure in the discovery of papers preserved by her grandfather, George du Maurier:

> I looked through every paper in the bureau for further evidence, and found a batch of letters from the émigré's son Louis-Mathurin who had been born in London, and who had returned to France at the restoration of the

monarchy. In three of the letters he mentions meeting an eighty-year-old aunt Sophie [Busson] for the first time . . . The pieces began to fit together. The aunt, having met her nephew, sent him the family history, and those parts that had displeased him he had scored through with his pen! My curiosity was now fully aroused, and I made several visits to France . . . Little by little the jigsaw fitted into place, and the pictures formed.[5]

The original eight pages of tatty, scored notes on the history of the 'Famille Busson',[6] allegedly in the hand of Sophie Busson, and numerous fragile cross-written letters of Louis-Mathurin to his sister Louise Wallace from the 1830s–1840s still survive within the archive.[7] In her account, Daphne du Maurier rather glossed over her grandfather George du Maurier's (1834–1896) keen interest in the du Maurier history, though he had written to French archives himself to try to establish the facts; various genealogical papers in his characteristic hand are included in the Exeter papers.[8] However, Daphne still had to undertake a considerable amount of research herself in order to check up on the claims (which proved unfounded) of the documents she had unearthed in the family collections. To do this, she employed research assistants in England and in France, who spent weeks ferreting through libraries and archives on the Busson trail:

> Helpers joined in the research, both in London, and in Paris, and in the provinces of France. Papers, leases, wills, long buried under dust in notary's offices, came to light, and what was more uncanny still certain wild guesses of my own concerning family history were proved correct.[9]

Here, as elsewhere in the archive, historical discovery fuses with the writer's powerful imagination:

It was not just mere deduction, it was as though something within me *knew*. I remember on one occasion having
the weird feeling that the black sheep, my great-great-
grandfather, sold glass in a boutique in the Palais-Royal. I
could see him there, swinging under the arcades, graceful,
blue-eyed, blond, just as his sister Sophie had described
him. Within a few weeks came word from my research-
worker in Paris. 'I have just turned up a letter from Robert
Busson, your great-great-grandfather, written from No. 255
Palais-Royal, where it seems he had a boutique'.
Coincidence or guess-work? I prefer to think it was neither,
and that memory, like colour of hair and feature, can be
inherited too. Love of family is a very personal thing. You
either have it or you don't . . .[10]

Two other manuscript notebooks in the archive collection illus-
trate du Maurier's transformation from historian to storyteller. The
first, a notebook containing rough notes by George du Maurier
and with blank pages reused by Daphne, contains her rather dry
research notes on the background to the historical period in which
Mary Anne Clarke lived.[11] In the second notebook, a black pocket
book so tiny it could easily have been lost over the years, we see
Daphne du Maurier change from historian to creative writer as
she reduces those 'shards of evidence'[12] into sharp character sketches
for Mary Anne, her daughter Ellen, son-in-law Louis-Mathurin
Busson du Maurier, grandson George du Maurier, and other
important family members who are all portrayed in detail in *The
Du Mauriers, Mary Anne* and *The Glass-Blowers*. Mary Anne is characterised as 'painted and passé, witty, shrewd', but the portrait for
her daughter, first named as Hélène but later as Ellen, is less deci-
sively drawn: 'Opinions differ as to her character. Round shoul-
dered (hump-backed?), a little querulous . . . sharp-tongued at
least!'. Her great-grandfather appears thus:

Louis-Mathurin du Maurier

Has either fallen in love with the face or the fortune of Hélène Clarke. He is a good-looking, charming young man, irresponsible and careless . . . He has no idea of saving money and runs completely through her little fortune.[13]

It is the correspondence within the archive that provides most of the 'biographical bones'[14] on which these vignettes are based. The letters record the du Maurier family leading a nomadic life, moving constantly between London and mainland Europe (mainly Paris) and increasingly facing financial difficulties. Relations between the young couple and Mary Anne Clarke become strained, as is shown in a letter from Louis-Mathurin to his sister Louise Wallace, written from London in June 1844:

Ellen as you may imagine is rather dull as I am obliged to be so often away from home but she bears it with patience. We have been quarrelling with Mother [Mary Anne Clarke] and brother [George Clarke] which makes it unpleasant. The Mother has gone to live in Bruxelles. However this will blow over as everything does in this world.[15]

In another undated letter from Paris, Louis-Mathurin asks his sister's advice on his two sons George and Eugene: 'I shall be glad to learn what you think of the boys' drawings – They still say the youngest [Eugene] has the greatest facility from a natural *coup d'oeil* tho' he'd be too young to expect application from him. The Eldest [George] works hard.'[16] Ironically, it was George du Maurier who went on to carve out an illustrious career for himself as an illustrator, and the author of *Trilby* (1894). By contrast, the correspondence in the archive shows that Eugene lacked application even in adult life. He entered the French army and relied heavily thereafter on his aunt Louise Wallace for financial support.

George du Maurier (1834–1896) is perhaps the most fully documented figure in the archive, through his literary manuscripts, large art portfolios and bundles of illustrated correspondence, particularly with his mother Ellen du Maurier and his wife Emma, née Wightwick.[17] Although Daphne du Maurier edited and published her grandfather's early family letters, many unpublished letters remain in the archive. For instance, George du Maurier, who later went blind in one eye, wrote from Malines (where he was studying art) in January 1859, as he was about to leave for Germany to see a specialist about his failing eyesight:

> I am going to Gräfsath next Tuesday or Wednesday, to know my fate – and in a fortnight hence shall probably have returned – what shall we be thinking of next Saturday next week at this hour? What shall I have seen, heard, done and be done to?

On arrival, he continued:

> Saturday 29 Jan
> ½ past 10
> [. . .] We are *thinking* that it's very jolly for me to paint a little as I did today [. . .] *Heard* [the doctor] say I shall soon be better. Did and was *done* to many funny things which I shall relate to my friends, with those little embellishments for which I am justly renowned – all of which is very satisfactory.[18]

George and Emma du Maurier had five children, two of whom, Gerald (1873–1934) and Sylvia (1866–1910), are represented in the papers. Two bound volumes of theatre programmes and newscuttings, later mined by Daphne du Maurier for her memoir *Gerald: A Portrait* (1934), record Gerald du Maurier's hugely successful theatrical career.[19] Gerald du Maurier's fame was more ephemeral than that of both his father and daughter, but in his lifetime he was one of the best-known figures of the British stage. Amongst the cuttings in these volumes are the programmes for *The Admirable Crichton* (1902), when he met and became engaged to the actress Muriel Beaumont (1877–1957), and for *Brewster's Millions* (1907), in which he was starring at the Hicks Theatre on Shaftesbury Avenue the night his second daughter, Daphne, was born.

The albums provide insight into the breadth of his stage career, but there are substantial and frustrating gaps in the record. The first volume concludes in 1914 and the second begins in August 1931. If it ever existed, the album of cuttings from his mid-career is missing. The only document in the archive representing Gerald du Maurier's middle years is a 1918 notebook containing his notes on military training, when he left the stage and briefly joined up as a soldier, aged forty-five.[20] There are other absences too: for instance, the albums remain silent over a series of private family tragedies, including the premature deaths in 1907 and 1910 respectively of his brother-in-law, Arthur Llewelyn-Davies, and his sister, Arthur's wife, Sylvia, as well as the deaths of his sister Beatrix Hoyer Millar in 1913, and his brother Guy du Maurier, during the First World War, in 1915.

The most potent glimpse of these family losses comes in the form of a photograph album which, with its haunting Impressionist and pre-Raphaelite style images, we knew to be something very special even before it was properly identified. The album was created by the Scottish playwright J. M. Barrie to record the life of the Llewelyn-Davies family. Barrie had a close relationship with Sylvia Llewelyn-Davies and particularly her five sons, who were later to become the inspiration for the Lost Boys in *Peter Pan*. The memorial album is similar to one held at the National Portrait Gallery,[21] but the du Maurier album holds extra copy drawings of Sylvia by her father, George du Maurier, and has some pages missing. Many of the photographs are taken of Sylvia Llewelyn-Davies and her boys in informal settings, including a series taken on the beach in 1899 whilst on holiday at Rustington, Sussex. Some of these photographs have been previously published,[22] but many have not, and they give a nostalgic glimpse into the life of a young family soon to be devastated by the death of both parents. The focus of the album is firmly set by Barrie on Sylvia – her face, the sensuous curve of her neck – and her sons; Arthur Llewelyn-Davies does not feature prominently, and Barrie himself appears only rarely as a subject, preferring instead to remain behind the camera.

When her father died in 1934, Daphne du Maurier went on to finish the incomplete narrative record of his life by pasting into the second album reviews of her memoir, *Gerald: A Portrait*. Reviewed at the time as a daughter's biography of her famous father, the excellence of the reviews quickly establishes her talent, and the album shifts in its subject emphasis from father to daughter. The final letter in the album symbolically secures the daughter's ascendancy. Dated 21 October 1935, the letter is from one Victor Gollancz, who is 'absolutely delighted' with her manuscript for *Jamaica Inn*, the breakthrough novel that in 1936 was to become her first really big commercial success.

The du Maurier archive reveals much about the private lives of earlier du Maurier generations and about Daphne du Maurier's own research into their history, yet the majority of papers representing her own generation are straight literary manuscripts. Her personal papers, such as letters and diaries, remain for the time being in private hands. However, the iconic value of her literary manuscripts is very high, particularly for her best-known works such as the original typescripts for *Jamaica Inn* and *Rebecca* (1938), the latter presented alongside the famous 'Rebecca notebook' and calling card from Mrs Nelson (Ellen) Doubleday as court evidence in the 1947 plagiarism trial.[23] In total, at least twenty-eight of her published books are represented in the archive by literary manuscripts, research notes and occasional editorial correspondence, and they uniformly provoke a sense of wonder from visitors; in the presence of such documents, it is possible to imagine the author alongside, and see her imagination unfolding on the page.

Of Daphne's siblings, there is much less evidence in the archive. Despite naming her 1951 memoir *It's Only the Sister*, Angela du Maurier (1904–2002) published thirteen books, including two volumes of autobiography. There are four minor manuscript items in the archive believed to be in Angela's hand, these being two cloth-bound neat copies of work by other writers and two smaller notebooks containing neat copies of her own poems, with a couple of loose sheets of rough drafts enclosed. Of their sister Jeanne du Maurier (1911–1997), who inherited her grandfather's artistic talent and worked as a painter, there is no obvious record here or in any other UK collection.

By their nature, archives become scattered and fragmented. Documents in the du Maurier family record have been burned, lost, discarded and sold, and others still remain in private hands. Archives rarely tell the whole story, but in this collection even the frustrating narrative gaps provided fuel for Daphne du Maurier's powerful literary imagination. Her own pleasure in the archive is as obvious as our own, and each time the boxes are opened, the ribbons untied, and the letters unfolded, she is brought close: as a writer, as a researcher, and as an archivist, too.

The View From Kilmarth:
Daphne du Maurier's Cornwall

Ella Westland

'I walked this land with a dreamer's freedom and with a
waking man's perception.'

These words were woven into the foreword of *Enchanted
Cornwall*, a collaboration between Daphne du Maurier and Piers
Dudgeon completed a few months before her death, to describe
the author's relationship of more than sixty years with her adopted
land.[1] Originally, they were the words used by Dick Young, the
narrator of Daphne's last great novel, *The House on the Strand*,
to define his experience of another world more dangerous and
desirable than his own.[2] A time-drug transports Dick to the
medieval past of Kilmarth, the last of Daphne's Cornish homes,
enabling him to explore this colourful land with growing excitement. He retains 'a waking man's perception' as he makes his
repeated journeys into this fourth dimension, but he comes to
dread his reawakening in the real world and the painful withdrawal from his other life. Daphne similarly relished that dreamer's
licence to roam in a different psychological terrain, the place
out of which her fiction emerged; she too, on her arrival at
Kilmarth, came to dread the denial of entry to that more vivid
realm.

At first, on falling in love with Cornwall, Daphne did not
differentiate between the subtly transformed land of the dreamer

114

and the physical presence of busy boatyards, gorse-scented cliffs and heron-haunted creeks. She was simply convinced that she had found the place where she was meant to be, where her imagination could at last be released. 'Here was the freedom I desired,' she wrote of her nineteen-year-old self, recording the epiphany on the bank of the River Fowey that espoused her to Cornwall for ever: 'Freedom to write, to walk, to wander, freedom to climb hills, to pull a boat, to be alone.' As she relives her entrancement with the view from Ferryside, the boathouse that was to become her family's Cornish home, Daphne's distinctive talents are at work, arousing the reader's senses with 'a smell in the air of tar and rope and rusted chain, a smell of tidal water', and stirring in her reader a deep, inchoate desire for the liberty of the open sea. As she writes on, her easy adoption of a male stance betrays the insouciant authority of the androgynous artist: 'I remembered a line from a forgotten book, where a lover looks for the first time upon his chosen one – "I for this, and this for me".' At this moment her emerging sense of selfhood, crystallising around her identity as a writer, is caught up, inextricably and for ever, with her idea of Cornwall.[3]

The rocky peninsula of the far south-west, especially the area around Fowey, which was to become Daphne's emotional home for the rest of her life, offered the natural beauty and remoteness from the metropolitan centre that many writers since the days of the Romantic poets have held to be prerequisites for literary inspiration. Cornwall became the setting for seven of her novels, from her first book *The Loving Spirit*, the saga of a local boat-building family, written at Ferryside, to her last, *Rule Britannia*, her fantasy of a militant Cornish resistance movement, which was written at Kilmarth, less than three miles from Ferryside as the crow flies. Half of her fictional output, and most of the famous du Maurier titles that made her such an extraordinary publishing phenomenon before and after the war – *Jamaica Inn*, *Frenchman's Creek*, *Rebecca*, *The King's General*, *My*

Cousin Rachel – have Cornish settings, though of markedly different places and periods. Her short story 'The Birds' and her play *September Tide* are set around Fowey; *Castle Dor*, the novel partly written by her old neighbour and mentor, Sir Arthur Quiller-Couch, which she completed on his death, takes its title from a nearby Iron Age fort; *Vanishing Cornwall*, which she researched, and worked on together with her son, Christian Browning, is a sustained tribute to her chosen home.

For twenty-six years of her career the author worked from the privacy of Menabilly, the secretive old house which she held on a long lease from the Rashleigh family. Much has been written by Daphne and her biographers on the significance of this greatly loved home in her writing life, but perhaps one of the most important and easily overlooked facts about the quarter-century of her residence is that only three of her Cornish novels were produced there, and two of these – *The King's General* and *The House on the Strand* – were conceived on the cusps of her tenancy. For Daphne's imagination thrived on the dangerous edge of things, and however fundamental her personal need for security, she seemed to write most evocatively when she was exiled from the place she longed for, or haunted by the nightmare of dispossession.

Rebecca begins, unforgettably, with the narrator's dream of passing with difficulty through Manderley's iron gate – 'for a while I could not enter, for the way was barred' – and following the drive that winds unmistakably through the overgrown estate of Menabilly. Daphne, who had always longed to live there, was fascinated by the deserted house, and her description is spiced with the frisson she must have felt as a trespasser in the grounds.[4] Her fertile imagination recreated this abandoned Eden when she was hundreds of miles away in Alexandria, reluctantly playing the role of a senior army officer's wife, and 'going through torments of creation in the very hot weather'.[5] *Jamaica Inn* had been written in Surrey three years earlier, out of frustration at living away from Fowey; and later, during the war, she conjured up the sea birds and pirate ships of *Frenchman's Creek* in land-locked Hertfordshire. *My Cousin Rachel* was the only Cornish novel to appear in the middle of her long Menabilly tenure; it was conceived at an emotionally turbulent time, and the estate she reinvented, far from being a place of contentment, was cursed by a corpse swinging on a gibbet at the crossroads – the site of the gateway to Manderley.

The King's General was the novel which marked the heady days of her wartime move to Menabilly, a transition from trespasser to resident fittingly financed by the huge success of *Rebecca*. Though the bombs had been falling on Plymouth, and American marines had been massing in Fowey in preparation for D-Day (*AM*, pp.237–46), Daphne managed to attune her mind to the Civil War three centuries earlier that had turned Cornish families one against the other. Her narrator, Honor Harris, mistress to the Royalist 'red fox', the King's General in the West, takes refuge in the Rashleighs' house during the hostilities. Despite the plundering of Menabilly by Cromwell's troops, Honor clings to her reassuring love of the countryside, sitting daily on the Gribben headland:

> The Parliament could strip the place of its possessions, take the sheep and cattle, glean the harvest, but they could not take from me, nor from the Rashleighs, the beauty that we looked on every day. [. . .] The sea is very white and still, without a breath upon it, and only a single thread of wash upon the covered Cannis rock. [. . .] Dusk comes slowly to the Gribben hill, the woods turn black, and suddenly, with stealthy pad, a fox creeps from the trees in the thistle park, and stands watching me, his ears pricked . . . Then his brush twitches and he is gone.[6]

Even in this peaceful scene, as Honor sits apart from the ransacked house, there are unsettling hints, heightened by the shift to the present tense: night is falling, and the comings and goings of the prowling predator, like the unpredictable appearances of Honor's 'red fox', bring tension into the evening calm. Rarely are the loveliest Cornish landscapes of du Maurier's novels allowed to console for long. Her renderings of place characteristically express incipient trouble and transience, reflecting changes as swiftly as the moods of the sea.

Daphne did not own Menabilly, and recognised only too clearly from the earliest days that her occupation of the house, ever dependent on the Rashleighs' plans, was as tenuous as Honor's. But in the end she was to bring up her three children there, and it was not until her husband's death that the crisis came. Philip Rashleigh's decision to return to Cornwall, forcing Daphne to contemplate his considerate offer of the dower house at Kilmarth, coincided with a phase of continuing grief over her widowhood and growing concern about her own ageing. Though she tried to be positive, her revealing correspondence with the younger writer Oriel Malet betrayed her underlying anxiety at the prospect of the move; Oriel sensed Daphne's alarm that the wellspring of her creativity was drying up: 'All that [she] wanted was to be left in peace at Mena [. . .]; above all, to hope that inspiration would come and set her mind brewing again' (*LM*, p.186). She had not long finished *Vanishing Cornwall*, which entailed taking a hard look, with 'a waking man's perception', at the region's storied past and problematic present. But she had deliberately started the project to get herself going on 'something that did not mean brewing too hard' at a time when she felt she could not cope with fiction (*LM*, p.198, 7/1/66), and she desperately needed to return to her dreamer's wanderings. Before she left Menabilly – typically, when she was approaching the threshold of her new home but not in full possession – she decided to access Kilmarth's past for *The House on the Strand* as she had once accessed Menabilly's for *The King's General*. She reported delightedly to Oriel that the scheme had worked and broken through her writer's block: 'I really am getting rather brewified about Kilmarth in olden days' (*LM*, p.212, 30/11/67). It was an immense relief; at the early age of sixty, she had feared that her powers were failing.

Menabilly had been a secluded place, perfect for brewing. Like Manderley, it lay like 'a jewel in the hollow of a hand'[7], concealed from curious walkers by its giant rhododendrons and the contours of the land, the sea visible only from the upper rooms. The view from Kilmarth was strikingly different. Sunnier, higher, more open to the winds above and the waves below, the house was exposed to the elements, and gave Daphne a marvellous sea vista.[8] But it was much closer than Menabilly to modern encroachments on the quiet coastal scenery. Walking on the west side of the Gribben, looking across St Austell Bay, Daphne could see Par Sands, edged with a 'row of bathing-huts, lined like dentures in an open mouth', the docks for the clay works, the buildings of Par village, and 'the sprawling tentacles of St Austell enveloping the countryside beyond the bay'. This description, taken from the opening chapter of *The House on the Strand*, exudes the disgust at the ravages of tourism and development that Daphne had expressed in *Vanishing Cornwall*. In utter contrast is the ancient landscape seen by Dick Young on his time travels, where he finds that all these features have been mercifully replaced by a higher sea, an unsilted river and a sward of grass and shrub. The diminished present is swept away by the seductive past, a place of brilliant colour, where hyper-real fields of 'sharp-edged silver grass' glisten under a psychedelic sky of 'blazing ecstatic blue' (*HS*, pp.1–2). The strident telephones and rattling railway tracks of modernity give way to a sparsely populated land of primitive cottages, monks and manor houses; instead of his own mediocre life of bickering and compromise, Dick finds himself overtaken by the intense passions and hardships of his medieval predecessors.

Though the younger, selfish and ineffectual protagonist of *The*

House on the Strand bears no obvious resemblance to Daphne, he stands nevertheless at a comparable mid-life crossroads. Escaping into another realm, he leaves his domestic responsibilities behind, growing obsessed with a past which his wife cannot share, and falling violently in love with a woman separated from him by several centuries. His reckless addiction puts his psychological and physical health at risk, and makes him deceitful in devising opportunities to keep taking the drug. In the end his brave new world betrays him, and he travels back once too often, only to find himself in a hopeless, desolate place. The wretchedness of his last time-trip might be construed as the author giving herself a salutary warning about the dangers of immersion in the illusory world of fiction; she understood how the Gothic tendencies of the imagination could play the dreamer false, leading into menacing shadows better left unexplored. And yet Daphne's gloomy premonition about her future creative life allowed her to empathise with Dick's plight. However she tried to rationalise it, she was rightly predicting that her comfortable routines at Kilmarth, supported by her caring family, helpful neighbours and beautiful surroundings, would be no substitute for that irresistible creative high.

From the day that Daphne made her pledge to Cornwall – 'I for this, and this for me' – the place had never failed her, but she feared that she might yet be deserted by her muse. Turning her back on the bathing-huts of Par Sands, she could walk on the Gribben to her life's end, enjoying the tranquil scenes that Honor had looked upon, or thrilling to the thunderous seas of a winter storm. But ultimately the view from Kilmarth was not enough; Daphne knew only too well, as she had once advised Oriel, that 'in the long run, a book is the only hope' (*LM*, p.178, 23/8/64). She needed to retrieve her imaginative world, those inner regions even more precious than the landscape around her, where for forty years she brewed her extraordinary fiction. But after the brave creative feat of *The House on the Strand*, she found to her dismay that inspiration was slow in coming; like the dreamer returning to Manderley, she 'could not enter, for the way was barred'. Fortunately for her readers, whatever scarred Cornish scenes may meet our waking eyes in the twenty-first century, we can regain at will those imagined domains simply by opening the pages of Daphne du Maurier's novels, and wander her cliffs and creeks with a dreamer's impunity.

Christianity Versus Paganism: Daphne du Maurier's Divided Mind

Melanie Heeley

'ἀπόστασις'[1] ('Apostasis')

I resent, and cannot be reconciled
Anymore now than I was as a child
To the Fatherhood of God, the God of the Sky.
Who Omniscient, All-Seeing, watches on High,
And causes the rain to fall and the sun to shine,
And with paternal pride sent upon me and mine
His only Son, a surrogate for sin,
To bleed within.
I protest, and will not suffer the Cross,
Nor put my hand to the plough, nor bewail the loss
Of the lambs who fled from the fold, and were saved by
     love,
Redeemed by the Sacred Heart, and the God Above.
Listen, it was not so when the world began,
When Chaos reigned in the night and the first man
Knelt on his bended knees and blest the earth
That gave him birth.
Monsters swam in the heavens and in the seas,
The planets reeled; the wingèd birds and bees
Fled from the weeping sky to the still sand,
To the forests, to the trees, to the warm land.
The mountain, with melting snow, uncovered her breast,

So that all things, crying for succour, should have rest,
And her caverns and her hollows gave place
To the human race.
Then Gaia, Mother of Man, rose from the deep
Untroubled earth, and smiled, and banished sleep,
Brought fire from the jagged flints and the crumbling
    stones,
Spilt seed upon the grass, and the buried bones
And shells of ancient matter turned to bread,
So were the naked clothed, and the hungry fed.
And Gaia, stanching the rising Flood
With her own Blood,
Gave increase to the world with her Body's heat,
Blossom, and flower, and fruit, and did entreat
The rivers to seek the sun and fall as rain,
Upon the mountains, valleys, and the plain,
Her children neither bowing, nor praying apart,
But flinging themselves upon her living heart
To share in creation's joy, creation's power,
Each mortal hour.
And that is why I protest, and must deny,
The Fatherhood of God, the God in the Sky.
I will not be mocked by fables of Palestine,
Of shepherds watching their flocks, of water to wine,
Of martyred saints, and sinners reconciled,
Of Mary the Virgin and Jesus the Meek and Mild,
When from the passionate earth came the Sound and Strife
Of Eternal Life.
Burn incense, offer candles, sing the Mass,
And purge the soul to vapour. Let it pass.
But may the body blend to the saffron soil,
The Child return to the Mother, the serpent coil
Protective limbs about the rooted Tree,
And when this earth dissolves to infinity,

May the last man cling to her molten crust
And kiss the dust.

Daphne du Maurier

Daphne du Maurier's novel, *Jamaica Inn* (1936), sees the creation of the spiritually ambiguous character Francis Davey, outwardly the vicar of Altarnun, but inwardly a worshipper of the old pagan gods. I wish to argue, with the aid of two poems, 'Apostasis' and 'Remembrance Day', that du Maurier's own spiritual experience was perhaps the model for Davey's divided mind, and that there is much in her literary legacy that is an expression of her thoughts on both Christianity and paganism, and indeed the tension between these two different belief systems. The poem 'Apostasis' was found amongst the letters between Daphne du Maurier and Victor Gollancz, her main publisher from 1934 onwards. Gollancz himself was the author of several works, mostly of a political and religious nature, and he was in the habit, like all publishers, of sending out advance copies of his works for review and comment. Du Maurier thus read some of these works before they were officially published. 'Apostasis' forms part of du Maurier's response to Gollancz's anthology of quotations, *From Darkness to Light – A Confession of Faith in the Form of an Anthology*.[2]

Gollancz's new anthology was read with close attention by du Maurier, and subsequently it greatly exercised her mind, as can be seen in her explanation behind the inspiration for writing the poem:

> Your anthology is having the most frightful effect upon me that I can't settle to working out the plot of The Double at all, but want to shout and proclaim the reason for living, and loving, and fighting, and dying – I truly am adoring every word of it – and while I agree with everything yet at the same time I become more pagan, an odd paradox

> which is in your nature too, and in a frenzy yesterday after
> sawing down a tree I write [sic] the enclosed poem.[3]

The poem itself is a passionate portrayal of the paternal god she resents, combined with an exposition of the maternal goddess she embraces. In an odd sense, however, the two versions of the deity – the Christian God and the pagan Gaia – are inextricably linked in her imagination, since the negative attributes of the one help to define, by way of contrasting opposites, the positive attributes of the other. The title, 'Apostasis,' seems to reflect this dual system, and points to the same self-consciousness of the paradox in her nature that is expressed in the letter. 'Apostasis' is a state of rebellion from a creed, and thus in using this word du Maurier shows that she remains always mindful of the tradition from which her pagan preference should liberate her. Correspondingly, the more she thinks of the Christian God, the more strongly she feels about Gaia, so that in her love for the goddess she can never forget that she is an apostate.

In rebelling against the traditional Christian religion, Daphne du Maurier enacts another series of paradoxes. In rejecting a religious tradition, she simultaneously follows a family tradition, that of apostasis of her own father, Gerald, and his father before him. Also, whilst embracing the apostatic views of her paternal ancestry, she oddly rejects a paternal concept of God. George du Maurier, her grandfather, wrote about his rejection of some of the central tenets of Christianity in his novel *Trilby*. The type of god he cannot believe in is one that seems to be a:

> self glorifying ogre in human shape, with human passions,
> and most inhuman hates – who suddenly made us out of
> nothing, one fine day – just for a freak – and made us so
> badly that we fell the next – and turned us adrift the day
> after – damned us from the very beginning.[4]

In her correspondence with Victor Gollancz, du Maurier implies that he shares the unconventional ideas of her grandfather, her father and herself, when she writes:

> I adore your ideas about God, they remind me of Daddy, and I know I share them to a large extent. So monstrous that bigotted [sic] view, rammed down one's throat as a child, and if one is a church-goer as an adult too, that the world was created, or rather Man was created by God, for the very un-laudable purpose of worshipping Him. It makes him such a monster, and the thing that infuriated Daddy was the abject humility expected of man, by the church.[5]

It seems apparent that du Maurier was influenced directly by her father, and also indirectly by her grandfather through his novel. Du Maurier's Christian God, like George du Maurier's in *Trilby*, has all the qualities of an egotistical monster.

In 'Apostasis,' du Maurier's rebellion is against the orthodox view that the Christian God is an authoritarian patriarch who makes demands of the people he is said to have created; she cannot countenance the 'paternal pride' inherent in a god who is supposed to behave in this way. Not for du Maurier is 'the God of the sky' who 'watches on high'. Such a god, by implication, is too distant, too cold, and seems divorced from the genuine life of earthly, earthy man. Nor will she 'suffer the Cross', which is associated with atonement for man's collective sin, since she does not believe that any genuine god could condemn man from the very instant of his origin. Hence du Maurier 'will not be mocked by fables of Palestine', or by 'martyred saints, and sinners reconciled', feeling perhaps that the god who condemns man then adds insult to injury by persistently drawing attention to the predicament in which He has placed him. A god who is capable of such injustices is not, in du Maurier's view, worthy of subservience and worship. In her essay, 'This I Believe', du

Maurier recognises in herself this 'contempt for authority imposed from above', even though she knows – paradoxically – that she cannot escape a certain 'respect for tradition'.[6] There is a lingering regard for Christianity, but in an attempt to thwart this ongoing 'return of the repressed', her denunciation becomes powerful and passionate.

Du Maurier's heart is reserved for the immanent goddess Gaia, who represents the Earth and is its essential sustaining spirit. Du Maurier's Gaia is always present wherever man himself is to be found, and freely offers herself as aid 'so that all things, crying for succour, should have rest'. She is thus a giving, not demanding, divinity, and is always at work 'stanching the rising Flood' of man's need '[w]ith her own blood'. Gaia does not expect eternal thankfulness from her children because she is not separate from creation; on the contrary, she is an intimate part of it:

> Her children neither bowing, nor praying apart,
> But flinging themselves upon her living heart
> To share in creation's joy, creation's power,
> Each mortal hour.

It is the immanence of the mother goddess which most assuages du Maurier's own spiritual need. Religion must be personal for du Maurier, not remote, and Gaia fulfils this necessary quality by her very nature.

There is, however, another reason why du Maurier feels personally involved with Gaia, and this can be found in the stories surrounding Daphne's namesake in Greek mythology – as du Maurier reveals in a letter to Gollancz dated 31 March 1958, sent just prior to his planned holiday in Greece:

> [A]s you stand in Apollo's temple at Delphi think of the first priestess, Daphne, who was defending it for the Earth-Mother, Gaia, when Apollo seized it. This was the original

legend, according to my many researches, and that chat about a pretty nymph is all my eye![7]

Du Maurier was extremely well read in the legends surrounding Apollo and Daphne, having made a special study of them in the 1950s. The legends had a considerable impact on her in this period, as can also be seen in her letter to Maureen Baker-Munton dated 4 July 1957, in which she writes that Daphne the nymph:

> was chased by Apollo and to save herself from waxing, called to her father – a river god – to turn her into a tree. Could be my story. Daddy-complex, and don't forget that the tree of life in Norse mythology is Ygdrasil.[8]

To clarify, waxing is du Maurier code for making love, and Ygdrasil was also the name of her husband's boat. Evidently, she was able to see her own life through the lens of such myths, identifying more closely with 'Daphne the nymph' in 1957 and then with 'Daphne the priestess' in 1958. Hence, the poem 'Apostasis' becomes a means of defending Gaia and her temple a second time, not from Apollo on this occasion but from what she saw as the ravening clutches of the transcendent god of Christianity. Perhaps, in du Maurier's divided mind, religions were always in perpetual collision, vying endlessly in her thoughts for a supremacy that could never be perfectly maintained.

Du Maurier's rejection of Christianity seems to contradict her previously expressed respect for tradition, but in a letter to Oriel Malet she explains her view that Christianity is merely a recent upstart when compared with paganism, and more specifically the idea of the mother goddess:

> The only thing is, I am so steeped in my queer London Libe [Library] books about Origin of Consciousness and

Great Snake Mothers that I feel Catholicism is too modern for me, like living in a block of flats instead of a cave![9]

Du Maurier's poem, being a celebration of the earth mother goddess, allows her to restore to her religious sense those aspects of the feminine and the chthonic which Christianity seems to deny. This way of thinking about spirituality is in accord with the writing of Carl Jung, whose work du Maurier began to read during the 1950s, the decade in which 'Apostasis' was written. Jung's essay on 'Mind and Earth' (1927), argues that the mind can be understood as a *'system of adaptation determined by the conditions of an earthly environment'*.[10] For Jung and du Maurier therefore, Christianity – as a transcendent religion – does not really appeal on a psychological level since it neglects the fact that the mind is attuned to a more immanent, physical environment.

'Apostasis' is not unique amongst du Maurier's works for its emphasis on the earth mother and the power of chthonic forces. Her first novel, *The Loving Spirit* (1931), relates how a mother's spirit communicates after death with the future generations of her family, thus foreshadowing her later sentiment in 'This I Believe' that:

The I who writes this essay lives and dies. Something of myself goes into the children born of my body, and to their children, and those children's children. Life, whatever shape or form it takes, goes on, develops, adapts.[11]

In a novel such as *Jamaica Inn* (1936), the land itself, in the form of Bodmin Moor, is both the dark mother and also the shaper of its inhabitants. For the main character, Mary, the bleak quality of the moorland seems to be echoed in the temperament of the moors men, whose minds are 'twisted' as a result of their subjection to 'marshland and granite, harsh heather and crumbling stone'.[12] *Hungry Hill* (1943) demonstrates what happens to several generations of a mining family in Ireland when they fail to respect the chthonic power of the hill in question. John Brodrick refuses to ask permission from the hill before starting his mining enterprise, and in return for his disrespect of Mother Nature his family is cursed throughout several generations. This novel portrays the Earth Mother in her negative, vengeful form rather than the nurturing form displayed in the poem 'Apostasis'. Finally, in *The Flight of the Falcon* (1965), the Apollo-esque protagonist of the novel, Aldo Donati, is a determined mother-despiser. In the novel, he decides to stage an episode in the life of his Renaissance hero, the Duke of Ruffano, for the student pageant, which entails dressing as a bird of prey and leaping from the tower of the Ducal Palace. When he takes 'the flight of the falcon', he deliberately fails to operate the costume's gliding mechanism and thus falls to earth, demonstrating perhaps his final meeting and reconciliation with the earth deities that he has so long despised. It can be seen from the above examples that du Maurier's fascination with the Earth Mother – her spiritual apostasis – took many forms over the course of her life, and found continual expression in her literary output.

Some ten years earlier than 'Apostasis', the *Observer* printed a poem by du Maurier entitled 'Remembrance Day':[13]

Let us no longer mourn the happy dead
But mourn the living; the dead will continue to sleep
peacefully, with smiling lips, and unseeing eyes,
Ignoring the many passionate tears we shed.
But the living come empty-handed, with a deep
Hunger they cannot express, and their puzzled sighs
Pitifully inarticulate, betray
That the victor is always vanquished. Once again
They're back where they started from, and may lose the way
The men who did not die at Alamein.

Let us no longer mourn the child who lies
Beneath the rubble; he cannot feel the cold.
But mourn the living, whose parents drifting apart
Give him no home for haven, so that he cries,
'What can I cling to in life, what can I hold?'
With a cynical twist to the mind and a husk for the heart
The scapegoats of this generation go drifting past.
The children for whom the war was apparently won,
And nothing is certain, and nothing is likely to last
For the child who was not bombed at Kennington.

Let us no longer mourn the Christ who died
Upon a Cross two thousand years from now
Crying aloud that God has forsaken Him.
There have been so many others who likewise cried.
From Golgotha to Belsen and Dachau
The way is short, monotonous and grim.
Mourn for the risen Christ, with the eyes of them.
The eyes of the living, calling to me and you.
Whom every day we continue to mock and condemn,
Whom every day we crucify anew.

This poem contains an unexpected reversal of sentiments, for du
Maurier asks her readers not to 'mourn the happy dead' on
Remembrance Day, but to 'mourn the living' instead. Du Maurier
is unafraid to invoke the name of Christ in support of her poem's
thesis, as she writes:

Let us no longer mourn the Christ who died
Upon a Cross two thousand years from now
Crying aloud that God has forsaken Him.
There have been so many others who likewise cried.
From Golgotha to Belsen and Dachau.

131

Du Maurier alters our perspective by asking us to 'mourn for the risen Christ' with 'the eyes of the living'; in this startling parallel du Maurier is suggesting that the living are the ones we 'mock', 'condemn' and 'crucify anew'. Christ is thus not a singular phenomenon, but one person amongst many who are now doomed to a death-in-life existence as the result of the horrific actions of their fellow men. Du Maurier's writing about Christ in this poem highlights yet again her ambiguous attitude towards Christianity, in that she is both mindful of its codes and also defiant of any orthodox stance. Alternatively, it is possible that du Maurier may see the Biblical Christ as just a literary device ripe for exploitation. Knowing the inevitable resonances that such a figure evokes would enable her to manipulate his story for dramatic impact. No doubt she was well aware of the disquieting effect that potentially heretical formulations would have on the orthodox mind. Many well-known works of literature have been subjected quite successfully to du Maurier's revisionist imagination, and perhaps the Bible, both here and elsewhere in her writing, was no exception.

The Loving Spirit

Michèle Roberts

Daphne du Maurier takes her title from a poem by Emily
Brontë:

> Alas – the countless links are strong
> That bind us to our clay,
> The loving spirit lingers long,
> And would not pass away.

Emily Brontë seems to be talking about how hard it can be
to find the freedom of death if we are at all frightened of dying,
how the beauties of the world can exert their pull on us right
up to the end. Daphne du Maurier's lushly written novel, on
the other hand, salutes the necessity of death as a conduit between
the generations through which the loving spirit can be poured.
While it is a rapturous celebration of the beauties of the Cornish
landscape, in particular, it is also about the drive towards aban-
doning the cares and duties of the daily, material world in order
to pin your faith on a transcendent symbol and a love so intense
it approaches the taboo, even the perverse.

First published in 1931, *The Loving Spirit* is both a romance
and a family saga, a novel about thresholds and changes. It begins
with one marriage and ends, three generations later, with another
one. The heroines who brace the story, like book-ends, are linked
by their semi-mystical appreciation of the power of love to inspire,
save and heal. The presiding goddess of this intense emotional

landscape is Janet Coombe, whom we meet, in the opening chapter, on her wedding morning. She is about to marry her sober, God-fearing cousin Thomas, a boat-builder, and has fled up to the cliffs above Plyn, her village, and the harbour it shelters, to say goodbye to her old life and begin looking towards her new one.

Part of Janet fears her soul is 'sinful and wayward' for drifting off in daydreams: 'her heart would travel out across the sunbeams to the silent hills'. She is chided by all the village gossips for loving to play truant, for running and jumping, for answering back, for envying male freedoms. Her mother scolds her and beats her, but Janet insists on becoming a woman in her own way. Her beauty and strength attract all the local boys and from them she chooses Thomas.

She is doubtful about marriage, at first: 'No more could she lift her skirts and run about the rocks, nor wander among the sheep on the hills. It was a home now to be tended, and a man of her own, and later maybe, and God willing, the child that came with being wed.' So far, so mapped out. But then:

At this thought there was something that laid its finger on her soul, like the remembrance of a dream, or some dim forgotten thing: a ray of knowledge that is hidden from folk in their wakeful moments, and then comes to them queerly at strange times. This came to Janet now, fainter than a call; like a soft still whisper.

So Janet recognises her conflicted desires and destiny:

. . . and it seemed that there were two sides of her; one that wanted to be the wife of a man, and to care for him and love him tenderly, and one that asked only to be part of a ship, part of the seas and the skies above, with the glad free ways of a gull.

This opening chapter, having thus introduced the main themes and symbols of the entire novel, closes on an epiphanic note: 'she knew in her soul that there was something waiting for her greater than this love for Thomas. Something strong and primitive, lit with everlasting beauty. One day it would come, but not yet.' Of course I'm not going to spoil the story for the first-time reader by telling you what that is. Suffice it to say that it's the fuel for the entire book and drives it unflaggingly, through episodes of cruelty, treachery, war and loss, towards its peaceful and triumphant end.

How does du Maurier achieve her effects? To begin with, she's an accomplished storyteller, keeping the narrative racing along with plenty of colourful characters, dramatic incident, cliff-hanging chapter endings, mystery and suspense. More importantly, I think, she relies on the Gothic and Romantic elements of personage, narrative and landscape employed by Emily Brontë in *Wuthering Heights*. Her entire novel is a homage to that of her great precursor. Janet Coombe is a free spirit like Brontë's Cathy, and her wild, rebellious son Joseph has a lot in common with Brontë's anti-hero, Heathcliff. The great love between Janet and Joseph defies death, destitution, and wretchedness to the point of madness, just as Cathy's for Heathcliff does. *Wuthering Heights* could in no sense be described as a family saga, but it shares with *The Loving Spirit* the inbuilt necessity for the plot to be worked out over more than one generation. Du Maurier is conscious and proud of her debt to Brontë. At the beginning of Book One, her story of Janet, it's no accident that she quotes one of Emily Brontë's greatest poems:

> No coward soul is mine,
> No trembler in the world's storm-troubled sphere:
> I see heaven's glories shine,
> And faith shines equal, arming me from fear.

As in *Wuthering Heights*, the weather plays a crucial part. The Romantic Fallacy is in full swing. Storms at sea mirror storms in the human heart. Plants and creatures feel just as we do. Du Maurier invokes 'the glad tossing of the leaves in autumn, and the shy fluttering wings of a bird . . . a pale forgotten primrose that grew wistfully near the water's edge'. Imagining that flowers can share our wistfulness, or birds our shyness, is consoling, of course. This is what we might call the banal side of the Romantic Fallacy. But Brontë turned it around into a profound statement of mysticism, in which people dissolve into the universe to become one with it, and du Maurier follows her:

> . . . the spirit of Janet was free and unfettered, waiting to rise from its self-enforced seclusion to mix with intangible things, like the wind, the sea, and the skies hand in hand with the one for whom she waited. Then she, too, would become part of these things forever, abstract and immortal.

Only Brontë, I think, would not have said 'hand in hand': much too tame. Indeed, du Maurier is a much more sentimental writer.

Brontë's use of Gothic in *Wuthering Heights* allowed her savagely to satirise the genteel bourgeois world she despised, to dream of a hero brutal enough to overturn the established order, and to hint at some of the secrets festering underneath the placid surface of normal domestic life. Women writers have tended to take up the Gothic with enthusiasm, since it allows them to peer down the cellar stairs and up into the third-floor attic and reveal some of the bad things that go on in seemingly respectable houses. Du Maurier employs Gothic hyperbole and excess to permit her decent, hard-working, artisan characters to express their turbulent emotions in dramatic and even violent language, accuse each other of evil and madness, and knock each other down. No point fretting she's hamming it up; she's in a tradition as much theatrical as literary. To emphasise her novel's reach towards the timeless and the sublime she mixes in biblical phrases, cadences and rhythms, lots of archaisms, repetitions and inversions:

> And she strove to banish these thoughts . . . the cold rain shut outside and the damp misty hills, and the sound of the wild harbour water coming not to her mind . . . And Joseph looked down on Christopher, and stifled the nigh-overmastering impulse to kneel beside the boy and ask him to place all faith and trust into his keeping, but it came to him that the boy might feel shy and embarrassed to see his father act in such a way.

Like other Gothic-influenced novelists, du Maurier uses the motifs of the form to conceal secrets as much as to expose them. Gothic circles around repression and may succumb to it. Du Maurier's rhapsodic descriptions of the love between Janet and her son Joseph hint at an incestuous element:

> She longed for the other one to be with her tonight, he who was part of her, with his dark hair and his dark eyes so like her own. He who had not come yet, but who stared at her out of the future, and walked with her in her dreams.

On one level this son-lover is an animus-figure like those found in Jungian interpretations of fairytales, he who helps make a bridge for the woman into the wider world. On the level of modern psychobabble, poor Janet would be characterised as a dangerously possessive mother. Feminists might think the male principle is being over-valued and might want to deprecate a mother placing all her desires, potency and ardour in the lap of her son. But the Gothic romance can soar away from this sort of questioning, which is of course part of its charm. It is not necessarily a subversive form; it all depends on what you do with it. And to turn the question around: perhaps a forbidden love may be deftly imaged by separating the lovers into different generations and time-frames; or, perhaps, the enforced separation and ecstatic reunion of mother and son depicted here by du Maurier is simply a powerful image for the losses that afflict us all and for our longing to repair them.

I'll Never Be Young Again

Elaine Dundy

Devotees of Daphne du Maurier will find in *I'll Never Be Young Again* a rich source of self-revelatory material. This second novel with its world-weary title was completed in 1930, when the author was all of twenty-three years old. Young as she was, however, it is all there, yet at the same time none of it is. She is a beginner. Nevertheless, it contains the strengths that will make her one of the great monologists in twentieth-century fiction, most endearing are the twists, turns and shocks of her plots, which are done in such a way that the reader grows to accept them as reasonable. It also reminds us again what a strong influence James Joyce had on our writers in the 1920s and '30s, with his stream of consciousness, a technique du Maurier uses to her great advantage.

Two decades later, about her novel in progress, *The Scapegoat*, she will write to her publisher Victor Gollancz describing her task as 'simply to take a fantastically impossible situation and make it read with utter conviction', a target which she hits bull's-eye in most of her novels, including this second one.

In form the novel is episodic; if a film, it would be called a 'road movie', with the self-described male narrator, Dick, driven from crisis to crisis. Starting as a would-be suicide on a London bridge, he moves to a posh cruise of Scandinavia. From there, as a deck hand, we find him on a run-down tug boat about to sink. Having survived, he goes on to Paris. Settling into café life, he enters into a year-long love affair with an American girl, simultaneously embarking on becoming a writer, buoying himself up on hot dreams of fame and fortune. His bubble bursts when a noted publisher tells him he has no talent. Then, when he returns to Paris, his girlfriend walks out on him. In a surprise ending, he becomes happier than he has ever been in his life as a bank clerk in London, listening to a bird who seems to be singing over and over, 'I'll never be young again.'

True, Dick is rather unsympathetic. Du Maurier will rarely make that mistake again. At the same time she will magically retain the weaknesses, dishonesties and peccadilloes in her characters that are unsympathetic, as she does with Dick. Fifty-seven years later, in her novel *The House on the Strand*, there is also a narrator called Dick who is similarly unsympathetic. Coincidence? Subconscious? Provocative?

This early novel is a forerunner of the later ones in that, as with all prolific writers, du Maurier employs favourite words in it which she will use throughout her work. It's fun to see which words here will become staples of her style. 'Fool', 'child' and 'brandy' are three. Her characters feel like fools, as often as they call other people the same. The word 'child' denotes everything from innocence to tantrums while brandy is, universally, the only drink characters swallow to pull themselves together. It is fascinating to see some phrases evolve: 'I'll never be young again' progresses to the second Mrs de Winter's 'I'll never be a child again'. Biting one's nails under stress, which appears as early as her second novel, turns up again full force in the second Mrs de Winter, who says, 'I didn't like it. I began biting my nails. No, I did not like it.' Nail-biting will apply throughout her oeuvre. In *The King's General*, one person even gets around to biting his hands. Daphne herself bit her nails when growing up. A touch of reality.

Another reality in du Maurier's books is that people die in them, sometimes in profusion! She kills them off with the brio of Dickens and Shakespeare. Babies, mothers and grandfathers fall dead just when we are becoming fond of them. Only two people die in *I'll Never Be Young Again*, but they are the two most important to Dick. Reading her novels, we become alerted to the real and present dangers that threaten her characters every time they mount a horse, climb a hill, step into a car or carriage, scramble up a balcony – or even walk out of a front or back door.

Important also are du Maurier's unhappy endings (which her husband teased her about). They leave us to ponder how invariably fate pays us back for our transgressions. Though her books were advertised as 'romances', boy rarely gets girl; in fact it is rare that two main characters go off together into the sunset. We realise she feels it would be *morally wrong* if they did. Du Maurier, schooled in the ways of the world, makes this sound sense, leaving a reverberation that haunts us; whereas a happy ending would merely signal closure.

After reading Margaret Forster's biography documenting du Maurier's hitherto unknown bisexuality, I confess that it sent me straight back to her novels sleuthing for clues of this interesting facet of her personality. And there are plenty. Nowhere is it more blatant and confusing than in *I'll Never Be Young Again*, when narrator Dick explodes about how he wished his father had treated him like a boy: 'I wanted to use my fists against the faces of boys,' he says, 'to fight with them, laughing, sprawling on the ground, and then run with them, catching at my breath, flinging a stone to the top of a tree.' The confusion here is that the author has mixed up her real-life plight with that of Dick's, and writes like a woman yearning to be a man. This kind of thing runs through her work. Often her heroines will declare they wished they were a man.

Looking for a context in which to place du Maurier in a literary and historic time frame, I suddenly came across a phenomenon I might otherwise have missed. Until recently, it seemed to me that all the full-drawn female characters such as

Becky Sharp, Hedda Gabler and Scarlett O'Hara disappeared after the nineteenth century. I see now that the twentieth century, specifically the 1920s and 1930s, produced two other star woman writers, who created wonderful female characters as did du Maurier; I am talking about Virginia Woolf and the poet Edna St Vincent Millay, both of whom were also Sapphically inclined. In order of their appearance, Virginia Woolf (1882–1941), in whose *Orlando* the protagonist begins a three-hundred-year journey as a man, but metamorphoses into a woman and who, in another work, gives us the arresting psychological insight that 'Women have served all these centuries as looking-glasses possessing the magic and delicious power of reflecting the figure of man at twice its natural size.' (*A Room of One's Own*)

As for Edna St Vincent Millay (1892–1950), whose wit, candour and genius made her the hottest ticket in the poets' lecture circuit, unseating Robert Frost; when a college girl, she asked herself the question: What will a scholarship student several years older than the other girls at a top women's college, Vassar, do to get noticed? The answer: use her attraction to and by women and fix on the same-sex spell they were all under. Her poem, 'A Few Figs from Thistles', containing the stanza

> My candle burns at both ends;
> It will not last the night;
> But, ah, my foes, and, oh, my friends—
> It gives a lovely light.

endeared her to females around the world and possibly gave rise to Dorothy Parker's comment: 'If the prettiest girls at Vassar were laid end to end, I shouldn't be surprised.'

Bisexuality surely added to their originality, idiosyncrasies, imagination and talent. Yet of equal significance was their strong sense of reality which is manifest to anyone who begins to study their careers. There was nothing fey about them. In fact, they were noticeably grounded. All needed a special place to lay their heads and all got it: du Maurier at Menabilly, a mansion in Cornwall, Millay at Steepletop, a farmhouse in upstate New York – two houses set in impressive surroundings. Both women renovated them to suit their own will. With Woolf, it was simply *A Room of One's Own*, yet I speculate it stirred up more emotion in women than the two other grander houses.

Another similarity: all three did a lot of suffering in their childhood, which seems to have stiffened their resolve to make up for it by working towards a kingdom, a power and a glory in their art.

As for husbands, each chose hers with a sense of practicality. We have all heard of Trophy Wives but not enough of Trophy Husbands. These three realists chose husbands that they loved and were proud of. Virginia married a publisher, Edna a Dutch businessman, Daphne a much-decorated war hero who masterminded an important wing of World War II Air Force and became a valued member of Queen Elizabeth's and Prince Philip's staff, for which he was knighted.

All three women on their own were powerful and entitled, yet desirous of what they saw fame could not purchase: respectability and acceptability. They married what seemed to them stable, non-participants in the arts, although appreciators of them. The men seemed the embodiment of what these women wanted – someone to lean upon, someone to guide them. Ironically, all three of the ladies became the breadwinners of the family.

And yet . . . suppose I ask us to forget, erase, wipe out all I've been writing before. Lest all self-revelations, the deconstructions and any other clues lead us astray from the only thing close to our heart: what's on the page? When we open books, we don't care about the mood of the authors, the events surrounding their creations or the people they loved and hated at the time. Who cares if they were unhappy, if they give us the finished masterpiece? For this special event, the trio not only achieved Trophy Husbands, they achieved Trophy Editors. They put themselves not in harm's but in help's way. Once writers have given themselves to the right person's eyes, something else happens. It also happened that these editors – Victor Gollancz, Daphne's publisher and editor; Edna's high-ranking editor at Harpers, and Leonard Woolf, Virginia's husband – became fathers, mothers, bankers, messengers and advisors. Cases in point: Virginia's homage to Leonard Woolf, ticking off in her acknowledgements all the ways in which he was vital to her novel *Orlando*; Edna's editor, always at hand to come to her financial aid when needed.

But best for me were Daphne and Victor Gollancz's flirty, sunkissed, delirious exchanges concerning a short-story collection. One story, 'The Birds', he called a masterpiece, but he didn't like and wanted her to drop two further stories, one of which jarred on him while he thought the other poor. She was 'one of the few authors . . . with whom I can be frank'. Daphne accepted his judgement and dropped them, adding that he was 'dynamic, exuberant, tender, intolerant and the only publisher for me'. To which Victor returned that she was 'beautiful, adorable, gracious, charming and good'.

Most of all, these Trophy Editors gave Virginia, Edna and Daphne the respect, adoration and veneration due to them.

Julius

Julie Myerson

I remember exactly who I was when I first read *Julius*. Winter of '73 and a skinny, bookish thirteen-and-a-half-year-old is lying on the floor of her lilac-wallpapered bedroom in Nottingham. Last week she took *Frenchman's Creek* out of the library, the week before that *Jamaica Inn* – she was transported by the pure Cornish romance and excitement of them. Now here's another Daphne du Maurier, one she hasn't even heard of. She flings herself down on the prickly nylon carpet and opens it enthusiastically.

And is plunged straight into a harsh and remorseless world of Paris under siege, starving peasants, Algerian child prostitutes, ruthless sex, cold murder and emotional sadism. I was, by then, quite a mature reader, but I'd never alighted on a novel as psycho-logically savage and uncompromisingly sophisticated as this one.

Of course, at thirteen, I was far too inexperienced to glean many of *Julius*'s deeper and darker meanings. I knew nothing of men–female sexuality, still less of money, class, deprivation and war. I am sure that back then in my adolescent bedroom, I read this singularly dramatic tale on a very superficial, one-note level. But the gist of it lingered – stayed with me right into adult-hood. All those years, at the back of my mind, I certainly remem-bered Julius – the uneasy flavour of him, his astounding capacity for money-making, his stark incapacity for anything approaching spontaneous human love. I think I knew even then that those pages contained the portrait of a monster, somehow all the more alarming for being emphatically, or at least, ambivalently, drawn.

There's something calculated and frightening about this book. It's intensely shocking in places. Its moments of violence and cruelty have, even today, more than fifty years on, an almost David Lynch-style kick to them. This is a tale of such emotional brutality and moral dislocation that it feels as if it's been wrought by a master, someone who has seen, known and grappled with the world. Chilling, then, to discover that Daphne du Maurier was just twenty-six years old when she wrote it.

So what did this young woman believe she was writing? Is *Julius* a straightforward account of a monstrous sadist, a man whose feelings of possessive love for his daughter veer danger-ously and desperately out of control? Or is it the tale of a life coming undone, the sad inevitability of a deprived child grown up to cold manhood and thankless, pointless prosperity – the story of a victim of poverty, circumstance and fate? And anyway, is Julius Levy the master of his own fate (and those around him) or is he in fact no more than face and bluster, no more in control than any of those people he destroys to get what he wants?

And, maybe most intriguingly of all, what exactly was in du Maurier's mind when she chose to make him a Jew? A young twenty-something woman scribbling away at her desk in windy Cornwall in 1932 was still safely innocent of the hideous drama to be played out only a few years later in Europe, but the choice can only set our post-Holocaust teeth on edge. 'Jew,' sneers Julius's Catholic grandfather to his hapless son-in-law, 'nothing but a miserable Jew.'

Even though the grandfather is portrayed far from sympa-thetically – at best a bestial, overbearing peasant – still there were mutterings, in du Maurier's later years, that this possible whiff of anti-Semitism should be excised from the novel. Apparently du Maurier even took them seriously. But thank goodness she never succumbed. Not only would it have meant bowdlerising a novel that is absolutely and innocently (in the best sense of the word) of its time, but there's a more important point. Rereading it in the twenty-first century, it seems to me that it's precisely Julius's Jewishness – and other people's attitudes to it – that redeems him, that makes him real and whole and fascinating. It's his rediscovery of his religion, as he wanders into a temple by chance, that gives him his few moments of calm and happiness. He is not at odds with the world because of his Jewishness but in spite of it.

In fact, far from being a one-dimensional baddie, this spirituality and longing to belong makes du Maurier's eponymous anti-hero so much grander: a questing, complex and, in many ways, touching man. Without this extra dimension, the novel would be far lighter and more brittle. As it is, it's a tragedy – a vivid and profound exploration of what it feels to be an outsider, accepted as neither Christian nor Jew, neither aristocrat nor millionaire.

Julius begins and ends the novel with his hands stretched out to the sky, reaching for the clouds, searching, always searching. A mixed-up, lonely, starving child, he responds instinctively to the music in the temple, feels something warm take hold of his heart, realises he is among 'his own people'. It is Julius's particular tragedy that he spends the rest of the novel struggling to re-attain this fleeting emotion. If Julius has a benign side, a sensitive side, there's no doubt that it's the Jewish side.

Interestingly, du Maurier always avoids the easy racist cliché. Though Julius amasses incalculable wealth, she never portrays him as a money-grabber. He is no blinkered and greedy lover of cash and property – just a man who simply can't help but work hard and do things well. His abiding code is 'something for nothing' but actually, it's rarely for 'nothing' – Julius works and works and works, forgetting even to spend his money. When a friend persuades him to match his lodgings to his newly acquired wealth, it's significant that Julius is uncomfortable. He's 'disturbed' by his 'first experience of luxury'. Julius is an ascetic, he's pure in his soul. He works out of a sense of personal pride and for mental satisfaction, for the chance to take control of his life, rather than the chance to shirk it.

But though Julius will always survive he has, in the best tradition of tragedy, a single undoing flaw. He can't love without wanting to possess and control. And if he can't possess then he'd rather destroy – and he's quite prepared to. As a young boy, forced to leave home and his beloved cat behind, he ties a stone around her neck and flings her in the Seine rather than leave her to an uncertain fate, or worse – to be cared for by someone else.

This act – an act of love in his eyes – is carried out unflinchingly, but it's the start of a lifelong and sinister equating of love with destruction. When Julius discovers his mother committing adultery and tells his father, it seems painfully logical to him that his father should throttle her there and then. He knows he'll miss his mother, but didn't she deserve it, and won't his father ultimately feel better if no one else can have her? Julius's reaction to this crime quickly becomes its most disturbing aspect. Here is a boy with an almost autistic lack of sensibility. Where he should connect with others, there is an icy vacuum. He knows he ought to feel something, but he wonders what it should be.

But it's precisely this vacuum that gives Julius his resilience and power. That's what lies at the heart of this novel – a study of power and powerlessness, which has little or nothing to do with Jewishness. The helplessness that this young boy feels as a starving child in turn-of-the-century Paris turns him into a sadistic character – someone who discovers 'a new thing, of hurting people he liked'. This destructive pattern – which ultimately bores him because it means he is always in control and life contains no surprises – continues until he finally meets his match.

His nemesis is his daughter Gabriel, his own flesh and blood, his alter-ego. At last Julius can take pleasure from the existence of another human being – even though the pleasure he feels is obsessive, a 'voracious passion' that gives him a 'sensation in mind and body' that is 'shameful and unclean'. It is said that the character of Julius is based heavily on du Maurier's own father, Gerald du Maurier, and the fact she was able to write it – such steady, concise prose – means she had come to terms with that intensely passionate relationship. It's an idea I find comforting if baffling. Such candour and control? The author must have been an admirably sorted-out twenty-six year old.

I said at the beginning of this piece that I was far too young when I first read the novel to mine its deeper, darker meanings. Well, not quite. It's true that I knew nothing of men and women, class, war and money. But I did know a little more than I'd have liked about the uneasy relations of fathers and daughters. The summer before, my mother had left my father and he – furious and unscrupulous – had begun a slow campaign to hurt me, to make me feel his pain. Fuelled by his own sense of powerlessness, it was his way of getting back; of punishing my mother for leaving, of punishing me, at almost fourteen, for looking and sounding more and more like her. I became increasingly afraid of my father – not so much of any single thing he did, more that I realised I did not know his limits. I did not know where he would stop.

I was seventeen when he decided not to see me any more. The rejection – signalling the end of so much pain and uncertainty – felt more like relief than trauma. It seems far too easy and unfair to brand my father a monster. I know now (more than a decade after his lonely suicide) that he wasn't. I know now that he was a sick, sad man who needed help. But, very like Julius, he'd felt powerless as a child – deprived of love, shown only coldness and dislike. And like Julius, he'd discovered that inflicting pain on those he loved was as good a way as any to take control, to give his life value and momentum.

I see this now, but did I recognise any of it as I lay on the carpet of my room reading my *Julius*? It's hard to remember, impossible to know for sure. I used my novels back then as comfort and, yes, escape. And the best, most vividly exciting thing about great novels is the way you don't always know what you've read until years later, when the sediment has drifted and settled. And you find what remains – what you really remembered – is the thing that most mattered. And what I remember is that I read a book about a hurt and hurtful man, a man who worked and strove for no purpose and ultimately was left bereft. I do not remember a book about a Jew.

Jamaica Inn

Sarah Dunant

Jamaica Inn opens with echoes of *Dracula*: a carriage rattling through a desolate landscape and wild weather to a place where even the locals won't go, so ferocious is its reputation. Inside rides Mary Yellan, newly orphaned and en route from the tame farmland of the Helford area to the rainswept moors of nineteenth-century Cornwall and the married home of her aunt, a woman once known for her rich curls and girlish laughter. We are in the territory of the Gothic novel, but one with an under-current of modern sensibility.

Mary's destination, Jamaica Inn, stands dark and forbidding at the top of the moor. It is the house from hell. At night the sign outside twists in the wind like a human body on a gibbet. Inside, the place reeks of neglect, drink and male violence. The lovely giggling Aunt Patience is now a gaunt, shaky wreck, her spirit destroyed by abuse, and her husband, Joss Merlyn, is a monster: physically overwhelming, lumbering, violent and drunk. By the end of the first day, as the light bleeds away and Mary barri-cades herself in her miserable little room, a pact has been made with the reader. This is going to be a journey into darkness, and it's going to deliver both violence and sensation.

It doesn't take long to find out why the Inn and its landlord are so feared. Early on, most readers will have guessed the reason. Cornwall, with its bleak, treacherous coastline and wild weather was for much of its history a law unto itself. Jamaica Inn may now be a tourist trap reduced to kitsch by the publicity of minor literary fame, but when du Maurier would have first seen it, in the 1920s, it would no doubt have been a more desolate place which, with the right imagination, could easily be transformed into Robert Louis Stevenson territory and the heart of a smuggling ring that not only hides the booty but runs a gang of wreckers who lure the ships onto the rocks to drown their crew and steal their cargo.

There's no doubt that many of the ingredients of Jamaica Inn – wild men, wild land, dark secrets and violent ends – are close to Gothic cliché and would have been even in 1936 when Daphne du Maurier wrote the book. But what makes the novel still vibrant is to see how in the hands of a master storyteller – because that is exactly what du Maurier is – the form can be revitalised and even to some measure reinvented.

The way she does it is twofold: first by sheer force of plotting. Mary, alarmed and demoralised, may have found herself in hell, but she has no option but to stay, held by her loyalty to her aunt and the need to protect her. In the eyes of the community that makes her virtually an outlaw herself. All good thrillers have to isolate their hero if the threat is really going to bite, and even when Mary manages to get herself out of the house, the desolation of the moors only mocks her helplessness, the landscape and the weather as much a force in this book as any of the characters. The only other people she meets are in their own way as bizarre as the inn's inhabitants. There is her uncle's younger brother Jem, a horse thief and an adventurer whose attraction keeps her on the wrong side of the law, and the strangely tender mercies of one Francis Davey, the Vicar of Altarnun, a fabulously unnerving character whose soft speech clashes with his bleached albino looks and his heavy whip on the horse's back.

But for most of the book it is Mary's battle with Joss Merlyn that keeps you turning the page. As a character he isn't to everybody's taste. Du Maurier's own biographer, Margaret Forster, finds him near to caricature, and it's true that he is larger than life. But there is also a terrible fascination to him. His brooding figure, craggy looks and wild temper are in their own way all attributes of the romantic hero inverted into violence and self-loathing – a Mr Rochester without a Jane to redeem him. Before guilt and drink disabled Joss he would have been a charismatic figure. (Du Maurier had lived too long with a glamorous, powerful father – the actor Gerald du Maurier – not to have understood that there is a price to be paid for charisma.) There is something in Joss Merlyn's torment that smells of damage done as well as inflicted. And it's here that *Jamaica Inn* pushes at the boundaries of the romantic genre to suggest how passion between men and women can lead to abuse. Joss's wife may now be a quivering victim, but at one point she was madly in love with this powerful man, believing she could somehow save him from himself. There is a hint of collusion here, and despite her fear Patience still makes excuses for Joss, trying to deflect his anger in a way that only provokes it further. Du Maurier herself doesn't excuse him. Admittedly, she gives him a childhood with its own history of violence, and an abused, helpless mother, but she never lets him off the hook. For all his physical strength he is a weak character, and though Mary may be morally and phys-ically repelled by him she is also up for the battle. And a battle it is, from the moment he latches on to her both as his prey, the next woman after his wife that he must break and destroy – and also in some desperate hope that Mary will match him and somehow bring him to redemption.

There is an extraordinary scene halfway through the book – in its way much more frightening than the real thing, which comes later – when Joss emerges from a drinking bout to accost Mary in the kitchen. Crazed by waking nightmares, he offers up a lacerating confession about the ships he has lured onto the rocks and the survivors he has bludgeoned to death in the roaring surf, their faces coming back to haunt him. His terror at that moment is much greater than Mary's, but it is her sentence to be the helpless listener. It is worth knowing as you read this scene that du Maurier's own husband, the affable, charming, good-looking Frederick Browning, had been a war hero; one of the things that marked the early years of their marriage was the way he would wake at night screaming, and she would have to try and comfort him. Some of du Maurier's own helpless horror is in Mary as she watches, repelled and overwhelmed by her uncle's raving confessions.

This painful realism of the relationship between men and women also underpins Mary's growing attraction to her uncle's brother, Jem. There is a quiet cynicism to du Maurier's description of their courtship. Mary knows that Jem will probably bring her as much pain as happiness, but she accepts it as part of how the world works. She has watched it unfold too many times around her to be fooled: seen how a teasing courtship down sun-drenched lanes will be replaced by the mundanity and exhaustion of married life, the man 'calling sharply that his supper was burnt, not fit for a dog, while the girl snapped back at him from the bedroom overhead, her figure sagging and her curls gone, pacing backwards and forward with a bundle in her arms that mewed like a cat and would not sleep'. Du Maurier had had her first child just a few years before she wrote this novel and while the nanny had done more caring than she ever did (the one time she was left with the baby it screamed its head off), there is a taste of experience to the vision. For a book which at one level is a romantic adventure story, *Jamaica Inn* is full of decidedly unromantic thoughts.

The novel doesn't dwell on them though. It's too busy winching the story ever tighter. Once you get past the second chapter it's almost impossible to read *Jamaica Inn* slowly. It is the burden of thriller writers to have the reader tell them admiringly how fast they read your books. 'I couldn't put it down' is both the greatest compliment and the cruellest cut of all, since it almost certainly means that a reader's greed to get to the end of the book will have made them careless with some of the best writing on the way. It's a trade-off thriller writers have to accept. But du Maurier never set out to write literary fiction. Her style is intelligent and fluid, sufficient unto the cause of telling the story. But then it wasn't her style that made her famous. That's not why she is still being reprinted when a hundred other writers of her age are footnotes in fiction. And while she has dated in certain respects – her dialogue can sometimes feel a little stilted and there are perhaps one too many dark nights and haunted moors for modern taste – almost seventy years have in no way dimmed her capacity to hook the reader like a fish and angle them in through the rising waters of the plot. There is virtually no spare action here. It would be invidious to give away the last twist, and while there will be those who see it coming, fore-sight doesn't rob it of its elegant baroque menace, with more than a touch of the Hannibal Lecter/Clarice Starling relation-ship thrown into the dark mix. Mary Yellan sups with many devils in this book and by the end there is not even a long spoon between them.

In the end – well, in the end the book resolves itself as any good Gothic adventure should, by bringing the reader out of darkness into at least a semblance of light. Mary Yellan survives. But even though the writer doesn't say it directly, you can be sure Mary will not sleep well at night. That is the price you pay for winning such battles. The good triumph but, like du Maurier's husband, they remain damaged by the fight. For all of her priv-ileged middle-class upbringing, by the time Daphne du Maurier wrote *Jamaica Inn* at the comparatively young age of twenty-nine, she too, already had something of darkness about her. She was, in fact, well on her way to *Rebecca*.

Frenchman's Creek

Julie Myerson

Back in 1975 when I was fifteen and already determined to Be A Novelist, I wrote a letter to Daphne du Maurier. I sent it care of her publishers, Victor Gollancz, and I didn't know if it would really get to her. So I was delirious with excitement when a small white envelope postmarked St Austell plopped through our Nottingham letterbox. She'd written back! She enclosed a grainy colour snap of Kilmarth, her grey Cornish stone house, explaining that it appeared in her novel *The House on the Strand* – 'which I think you would enjoy as much as the others'. She also wished me luck with my O Levels.

Normal teenagers might have been very grateful and left it there. But not me. I got back to the poor woman immediately, enclosing my pencil sketch of 'Rachel' in *My Cousin Rachel*. Very kindly – where on earth did she find the time? – she replied straightaway, this time sending an autographed photo of herself sitting on the beach at Par.

I gazed at it for ages, at this photo that her fingers had actually touched. I gazed at her face – wise and wistful with just a hint of defiance. At her boyishly sensible brown wool trouser suit. At her eyes, mysteriously fixed – just as they should be! – on some point far out to sea. She thanked me for the drawing, generously remarking that it was 'more attractive than the actress Olivia de Havilland who took the part in the film!' And, best of all, she wished me good luck with my 'book'.

This was the 'novel' I was writing – in painstaking biro in a spiral-bound exercise book. It was called 'Samantha' and, yes, it owed an embarrassing amount to *Rebecca*. I didn't tell her this.

Our correspondence continued sporadically across almost two years, as I turned sixteen and then seventeen. I still have the clutch of postcards, letters and photographs she sent me. The small white envelopes with my name typed on the front, the 6p stamp, the St Austell postmark, the spidery handwriting.

Handling and reading them now is strangely moving – an eerie shortcut back to the girl I was then. I am reminded of how profoundly du Maurier changed the way I felt about myself – how she engaged and excited me with her writing, how she was the first novelist I'd encountered who seemed to delve into the darkest stirrings of the human heart – its most monstrous passions, its most restless yearnings – in a way that I could touch and understand. Somewhere deep in those novels, I found a taste of something that shook me up: a sense of romance, of spirit and place and, I suppose, a hint of what sexual love between men and women might actually be like.

I first read *Frenchman's Creek* in the summer of 1974. It was a big yellow cellophane-covered hardback from the Nottingham Library in Shakespeare Street. We had just started spending summer holidays in Cornwall – my stepfather had bought a small yacht and decided to moor it in the harbour at Fowey. I remember those holidays as always hot, always perfect. The sailing, the swimming, the mackerel fishing off the back of our boat, the hot walks on the cliff paths, the picnics at Lantic Bay. I'd never been anywhere more beautiful, more exotic and inspiring. The fierce aquamarine skies, the jagged landscape took my breath away.

But then so did the novel. I read it as pure, exhilarating adventure story – a swashbuckling tale of exquisite danger and tangled love. The beautiful and headstrong Dona St Columb, trapped in a marriage to a fat and mindless fop, bored by the shallowness of Restoration court life, escapes to the family seat in Cornwall and finds a place to satisfy her restless soul. Soon she has morphed

Julie Myerson

into someone else – a woman who thinks nothing of leaving her children at home, dressing up as a cabin boy and going on escapades with a Frenchman about whom she knows almost nothing. Except, of course, that he's a pirate (a sensitive and romantic one) who spends his spare time sketching birds. Enough to make any girl fall head over heels.

And why not? At fourteen, moodily tramping the cliffs above Fowey with the sun in my eyes and poppies in my hair, I understood Dona perfectly. Life was about spontaneity, about the romance of simply following your heart. Well, what else was there? If the white sail of La Mouette had appeared in the harbour below me just then, I would not have hesitated. I would have stuffed my curls under a hat just like Dona and sailed off in search of adventure.

That was then. Coming back to *Frenchman's Creek* now – almost three decades, three children and five novels of my own later – I'm amazed to find a quite different book, something infinitely deeper and darker and more daunting. Here is a tale of emotional and sexual awakening, of loss and risk and compromise. It's a much more poignant and slippery novel than I'd ever realised – far more uneasily sophisticated in its exploration of the human heart.

And at the centre of this exploration stands Dona St Columb, one of the greatest du Maurier heroines – headstrong, beautiful and brave with a surprising sense of humour and mischief. But she is also uptight, unhappy, quietly furious with herself. Escaping London and its wearinesses and bringing her children to Navron House in Cornwall changes her inner world unexpectedly and profoundly.

But the joy and release she discovers in the wild Cornish landscape is just the beginning. Suddenly there seem to be no limits: everything she once thought closed is suddenly open, the impossible becomes possible. By the time the Frenchman walks into her life, she's ready for him. She's met her match and so has he.

'Why are you a pirate?' she said at last, breaking the silence.

'Why do you ride horses that are so spirited?' he answered.

'Because of the danger, because of the speed, because I might fall,' she said.

'That is why I am a pirate,' he said.

Yet though Dona may be a rebel, a free spirit – evoking that streak in all of us that strains at the leash, wants to gallop and risk the fall – she is also a wife and mother. Du Maurier does not make light of this. Dona's escapades in the night, with the trusty William covering for her, are not without risk. We are never allowed to forget that there is a potentially vengeful husband in London and, more urgently, two small children tucked up at Navron. So Dona takes her freedom, her adventure, but at a price.

For that's what this is – a novel about the queasy relationship between freedom and responsibility, between choice and no choice. Dona had thought herself trapped forever in her loveless marriage and had therefore hardened herself against the possibility of being opened, touched, awakened. Instead she had become feckless – drinking with her husband's friends, carrying out silly pranks at Court – all in order to avoid having to think about her own intrinsic unhappiness. Now, though, she must. Think, that is.

But this is also a love story, a story about what happens when you recognise passion, when you stumble upon a kindred soul. Before the Frenchman, Dona knows nothing of love, she has never encountered it. Now, though, she sees that it is 'a place she had known always, and deeply desired, but had lost, through her own carelessness, or through circumstances, or the blunting of her own perception'.

When Dona is with the Frenchman, she feels still, at peace – she feels completed. 'She would be playing with the children at Navron, or wandering about the garden, filling the vases with flowers, and he away down in his ship in the creek, and because she had knowledge of him there her mind and her body became filled with life and warmth, a bewildering sensation she had never known before.'

These passages, so astute and precise, contain as intelligent a description of the way it feels to love, really love, as any I have read. This is where du Maurier excels – in describing human ardour in a way that is at once both mad and unearthly, warm and realistic, bitingly erotic and beautiful. It's the part of her writing I could never have properly understood or appreciated at fourteen.

'I hope you will be able to live in your dream house one day,' she wrote to me at the very end of her last letter, 'Menabilly was mine but I have settled very happily here.'

I haven't yet lived in my dream house but there's no doubt that her encouragement and generosity helped me achieve another dream. This thrilling contact with a Real Writer – so crucial, so exhilarating to a shy, intense teenage girl – kept me going for years. In a world where no one really believed I could or would write – people we knew in Nottingham didn't! – it gave me real hope.

I would give anything now to be able to tell her that I made it, that I wrote my novels. Not only that, but I wish she could have known that her relentless, probably irritatingly persistent, Nottingham pen pal was one day enough of a Proper Writer to be allowed to write a new introduction to this, one of the most bewitching and heart-squeezing of all her novels.

The King's General

Justine Picardie

The first time I read *The King's General* was on a melancholy autumn day, not long after I'd started at a new school, in a town where I knew no one, at the age of fourteen. Daphne du Maurier's landscape – seventeenth-century Cornwall, last refuge of brave Cavaliers – was entirely distant to mine; hundreds of years and miles away, further by far than the home I'd left behind. But as I sought refuge in the school library, escaping the rain and all the people I didn't know, and who didn't want to know me, the book seemed more real to me than the unfamiliar place I had found myself; offered more solace than anything else at the time.

Returning to *The King's General,* decades later, reminds me of how well it expresses the sadness of the dislocated and dispossessed. That might sound melodramatic – and the book is melodramatic, at times; just as I was as a teenager, about the dismal misery of my new life – but *The King's General,* so often overlooked by literary critics, is more than a melodrama, more subtle and unsettling. Widely regarded as a straightforward historical romance – which it can be, if that's simply what you want it to be – the novel also does something unusual, creating a story that feels timeless, for all its period detail. The description of the Cornish setting – always vivid in du Maurier's writing; far more than a backdrop, as crucial as any of the main characters – seems as atmospheric and as true now as when *The King's General* was first published in 1946. Anyone who loves Cornwall, as I do (both as a real and imaginary landscape) will be comforted by the idea that the hills and the moorland, the beaches and the cliff tops, remain, in essence, those that du Maurier's heroine, Honor Harris, gazed upon as her story opens in 1653; and I like to think that future readers of the novel will feel the same way.

That opening is also an ending – or close to an ending, it seems; though du Maurier is unsurpassed at keeping secrets, at the same time as hinting at revelations to come. At fourteen, I found it impossible not to look at the ending, so intriguing was the first chapter: but unlike any other writer that I can think of, du Maurier still managed not to give the game away; at least not to me, the cheating reader; not then, for it is only when you read the whole book that the final page makes sense.

So it would be entirely wrong of me to break the suspense now, in this introduction; though I think it safe to say that the first few pages, with their description of a summer's end, and the encroaching chill of autumn, are a perfect indication of what is about to unfold. 'The first clouds of evening are gathering beyond the Dodman,' observes the novel's sole narrator, Honor Harris, an ailing woman writing by candlelight. 'And the surge of the sea, once far-off and faint, comes louder now, creeping towards the sands. The tide has turned. Gone are the white stones and the cowrie shells. The sands are covered. My dreams are buried. And as darkness falls the flood-tide sweeps over the marshes and the land is covered.'

Faraway, across the sea, Honor imagines her former lover, Sir Richard Grenvile – the King's General no longer – banished from the land he loved. 'My heart aches for you in this last disgrace,' writes Honor. 'I picture you sitting lonely and bitter at your window, gazing out across the dull flat lands of Holland . . .' As an opening, it is as brooding as the first pages of *Rebecca*; and the darkness of that more famous novel, published eight years previously, casts a shadow over *The King's General*, too. There are other similarities, as well: for like the hero of *Rebecca*, Sir Richard Grenvile is a ruthless, powerful man; more powerful, apparently, than the woman who loves him.

Daphne du Maurier dedicated *The King's General* to her husband, Sir Frederick Browning, a Grenadier Guards officer, otherwise known as Tommy: 'To my husband, also a general, but, I trust, a more discreet one'. Margaret Forster's marvellous biography of Daphne du Maurier reveals that Tommy (who had been knighted in the 1946 New Year's Honours List) guessed that his wife's dedication would make people assume that Richard Grenvile, 'first a soldier, second a lover', a man 'violent from his youth . . . cruel . . . hard', was based on him. Tommy (a likeable chap, by all accounts, though prone to depression) was amused; at the same time as expressing the hope, in a letter to his wife, that her latest novel might 'have a nice ending for a change, because you know what I think of your sad endings'.

But there was to be no happy ending for Honor and her general; an indication, perhaps, that Daphne (who wrote the book while Tommy was still stationed abroad) was fearful of what might happen to their marriage when he finally returned to Menabilly, their house in Cornwall. And Menabilly was to play a crucial part in *The King's General*: it is where much of the action takes place, and Daphne immersed herself in its history when she was researching the novel. The house had fascinated Daphne ever since she first discovered it, soon after her parents bought a holiday house in Fowey in 1927, and its original owners, the Rashleighs, were also to appear in *The King's General*. She was particularly intrigued by the tale of a skeleton found in Menabilly in the nineteenth century, apparently discovered by builders, in a bricked-up room. As she explains in her postscript to the novel, the workmen 'came upon a stair, leading to a small room, or cell, at the base of the buttress. Here they found the skeleton of a young man, seated on a stool, a trencher at his feet, and the skeleton was dressed in the clothes of a Cavalier, as worn during the period of the Civil War'. The rest – in Daphne's version, anyway – is not history, but romance; though the story as she told it seemed entirely convincing to me, as a teenager (far more so than those dreary history text books about the struggles between Royalists and Parliament that I should have been reading instead).

Given the success of other du Maurier stories that were turned into films – *Rebecca*, *The Birds*, *Don't Look Now* – I'd always half expected to see *The King's General* as a swashbuckling Hollywood movie. But despite the sale of the rights for what was then the enormous sum of £65,000 – part of which was spent on a new boat for Tommy after the war – the film was never made. (After years of setbacks and delays, Elizabeth Taylor was suggested to play the heroine in 1958: Daphne was horrified by the prospect; nor did she like the script.) I still think it would make a good film – it has the right blend of epic and intimate qualities – but there is pleasure, too, to be had in feeling the book to be one's own private discovery. When I first read it I knew no one else who had, so its revelations and secrets remained mine alone. This, of course, is part of the conceit of the novel, from the beginning: Honor Harris, she tells us in the first chapter, knows 'this autumn will be the last' for her, and her memoir 'will go with me to the grave . . . rotting there with me, unread'. Honor's purpose, in writing down her secrets, is, she says, 'to rid myself of a burden'; and though Daphne du Maurier chooses not to reveal why, or how, the story escapes from the grave, the reader is left with the sense that we have been given not a burden, but a gift.

It's a remarkable achievement – and all the more so, I realise now, as I reread *The King's General* in my own middle age. As a fourteen year old, I adored the novel's early chapters that describe Honor Harris as a spirited teenager, before tragedy had torn her life apart; now, while I still love that part of *The King's General*, I also appreciate du Maurier's account of growing older. Towards the end of the book, when Sir Richard Grenvile has remarked in a letter to Honor that doubtless she finds her days monotonous, alone in Cornwall, she observes:

> I have seen the shadows creep, on an autumn afternoon, from the deep Pridmouth valley to the summit of the hill, and there stay a moment, waiting on the sun ... Dark moods too of bleak November, when the rain sweeps in a curtain from the south-west. But, quietest of all, the evenings of late summer, when the sun has set, and the moon has not yet risen, but the dew is heavy in the long grass.

You could not ask for a better, swifter description both of the passing of the seasons, and the turning of the years. Daphne was in her late thirties when she wrote the novel – 'a dull, grey-haired, nearly-forty wife', she wrote in a letter soon after Tommy arrived home from the war – and while by no means close to death herself, it cannot be coincidence that she chose to write about Honor Harris, who died at the age of thirty-eight. (Like the other principal characters in the novel, there was a real Honor Harris, who was buried in a church near Menabilly, in the parish of Tywardreath, on 17th November 1653.) Daphne herself lived on until the age of nearly eighty-two: a long, extraordinary life, in which she became one of the most wildly popular authors of her time. Yet nowhere in her writing, it seems to me, than in *The King's General* will you find better expression of that bittersweet blend of foreboding and hopefulness, of passionate love and anguished loss, that marks what it means to grow up. 'Come now, take heart,' says Honor's brother-in-law Jonathan, on the final page of the book, when we know she is nearing her end, fading into the twilight that has shaded her story from the start. 'One day the King will come into his own again; one day your Richard will return.'

'One day,' replies Honor, repeating lines that have echoed throughout the novel, 'when the snow melts, when the thaw breaks, when the spring comes.'

The Parasites

Julie Myerson

I first encountered *The Parasites* in the Nottingham Library, summer of '76. A fat, yellow Gollancz hardback wrapped in thick, cloudy polythene and date-stamped inside, it would have been one of six novels I borrowed that week from the tall Gothic building on Shakespeare Street. It was the summer I finished my O Levels – a long, parched scorching heatwave of a summer. Every day you thought it couldn't get any hotter but it did. I was a tense, nail-chewing teenager who shunned boys and wrote 'novels' in exercise books. To me that city library was a sanctuary, the safest place in all the world – and icy cool to boot.

I haunted it like a ghost. I knew its opening hours, where its toilet was, and which of its haughty librarians was most likely to let me lurk in peace. I learned to dodge its furthest aisles, where the tramps punctured the air with their snores and musty urine smells. Instead, breath held, I loitered in Fiction, fingering every single, grubby spine on those shelves as I looked – for what? A way into a secret world? Dispatches from the front line of personal experience – a place I had yet to get to myself?

Probably both. But most of all I remember searching for novels that might in any way touch on my pet obsessions: dance, writing, painting, theatre, ghosts, Cornwall, sex – especially sex. I can see now that *The Parasites* – a strange, ambiguous love story set in a world of dark, Lutyens houses, Morny soap and brittle, fading theatrical glamour – would, in its sly way, have satisfied quite a few of these criteria.

I do know that I thought it was a very grown-up novel. Infinitely dark and sexy and weary – in the very most attractive sense of the word. Weary and worldly. Here was a world of cocktails and dinners, of matinées and debutante's feathers, of virginities lost in Paris apartments. In fact the precise flavour of weary-worldliness I sensed lurking in those pages made me feel reckless, daring, chaotic – everything a romantic, provincial sixteen-year-old fantasised that grown-up life might one day be.

What I didn't see then – probably because I was too wrapped up in my adolescent self to get it – was how mischievously comic a novel it is, how successfully and enjoyably it sends up the upper classes, actors, theatrical types, the rich by birth, the terminally self-absorbed. I think at that age I would have completely missed the savage and satirical anger that lies at its dark heart – a ferocious, sometimes surprising fury which keeps it bubbling, never lets it become glossy, camp or self-indulgent in the way that novels about theatricals and show business so often are.

But that's not all. Another aspect struck me even more forcefully when I picked the novel up again, now, in 2005. I found myself moved and shocked by its central relationship and I experienced a sense of déjà vu I couldn't shake off. What did it remind me of? Where had I come across this kind of bond before?

This is the story of a strange and powerful, quasi-incestuous love. Here are a girl and a boy who grow up as siblings but are not blood related – whose bond is intense, passionate, unstoppable. They understand each other intuitively, like twins, but the love itself is immature, hopeless and selfish, irresponsible even, leaving no room for others. It's the story of two people who spend their whole lives both in thrall to and in denial of, this central passionate relationship – because however hard they try to pull apart, whatever other relationship (or marriage) each tries to forge, they always spring back together again, helpless. Who else does this remind you of? Doesn't another English novel spring immediately to mind?

Of course there are many differences between Maria and Niall and Cathy and Heathcliff, but still I find the similarities curiously impossible to ignore. These are harsh and possessive loves, devastating at times. There is a darkness here that seems to blot out the possibility of any kind of future. Both Maria and Niall are perplexed to find that now and then they want to hit the other 'very very hard'. Except to think it's a relationship of violence is to misunderstand it – the hitting never happens. It's about frustration, sexual and logistical: how else to get sufficiently inside each other's skins? When Maria is on the stage, Niall can't watch but has to leave, so closely and painfully does he identify with her terror. Maria is the only person who always knows what Niall is thinking – sometimes even before he does. And yet, just like Cathy and Heathcliff, Maria and Niall sometimes don't seem separate enough to be able to form a normal, useful adult relationship. Indeed, if family servant Truda is Nellie Dean's counterpart, then you can almost hear Maria declaring to her, 'Truda, I am Niall!'

I also see more to link Brontë and du Maurier. Both authors use landscape to invoke passion – and libido. Both have an inherently and fascinatingly queasy relationship with their characters. Du Maurier apparently admitted that all three Delaneys were probably facets of her own personality – and she is certainly rare among women novelists in that she seems to inhabit her male characters at least as fully as her female ones and with absolute authenticity and ferocity. The same could certainly be said of Brontë. Not only that, but it's undeniable to anyone who knows their work that a prime strength of both Brontë and du Maurier is their ability and willingness to imagine and mine the darkest reaches of the human mind, of passion and sexuality (the male and the female side) and of life and death. These are brave writers, unafraid to look over the edge into the abyss.

But there the similarities end, because there's certainly no comedy in *Wuthering Heights*. And yet some of the most unsettling scenes in du Maurier's novel are also its funniest. My favourite is the one where Maria, who has married the Hon Charles Wyndham (for reasons very similar, by the way, to those that drive Cathy into a marriage with Edgar Linton) and given birth to a daughter, Caroline, finds herself left alone with that baby one afternoon. Spoilt, immature and inexperienced, she is quite unable to cope. Without even thinking twice about it, she calls Niall who, also without a thought, drops everything and comes running to help.

But it's no good. Here are two children in charge of a child. When Caroline won't stop crying they stop the car and, in desperation, ask a passing woman what they should do. Unsurprisingly, she gives them short shrift and threatens to call a policeman. They drive on. Maria remarks that she can see now why mothers leave their babies in shops. 'They can't stand the strain.' Only half joking, Niall suggests they leave Caroline in a shop. Both agree that no one would miss her. Eventually Maria has an idea and asks Niall to stop at Woolworths so she can buy a comforter. 'You know, those awful rubber things that common babies have stuck in their mouths.'

They get the comforter and it works. Caroline stops crying.

'How easy it would be,' said Niall, 'if every time one felt on edge one could just go to Woolworths and buy a comforter. There must be something psychological about it. I think I shall get one for myself. It's probably what I've wanted all my life.'

It's a laugh-out-loud scene – and rather novel and startling suddenly to be reading du Maurier on childcare and the oral comforting of babies – but it's also a very damning one. Nowhere else in the novel is the parasitical nature of du Maurier's protagonists better expressed. These are selfish creatures who are reluctant to fulfil anyone's needs but their own. But take away the comedy and you begin to wonder, what does du Maurier herself feel about all of this? What does she want us to think, and whose side is she on anyway?

A tricky question because, more than anything, *The Parasites* is stylistically on the edge, an exercise in narrative sleight of hand. The clue lies in that very first sentence: 'It was Charles who called us the parasites.' Called who? Well, the three Delaneys: Maria, Niall and Celia, obviously. But which Delaney is talking? You read on, expecting to have the question answered, to have it all made clear – and very quickly realise it's impossible to tell.

Because this is a tale told by three people and therefore, in a sense, never really told by anyone. Just when you think you're getting close, the invisible narrator swerves away and disappears. You can almost hear du Maurier laughing. And, though we spend time in the heads of all three Delaneys in turn, there is never a single moment when that bold, all-encompassing 'We' begins to feel like an 'I'. So who, ultimately, does the author sympathise with most? Brittle, fragile Maria? Dogged, lonely Niall? Unfulfilled, put-upon Celia? Whose skin is she in? And does it matter if we never find out? It's a tribute to the complexity and breadth of this strange, unnerving novel that I'm still trying to decide.

My Cousin Rachel

Sally Beauman

My Cousin Rachel is a novel of great technical assurance. As the *Guardian* reviewer wrote at the time of first publication in 1951, it is 'a consummate piece of story-telling'.

A double-edged remark, perhaps, the ability to plot well being regarded with suspicion outside the confines of 'popular liter-ature', but for Daphne du Maurier, even such backhanded compliments represented an advance. At least *My Cousin Rachel*, unlike earlier successes such as *Jamaica Inn* and *Rebecca*, was not entirely consigned to that critical netherworld reserved for 'romance' or 'women's fiction' or (to use George Eliot's sexist terms) 'Silly Novels by Lady Novelists'. Its ingenuity of construc-tion, if not its darkness and complexity, was acknowledged from the first.

Du Maurier was forty-four when *My Cousin Rachel* was published, and, although she would continue writing novels for another twenty years, this would be the last of her great best-sellers. It marked a watershed in her creative abilities too: only one of her subsequent novels (*The Scapegoat*, 1957) and some of the short stories (particularly the collection *The Apple Tree*, 1952) show her writing at full imaginative power, and these, rich, strange, and perturbing as they are, never found great popularity with readers. So *My Cousin Rachel* marks a crucial divide, a kind of climacteric: it comes exactly at the mid-point of her novel-writing career; it crowned her earlier successes, and it is, in many ways, a last throwing-down of the novelistic gauntlet. Here, for the last time, du Maurier applies the full battery of skills that made her a bestselling author. The result is dazzling.

Using one of her favourite devices, a male narrator, du Maurier, *en travestie*, shuffles the cards of plot, theme and character, and makes them dance. Each chapter teases our understanding of what has gone before; each revelation undermines or seems to contradict the one that preceded it. The novel is an object lesson in the difficult art of dovetailing timescheme and plot to lethal effect. Like *Rebecca*, it perfectly demonstrates du Maurier's ability to conceal unpalatable social truths within a page-turning format. It is a razorblade of a novel: the blade is carefully hidden, but it is there, inside the packaging, and, fifty years later, its capacity to draw blood remains unaltered.

The novel begins conventionally enough. Clearly, this will be an historical novel, and its location will be familiar du Maurier territory – Cornwall, at du Maurier's own home, Menabilly (fictionalised in other novels, most notably in *Rebecca*). But from the first, there is a sense of displacement. We never learn the exact era in which the novel's events take place, which gives it a curious, dreamlike air of timelessness. And this Cornish estate, unnamed in the novel, has had all fictional allure ruthlessly scraped away: anyone expecting another Manderley (and many readers will expect just that: du Maurier plays with such expectations throughout) is in for a shock. We first approach it via a gallows, on which the decaying corpse of a wife-killer swings; then, passing down the drive (the same drive that features so memorably in *Rebecca*), we discover a house from which women have been banished. There, two men, served entirely by male staff, lead an isolated, philistine, inward-looking existence. The older man, Ambrose Ashley, is in poor health; he is only in his forties, but the damp Cornish climate is, literally, crippling him. The younger, his cousin, surrogate son, protégé and heir, Philip Ashley, is twenty-three, but old before his time, willingly imprisoned by the reactionary,

Sally Beauman

chauvinistic, anti-intellectual and misogynistic beliefs of the older cousin-guardian he worships.

No sooner has the reader adjusted to this masculine redoubt, than he is whisked away to a very different world, to Florence. There, Ambrose travels in search of plants for his garden, and an improvement in his health. Philip Ashley, left behind, learns of events in Italy only intermittently by letter, and these gaps in communication, characteristic of a novel in which 'truth' is always elusive for characters and readers, will have profound and lasting effects. Within months of his departure, Ambrose meets and – astonishingly – marries the eponymous Rachel (a distant cousin, half Cornish, half Italian, impoverished widow of the Count Sangalletti). Marriage does not suit him, however: the early rapture of his first letters rapidly gives way to reports of worsening health, and veiled accusations against his new bride – accusations that may have substance, or may merely be paranoid. An incoherent plea for help finally arrives: Philip leaves Cornwall immediately. On arrival in Florence, he finds the Villa Sangalletti closed up, Cousin Rachel absent, and Ambrose dead. But is it true, as Philip is informed, that Ambrose died of a brain tumour – or could his death have another, more sinister, explanation?

From that moment onwards, two worlds collide and for the remainder of the novel, those two worlds, and their two sensibilities, will struggle for dominance. On the one hand, we have England and the Ashley estates, a dour, feudal enclave fiercely resistant to social or political change, a world in which women are marginalised, their influence regarded with a distaste bordering on revulsion. On the other, we have a Florence redolent of such Browning monologues as *My Last Duchess,* a place of profligacy, deadly intrigue and sexual sophistication. In England, we found ourselves on a man's estates; in Florence, crucially, we are on female territory, for the Villa Sangalletti belongs to that black widow who gives the novel its title. This is Cousin Rachel's domain, and once in it, or under its Circean

174

influence, first Ambrose then Philip will be unmanned – with fatal consequences for both of them.

To the jingoistic, arrogant and inexperienced Philip, the Florentines he encounters exhibit slippery un-English character-istics: unlike the Ashleys, they resist easy definition by social class, occupation, or beliefs. Their gender roles shift; their sexual orien-tation and their motivation is uncertain – but, as he will learn, they seem to enjoy a stereotypic Borgia-style taste for murder, their chosen method being equally stereotypic: poisoning.

So far, so clear – and, possibly, so melodramatic – one might think. But is that the case? This story wears layers of disguises, and no sooner does one mask come off, than another is revealed beneath it. The central mystery of *My Cousin Rachel* is usually perceived as relating to its female protagonist. It is a question of *poisoning*. Did Rachel first murder Ambrose, and then set out to murder his heir, Philip? *Cherchez la femme*: is Rachel pure or impure, is she innocent or guilty? But this question, fascinating though du Maurier makes it, is an authorial sleight of hand: it disguises the far more interesting issue of *male* culpability – as the title, with its deliberate echoes of Browning, suggests. Both Ambrose and Philip exercise a financial stranglehold on Rachel: in turn, they seek to own and control her, their weapons being money and marriage. This male hegemony (in a novel deeply concerned with wills, testaments, and inheritance) continues after death, and much of the novel explores, with great subtlety, Rachel's efforts to resist it. So who is doing the *poisoning,* the corrupting, here? Is it Rachel, with her *tisanas* and witchy herbal pharmacopoeia, or is it the Ashleys, with their conditional gifts of jewels, land, houses, money and status?

Rachel, shimmering, enigmatic and elusive, does not appear in the opening chapters; she is absent when, after Ambrose's death, Philip goes to Florence in search of her, though he encoun-ters her double, or alter ego, in the shape of a young beggar-woman by the Arno, a ghostly figure, glimpsed then gone, who will haunt the rest of the novel. When Rachel finally does appear, on a prolonged visit to Cornwall, Philip is predisposed to hate her, but once they meet, is bewitched by her. We watch Rachel make an assault on a charmless, uncomfortable house; we watch her tame and feminise it, winning over the servants, civilising its routines, introducing guests, good meals, good wines and Italianate luxuries. We watch her adapt at will to a range of male-determined female roles, so she is mother and seductress, widow and waif, chatelaine and – possibly – charlatan. As we do so, our male narrator invites us to share his uncertainties: is Rachel grieving, or deceiving? Is she a visitor, or a usurper? Could she love Philip – or is she merely using him?

Du Maurier withholds the answer. We see Rachel, and hear her speak (as we never do that other female chimera, Rebecca de Winter) yet she remains essentially unreadable, her features distorted by the male gaze of the possessive, jealous and infatu-ated man describing her. We can never see her because Philip Ashley, blind to his own Oedipal impulses, obscures her – in which context, the semiotics of the possessive pronoun used in the title is not, one feels, accidental. As that 'My' signals, an act of appropriation takes place in this narrative, one that denies Rachel autonomy. Forced to fit inside the fictive prison Philip Ashley constructs around her, she *cannot* be herself; she has to be his belonging, his adjunct and chattle – and she is merely another item on a long privileged Ashley list: *my* house, *my* estate, *my* money, *my* family jewels . . . *my* cousin Rachel.

How much can the reader trust Philip Ashley, in any case? It is almost always a mistake to pay too much credence to du Maurier's narrators. Her skill renders them plausible but to read du Maurier properly, and understand just how heretical a novelist she is, it is necessary to watch for the correctives, the destabil-ising devices she builds into her narratives. And, in *My Cousin Rachel*, they are there: Philip Ashley is no objective observer of these events, after all; he is deeply enmeshed in them – it is he who will propel events to their tragic conclusion, influenced to the last by the claims of his cousin Ambrose. But Philip and Ambrose are doubles. The cousins' physical resemblance is strong; their mindset is near identical; Philip's character may have been warped by his upbringing, but insanity and paranoia run in the male Ashley line, so an ugly genetic inheritance may also link the two men. What we are reading is certainly a confession – but is it sane or mad, truthful or profoundly manipulative?

Such questions undermine the entire text, yet the unbalanced suspicion and disregard for women that both men exhibit are scarcely peculiar to them: they are shared, to varying degrees, by every male character in the novel, regardless of age, class or nationality. Misogyny is not a British disease, it seems: it infects even Rachel's worldly-wise advisor, the Italian, Rainaldi; and it affects, adversely, every female character in the book. The damage inflicted here is not confined to one woman, Rachel; it extends to an entire sex, and it poisons a society. It is *this* poison that is the central concern of du Maurier's novel. At a plot level, she will tease the reader with the question of laburnum seeds, and whether or not Rachel brews them up in her *tisanas* to rid herself of a husband or a lover; but in counter-point, at a thematic level, she examines male-administered poisons that are equally deadly, and whose victims are more numerous. Yet this, the central mirroring device of the novel, has scarcely been noticed, let alone examined.

· Du Maurier's cunning as a writer is very evident here: such was her sleight of hand she could disguise the true nature of her work. *My Cousin Rachel*, with its cool contempt for romantic conventions, is the most overtly feminist of her books, yet it is rarely perceived as such. But then, as its author had every reason to understand, the male misreadings she satirises throughout her text would be mirrored by the misreadings of prejudiced, misogynistic critics, male and female. It is typical of du Maurier's approach that she should write in the guise of a man, in a novel that explores, *inter alia*, the full implications of male authority. And it is typical of du Maurier's bitter venomous wit that she should use *poison* (famously a female weapon) as the central metaphor for a novel that is clever, cold-eyed, prescient – and unputdownable.

Mary Anne

Lisa Hilton

Mary Anne Clarke, the notorious mistress of the Duke of York, had much in common with her descendant, Daphne du Maurier. Both women wrote bestsellers, both combined lucrative careers with motherhood, both saw themselves, accurately, as the principal breadwinners in their families. It seems natural that du Maurier would have found a sympathetic subject for a biographical novel in her scandalous ancestress, in particular because she believed the defining characteristic of Mary Anne's personality to be one she herself shared, that of a woman alone and embattled in a world of men. In 1954, before the feminist explosion of the sixties and seventies, du Maurier interpreted the life of Mary Anne with a surprising prescience, an identification of the issues surrounding male and female power that were to galvanise the next generation of women writers. Du Maurier was no more a purely 'feminist' writer than she was a 'romantic' one, and she expressed contempt for such lazy and, in her eyes, dismissive categorisations. But just as *Mary Anne* is self-declaredly an unromantic book, it might be said that it is du Maurier's most overtly feminist work, in its suggestion that the world that elevates and eventually crushes the heroine might not, in two centuries, have changed a great deal.

Mary Anne was written at a very troubled time in Daphne du Maurier's life, and it seems clear that the concerns of the biographer often inform her interpretation of her subject. Eight years after his return from the war, Daphne had still not managed to repair her partial estrangement from her husband, 'Tommy' Browning, and though outwardly they appeared an ideal couple, their separate careers, he in London, and she in her beloved Cornwall, and the absence of a sexual relationship between them, were a source of great private strain. It is possible that the problems in Daphne's marriage were heightened by the fact that she had become intensely involved with two very different women. Ellen Doubleday, the wife of her American publisher, was a great unrequited passion. After meeting on Daphne's first voyage to America in 1947, they began a torrid epistolary relationship, but Ellen made it quite clear that her love for Daphne contained nothing physical, a rejection that infuriated Daphne at the same time as she denied fervently that she had any lesbian tendencies. She explored her feelings for Ellen in her successful play, *September Tide*, which starred Gertrude Lawrence, with whom Daphne quickly began a relationship of the sort that Ellen refused to countenance. When Gertrude died in 1952, aged only fifty-four, Daphne suffered from a profound and agonisingly private grief. She had discussed the relationship between herself and Gertrude with Ellen, but none of her family understood why she suffered so dreadfully at the death of a woman whom she had, after all, known only four years. Daphne had enjoyed great success with her novel *My Cousin Rachel* in 1951, and she knew that the way to recover was to write herself out of her depression. It is unsurprising, though, that *Mary Anne* proved a difficult book. With Gertrude, Daphne had discussed the possibility of turning Mary Anne Clarke's life into a play for Gertrude to star in. The story was to have been a lover's gift; yet two years later, lonely, ill and in mourning, Daphne shut herself up in her freezing garden hut in Cornwall to turn what had been intended as a tribute to her friend's dauntless exuberance into a form of elegy.

Mary Anne Clarke is a furiously ambitious woman, who learns

early that the only way to drag herself away from her mother's lot of dreary drudgery is to beat men at their own game. She despises men as 'a race to be subjected', whilst recognising that the world is run on their terms, and that the alternative to attempted equality is her mother's passive, craven weakness. This ambition is at once intensely feminine, concerned with protecting her family at all costs, and inappropriately masculine, determined upon power and a place in the world beyond the dreary kitchen of her childhood in Bowling Inn Alley. If Mary Anne is to prostitute herself, it will be on her own terms, and she refuses the pimping service offered by 'Uncle Tom', to maintain, at least, a determined independence in her choice of lovers. Her audacity is both her success and her ruin. She learns that it pays to deceive, to be cunning, to beat men's injustice by matching it, yet eventually this *idée fixe* destroys her judgement and her wit, and she is brutally punished by a masculine culture that is 'antagonistic because they knew her worth'.

Men, thinks Mary Anne, are all little boys, who need to be cosseted and protected from their own irresponsibility. Time and again, the men in her life upset her careful plans, from her drunken husband Joseph – whom she successfully leaves, only to have him reappear and destroy, with unbearable stupidity, her relationship with the Duke of York – to her whingeing, lazy brother Charley, whose adolescent pomposity du Maurier brilliantly captures in his proud use of military acronyms, and whose arrogance is such that he dares to criticise his sister, who has fed, clothed and kept him, for losing the Duke on the grounds that 'You were only a woman, his mistress, but we were men'. Even the Duke, the all-powerful Prince, the great commander, is weak and indecisive, easily swayed by his acolytes, and with an aristocratic disdain for money (initially imitated by Joseph Clarke) that forces Mary Anne into surreptitious commission-broking in order to maintain the vast, expensive household he so casually demands.

It is interesting that some time before the theories of psycho-sexual linguistics became fashionable in academia, du Maurier located Mary Anne's awareness of gender difference in language. The young Mary Anne teaches herself to read from printers' proofs, observing that the vowels are like women, and the consonants the men who depend on them. Since society conceals this dependence, it is a masculine language that Mary Anne must learn, a language of politics and newspapers and legal terms. It is crucial that du Maurier places such emphasis on Mary Anne as a writer, first of scurrilous pamphlets and then her own sala-cious memoirs, since the anonymity of print is the one place a woman can be seen, or unseen, as an equal. The compatibility of writing and femininity was always a treacherous issue for du Maurier herself, who often said that she wished she had been born a boy, a wish her father Gerald confessed to sharing in a poem he wrote for her as a child. Daphne felt ambivalent about her roles as a woman and a writer, an ambivalence that was re-inforced in later life by her sexual feelings for Ellen and Gertrude. The first time she met Ellen, Daphne confessed that she felt 'a boy of eighteen again with her nervous hands and a beating heart'. 'Again' is the telling word. As a child, Daphne had appar-ently convinced herself that she was a boy, and her biographer Margaret Forster comments on the devastating psychological consequences of puberty on this belief.

In the novel, Mary Anne makes her first error of judgement by falling in love with Joseph, impelled like Mary Yellan at the conclusion of the earlier novel, *Jamaica Inn*, by an irresistible sexual urge that represses her intuition. In *Jamaica Inn*, Mary abandons the prospect of a secure life to follow her wild lover Jem without fully understanding why; 'because I want to, because I must', and it is this weakness in women that Mary Anne initially despises, only to succumb to it in adolescence. Daphne du Maurier famously compared the masculine side of her person-ality to a jack-in-the-box, whom she would release, when alone, to caper through the silent rooms of the night, and one wonders whether she saw this image as being her writer's self, unhampered by gender. 'It's people like me,' she wrote, 'who have careers, who have really bitched up the old relationship between men and women. Women ought to be soft and gentle and dependent. Disembodied spirits like me are all wrong.' Mary Anne is another career woman, another disembodied spirit, and her frustration at the limitations of her femininity recall Daphne's own continued and complex dialogue between what she perceived as her own sexes.

Much of the vividness of Mary Anne's story is due to the fact that du Maurier was able to bring practical, as well as emotional experiences to bear on the book. Her portrait of the Duke of York – bluff, boisterous, a whirlwind of energy in the quietness of a feminine household – might owe something to the return of her own soldier husband to Cornwall after the war. As Tommy worked in the household of Princess (later Queen) Elizabeth, du Maurier also had first-hand experience of royalty off duty, enabling her to convey not only a confident sense of a royal prince as a human being, but also Mary Anne's disappointment at what she is surprised to find are the Duke's rather bourgeois tastes. Similarly, du Maurier could draw on personal knowledge of the courtroom scenes in which Mary Anne is a witness in the Duke of York's trial at the House of Commons for military broking. In 1947, on the same trip during which she met Ellen, Daphne had been forced to answer charges that she had plagiarised forty-six episodes in her bestseller *Rebecca* from a 1927 novel called *Blind Windows*. The charges were a farce, but Daphne found the experience of discussing her writing in public 'degrading'. 'When I got up on that bloody stand,' she wrote, 'I wasn't just fighting a foolish charge for plagiarism, I was fighting all the evil that has ever been, all the cruelty in myself.' Her image of Mary Anne on the witness stand, pathetic and vulnerable yet self-consciously culpable, highlights the way in which the law can make victims of women whilst being too unsophisticated to determine questions of personal morality. Mary Anne has connived at corruption, but she sees herself as having no option in a world in which the men who make the rules are also those who consistently betray her.

Du Maurier is also concerned in *Mary Anne* with the correlation between the physical and the psychological constructions of the feminine self. Mary Anne's ambition is her downfall, and her punishment is made physically manifest on the means by which she has achieved that ambition: her body. She is cheerfully untroubled by selling sex, a transaction which for her has nothing to do with love. The snores of a peer, she observes, are less grating than those of a mason, and she is practical in estimating the amount of time it will cost her to satisfy her lovers. Poor Lord Folkestone has to make do with a skimpy half hour. The hypocrisy of the men who condemn her in the House of Commons whilst still trying to buy her favours is highlighted by Joseph, who infects her while she is still his faithful wife with the venereal disease that causes her two miscarriages and, du Maurier suggests, leaves her infertile. Mary Anne's rebellious body is ultimately punished in prison, which her daughter recalls as 'horror beyond description, someone white and wan who could not stand, whose eyes were glazed, who stared without recognition when carried out of hell into the world'. Mary Anne has indeed climbed high, and the proof of her achievement of equality is the necessity of her destruction.

Daphne du Marier herself did not much care for *Mary Anne*. 'The whole thing,' she wrote, 'is lacking in human interest and reads like a newspaper report.' Indeed, much of the latter part of the novel, meticulously researched from old court documents and articles, does read this way; yet while it lacks the tight, gripping plot beloved of du Maurier fans then and now, the novel never quite manages to achieve the dullness its creator so harshly claimed for it. Daphne consoled herself with the thought that whatever else the book's shortcomings, it was definitely not 'romantic', a word which had already begun to plague her by the time of *Mary Anne*'s publication in 1954, and which has dogged serious appreciation of her work ever since. There never was a less romantic, even, one might say, downright unappealing heroine as Mary Anne Clarke, a quality which perhaps contributed to *Mary Anne* being the least commercially successful of her books in the first year of its publication.

Why, then, amidst such a distinguished oeuvre as du Maurier's, is it worth reviving? Perhaps because, like its heroine, the book is possessed of such unforgettably vivid charm that one is seduced, despite oneself, into forgiving its faults. Du Maurier compared the change in her style in this novel to 'a lush painter turning abstract'. Whilst *Mary Anne* does not attempt to form an historical composite, a portrait of an age, Daphne never makes the common historical writer's mistake of describing as surprising details that would have been commonplace to contemporaries, and we see always, with marvellous economy, through Mary Anne's cynical but lively eyes. The prose has a sense of eagerness, of rush, the clauses tumbling impressionistically over one another, so that in the most successful sections we inhabit the heroine's thrilling, rackety existence with the urgency and excitement of Mary Anne herself. Mary Anne may have been almost finished by her attempts to get even with the world of men, but, as du Maurier points out, she has the last laugh on her lover, as a raffish middle-aged Cockney woman cheerfully picnicking by his grave. The men in her life are agreed only on the enchantment of her smile and that gay insouciance with which she flips her champagne flute over her shoulder to toast the future in splinters. Daphne du Maurier has collected the shards, and though there are cracks in her portrait, it still scintillates, a captured prism of words that joyously illuminate another world.

The Scapegoat

Lisa Appignanesi

The Scapegoat, Daphne du Maurier's eleventh novel, first appeared in 1957. Almost twenty years earlier, *Rebecca* had rocketed to bestsellerdom and made the du Maurier name synonymous with romance. It is this expectation of intrigue and high passion which makes the later novel so startling. *The Scapegoat* is more Graham Greene than romance. It has a terse economy of style, great literary sophistication and an alienated post-war male conscience at its core. It also has gripping narrative pace. What is perhaps surprising is that all these are put at the service of a complex of themes already present in *Rebecca*. What is more surprising is that this fine book has so far failed to find the wide acclaim of its predecessor.

If in one light *Rebecca* is the story of the second and name-less Mrs de Winter's wistful longing to be like the dramatic and unforgettable wife she has never quite managed to replace – that Rebecca who left a mark on all who knew her – then *The Scapegoat* is the story of her male counterpart, John.

Plain, English John, like the second Mrs de Winter is name-less, but in reverse: he has no family name, no patronymic, as the Russians would say, no identifying male line which is the sign of belonging as well as the sign of power. Diffident, family-less, orphaned John is a lacklustre historian of France. At the start of the book, he is on his way back to a London he would rather not reach and considers stopping off at a Trappist Monastery for succour. He is depressed, indeed suicidal. He

186

doesn't 'know what to do with failure' and wishes, like the second Mrs de Winter, he were other. To use E. M. Forster's term, he wants to 'connect': somehow to form relations, perhaps to love, certainly to take part in that French life he can only observe from the outside and record.

With the perversity and panache of an Edgar Allan Poe or a Dostoevsky, du Maurier quickly gives her hero what he wants. She gives him another life. She gives it to him through a double. To want otherness enough is somehow to become other. But as fairytales always knew and we post-Freudians iterate, the fulfilment of a deeply held wish may well be the most dangerous thing that can happen to you.

John's double arrives on the scene without magic Jekyll and Hyde potions or devilishly dreamy lightning and thunderclaps or even deep rumblings of Russian anguish. He simply materialises beside the hero at a crowded station buffet in Le Mans and makes him feel slightly 'sick' at the 'looking at himself'. Du Maurier's understated matter-of-factness, her edge of humour, is what gives the scene such force and plausibility, together with an undertow of threat. 'You don't happen to be the devil, by any chance?' Jean de Gué asks John who answers, 'I might ask you the same question.'

The two men drink and dine together, stare and drink some more. What John learns is that his mirror image is both altogether familiar and profoundly unfamiliar. The Comte de Gué – and it is the one thing he reveals in response to John's garrulous self-confession – suffers from what John desires: 'too many possessions. Human ones.' In the presence of this bold and domineering twin, burdened with relations, the hero feels insubstantial, like a shadow without a will. When this shadow wakes from drunken stupor, it is to find itself substantiated, made over, as the Comte de Gué.

What du Maurier does brilliantly is to show us that identity (mistaken or not) is largely based on what others want and expect of us, what they project onto us. Hell may be other people, but so is life. It is no use John telling the chauffeur who has come to fetch him that he is not the Count: the man just respectfully asks if *Monsieur* would like to rest a little longer or have something brought from the *pharmacie*. Nor is there any point his protesting when he reaches the moated chateau which is the home of his double. Whatever conflicts he may experience inwardly, whatever his trepidation at each step of the unknown way, he behaves largely as the family demand of him and is accepted, even when he surprises, with equal measures of love and loathing.

John's journey as another into the depths of the extended family which is his new world is deeply disturbing in the echoes it sets up in us. Each step in his discovery of the familiar increases the threat that he will be uncovered as an impostor, neither husband nor father, son nor lover, nor indeed any of the other shifting, unstable and demanding parts in the great generational Oedipal drama. John masquerading as Jean is du Maurier's means of tapping the deep reservoirs of the uncanny which flow through the family: on occasion any of us may wake to find our nearest unknown, unfamiliar, frightening, wondering who they or we are.

The domestic, as du Maurier knew too well from her own childhood and marriage, is haunted terrain whether it's a two up, two down in Balham, Manderley or a French chateau with Gothic turrets and paintings of bloodied martyrs, here described with a spareness usually applied to the first. Dark murderous secrets, shafts of prohibited desire, make their home in each, turning the safe into the hazardous with the merest flick of a table knife or bedroom light.

John's gradual discovery of who the main players are in the chateau and its accompanying glass works, not to mention the secrets which drive them, is a process punctuated by the dangers both of repulsion and attachment. Du Maurier draws her characters with the deft strokes of a master, showing them as at once monstrous and ordinary. Through them, she has John wake to feeling. Here is John meeting the ailing bulk of sagging and demanding flesh who is his mother:

'Drawn to her like a magnet, I went instinctively to kneel beside her chair, and was at once caught and smothered, lost in the mountain of flesh and woollen wraps, feeling momentarily like a fly trapped in a great spider's web, yet at the same time fascinated because of the likeness, another facet of the self, but elderly, female, and grotesque.'

John is also this controlling, repellent woman who needs the love and power the Count won't give her and displaces need into an addiction her newly awakening son may help to cure.

The Scapegoat has a memorable cast of characters: the resentful younger brother, the sister whose religious ardours are a veil for rage and repressed desires, the frail, depressed, jealous wife trapped in the emotional maelstrom of her husband's kin, two mistresses, one histrionic and demanding, one a still centre, not to mention a sweetly unflappable curé de campagne, workers and retainers. Amongst all these vivid creations, it is Monsieur le Comte's daughter who leaps out at us with a mixture of poignant force and Puck-ish mischief. At the cusp of puberty, Marie-Noel is neither male nor female, but somehow both, undoubtedly her maker's preferred state. She is caught between her aunt's blandishments towards a saintly, self-flagellating life, for which she shows a marked talent, and her love for her all-too-worldly father whom she openly wants all for herself. Like a child, Marie-Noel speaks the household's secret truths. Like the dawning woman she also is, she is poised to love and control or throw herself to her end. Like her creator, she knows the tugs of father-love almost too well, and can also 'dream true' – somehow make her father into a good man and her own. Marie-Noel is prescient and her wishes dream the future too acutely.

If all this put blandly has the ring of melodrama or the novel of sensation, it is to du Maurier's credit that she grounds the whole not only in a psychological realism, but in a knowledge of France which came to her with the ancestral line. The du Mauriers had once had a *verrerie*, a glass works, and indeed, it was while she was on a trip to France to find out more about her forebears, that the seeds of *The Scapegoat* were sewn. One of the secrets the novel probes has to do with sides taken during the occupation in the Second World War, of who collaborated and who resisted and whether absolute moral values can be read from those allegiances. In du Maurier's world, good and evil are never quite that clearly demarcated. Seemingly good political acts can mask evil personal passions. Both percolate through the generations and distort lives.

But what of the scapegoat, thrust from the fold in order to take on its sins? Du Maurier gives us at least two contenders for the role. At the end, English John is forced out of the field of his new connectedness, having left everyone in a far better state than he found them. Is he to be pitied as our scapegoat? Or does the role really belong, as so often in du Maurier's work, to the pregnant, benighted wife who falls to her sacrificial death, leaving her husband the wherewithal to make his mother and daughter and the rest of the family far happier (which in the women's case, also means busier) than such a calamity should allow?

Conventional morality was never something du Maurier succumbed to. She was always a quintessential doubler, like some of the characters her beloved father played. In the shifting landscapes of life, good and bad, like wife and mistress, or male and female, can play out surprising metamorphoses. At the end of *The Scapegoat*, when John goes to see Béla the mistress who could be seen as the moral centre of the book – the independent and loving mistress who admits to having recognised him, and who has repaired the animal figurines, broken by Marie-Noel, which stand in for maternal love – it is clear that she doesn't judge his double, the Count, as harshly as he does. Jean de Gué may callously think that all relations are in the last instance based on greed, but there is only a fine line between his cynicism and John's newly acquired tenderness. It may be an important line and, in John's case, it is the line of self-recognition, but at any moment, it can slide into its opposite. After all, both John and Jean have contemplated murder.

In a letter written the year of the publication of *The Scapegoat*, du Maurier notes of herself and her husband, 'We are both doubles. So is everyone. Every one of us has his or her dark side. Which is to overcome the other?'

In du Maurier's case, there are not only dark doubles, but sexual doubles too, male vying with female in role and desire. She always talked of the 'boy-in-the-box' she contained inside herself, a boy who loved women, while she also loved men.

But perhaps the idea of the double, which has so preoccupied artists, is the ultimate image for the writer herself. Du Maurier's marriage was in difficulty at the time she wrote *The Scapegoat*, and it would hardly be surprising if she felt the always uneasy split between loving, engaged wife and coolly observant, disengaged writer as more than usually troubling.

As Margaret Atwood has noted: 'There has been a widespread suspicion among writers . . . that there are two of him sharing the same body, with a hard-to-predict and difficult-to-pinpoint moment during which one turns into the other. When writers have spoken consciously of their own double natures, they're likely to say that one half does the living, the other half the writing, and . . . that each is parasitic upon the other . . . The double may be shadowy, but it is also indispensable.'[1]

For du Maurier, throughout her life, doubling was indispensable. The force of her understanding of what it meant is perhaps what gives *The Scapegoat*, a mature novel, its power.

Neither part of me could put it down.

Castle Dor

Nina Bawden

Castle Dor is a double find for me. Not only is it a novel written – or partly written – by Daphne du Maurier that I had not read before, but it is one that had been begun and half completed, before she took it over, by a hero of my youth, the writer and critic Sir Arthur Quiller-Couch. When I was at school in the forties, 'Q', as the great man was more generally known, inspired me to read – and I hope to recognise – the best in English literature. I still possess three of his excellent Studies in Literature, old and with yellowing pages but still serving as the best guide to literary judgement that I know. In his foreword to the earliest volume, first published in 1918 and reprinted many times since, he states his own position with beautiful clarity: '. . . before starting to lay down principles of literature or aesthetic a man should offer some evidence of his capacity to enjoy the better and eschew the worst.' And, as an example – he always gives examples: 'By "poetry", in these pages, I mean what has been written by Homer, Dante, Shakespeare and some others.'

That this exceptionally scholarly man whose judgements, always rich and sensitive, though sometimes austere, should have embarked on an intensely romantic retelling of the old Cornish legend of that famous pair of tragic lovers, Tristan and Queen Iseult, is intriguing in itself. But what makes it even more fascinating is that Daphne du Maurier, asked by 'Q''s daughter long after her father's death to finish this novel that he had set aside 'near the end of a chapter, halfway through', did so in such a skilful fashion that it is impossible to guess with any certainty the exact point at which she began to write. She says, in a modest foreword, that she 'could not imitate "Q"'s style . . . that would have been robbing the dead', but she had known him when she was a child, remembered him as a genial host at many a Sunday supper, and 'by thinking back to conversations long forgotten' she could recapture something of the man himself and trust herself to 'fall into his mood'.

She has succeeded superbly. 'Q' had set his retelling of the ancient legend in the early 1840s, in the Cornish countryside around the Fowey river that he loved and knew so well. The Tristan of the legend has become Amyot Trestane, a young Breton onion-seller from the *Jolie Bris*, a small schooner that plies the Breton coast and sails to Cornwall regularly with seasonal cargoes of strawberries, apricots, onions and lime – the last in great demand by the Cornish potteries, since the kilns which had once burned at the head of every creek had by this time been abandoned. The Captain of the *Jolie Bris* is a monster, a vicious drunk, and Amyot jumps ship to escape from his sadistic cruelty. After rescuing her when her horse runs away with her carriage, he falls in love with Linnet Lewarne, the beautiful new bride of Mark Lewarne, the landlord of the Rose and Anchor inn at Troy. Mark dotes on his young wife but he is a cantankerous old man and wildly jealous. And so the stage is set.

Each of the doomed lovers has moments when he or she is seized by confusing sensations of being part of something older and stronger than themselves, some force that links them with the past, and sets them on the same tragic path as the legendary pair who lived and died so many centuries before. Central to their story is a certain Doctor Carfax, who seems to have been intended by 'Q' as the main mover and shaker, controlling events, Daphne du Maurier suggests, a little like Shakespeare's Prospero. He is, for her, the most sympathetic and rounded character in the novel, which opens with him in his role as the local doctor, waiting one night upon the earthwork of Castle Dor for the blacksmith's wife to give birth, and being seized by wonder at the earth that holds so many universal secrets that might 'never flower again, yet be unable to forget or desist from the effort to throw up secondary shoots'. Doctor Carfax is present throughout the story, explaining, holding it together, and at the end he is still there, an old man pondering the mysteries of love, and dreaming about one of the 'saddest love stories in the world'.

There are a number of different versions of the Tristan and Iseult legend and Daphne du Maurier tells us that she read all she could discover before she took on the task of completing the novel, and found inconsistencies and confusions that she had to resolve in order to satisfy her own 'sense of order'. In 'Q''s unfinished half of the novel, the earthwork of Castle Dor where King Mark, Queen Iseult's husband, had his palace in the legend, has become the site of Lantyan, a farmhouse that belongs to Bosanko, a local farmer with whom Amyot finds refuge and a job. Although Bosanko and his wife and two children play no part in the original story, there are many deliberate connections between the old tale and the new. In 'Q''s version, Linnet contrives to fall from a hay wain into Amyot's arms, and when her jealous husband accuses her of infidelity, she laughs at him, saying that she can hardly claim no other man has touched her, since the lowly farm hand, Amyot, has just saved her life. Centuries before, Queen Iseult had made the same mocking answer to King Mark after she had been helped ashore from the Fal by Tristan, disguised as a leper, and had tumbled with him, wrapped in his arms, on landing. A somewhat more laboured connection is made between Tristan's unintended death by a friend's poisoned spear, and Amyot's death, after he has misunderstood Doctor Carfax's attempts to rescue him from a disused mine shaft and inadvertently cut himself with the doctor's clasp knife that had just been used to remove a stone from a horse's hoof. There were no antibiotics in 1840, as Carfax's musing over the results of the terrible accident reminds us.

Daphne du Maurier is often – and automatically – dismissed as a 'romantic novelist'. Sir Arthur Quiller-Couch is, above all, a scholar. In the first of his Studies in Literature he includes an essay, or discourse, on the terms 'Classical' and 'Romantic'. He considers these labels, as they are often applied to great poets, novelists, playwrights, to be meaningless, and is against considering literature as if it were something that could be studied in compartments under abstract headings: 'influences', 'tendencies', 'isms'. Books, plays, poems, he insists, I think rightly, are written using the rare skills their authors were born with and have honed over the years. 'Shakespeare, Milton, Shelley did not write "classicism" or "romanticism". They wrote *Hamlet*, *Lycidas*, *The Cenci*.'

This immensely complex but extremely readable novel is a splendid story of love and loss with fascinating links to two widely separated centuries by two very different, but very skilful writers.

The Glass-Blowers

Michelle de Kretser

Daphne du Maurier was the fifth-generation descendant of a French master craftsman who settled in England during the Revolution. *The Glass-Blowers*, the fictionalised story of his family, was originally published in 1963, but du Maurier first conceived of writing about her French forebears in the mid 1950s. She had recently completed her novel about Mary Anne Clarke, her famous great-great-grandmother, and a complementary work about the French side of her family seemed logical. It was also providential. Since the runaway success of *My Cousin Rachel* at the start of the decade, no new idea had arrived to spark du Maurier into fiction. A book with family history as its impetus would fulfil her ever-present need to write, as well as providing a factual skeleton that could be fleshed out with novelistic detail. But when du Maurier visited the Loir-et-Cher region to research the lives of her glass-blowing ancestors, a chance encounter there waylaid her imagination. It led to *The Scapegoat*, a novel about real and assumed identities. No wonder, then, that when she finally returned to her French novel, the tension between history and story, fact and fiction, etched itself on to her narrative.

The Glass-Blowers takes the form of a letter written by Sophie Duval to her nephew, Louis-Mathurin Busson du Maurier, in which she sets out the history of his father's family. Sophie's narrative is impelled by the need to distinguish reality from fantasy. Her nephew has been brought up to believe that his father, Sophie's brother Robert, was an aristocrat who fled to England to escape guillotining during the Revolution. Not that young Louis is much interested in the turbulent events that predated his birth: 'What was past was past.' For Sophie, however, who has lived through those 'bitter and exciting days', it is important that they be remembered accurately. She dutifully hands over the engraved crystal tumbler that is her nephew's inheritance, but the more significant legacy she leaves him is the truth.

Pride plays its part in Sophie's decision to disclose her family's story. Louis will learn that his father was a bankrupt, once jailed for his debts, who emigrated to avoid a second prison sentence. He will learn that he comes from a family of 'ordinary provincial folk' and that his father had no right to the aristocratic name of du Maurier. What I find interesting is that Sophie considers this rather sordid story morally preferable to the glamorous tale concocted by Robert. Half a century after the Revolution, she remains true to its spirit. It is better, in her view, to be a bankrupt than a royalist, better to be an artisan than an aristocrat. She wants Louis to know that his father emigrated because he feared the loss of his freedom, not the loss of his privileges. Her condemnation – and by extension du Maurier's – of a corrupt and indolent aristocracy is absolute.

It seems to me that this story about lineage is positioning itself right at the outset in relation to two eminent ancestors. The turn of the twentieth century had seen the publication of Baroness Orczy's *The Scarlet Pimpernel* (soon followed by several sequels). Du Maurier's narrative scorns the sentimentalisation of privilege that lies at the ideological heart of Sir Percy Blakeney's adventures; it counters rose-tinted romanticism with clear-eyed realism, focusing its gaze on a modest social milieu. That focus also serves to ease *The Glass-Blowers* out from the formidable weight of a novel written a century earlier, Dickens's *A Tale of Two Cities*.

While Dickens brings his characteristic sharpness to bear on the abuses of the Ancien Régime, his narrative, like Orczy's, is organised around the spectacle of innocent lives menaced by the guillotine. Both novels derive their energy from their oppositional engagement with the public sphere. *The Glass-Blowers*, on the other hand, is essentially a private drama. The paraphernalia of domesticity is prominent: family relationships, furniture and linen and household management, pregnancy and childbirth. The narrative carves itself a space that is marked as female and interior, in contradistinction to its predecessors.

Du Maurier was conscious of avoiding the trajectory laid out for French Revolution fiction, warning her publisher not to expect 'a suspense story . . . with heads falling'.[1] It would have been easy to raise the emotional pitch of *The Glass-Blowers* by inventing an episode along those lines. Instead, the tragedies that befall the Bussons are commonplace: babies die in infancy, a woman doesn't survive childbirth, family loyalties give way before political differences. Emile, whose death is the most dramatic in the book, isn't killed by the guillotine but by a reactionary's bullet. The manner in which characters die is one way du Maurier expresses moral and literary choices in *The Glass-Blowers*: realism, progressive politics, and fidelity to family history are preferred over the cranked-up emotion of 'a suspense story'. It is ironic — and surely not accidental — that 'suspense stories', a label used dismissively by the literary establishment, were synonymous with du Maurier's name. So one way to read *The Glass-Blowers* is as a resolute attempt by du Maurier to dampen her dramatising instincts. One of the powerful literary ancestors she is taking on here is herself.

The book's preference for the minor key is also evident in its provincial setting. When we think of the French Revolution we think of Paris. The city is inseparable from moments that are symbolically as well as politically crucial: the Tennis Court Oath, the fall of the Bastille, the guillotining of Louis XVI, the murder of Marat; also, of course, the whiff of grapeshot that ended the dream. In Paris the Revolution modulates from history into mythology.

The originality of *The Glass-Blowers* is that it is not primarily concerned with that grand, mythologising narrative. In fact, those passages that invoke it are stiffly self-conscious: Robert's arch reference to Robespierre as a young deputy to watch exemplifies the problem. Mostly, however, the Revolution du Maurier conjures has escaped the frozen status of iconography. Chapters that describe the looting of provincial châteaux or the Vendéan uprising decentralise the Revolution and render it vivid. Here is writing that captures politics as a lived experience, not yet fixed in the embalming fluid of history.

One such episode portrays the Great Fear that follows the storming of the Bastille, when stories of rampaging 'brigands' sweep the countryside. The panic is specifically provincial, engendered by distance from Paris and lack of reliable communication with the capital. For provincial France, the need to distinguish between fact and rumour takes on life-or-death urgency. In other words, the Great Fear stages the novel's key opposition between history and hearsay.

The episode also reinforces Robert's role as an 'incorrigible farceur', an inventive fabricator of stories. The lies he tells are symptomatic of what Sophie diagnoses as *folie de grandeur*. They are linked to Robert's attitude to money, to his inability to live within his means. He operates on credit, which is to say on promises – another kind of storytelling. His lies are therefore a symbolic sin against thrift just as his overspending is a literal one. The store Sophie sets on fact – 'I have always preferred the truth' – might therefore be understood as a metaphor for the bourgeois virtue of financial responsibility.

That interpretation is reinforced by the impersonal narrator of the Prologue who compares Sophie's status as a landowner who has paid for her property with that of 'any outdated seigneur' who has inherited his. It is a neat metaphor for the passage from feudalism to capitalism, of which the French Revolution is the iconic expression. It also marks the limits of the Revolution's drift towards social equality: since property that has been paid for makes a bourgeois the equal of an aristocrat, those who possess neither land nor capital have no status.

With that limitation in mind, it is illuminating to consider the disapproval that flashes through the narrative (via Sophie) whenever excess is depicted. It is present in the scene where a revolutionary crowd inadvertently tramples a woman to death; also in the fanaticism of the Vendéan rebels. Note that excess is not in itself politically charged; it occasions censure as a sign of itself, as a lack of control. Sophie's initial support for the Revolution wanes as the enlightened reforms of its early years evolve into the excess of the Terror. Historical orthodoxy has always presented the Revolution as a movement from reason to unreason, from the thrifty management of reform to its passionate squandering. Only, of course, the development was not antithetical but organic: 'Revolutionaries always demand more,' says Sophie, which I take as recognising that passion cannot be excised from reason, excess from control.

On the political plane, then, the 'excess' of which the narrative disapproves may be either the aristocratic abuse of privilege or the proletariat zeal that would abolish privilege altogether. There is a 'proper' revolutionary middle course, represented in the novel by Pierre. But wariness of political outcomes alone does not strike me as an adequate explanation of the novel's concern about excess, which is itself excessive, overdetermined.

This narrative anxiety coalesces around Robert. He has a profoundly unsettling effect on Sophie, who worries far more about his financial and narrative extravagance than about Michel or Edmé; even though they court danger more directly, even though Michel's revolutionary fervour causes him to act in ways that Sophie finds morally dubious. But Michel and Edmé represent a purely political extreme. Robert, on the other hand, the most gifted glass-blower of the three brothers, is the novel's portrait of an artist.

When he creates beautiful glass, Robert demonstrates masterly control of his medium. He knows that the same breath that gives shape and form to his art will destroy it if he does not exercise caution, for the first lesson glass-blowing teaches is that 'Control is of supreme importance.'

Glass-blowing serves as du Maurier's metaphor for art, in general, and specifically for fiction. And where Robert fails to exercise control is precisely in the invention of stories; his financial difficulties are the by-product of a seductive tale he has told himself about his rightful place in the world. He refuses the distinction between fact and fantasy, revealing himself as a literary spendthrift who ignores 'the limits proscribed'. Here, it is useful to recall that the wild, dramatising quality of du Maurier's work was what critics cited when denying her literary respectability. Excess is characteristic of the Gothic, of its energetic deployment of suspense and melodrama; excess is shorthand for the triumphant storytelling that had made du Maurier's name. Consider that it was a name derived literally from a historical fiction authored by Robert, and *The Glass-Blowers* begins to look like a self-directed blow. In exposing the lie that constituted her name, in slanting the moral of her tale towards exactitude over extravagance, du Maurier is restaging the criticism that considered her reputation worthless, founded on gaudy excess.

But here's the thing: Robert is easily the most compelling character in the novel. When it isn't focused on his imaginative fictions *The Glass-Blowers* loses its verve, settling into a dutiful chronicle of family and revolutionary history. Du Maurier might have wanted her work to be taken seriously but I think the storyteller in her rejected the terms of assessment. And so Robert reaches through time to steal Sophie's story. Beside his flash lies, her account-keeping looks a little niggardly.

* * *

Finally, a personal coda. I first read du Maurier when I was twelve or thirteen, drawn by those lurid Pan jackets on my older sister's bookshelves. The novels that held me enthralled were the famous ones: *Rebecca*, *My Cousin Rachel*, *Jamaica Inn*. Of *The Glass-Blowers* I retained only the haziest picture; I suspect I didn't finish it. When it came to fiction about the French Revolution, I was for the high-octane drama of Sidney Carton and Sir Percy. Until I was invited to write this introduction, I had forgotten du Maurier's reworking of the subject.

And yet, and yet. Years later and in another country, I wrote a novel set in provincial France during the Revolution, with a heroine called Sophie. My book had its immediate origins in quite other sources. But surely some tendril of memory, however frail, linked it to a day I can no longer remember when a girl lay on her bed reading *The Glass-Blowers*.

So in the end what I find moving about this novel is its understanding of the tenacity of the past, how it keeps us company even when we neglect it. When Robert asks Sophie where our younger selves go, how they dissolve and vanish, she answers that they don't. 'They're with us always, like little shadows, ghosting us through life.'

The Flight of the Falcon

Amanda Craig

The Flight of the Falcon was published in 1965, coincidentally the year my own family moved to Italy, to the very city where the novel opens: Rome. The shadows of the Second World War, and the appalling poverty that made Italy so vulnerable to Fascism, were on the wane. Rome was incomparably lovely, a place where artists still came to learn from antiquity, where the privileged enjoyed the *dolce vita* celebrated by Fellini's film of that name, and the less privileged were desperate for American dollars. Mass tourism was in its infancy then, and the kind of tours that du Maurier's hero, Fabbio, takes around Italy were more innocent, less commonplace and less world-weary than one suspects they are now. Those were the days in which the waspish whine of a Vespa in the Eternal City carried young couples as beautiful as Cary Grant and Audrey Hepburn, not a pair of muggers out to rob the unwary walker. Bliss was it in that dawn to be alive.

Curiously, *The Flight of the Falcon* is the only one of du Maurier's novels to be set in Italy – though 'Don't Look Now', her masterpiece short story, had Venice for its setting. Du Maurier loved Italy and visited it many times, though it is uncertain whether she went to Urbino before she wrote *The Flight of the Falcon*, for which she seems to have used a researcher. Her son, Kits Browning, visited the city with her in 1964 to check on the details after the novel was completed, and remembers being asked to take 'lots of stills' of it.

Fabbio is a Germanicised Italian, shamed by his mother's wartime affairs with German and American officers. He begins his story with a small bet and ends it with a desperate gamble for freedom. A tour guide, or courier, he is good at his job, which involves impressing his charges by sheer force of personality in acting as their shepherd, conductor and mediator. His elder brother, Aldo, is meanwhile plotting a much more sinister kind of leadership, revolving around the cult of personality all too familiar to survivors of the War. There are still elderly Italians alive today who complain that the country has never functioned so efficiently or so proudly as in the time of Il Duce, Mussolini. If du Maurier's plot can seem too Gothic, too improbable in its conflict between the good brother and the bad, it may not seem too extreme to those who remember how nations have been swayed to commit and justify acts of atrocity under the influence of a single charismatic leader.

What I particularly admire about *The Flight of the Falcon* is the way its drama seems to spring from a geography and architecture that exist in real life. Just as the second Mrs de Winter's tale is indelibly marked by Manderley, and Cornwall, so Ruffano is intrinsic to *The Flight of the Falcon*. Du Maurier's city is virtually indistinguishable from Urbino, the remarkable city east of Florence and south of Bologna, transformed and largely built by Federigo da Montefeltro. Montefeltro was a supremely successful soldier who had his marriage celebrated in a famous double painting by Piero della Francesca, featuring the Duke and Duchess in profile on one side, and shining white horses, representing Fame and Virtue, charioteered by cupids across an idyllic Umbrian landscape on the other. Montefeltro became Florence's favourite mercenary, and poured the wealth and plunder he obtained from war into expanding and beautifying his native city of Urbino. His Ducal Palace is a marvel of Renaissance architecture, largely paid for by decades of ruthlessness as a hired soldier. The Duke was a true Renaissance man, whose enthusiasm and genius as a *condottiere*, or hired general, was matched by an intelligence as subtle as it was fine. The greatest pupil of the greatest teacher of his age, Vittorino da Feltre, he personally conceived his Palace's architecture and design. You cannot walk through its rooms without being struck by the beauty of their proportions, their rare combination of taste and opulence, their theatrical sense of drama and restraint.

Certainly, du Maurier's description of the Ducal Palace is one that many visitors to Urbino will recognise:

> The silhouette might be that of some fantastic back-drop at a theatre . . . Fragile, ethereal at first view, the true impact came later. These walls were real, forbidding, with all the ingenuity of a fortress, concealing strength within. The twin turrets above their encircling balustrades pierced the darkness like sharpened blades. Beauty was paramount, menace lurked within.

Above all there is the small room overlooking a drop of over a hundred feet to the ground below. What precisely was this room? Was it a tiny private chapel, as some think? It contains virtually nothing but Piero della Francesca's haunting painting, *The Flagellation of Christ*, which John Mortimer observed in his novel, *Summer's Lease*, is 'undoubtedly the best small painting in the world'. In *The Flight of the Falcon*, the Palace's great painting (by an unnamed artist) is of an imaginary Temptation of Christ, in which Christ is shown being tempted by his double, the Devil, to fly down to the rooftops of Ruffano. This parable will be re-enacted for real in the climax of the novel, when Aldo's evil madness becomes irresistible. Temptation and guilt, rather than suffering and self-sacrifice, are what set du Maurier's imagination alight. She was drawn to polar opposites, often of a domineering sexual nature but also of a familial kind, and her fiction is almost always concerned with the liberation of a secret or hidden self which emerges through conflict. It is easy to see how in Urbino such a combination – a controlled, profoundly beautiful meditation on suffering, and a balcony whose height invites thoughts of flying and falling – could have inspired her to write what is essentially a Gothic tale set in Umbria. The rivalrous bond between the two brothers is as old as myth, but here, too, Montefeltro's history may have suggested her plot.

Born the illegitimate son of the Count of Urbino in 1422, Federigo da Montefeltro inherited his father's title at the age of twenty-two following the murder of his legitimate half-brother, Oddantonio. His people, as rugged and resilient as the landscape they inhabited, had their taxes kept low, which may account for Federigo's confidence that he could walk about his city without bodyguards or fear of the kind of assassination attempts that haunted other leading Italian families. (Du Maurier's duke has a very different attitude to his people, and is guarded accordingly.) Montefeltro's iron discipline over his troops ensured a minimum of bloodshed and destruction during conquest. His rule was informed by a superb intelligence and scholarship: the library he created now belongs to the Vatican. Perhaps it was the creation of this library, once one of the best in Europe, that gave du Maurier the idea for Fabbio's job as a temporary librarian's assistant in the Ducal library.

The pattern of many of du Maurier's novels is to set up an opponent, often fiercely desired or admired, who turns out to be a Lucifer-figure. Du Maurier experienced intense feelings for her charismatic actor-manager father, Sir Gerald du Maurier, and was herself overwhelmed by the memory of his commanding presence, so it is tempting to see her novels as a means of playing out an eternal fluctuation between love and hatred. Between these two magnetic poles, the world of her story spins into eventual disaster before coming to rest. If the usual sexual attraction between victim and predator is missing here, the fraternal bond more than makes up for it. Abel to his brother's Cain, Fabbio (or 'Beo', short for *beato* or 'blessed' in Italian) is, in fact, almost puerile in his lack of sexuality. He has, as we later learn, literally been usurped by his older brother. He is the opposite of the stereotypical Italian male, and the driver of his coach tour jokes that they should change places, so that Fabbio can drive while the driver makes love to the clients. His most passionate relationship is still his bond with the past, and his adored brother, Aldo. Their childhood games involved the younger brother dressing up in dirty linen and pretending to be Lazarus, raised from the dead by Aldo as Christ – or, tellingly, dressed as the Devil in the dark shirt of the Fascist Youth organisation to which he belonged. 'He was my god, he was my devil too,' Fabbio realises. Where Aldo is two-faced and double-natured, Fabbio, like the nameless heroine of *Rebecca*, has grown up in his brother's shadow and has barely enough personality to make an impression on those he meets. Doubles haunt du Maurier's stories, but Fabbio is surely the most colourless until, fighting back, he finally acquires some style. He notices women if they possess a Madonna-like beauty, like Signora Butali, but otherwise they are to be feared and despised, like Carla Raspa. Sexually attractive women are rarely rewarded in du Maurier's world, perhaps because of her troubled bisexuality, yet this portrait is a savage one.

Everyone in *The Flight of the Falcon* is obsessed by someone else, mostly Aldo, and Aldo himself is obsessed with the Duke of Ruffano, known as 'the Falcon'. He insists that, contrary to reason, the wicked Duke flew from the balustrade of his palace when tempted by Lucifer to show himself as the Son of God. Aldo became a pilot, believed to have been killed in a flying accident during the War. His return and rebirth as the city's Director of the Arts Council makes him appear more than mortal, a Lazarus or Lucifer. Ostensibly a good citizen, Aldo has modelled his behaviour on the first Duke of Ruffano, a character whom we are told 'cast off his early discipline . . . and dismayed the good citizens of Ruffano by licentious outrages and revolting cruelties'.

Fabbio's emotional and spiritual entrapment by his brother, his desperate attempt to hold on to sanity and virtue, are also foreshadowed by the fictitious history of the ducal brothers. If Duke Claudio was mad and bad, his half-brother Carlo was known as 'the Good'; it was he who rebuilt the city and made Ruffano famous. Du Maurier split the character of the real-life Montefeltro into two, which, given that he fascinates us by embodying violently contrasting natures, one regrets – but her fiction needed opposites to spark its dynamics. As it is, *The Flight of the Falcon* is du Maurier's most political novel, one in which the consequences of breaking the accepted order of things is not solely a personal, emotional choice but has repercussions on a small society. Though they fought in the Resistance against Fascism, Aldo's followers want to rid Ruffano of 'scum'. They accuse the old of hypocrisy, abuse of power and lack of passion. They fail to see that there are other virtues, without which a civilisation cannot continue to exist and develop. Du Maurier, who had written *The Glass-Blowers*, a novel set against the background of the French Revolution, was perhaps thinking of where such attitudes can lead. In order to punish those who fall short, Aldo's followers carry out acts of cruelty and violence which cannot possibly be justified – or do they?

'Don't imagine I'm here to bring peace to this city . . .' Aldo says. 'I'm here to bring trouble and discord . . . to bring all the violence and hypocrisy and lust and envy into the open.' His words echo those of the deranged Duke, or Falcon: 'The proud shall be stripped . . . the haughty violated . . . the slanderer silenced, the serpent die in its own venom.' Ironically, the person who seems to partake of these vices most of all is Aldo himself.

208

At the start of the novel, Fabbio knows he is engaged in a 'flight without purpose'. It is only when he is forced to fly for his life that he discovers what really matters to him is not the past but the future, not the soaring glamour of insanity but the earth-bound humility of the sane. His initial mistrust of the present, 'slick, proficient, uniform, the young the same the world over, mass-produced like eggs', and his fascination with the past, 'that sinister and unknown world of poison and rapine, of power and beauty, of luxury and filth', has been felt by many visitors to Italy. Du Maurier, for all the high drama of her imagination, always surprises the reader by ultimately turning away from passion and elation. Aiming too high, in her fiction, is the prelude to catastrophe and downfall. It is the humble, almost anonymous characters, poised between the sweetness of hope and the bitterness of experience, who survive to tell their version of the story before us.

The House on the Strand

Celia Brayfield

The simple and instant response to *The House on the Strand* is that it is a novel revisiting the themes expected of Daphne du Maurier, all about Cornwall, set in a mysterious mansion, and featuring romantic episodes in the region's history. Ever since the publication of *Jamaica Inn* in 1936, *Rebecca* in 1938 and *Frenchman's Creek* in 1941, du Maurier has occupied this territory in the public imagination.

The huge commercial success of these early novels, written in her late twenties and early thirties, overshadowed the rest of du Maurier's career and, for the incurious reader, obscures the achievements of her maturity. While remaining a writer rooted in a landscape, she began *The House on the Strand* in 1967, at the age of sixty, when her interest had moved on to the complexities of human identity and the possibilities of paranormal experience.

Certainly, there is a house of secrets, loaned to Dick, the narrator, by his charismatic friend Magnus, ostensibly for a family holiday but in reality as a strategy to tempt Dick to take the psychedelic drug which is the focus of Magnus's research. The drug produced hallucinations of time travel, taking Dick back to the fourteenth century and immersing him in a conspiracy that threatened a beautiful young noblewoman, Isolda.

The real material of *The House on the Strand* is the relationship between its narrator, Dick and his brilliant friend from student days, Magnus. Their attachment was probably unique to middle-class England in the twentieth century, the kind of relationship which Evelyn Waugh portrayed more floridly in *Brideshead Revisited*, an attachment that was the product of emotional denial, single-sex boarding schools and a paralysing awareness of social class.

Magnus is clearly the dominant partner, manipulative, amoral, both socially and intellectually superior to the weak-willed Dick, who is described as 'highly suggestible'. Dick is a failing publisher, Magnus is a leading research scientist. Magnus is single; relatively late in life, Dick has married Vita, an American with two sons from an earlier relationship.

These names have symbolic meanings: in Latin, still a common currency in education at that time, Magnus means 'great' and Vita means 'life'. In American slang, Dick has three meanings – a detective, a penis, or an irritatingly stupid person. A sophisticated woman, who had travelled in the US and made close and rather racy American friends, du Maurier would have been well aware of these implications and it is possible that she chose her characters' names as a private aside to her more worldly readers.

The tensions in this marriage, maintained with a grudging sense of obligation rather than any evident love or joy, frequently swell into outright alienation, encouraged by Magnus. 'Three years of marriage and the dishwasher means more to your conjugal life than the double bed,' he scoffs. 'I warned you it wouldn't last.'

Destructive as the relationship with Magnus is, its comfort is addictive and the trips into the past become an extension of the process. Dick escapes with growing compulsion to the simpler, more vivid and less challenging other world. His real life is one of stunted and bitter feelings, most convincingly evoked, as is the honest bewilderment of his wife. Dick dismisses her as a 'hot house flower' but Vita behaves more like a cornfed nurturer coming to the end of her patience. At forty years of age, Dick wavers between a relapse into his adolescent bond with Magnus and the supreme effort of growing up into a husband and father.

No strong sexual inclination draws him in either direction. This is a man who professes mostly cerebral pleasures, who would rather pore over an old map than caress a young body. There is subtle but cruel comedy in the scene in which Vita hints to her husband that it's bedtime and she's in the mood for love, while he, oblivious, peruses his manuscripts. At times this unexamined lack of libido provokes a vinegary misogyny. 'The trouble was, with women, they had one-track minds, and to their narrow view everything male, be it man dog, fish or slug, pursued but a single course, and that the dreary road to copulation. I sometimes wondered if they ever thought of anything else.'

The liaison between the two men has a strong sexual element and Dick often seems to protest his heterosexuality too much, as when he describes their meeting at Cambridge, at the Christmas carol service at King's College Chapel. 'We had not gone for the carols, but to stare at one particular choir boy with a golden aureole of hair,' he remembers, immediately feeling the need to add 'not that my tastes inclined to choir boys.'

Allusions to gay sex reoccur throughout the text, in modern and mediaeval scenes; monks who occupied the priory which once stood on the site of the house are discovered in sadistic horseplay with a half-naked boy, and when Dick and Magnus compare their trips, Dick decides: 'I think we found what we deserved. I got His Grace the Bishop and the County awaking in me all the forgotten snob appeal of Stonyhurst, and you got the sexy deviations you have denied yourself for thirty years.' To which Magnus replies, 'How you do know I've denied them?' The implicit suggestion is that Magnus, finding Dick sexually evasive, is trying to possess him more completely through their shared drug experience.

The novel was written at the height of the Sixties drug culture, begun just before the famous Summer of Love in 1967 and published in the year of the historic pop festival at Woodstock. Psychedelic drugs, especially LSD, were a mainstream recreation for the young and an essential influence in art in every medium.

Du Maurier, a grandmother who despised fashion and lived in isolation in Cornwall, was in no sense part of this scene but was clearly aware of the interest in mind-expanding drugs which had already been current in some intellectual circles for more than a decade. Aldous Huxley's *The Doors of Perception*, describing his experiences with mescalin, came out in 1954.

It was widely recognised that psychedelics are not chemically addictive, and the text suggests a dependence that is psychological rather than physical, though Dick's struggle to resist temptation is vividly evoked. With a father, husband and son-in-law who had all struggled to control their drinking, du Maurier had a close acquaintance with the addictive personality.

She portrays Dick's increasing obsession with time travel as a response to a stressful life-passage, a time when his own failure is about to deliver his whole life into the hands of his well-connected wife. Rather than confront this fate, he prefers to live through the idealised historical figures of Roger, his loyal and stalwart alter ego, and Isolda, the woman in jeopardy.

In the book's final scenes the local doctor (not the most plausible figure in the landscape) suggests to Dick that the process has been beneficial. 'The world we carry inside us produces answers, sometimes. A way of escape. A flight from reality. You didn't want to live either in London or in New York. The fourteenth century made an exciting antidote to both. The trouble is that day-dreams, like hallucinogenic drugs, become addictive; the more we indulge the deeper we plunge, and then ... we end in the loony bin.'

His reasoned analysis falls on hostile ears. Dick says, 'I had the impression that everything he said was leading up to ... some practical proposition that I must take a grip on myself, get a job, sit in an office, sleep with Vita, breed daughters and look forward contentedly to middle-age, when I might grow cacti in a green house.'

Magnus names two drugs comparable to his concoction – teonanacatl and ololuiqui, and dismisses them, saying 'these only push the brain around in different directions – quite chaotic'. Both of these are naturally occurring hallucinogens derived from Central American plants. Teonanacatl is the Aztecs' name for their sacred mushroom, from which psilocybin is derived, while ololuiqui is extracted from the seeds of the morning glory, Ipomea, and is chemically close to the man-made LSD.

The physical effects of the compound Magnus is investigating – loss of the sense of touch, enhanced sight and the sense of hyper-reality at first, with nausea and vertigo on coming down – are realistic. Where the scenario moves firmly into fantasy, however, is in the description of the drug's action as a chemical time machine, producing a narrative hallucination that continues through each trip, and taking both men to the same time, place and cast of characters.

The inspiration for *The House on the Strand* came from the discovery of some glass jars containing biological specimens in the basement of Kilmarth, the house in which du Maurier lived from 1969 until the end of her life. She did not move there willingly.

The great love of her life was Menabilly, the Manderley of *Rebecca*, into which she moved at the end of 1943. Much as she adored Menabilly, she did not own it. In 1960 she believed that she had negotiated a long extension of the lease, but the owner never signed the document and after his death his heir, a young World War II veteran, reclaimed Menabilly, to her great grief and distress, and proposed that she take Kilmarth, the dower house, instead.

This she did only after long and bitter negotiation which she compared at one point to the war in Vietnam. Kilmarth was smaller and lighter than Menabilly, with a magnificent view across the bay of St Austell, but she hated the enforced change and feared that it would affect her writing. Even before she moved, however, the new house began to exert its own fascination. She researched its history and obtained the old maps that she has Dick decipher with such pleasure.

At the age of sixty and two years a widow, du Maurier was convinced that her popularity had waned and was afraid that her well of inspiration would run dry. She was anxious about money, despite reassurances from her publisher that *Rebecca* was still selling 2,000 hardback copies a year. Once she began *The House on the Strand*, however, the writing took hold of her and she recaptured the feeling of exhilaration that had powered her earlier work. 'I got so hooked on the story I actually woke up one day with nausea and dizziness,' she recorded.

The device of scientific research was one she had used only a few months earlier, in a short story titled 'The Breakthrough', which was eventually published in a collection of paranormal and sci-fi stories that included her last great popular success, 'Don't Look Now'. *The House on the Strand* also returns to many of the elements in *The Scapegoat*, her breakthrough novel of 1957, which is narrated by a man on the verge of suicide who swaps his life with that of a double. Both novels exercise du Maurier's sense of the duality of human nature. From the start of her writing career, she created male central characters and achieved a male voice and point of view with complete credibility. The hero of her second novel is also named Dick. These are the voices of her own second self, an identity of which she was aware from her teens.

Du Maurier was born at a time when women did not have the vote, and Victorian beliefs about gender roles were still current. The official and conventional concepts of womanhood were so far from reality as to deny anyone female full human status. Many thoughtful women, who recognised their own instincts to be active, independent or courageous, concluded that their character must include some aberrant masculine strand.

As a child, du Maurier dressed and behaved like the son her father had wanted. As a teenager she consciously suppressed her masculine side, but as an adult she formed close relationships with both men and women. Once she wrote to a woman with whom she had fallen in love, asking her to imagine 'D du M as a little girl . . . growing up with a boy's mind and a boy's heart. And then the boy realised he had to grow up and not be a boy any longer, so he turned into a girl, and not an unattractive one at that, and the boy was locked in a box forever.

'D du M wrote her books, and had young men, and later a husband, and children, and a lover, and . . . when she found Menabilly and lived in it alone, she opened up the box sometimes and let the phantom, who was neither girl nor boy but disembodied spirit, dance in the evening when there was no one to see.'

The House on the Strand is a delicate but satisfying exploration of these tensions, wrapped in a double narrative of masterly devising. Sadly, it was to be du Maurier's last successful novel. She followed it with a comedy, which was not well received, and she did not find the inspiration for another full-length work of fiction. Short stories, memoirs and biographies followed, but the phantom she kept in a box never again took hold of her imagination.

Rule Britannia

Ella Westland

This is a Daphne du Maurier novel in disguise. In *Rule Britannia*'s sardonic scenario for the 1970s, the United States administration sets up an alliance with the UK government over the heads of the British people, and sends in the marines to quell any troublemakers. But the authorities reckon without the truculence of the Celtic fringe. In a big house in Cornwall, between the spectacularly beautiful south coast and the clay-mining country (where Daphne du Maurier herself lived throughout her writing life), an eccentric ex-actress named Mad and her crew of adopted boys throw in their lot with the emerging Cornish Resistance.

Understandably, readers of *Rebecca* might fear that *Rule Britannia* will not transport them back to Manderley. Despite its dream opening, dangerous cliffs, dead bodies, and the slanting of the story through a young woman's eyes − all elements in common with *Rebecca* − Daphne du Maurier's last novel is indeed very different from the book that made her world-famous. Her biographer, Margaret Forster, shows from her letters that she deliberately tried to write a lighter work than usual, one which 'takes the mickey out of everything'. However, the novel she produced has more bite than she realised − she was closer to the mark when she called it 'mocking' − its tone shifting from the funny and farcical to the bleak and bizarre. Her publishers were worried by the implausible plot, and many of her faithful readers were

217

bemused. Yet what holds *Rule Britannia* together is its very absurdity, the bold concept of an eighty-year-old actress in league with the locals, which combines in one last gloriously defiant statement both the theatrical environment of the writer's London childhood and the grand passion of her adult life, Cornwall.

In the zany Cornish world of *Rule Britannia*, Peter Pan meets the marines. Mad's cool and sensible granddaughter plays Wendy to Mad's Peter Pan, the lovable and exasperating fantasist who refuses to grow up. The killing of an American by an arrow loosed by one of Mad's adopted children (the act that winds up the tension to propel the plot) is a black parody of the Lost Boys winging Wendy as she approaches Neverland. But the reality of the marine's murder marks Neverland's shocking end – this is Death in Arcadia. It works, in this oddly truth-telling book, as a reminder that Cornwall in the 1970s had to face its own realities, and that even a secluded writer must face them too.

As daughters of the celebrated Gerald du Maurier, theatre manager and matinée idol, Daphne and her two sisters were devotees of Peter Pan from childhood. Brought up in the glamorous milieu of the London stage, they knew J. M. Barrie as a kind of honorary uncle. He had created Peter for Daphne's Llewelyn-Davies cousins, later becoming guardian to the five brothers when they were tragically orphaned, just as the Darlings adopted the Lost Boys – and as Mad in *Rule Britannia* took on her parentless tribe. In the du Maurier nursery, Barrie watched the girls act out his story, with Daphne always claiming the part of Peter for herself, and her older sister Angela as Wendy; in the 1920s, Angela actually had the opportunity to play Wendy for three seasons on the London stage. Gerald had been cast in the dual roles of Captain Hook and Mr Darling in the very first production of 1904, before Daphne was born, making himself the definitive diabolical

Hook; he returned to the parts many times, and the show became an annual winter ritual, which the family would never forget.

Daphne's fascination with the theatre would stay with her for the rest of her life, and she occasionally tried her hand at writing plays herself. *September Tide* – set in a Ferry House based on her family's converted Cornish boathouse on the River Fowey – was staged in Oxford and London in 1948, bringing Daphne back in touch with an old flame of her father's, Gertrude Lawrence. Daphne was captivated by Gertie, whose sudden death a few years later devastated her, stirring up feelings about her father's death twenty years before. As Margaret Forster observes, she had recognised an affinity between their personalities: both Gerald and Gertie were types of Peter Pan, the everlasting boy, and in conceiving the spritely character of Mad, Daphne was to make that eternal childlikeness a dominant trait of her imaginary actress.

Rule Britannia was dedicated to another of Gerald's lovely leading ladies, Gladys Cooper, who had died the previous autumn. 'Gladys came into our lives in 1911 and never left,' Angela recounted in her delightful autobiography, *It's Only the Sister*: she was to remain a close family friend for the next sixty years. Gladys was as bewitched by *Peter Pan* as the du Mauriers, taking the role of Peter for two consecutive seasons at the Adelphi Theatre; in the second production of 1924, she acted alongside Angela's Wendy, under the direction of Gerald himself. In later days, she was to play the supporting role of Maxim's sister, Beatrice, in Alfred Hitchcock's 1940 film of *Rebecca*. Then in 1970, at the age of eighty-one – and incredibly with more stage appearances to come – Gladys spent her summer holiday with two granddaughters in Cornwall. She was staying near Daphne's home, and their conversations inevitably revived memories of old theatrical days in London. The outcome was *Rule Britannia*, with a larger-than-life 'Glads'

and her granddaughter Emma in the two starring roles. The
fictional Emma may also bear traces of that other Wendy,
Daphne's sister Angela, and, intriguingly, even deeper traces of
young Daphne herself, who had been told she resembled
Gladys and daydreamed of being her secret daughter. So when
we enter Emma's dream on the first page of *Rule Britannia*,
while she holds her famous grandmother's hand on stage, to
an audience's rapturous applause, we may be participating in
Daphne's teenage fantasy of being acknowledged as the
daughter of her true mother. At the same time we are undoubtedly witnessing a moving tribute to the late Gladys Cooper,
as she takes a final curtain call.

It was clear to Daphne's family and friends that her own
grandchildren had their counterparts in *Rule Britannia*. She
was sixty-four when she wrote it, with one teenage granddaughter a little younger than Emma, and five boisterous
grandsons. Certainly, one motive behind the book was to
explore her own feelings about the Britain that her grandchildren would inherit. A germ of the idea – 'the faintest,
faintest brew' – is recorded in a letter to her friend Oriel
Malet seven years earlier but, by the time the book was written
in 1972, it was very much a 'state-of-the-nation' novel,
projected forward into the later 1970s and anticipating an era
after US disengagement from Vietnam and the death of Mao
(whose style of jackets Mad provocatively adopts). The
Conservative Party had been returned to government in 1970
on a manifesto promising to pursue entry into the European
Common Market, and the plot is predicated on wholescale
public rejection of the move (though the 1975 referendum,
two years after Britain joined, would actually produce a
resounding vote of support). However, the real political
interest of the book, rather than its somewhat crude analysis
of the global situation, lies much closer to home, in Daphne's
determined attempt in her eighth Cornish novel to under-

stand more objectively the place for which she felt such a powerful attachment.

While the novel was 'brewing', the Mebyon Kernow ('Sons of Cornwall') movement had adopted a more focused political strategy and put up their first parliamentary candidate, encouraged by the recent success of Scottish and Welsh nationalist parties at the polls. During the 1960s, their broad agenda had attracted a thousand members, successfully tapping into a proud sense of Cornish difference and rousing pragmatic resistance towards up-country policies that threatened interference in the region. Daphne had come to share many of Mebyon Kernow's values, whose arguments infused the illustrated commentary on her adopted home, *Vanishing Cornwall* (1967). Though she was quick to criticise Mebyon Kernow for harking back to a mythic past, wanting to 'put the people into black kilts, speaking the old Cornish language, with a Parliament west of Tamar', in 1969 she accepted, not without wry amusement, an invitation to join the party, and even tried her hand at writing a political piece in their magazine, *Cornish Nation* (vol.I, no.5).

She could hardly be expected to come up with any solution to the conundrum that has frustrated Cornwall into the twenty-first century of 'seeking ways and means of preserving Cornish individuality and independence, keeping the coast and countryside unspoilt, with people fully employed' (*Vanishing Cornwall*). But along with many other members of Mebyon Kernow, Cornish and non-Cornish alike, she loathed the superior attitude of the London centre to the periphery, represented in *Rule Britannia* by the establishment figure of Emma's father, who thinks that crossing the Tamar takes him out of the civilised world into Tibet. She disliked the unimaginative politicians appointed to represent Cornwall's interests in Whitehall, satirised in the novel by the 'on-message' woman MP for Mid-Cornwall, who is quick to toe the government line. And most of all she resented crass interventions from up-country – the kind of London-centred thinking that had planned in the sixties to rehouse overspill populations in the South West peninsula – and despised the local people who colluded with such damaging projects for short-term gain. The publican in *Rule Britannia* who sees a future in selling drink to the marines and importing Californian wine, rather than joining the Cornish farmers and fishermen and clayworkers in a principled resistance movement, bears the brunt of Mad's scathing dismissal of collaborators.

The anger felt by Daphne at the lack of political will to regenerate the local economy fuses in *Rule Britannia* with her dread of a 'mass invasion' of tourists, a short-sighted economic solution which would turn Cornwall into 'the playground of all England' (*Vanishing Cornwall*). There is, of course, much more at stake than an altruistic concern for Cornwall in her savage vision of an American take-over bid for Britain, which plans to convert the entire country into a gigantic theme park. As early as 1952, in a defensive letter to her socialist editor, Victor Gollancz, she admitted to her gut reaction against the 'very noisy smelly people' who 'strew the beach, once so white and lovely, with sandwich papers, cartons, corn-plasters, contraceptives'; indeed, in prewar *Rebecca* (1938), the de Winters recoil from the summer visitors on the margins of Manderley. She would surely have hated 'Eden', the millennium project that, little more than a decade after her death in 1989, converted one of the abandoned Cornish clay-pits into a tourist attraction in the name of environmentalism, bringing a million visitors a year to the doorstep of what is now commodified as 'du Maurier country'.

It is easy to lampoon the perennial hostility of Cornwall's incomers to lower-class visitors, an attitude which has been as common among the less well-off writers and artists who have colonised different areas of Cornwall since the 1880s as among the more privileged owners of private rural retreats. This may be construed as a politically reactionary withdrawal from everything repellent in a more egalitarian, crowded Britain. But in Daphne du Maurier's case, the desire to defend Cornwall welled more directly from her personal commitment to the rugged coastal landscape and the mysterious house she loved. 'I do believe I love Mena more than people', she once said of the Menabilly estate, the primary inspiration for Manderley, and her life was lived in the shadow of its inevitable renunciation.

Her passionate possession of Menabilly, initially made possible by *Rebecca*'s sales and Hitchcock's film, was prolonged by a generous lease for a quarter of a century. But she had already mourned its destruction in the opening of *Rebecca*, when she was merely a trespasser in Menabilly's deserted grounds; and in *The King's General* (1946), written at the time when she first moved into the house during the war (and the Americans were massing around Fowey in anticipation of D-Day), she visualised the sacking of the earlier gracious building by Roundhead soldiers in the Civil War. In 1969, before the writing of *Rule Britannia*, she was finally forced to relinquish her tenure to the Rashleighs and move to the brighter dower house, Kilmarth, a little closer to Par (the 'Poldrea' of *Rule Britannia*). She became apparently reconciled to the move, and bravely repopulated Mad's fictional house with the troop of sons she had once wanted, but she never ceased grieving for Menabilly. And the apparently irrevocable vanishing of 'her' Cornwall, a land of lonely cliffs and farms, in the face of modernisation, immigration and tourism, actualised for her on a huge scale the nightmare of the second Mrs de Winter – that she could never return to Manderley again.

In *Rule Britannia*, du Maurier tries hard to give her Cornwall back to the Cornish, and let them defend their own land. The locals' voices are heard through the heroic figures of Jack Trembath, the farmer 'with powerful shoulders who used to wrestle for Cornwall against Brittany in his younger days', and Tom Bate, the fishmonger who skippers his own boat. Both are perilously close to ethnic caricature – though perhaps her strange creation of a Welsh beachcomber, representing a pan-Celtic alliance, calls such carping criticism into question. Mad's embarrassing insistence on nicknaming him Taffy mocks Daphne's own tendency to stereotype, a caution to the too literal reader that the whole novel, not only its extrovert heroine, is designed to be larger than life.

Taffy also becomes the interface between a hard-edged view of 1970s Cornwall and the haunting 'other Cornwall', saturated with Daphne du Maurier's imagination. As Emma struggles to seek a path of certainties through her brave new world, she has her suspicions about Taffy's authenticity, and challenges her grandmother's grasp on reality:

> 'You imply that nothing is ever true, that we are all misled, that each one of us, guilty or innocent, follows some will o' the wisp and then vanishes off the face of the earth for evermore?'

However, Mad has no difficulty with holding truth in suspense: 'I neither believe nor disbelieve. Taffy's a mountebank, so am I. Rogues, vagabonds, strolling players, we're all alike.' Their exchange is unresolved, dramatically broken by terrifying, anarchic explosions.

The author is here both the critical observer and the maddening actress. As Oriel Malet knew, she had 'put more of her own character into Mad than she realized', and in this distinctively du Maurier moment, Daphne is claiming the writer's prerogative to fuse real and imaginary worlds. What is 'the real

Cornwall' anyway? For thousands of readers, many of whom will never go there, Cornwall is not a region of clay-pits and tourist attractions, but Daphne du Maurier's Manderley, the place of her dreams.

The Rendezvous and Other Stories

Minette Walters

One of the reasons I'm such a fan of Daphne du Maurier is that her stories are never comfortable. Even in those which are commonly described as romances (erroneously, since she herself said *Frenchman's Creek* was the only romantic novel she ever wrote) there is always something to unsettle the reader. It adds to the suspense but, more importantly, shows how truly she understood human nature. The flaws and weaknesses in her characters are as skilfully drawn as their strengths, and the sinister elements in her plots invariably develop through these imperfections.

In *Rebecca*, it's the painful immaturity and lack of confidence of the second Mrs de Winter that set events in motion; in *The Scapegoat*, the selfishness of one man and the needy loneliness of another; in *The House on the Strand*, a husband's attempt to escape a wife he no longer loves. But Daphne's ability to create unease out of human frailty is demonstrated most powerfully in her short stories. Even in 'The Birds', which on a surface level depicts a bizarre natural event – birds provoked into attacking people during a harsh winter – it is man's complacency about his own superiority that leads to the huge number of deaths.

Biographers, students and reviewers often seek to explain Daphne du Maurier's stories through her relationships with the men and women in her life. Yet, were she still alive, this would undoubtedly irritate her, for it takes little account of

226

her powers of observation or the extraordinary imagination that allowed her to expand a single phrase or small event into narrative fantasy. It's this explanation that she gives in her preface to the first publication of *The Rendezvous and Other Stories* in 1980. 'Something observed, something said, would sink into the hidden places of my mind, and later a story would form.'

She talks of staring up at a seedy hotel in the Boulevard Montparnasse, and imagining what might go on inside. Or seeing a middle-aged man and a young woman dining together in a Geneva restaurant, and wondering what they're talking about. I do this myself – we all do – and like Daphne we tend to assume that the middle-aged man is after sex and the 'seedy' hotel is the type of place where he'll go to get it. But it's the way she transforms these people and places, and the often chilling twists of plot and character, that lifts her work above the ordinary.

In the same preface, she says that several of the stories were written before she embarked on her first novel (*The Loving Spirit*, 1931), when she was under twenty-three, and the rest between 1937 and 1947, adding: 'The early ones especially show something of my development as a writer.' There were ten of these which appeared as part of a Bantam Books collection (*Early Stories*, 1959). They are: 'Panic', 'The Supreme Artist', 'Adieu Sagesse', 'Fairy Tale', 'La Sainte-Vierge', 'Leading Lady', 'The Lover', 'The Closing Door', 'Indiscretion', 'Angels and Archangels'.

With no dates to guide us about the order in which they were written, the most interesting development seems to be her growing confidence in the portrayal of character. To my mind, the least sophisticated and successful of these stories are the two least cruel, both of which depict physically weak and naïve young people: 'Fairy Tale' and 'The Closing Door', while the two most successful show tough, egoistic older characters, bent on the ruthless destruction of rivals: 'Leading Lady' and 'Angels and Archangels'. There also seems to be an increasing awareness of the dramatic possibilities of one character's sexual exploitation of another. The most poignant are 'La Sainte-Vierge' and 'Panic', although this theme is at its most vicious in 'Leading Lady' and 'The Lover'.

These early stories are comparatively short because they were written for magazines, but Daphne's talent for exploiting imperfection is evident in all of them. 'Panic' tells of a first attempt at sex which ends in rape and death when a young woman enters into a tryst out of bravado and realises, too late, that she can't change her mind. 'The Supreme Artist' depicts a middle-aged actor, desperately trying to hang on to his youth; 'Adieu Sagesse', a henpecked husband looking for escape; 'Fairy Tale', the plight of a woman married to a gambler; 'La Sainte-Vierge', the easy betrayal of an ill-educated French wife; 'Leading Lady', a beautiful, but corrupt, woman's manipulation of men; 'The Lover', a young man's careless abuse of women; 'The Closing Door', a terminal illness and a butterfly-brained girl's insensitivity to it; 'Indiscretion', an employer's discovery that his assistant has slept with his wife; 'Angels and Archangels', the jealousy of a vicar for the popularity of his curate.

Some work better than others, although none is as sophisticated as later stories like 'The Apple Tree' and 'The Little Photographer', which have similar themes. Nevertheless, they're extraordinarily mature for a young writer, largely educated at home, who had just turned twenty when they were conceived and written. Daphne is often described as coming from a richly creative and artistic family – her father, Sir Gerald du Maurier, was a famous actor-manager, and her grandfather, George du Maurier, was an artist and the author of *Trilby* – but it's too easy to ascribe her talent to genes. Comparatively few actors, artists and writers produce children who emulate their success, and even fewer produce children who outshine them.

Like all great authors, Daphne's secret can only have been hard work and dedication to her craft. Even in these early stories, her prose is too elegant and her perceptions too acute for her to have taken a slapdash approach to writing. Her control of her plot is loose in places, notably in 'The Closing Door', where the story's direction seems to shift half-way through as if a better ending had suddenly occurred to her, but it's fascinating to chart her progress from these beginnings to the extraordinary later works like 'Don't Look Now', 'The Birds', and one of my personal favourites, 'The Way of the Cross'.

The four remaining stories in the collection were written from 1937 to 1947 when Daphne was in her thirties, married to 'Boy' Browning and the mother of three children. For some of that time she lived in London, but during the war she moved permanently to Cornwall where she set up home in Menabilly, the model for Manderley. She was already well established as a writer by 1937, with four novels to her name, but over the next ten years she published another four: *Rebecca* (Gollancz, 1938), *Frenchman's Creek* (Gollancz, 1941), *Hungry Hill* (Gollancz, 1943) and *The King's General* (Gollancz, 1946).

Unsurprisingly, since this ten-year period spanned World War II, three of the later stories in *The Rendezvous* collection – 'No Motive', 'Escort', 'Split Second' – dwell on death. Daphne's husband 'Boy' Browning was away for most of this time, in command of airborne troops, and despite the suggested rifts and infidelities within their marriage, there seems little doubt there was a strong bond of mutual admiration and affection between them, which may explain the wishful supernatural elements to 'Escort' and 'Split Second' that allow the characters to reach a safe harbour or make a last contact with someone they love.

In 'Escort' – an unashamed war story – a lone merchant ship

leaves a Scandinavian port and braves the U-boats in the North Sea. Help comes from an unexpected quarter when the skipper loses consciousness, and responsibility for the ship's safety falls to his Number Two. In 'Split Second' – which relates tangentially to the war – a pleasant but not overly bright woman, who can only function in a structured environment, comes home from an hour-long walk to find her house inhabited by strangers.

Both are intriguing, if a little fey, as they focus on the supernatural, but 'No Motive' deals with the harsh reality of death. It opens with the inexplicable suicide of a happy young wife who is expecting her first child in the spring. Her distraught husband, unable to account for it, instructs a private detective to investigate her background. What he finds is tragic.

The lead title in the collection, *The Rendezvous*, has all the elements that appear and reappear in Daphne's work. An unequal relationship, both in age and social standing; the exploitation of one character by another; a fairytale setting; sexual tension, misunderstandings and deep insecurities. It's the story of Robert Scrivener, a famous middle-aged British author, and his pursuit of Annette Limoges, a youthful shop assistant from Zurich who admires his work and longs to meet him.

It is a funny, brilliantly observed, and very cruel story, which serves as a warning to anyone who believes his own hype. Daphne was famous for hating publicity. She particularly hated promoting herself (that means of advertising so loved by publishers) and to avoid it, she shut herself away in Cornwall, eschewed the literary circuit and gave very few interviews. Perhaps because I have so much sympathy with this view, I love this story for its mockery of pseudo-celebrity . . . even if it is cringingly embarrassing to read!

One of the joys of writing this introduction was to come across stories I hadn't read before. I know all of Daphne du Maurier's novels and later short stories, but these early narratives were new to me. Understandably, because of her young age when most were written, they lack the polish of the more famous ones, but it's intriguing to see the birth of her writing style and the many themes and settings that were to reoccur in her work.

I've been a du Maurier fan since I read *Frenchman's Creek* when I was thirteen years old. I rushed to read *Jamaica Inn* and *The King's General*, but I can still remember the breathless excitement with which I read *Rebecca*. It's a book that deserves its hype. It has one of the most famous opening lines in literature – 'Last night I dreamt I went to Manderley again' – and one of the most brilliantly conceived characters, Rebecca de Winter. She is ruthless, vicious and deceitful, but so charismatic that, even dead, she dominates the book.

Although much of Daphne du Maurier's fame rests on that novel and the two short stories that were adapted into memorable films, 'Don't Look Now' and 'The Birds', it's the totality of her work that earns her a place as a 'classic' English writer. My favourite du Maurier novel is *The House on the Strand*, where Cornwall's geography and history are seamlessly woven into a page-turning narrative that works on every level. My favourite short story is 'The Way of the Cross' for its masterful depiction of a disparate group of pilgrims in Jerusalem. Yet none of the characters in either story is entirely sympathetic.

Daphne's strength was to paint people, warts and all, and that strength showed itself first in *The Rendezvous and Other Stories*. She doesn't offer one-dimensional puppets whose only purpose is to move a plot forward; instead she gives us multilayered protagonists who win and lose in equal proportions. We may not always like her characters, but we can't ignore them. It explains why her work still resonates so strongly with readers, for the human condition never changes. Our emotional responses and imperfections are the same today as they were fifty years ago, or even two centuries ago. Marriages will continue to fail, middle-aged men will lust, young girls will hesitate and everyone dreams of escape.

But it's an extraordinarily talented and perceptive writer who understands that at twenty when, for most of us, it takes a lifetime.

Tales of Awe and Arousal: Animals Invade

Nina Auerbach

Daphne du Maurier is scrupulously human in her novels. Her stories are laced with killing, but their murders are urbane offspring of incest or envy – uniquely human sins – never the sheer bloodlust we associate with animals. Du Maurier's murderers kill because they want to, not because they have to. We can live with their motives. In fact, many of us do.

The tales, though, open the door to transformations. For the most part, these stories are so uncharacteristically opaque that, compared to the popular short fantasies of Angela Carter or Shirley Jackson, they were little read even in their lifetimes. With little transition or overt moral commentary, the urbane protagonists of the tales expose themselves, if fitfully, as beasts. Why they become bestial is far from clear; the fact that they do is a twist forbidden to du Maurier, the well-bred sophisticate most of us know.

Her popular, if sadistic, novel *Jamaica Inn* features a repulsively bestial criminal named Joss Merlyn, but the maddest character is the supposedly spiritual vicar, Francis Davey. The vicar is aloof from animals, but he sees them everywhere. Spying around the vicarage, the robust heroine Mary Yellan is appalled by secret visions. The holy man is a monster, not because of what he does or is, but in what he sees:

> This was not a drawing at all, but a caricature, grotesque as it was horrible. The people of the congregation were

bonneted and shawled, and in their best clothes as for Sunday, but he had drawn sheep's heads upon their shoulders instead of human faces. The animal jaws gaped foolishly at the preacher, with silly vacant solemnity, and their hoofs were folded in prayer. The features of each sheep had been touched upon with care, as though representing a living soul, but the expression on every one of them was the same – that of an idiot who neither knew nor cared. The preacher, with his black gown and halo of hair, was Francis Davey; but he had given himself a wolf's face, and the wolf was laughing at the flock beneath him.

The thing was a mockery, blasphemous and terrible. Mary covered it quickly . . .[1]

Like her Mary, the novelist quickly covers the 'blasphemous and terrible' mockery that expunges known faces. Her characters can be stupid, mean, violent, with impunity as long as they look like people. Only the tale-teller accepts the bestial heads that replace or express 'living souls'.

In 'The Blue Lenses', du Maurier's heroine becomes the mad vicar whose paintings Mary Yellan could not look at. Marda West, the terrorised central character, is recovering from eye surgery; thus the eyes through which she sees humans fading into animals are either terminally diseased or fatally clear. She is blind when her story begins; as her vision clears, she sees her caretakers – nurses, doctors, her solicitous husband – wearing the heads of increasingly predatory animals. Once she is officially healed, human heads return to everyone but herself: 'Then Marda West took up the mirror and looked into it once more. No, she had not been mistaken. The eyes that stared back at her were doe's eyes, wary before sacrifice, and the timid deer's head was meek, already bowed.'[2]

Marda, through whose eyes we see the rapacity within rituals of care, is one of du Maurier's many victimised wives. Since she is a patient, she is even more passive and helpless than *Rebecca*'s nameless narrator. Yet broken, bedridden Marda sees when strong women close their eyes, confronting brutality more unflinchingly than does Mary Yellan, the spunky girl who has adventures. In the same spirit, the Daphne of the tales – most of which are so inchoate they feel unfinished – is an uncompromising seer compared to the popular author of polished novels whose animal heads disappear into villains' mad visions.

What do these animal-humans mean? They don't quite fit the rapture or the malice of traditional British hybrids. Du Maurier uses animals to menace the helpless, but what kind of terror do they share with better-known visions of metamorphosis? When Titania, the fairy queen of Shakespeare's *A Midsummer Night's Dream*, falls into enchanted love with Bottom, a low character wearing an ass's head, her infatuation is no more than transient silliness: in an unintoxicated world, fairies and donkeys, like royalty and weavers, never mingle. Hierarchy fixes who we are and whom we love. Midsummer night's dreams exist to warn us that we will wake up in colder weather.

Ben Jonson is more uncompromising than Shakespeare; his animals are harsh indictments of apparent men. In *Volpone*, the characters are too stupid or too mean to wake up: Shakespeare's Bottom may clutch at an elusive transfiguring dream, but Volpone is locked in the name that makes him a fox. To be a fox, a fly, a crow or a vulture is, for Jonson, contemptible. His reduction of his characters to acquisitive animals may anticipate the sheep and wolf of du Maurier's mad vicar, but there is no tinge of madness in *Volpone*; it exudes the unforgiving integrity of satire. Jonson is not metamorphic; he is mean.

When, in the twentieth century, D. H. Lawrence regenerates animals, he does so not with Jonson's scorn, but with a moral purpose that is equally simple: Lawrence's foxes, his snakes, his horses, infiltrate lost men and women to exalt them.

235

Right-thinking Lawrence characters are saved, not condemned, into animal life. His final bible of beatitude, *Lady Chatterley's Lover*, rectifies Shakespeare's impossible dream. The union of the lady and the gamekeeper allows Titania and Bottom to stay together at last.

When Daphne du Maurier's characters turn into animals, we feel neither scorn nor exaltation, but some wavering unease in between. In the suggestive conclusion of 'The Blue Lenses', when the put-upon wife confronts her doe-self, the doomed animal she sees is more sinuous than the woman was: 'The eyes that stared back at her were doe's eyes [. . .] the timid deer's head was meek, already bowed.' The woman's eyes were blind and shrouded. The doe's eyes see destiny; they can mirror what they see. The bedridden wife was immobilised; the deer's neck and head perform her fate. Moreover, in our modern world, deer are no longer sacrificed; they are simply shot. Du Maurier's victimised animal is a shadow of antique times that were no less cruel, but lovelier, than plotting contemporary human hunters.

Du Maurier's animals are not quite animals, but neither are they humans in satiric guise. They come from some semi-holy past that transfigures humans, if fitfully, without improving them. They bring ritual and grace to viciousness. Du Maurier's other animal tales are more cryptic and semi-mystical than 'The Blue Lenses' because in them, as in H. Rider Haggard's adventure stories, no hybrids come to England; tarnished humans travel to lands of transformation.

In 'The Chamois,' a coolly unhappy married couple goes hunting in the rugged Greek wilderness. Their goatherd guide, suggestively named Jesus – and called, even more suggestively, 'Zus' – is an enigmatic emanation of the landscape; he may incarnate eroticism, he may be a god, he may be a chamois. If this were a story by Lawrence or Hemingway, Zus would sweep the wife away and into fulfilment, but because the author is Daphne du Maurier, the wife collaborates in his murder, rejoicing when her husband Stephen shoots a chamois who may also (we never know) be Zus. She knows that Stephen is a cruel coward; still, she celebrates their union through the murder of an alien:

> ... I knew, with sudden certainty, that we were after different quarry. Stephen was after chamois. I was after Man. Both were symbolic of something abhorrent to our natures, and so held fascination and great fear. We wanted to destroy the thing that shamed us most.[3]

The chamois–goatherd–god is opaque. He never proclaims himself; he does little but slither through the landscape; he is neither a damning Jonsonian fox nor a saving Lawrentian one. Like the doe in 'The Blue Lenses', or the birds in 'The Birds', he is strange and familiar, arousing and shaming. This chamois is unfulfilled suggestiveness, with none of the eerie promise that makes the stylish hybrids in contemporary fantasy so arousing.

The glittering animals in Angela Carter's modernised fairy tales seem on first reading more vividly shocking than du Maurier's, but they are less disturbing because Carter tells us exactly what they are. In 'The Company of Wolves', a variation on 'Little Red Riding Hood', attack consummates itself in seduction. From the beginning, however, we know the attacker's nature: 'The wolf is carnivore incarnate and he's as cunning as he is ferocious; once he's had a taste of flesh then nothing else will do.'[4] Angela Carter's carnivores are gorgeous embodiments of erotic hunger. But what does du Maurier's chamois eat, what does he want, whom does he seduce and how? Hunger evaporates into mystery.

Du Maurier's animal transformations are generally observed from a distance rather than experienced; we watch them askance without longing to participate. In 'Not After Midnight' and 'The Old Man', these transformations might be sinister or saving; we know only that they mortify the observer. The narrator of 'Not

After Midnight' is du Maurier's usual maimed man. A failed schoolteacher with a vaguely unsavoury sexual secret (he is probably a paedophile) travels to Crete, ostensibly to paint, really to find doom. He encounters Stoll, an obese, drunken and generally repulsive American who may be an incarnation of the half-equine Silenus, satyr-tutor of the ancient god Dionysus. Animal, god and monster, Stoll, like the chamois, has no flagrant powers; this passive monster does nothing but be, and then die.

His indeterminate drowned face becomes the frail narrator's magnet of doom:

> Not innocuous but evil, stifling conscience, dulling intellect, the hell-brew of the smiling god Dionysus, which turned his followers into drunken sots, would claim another victim before long. The eyes in the swollen face stared up at me, and they were not only those of Silenus the satyr tutor, and of the drowned Stoll, but my own as well, as I should see them soon reflected in a mirror. They seemed to hold all knowledge in their depths, and all despair.[5]

The narrator makes the myth he wants to live in, for in reality Stoll's eyes are likely to hold deadness rather than knowledge, despair or evil. Stoll's animal transfiguration may not be quite illusory, but neither is it incarnate, mystically or morally. Animals in du Maurier's tales have nothing clear to teach us. They assume human form only to embarrass humanity.

In 'The Old Man', metamorphosis is more amoral still. A fond old couple solidifies their union by disposing of their children. At the tale's climax, they kill their hulking, needy son, spout wings, and soar toward the sun, two beautiful swans. In pagan legend, it is the beautiful or otherwise deserving who become animals or sinuous plants; in Daphne du Maurier's mythology, such transformations are unnervingly arbitrary. They seem unearned, with no discernible purpose. Instead of merging humanity with other, perhaps richer, orders of being, they shrivel us into shame.

Since these haunting stories don't quite make sense, they are hard to interpret. How do they fit into du Maurier's more fully realised novels? What material, what dangerous impulses, did she cleanse from the novels and siphon into the tales? Do they help us know a Daphne du Maurier who reached beyond the roles she played?

Perhaps the tales express the luxury, for a popular writer, of not making immediate sense. Du Maurier the consummate storyteller spurs us on to find out what happens next, but in these stories, what happens next blots what came before without revealing its pattern. Their animals bring perplexity; they are not the creatures we thought we knew. They tell us only that we too are not the creatures we thought we knew. I read these tales of metamorphosis as the vehicles of an outrage the novels only hint at, for though their plots are wilfully opaque, their characters embody an explicit feminist resentment foreign to the public du Maurier.

The wife in 'The Blue Lenses' is a more consummate victim of the collusion between lying husbands and self-important doctors than the wife in Charlotte Perkins Gilman's feminist classic 'The Yellow Wallpaper', for du Maurier's Marda can only, silently, see; she doesn't have the luxurious solitude of madness. 'The Chamois' is a more oblique tortured-wife story. Through most of it, the narrator hates her husband, who cares only about killing. Feeling abandoned with and without him, she articulates her rage only once, during the killing of the chamois-guide-god: 'Stephen was after chamois. I was after Man.' The wife's exultation encompasses all men, but since Stephen is presumably less of a man than Zus, she becomes his ally, killing him in spirit while she watches him kill. Her sudden cry against Man doesn't make entire narrative sense, but her embracing rage is the heart of her story.

No animals invade 'Kiss Me Again, Stranger', a wartime story about a femme fatale. Seen through the eyes of a romantic young man, this gorgeous killer of soldiers is as opaque to the reader as the chamois, but a jolly conversation at a pub fills in the world that makes her:

'I blame the war for all that's gone wrong with the women . . . Turned a lot of them balmy, in my opinion. They don't know the difference between right or wrong.'

''Tisn't that, it's sport that's the trouble . . . Develops their muscles and that, what weren't never meant to be developed. Take my two youngsters, f'r instance. The girl can knock the boy down any time, she's a proper little bully. Makes you think.'

'That's right . . . equality of the sexes, they call it, don't they? It's the vote that did it. We ought never to have given them the vote.'

'Garn,' said the Air Force chap [who will be the girl's next victim], 'giving them the vote didn't turn the women balmy. They've always been the same, under the skin. The people out East know how to treat 'em. They keep 'em shut up, out there. That's the answer. Then you don't get any trouble.'[6]

These brave men talk like caricatures in a feminist cartoon, not like the usual suave du Maurier misogynists. Only in the stories does hatred between the sexes become so incessant, so explicit. The girl responds with the weary insistence that gender, not nation, is the heart of war:

'Why what's wrong with them?' I said. 'What's the RAF done to you?'
'They smashed my home,' she said.
'That was the Germans, not our fellows.'
'It's all the same, they're killers, aren't they?' she said.

Virginia Woolf makes the same unpatriotic point in *Three Guineas*. Daphne du Maurier boldly echoes it only in the lurid obscurity of a tale about cockneys; in her cool novels about tarnished nobility, murder is not 'all the same', but stylishly personal.

The metamorphoses that dominate her stories twine with their explicit feminism. For du Maurier, who had little interest in politics or legislation, feminism involved transformation, not social change. When she subverted her own proper marriage by falling in love with women, she said she had turned into a boy.[7] Feminism similarly meant for her becoming a creature apart from the intact wife, mother, and châtelaine. As in her stories, she didn't bother to explain herself; she simply and deftly became something else. The transformation she imagined was tentative, unstable, and utterly destructive to the mere humans in its wake.

Glimpses of the Dark Side

Avril Horner and Sue Zlosnik

'It's like something out of that Daphne du Maurier story.' So thinks the main character in Stephen King's Gothic novel, *The Dark Half* (1989), as he witnesses the disquieting sight of sparrows massing into an army, guided by some unseen force. Although it is Alfred Hitchcock's film of du Maurier's 'The Birds' that most people remember, it is significant that King, contemporary master of dark narratives, should choose to pay homage to the power of du Maurier's talent and influence. Both fellow writers and academics now recognise that she was a skilled author of short stories as well as a gifted novelist. Her stories, written over four decades, reveal a marked ability to present character economically and convincingly, distil plot elements, endow certain incidents and settings with heightened significance, sustain narrative suspense, and work skilfully with the 'turn' of a plot. As in her novels, she uses both male and female narrators to articulate different aspects of the uncanny, often in an attempt to unsettle the reader's conventional beliefs and expectations. Many of her stories are characterised by a fascination with the macabre and sinister, by irruptions of the irrational, and by a knack of presenting the chill of the unfamiliar within the familiar. Readers new to the stories might well be surprised by their subject matter, since they often deal with violent deeds and emotions, incest and death. Those dark elements of her novels – which include a father's sexual desire for his daughter in *Julius*, the freakish vicar in *Jamaica Inn*, the incarceration of a son by his father in *The King's General*, and the murder of a wife by her husband in *Rebecca* – are presented undiluted in her short stories. Through them we glimpse a disturbing world in which people are cruel and exploitative and in which family life is far from benign.

'The Old Man', for example, published in 1952, acts out the classic Oedipal drama: a father kills his adult son, prompted by jealousy of his close relationship with his mother. It is only at the very end of the story that the anonymous narrator divulges that these characters are swans and that the 'father' is therefore subject to no human law. In this story, from du Maurier's middle period, the violence inherent in nature itself is acknowledged in a Cornish lakeside setting far removed from the sentimentalised tourist image of 'Daphne du Maurier Country'. Only in the last brief paragraph is the trick revealed, apparently recuperating this depiction of destructive family dynamics into a vision of the majesty of nature. Nonetheless, the matter-of-fact narrative has revealed in their rawest form the consequences of emotions that can lie beneath the surface of the nuclear family, particularly with regard to the possessive jealousy and violence of the dominant male.[1] This is a distilled version of a Gothic dynamic which is represented more obliquely in the longer works. In *The King's General*, for example, the motif of the father's disappointment in his son is placed in the sweep of an historical novel, and the murder of the son is implied rather than directly represented.

In 'The Apple Tree', a story which gave its name to the 1952 collection containing 'The Old Man' and 'The Birds', events are focalised through the eyes of a widowed husband in order to present an anatomy of a bad marriage and the passive–aggressive power of the apparently meek.[2] According to this nameless narrator, his wife had been a joyless person who had revelled in martyrdom; after her sudden death, he relishes his new-found freedom. He is, however, strangely reminded of her by the old apple tree in the garden. This 'humped' and 'thin' tree, with 'skeleton's arms raised in supplication', becomes a malignant presence in his life. He believes that his wife has passed into the old tree to haunt him: its new lease of life, buds sprouting from the apparently dead wood, seems to have no obvious explanation. Yet only he can smell the intolerable odour of its burnt branch; only he is affronted by its heavy load of blossom 'like wad upon wad of soggy cotton wool' and nauseated by the 'pulpy rotten tang' of apples. The following winter, obsessed by the tree, he fells it. One bitterly cold and snowy night in December he arrives home from a convivial evening in the pub and catches his foot in the split stump. As he lies trapped, doomed to die before dawn, he feels a stray piece of brushwood touch his lips, 'like a hand, hesitant and timid feeling its way towards him in the darkness'.

The telling of the tale encourages us to accept the events as uncanny. The female monstrosity the narrator perceives in the tree is ultimately confronted in his felling of it, an act of extreme misogynist violence in which the tree is a 'she' subjected to hacking, gouging, splitting, booting, and which groans and bleeds. For him, the tree *becomes* the loathed and abject older female body. Ultimately female nemesis triumphs, however, as the wife forces him to join her in death and he becomes the victim in this tale of a woman who is dead but will not go away. In contrast with the sanitised murder of Rebecca by Maxim de Winter (his second wife's acceptance of it being proof that Rebecca was evil and that he did not love her), the violence in 'The Apple Tree' is raw and immediate in its impact, although displaced from being an outright description of a man's abuse of a woman by the story's central conceit. Du Maurier's choice of a male narrator is also a strategy that may have enabled her to confront violently her own fear of being trapped by the role of the domestic woman – and her anxiety that she might ultimately succumb to it.

The whimsical 'The Blue Lenses' (1959) tells the story of a wife's epiphany.[3] A middle-aged woman recovering from an eye operation sees the people around her as having animal heads, which uncannily reveal their bearers' true nature, including the 'vulture' that is her husband and his lover (her nurse) who is revealed as a snake. No one else is privy to this strange world, but its optical distortions allow the main female character to understand that she is about to become a victim in a culture that discards the older woman. Even when her eyesight returns to normal, she sees herself as a doe, 'wary before sacrifice'. Thus the misogyny explored from the male perspective in 'The Apple Tree' is here presented from the female point of view. The 'lens' of the supernatural may appear to distort fantastically, but in so doing it can offer, through metaphor, uncomfortable insights into the values of a 'civilised' society.

The theme of 'A Borderline Case' (1971) is incest, although du Maurier avoids representing *knowing* incest, preferring to present her characters as victims of fate – as in Greek tragedy.[4] After the death of her father, aspiring actress Shelagh Delaney sets out to find his old friend, the now reclusive Nick Barry, described to her by her father as, 'Gallant as they come, but mad as a hatter. A borderline case'. The search for Nick takes her into deepest rural Ireland where, posing as a journalist under an alias, she discovers a small community run with naval precision by the charismatic Nick. Waiting to meet him in his sitting room, she is disturbed to see her parents' wedding photograph with Nick's head transposed on to her father's body. Failing to see the significance of this, she experiences 'a feeling of revulsion, a strange apprehension'. However, on meeting Nick she is fascinated by him. His apparent reclusivity masks his covert terrorist activities and in the course of an ensuing expedition he makes love to Shelagh. She is entirely willing and the sex is good.

It is only on returning home that she discovers the truth – she is the product of an affair between her mother and Nick – and understands the significance of her 'father's' horrified last words. He had recognised Nick in her when she posed as *Twelfth Night*'s

Cesario. Finally, Nick's gift of a photo of himself in that very role decades earlier reveals the truth to her. This traumatic revelation that she has indeed slept with her own father produces a self-loathing and desire for indiscriminate violence. 'A Borderline Case' is a tale built up from a tissue of deceptions cleverly represented through tropes of performance and representation – the stage and the photograph. These are both duplicitous: at one and the same time fake and truth-telling. Here du Maurier uses to powerful effect her own theatrical background as daughter of the charismatic stage actor, Gerald du Maurier. The instability of boundaries indicated by this and by the story's title refers to licit and illicit desire – a topic which fascinated du Maurier throughout her writing career.

Du Maurier's best-known stories are 'The Birds' (1952) and 'Don't Look Now' (1971), due in part to Hitchcock's memorable version of the former (which du Maurier disliked intensely) and to Nicolas Roeg's brilliant film of the latter (which she much admired).[5] 'The Birds', another middle-period story, hinges on one idea: that a species harmless to mankind can suddenly turn. The appalling destructive potential of the meek demonstrated in 'The Apple Tree' here comes into its own with terrifying and uncanny force. The power of 'The Birds' combines the destructive energy of the classical Furies with memories of being bombed from the sky during the 1940s and fears connected with the Cold War of the 1950s ('"Won't America do something?"' asks the terrified wife). For twenty-first-century readers there is an added *frisson* as anxiety about the effects of climate change and the impotence of governments in the face of them is evoked: 'It was unnatural, queer . . . The change was something connected with the Arctic circle'; '"Why don't the authorities do something?"'. The gendered aspects of this inversion of power are subtly invoked by Nat's deep anxiety about his eyes ('If only he could keep them from his eyes.'); the Oedipal fear of castration makes itself felt in this ordinary man, already undermined by an unspecified war wound, who is trying to protect his family.

'Don't Look Now', a story in which parents' grief at the death of a child is linked with a voyage into the unfamiliar, shows du Maurier at her most skilful as storyteller. John and Laura visit Venice after the death of their five-year-old daughter but find themselves ill at ease in a city stalked by a serial killer and disorientated by the labyrinth of dark alleys and canal boats that look 'like coffins' at night. Their acquaintance with the strange middle-aged twin sisters who keep appearing in their path makes them only more so, especially as one of them is blind and claims to be psychic. They react differently to her insistence that she has 'seen' their daughter: Laura is comforted, but it annoys and disturbs the super-rational John. The most uncanny element of the plot, however, is the little girl with the pixie-hood whom they glimpse from time to time. Believing her to be in danger, John chases her and, cornering her and himself in a small room, comes face to face with her and with his own death. As he turns to reassure the 'child', her pixie-hood falls away from her head and he sees the unveiled, monstrous spectacle of a 'little thick-set woman dwarf' with long grey hair and a huge head, who draws a knife and slashes his throat. The story closes with his fading consciousness as he bleeds to death. Much of the power of 'Don't Look Now' derives from this shocking ending and turns on the meaning of the freakish dwarf woman's strangeness, which suggests many things, not least John's own propensity to 'see' his dead child every-where, despite his supposedly rational approach to life. As in many of the best Gothic stories, there is a 'doubleness' to every-thing in 'Don't Look Now': the puzzling 'doubleness' of the ageing twins gives way finally to the sinister 'doubleness' of the dwarf whose childish clothes veil an aged murderess. But the dwarf also perhaps suggests the horror of ageing itself, some-thing that du Maurier dreaded.

For Daphne du Maurier, aged sixty-three when she wrote 'Don't Look Now', age itself – and the loss of mental creativity it signalled – was a terrifying glimpse of the dark side. She had already been shocked by some recent photographs that had made her look 'just like an old peasant woman of ninety' with an 'expression like a murderess'.[6] With the death of John, we see du Maurier anticipating the death of her writing persona – an aspect of her identity which she referred to in letters and auto-biographical writing as the 'boy-in-the-box'.[7] It was, indeed, her last and best short story and one in which she foresaw her own decline, a sad but fitting climax to several decades of short stories that had explored the darker side of herself as well as that of the world.

Gerald: A Portrait

Margaret Forster

Sir Gerald du Maurier, the most famous actor-manager of his day, died in April 1934, aged sixty-one. His daughter Daphne did not attend his funeral in Hampstead but instead went onto the Heath and released some pigeons, aware that this might seem an affected thing to do but believing it to be a gesture in keeping with her father's spirit. After she'd helped her mother and two sisters answer letters of condolence, she went home to Frimley, in Surrey, where her husband, 'Boy' Browning, was then second-in-command of the 2nd Battalion Grenadier Guards. A week later, leaving her baby, Tessa, with the nanny, she went into her local church, not to pray but simply to think about her father in peace and quiet. She also wanted to turn over in her mind an idea that had been steadily growing ever since she knew he had died: should she write about him? Should she attempt a biography of him? But would this seem disrespectful, so soon after his death? Could a daughter do such a thing without the result being embarrassing? Could a daughter do it and be truthful without hurting people still alive?

By the time she left the church, Daphne had decided to accept the challenge. Up to that time, she had only written fiction (three novels, published by Heinemann, all well received without making any real impact). She consulted her agent, Curtis Brown, who suggested that Victor Gollancz might be a more suitable publisher for the proposed biography, and a contract with him was duly signed in May, the month of Daphne's twenty-seventh birthday. She set to work immediately and within a mere four months had finished the book, delivering it to Gollancz in early September in time for publication on November 1st (which neatly caught the Christmas trade). Gollancz knew, the moment he read the manuscript, that here was a remarkable book, original in concept, containing some brilliant comic passages, and full of deep psychological insight.

But he also recognised that it was a strange book. Daphne had chosen to write it in the third person, to try to be objective, and yet her heavy personal involvement made it awkward when she was obliged to refer to herself (which she hardly ever does). The other odd thing was how she had combined fact with what amounted to fiction. She imagined dialogue, and invented thought processes, and presented them as real, sometimes in a bewildering way. But this often novelettish approach to her material was balanced by using quotes from Gerald's actual letters, and by carefully tracking his career in more or less chronological order so that the biography did have a solid centre. This combination made for an entertaining and immensely lively read, and was the very opposite of the solemn, laudatory style of biography then prevalent.

Daphne had never wanted merely to praise her father, or simply list his successes. On the contrary, she had been determined to try to catch his essence, to show him warts and all, believing as she did that otherwise there was no point in writing about him. But there were problems: easy enough to convey Gerald's charm, and demonstrate his sense of fun, and not so difficult to capture his particular talents, but much more difficult to explore the violent contradictions she knew had existed in his character, and it was these contradictions which interested her most. In them lay that very essence she was seeking to catch. When she was a child, her father had seemed straightforward – the perfect father, affectionate, happy, a man who adored his three daughters and lavished upon them every kind of care. He played wonderfully imaginative games, took them to his theatre, showed them off to his friends, talked to them for hours about everyone and everything. He left them breathless with his energy and vitality. But then, in adolescence, Daphne had seen another Gerald. She was not quite sure whether this other man had always been part of him and she had not realised, or whether he had emerged in middle age. Either way, she'd begun to be aware that her father was far more complex, and less attractive, than he had seemed to her young, devoted eyes. Exposing this complexity was what she saw as the real purpose of her biography.

To understand Gerald, she thought it important to emphasise the circumstances of his birth, and his family background, to show how spoiled he had always been. He was the fifth and youngest child of George and Emma du Maurier (who are never given their proper names but referred to, confusingly, by their nicknames). She relates how he was his mother's 'ewee' lamb, overindulged by her from the start with consequences Daphne saw as disastrous. He never knew, she writes, any form of hardship and never had to discipline himself in any way. He was a boy, and then a man, who could never relax, someone who needed (and expected) constant distraction to prevent the boredom he dreaded. Inconsistent in all he did, he counted on his charm to make people forgive him whatever he did.

All this is described in amusing detail, with plenty of examples to draw on, but what Daphne drew back from confessing was the effect Gerald's personality had had on herself. She loved him passionately, but not as passionately as she finally realised he loved her. It was not a comfortable feeling. His need of her became a burden and by the time she had grown up it was no longer delightful to be his favourite. It was confusing to be told he wished he was her brother, and that he also wished she had been a boy, a boy who would never grow up. His expectations of her were extravagant and when she failed to fulfil them, wanting as she did to be independent and to lead her own life, he made her suffer. His mood could, and did, turn ugly, and there were scenes far more unpleasant than any she described in her book. They all came back to her as she struggled to be fair to her father, and yet, within limits, hint at the truth.

At least the truth about his career was a pleasure to tell, and she enjoyed paying handsome tribute to his talent, though even here not without a critical edge. She judged that Gerald had gone on stage because it amused him but also because he'd been too idle to do anything else. He could never, she surmised, have been a truly great actor because of his cynicism, but she credited him with having introduced a new, naturalistic style of acting. As a manager, she thought him faultless when it came to choosing plays that would entertain, but not so good, because of his liking for plot and action, at spotting artistic worth. It upset her not only to have to trace Gerald's decline after he gave up Wyndham's Theatre (where he'd been actor-manager for fifteen years), but also what she saw as the general decline of the theatre due to the advent of the talkies in the cinema and what she refers to, with some fury, as 'the American invasion'.

When the book was published (Daphne received £1,000 plus twenty per cent of home sales) attention was focused not on the account of Gerald's career but on what had been written about his private life. Daphne had, in fact, been discreet, only mentioning in a light-hearted way how she and her sisters had been fascinated by what they called their father's 'stable' of young actresses. She did not go into his infatuation with them, or spell out what everyone in the theatrical world knew, i.e. that he had mistresses. She'd been deeply distressed, as a teenager, when she had learned the truth – it had made her see marriage as a sham, and believe love did not exist but was instead only lust. She was never close to her mother (though this is not admitted in the biography), but Gerald's behaviour made her sympathetic towards her. Everything she wrote on these delicate matters was tactful

– the truth was between the lines – but many of her father's contemporaries were outraged on his behalf and regarded what had been written as a betrayal.

The reviews, however, were excellent, with the most praise being for how Daphne caught her father's eccentricities perfectly. Critics laughed at her description of what it was like going on holiday with Gerald (she writes that he travelled like a typical scion of the eighteenth century) and at her account of his time as a cadet in the Irish Guards towards the end of the First World War. They commended her honesty, and her insight, but what they perhaps missed was the significance for her in having written this book. Her writing gained a new maturity which was to become evident in her next work, though for a while after she'd finished *Gerald* she felt so depressed and low she couldn't write at all. An era had ended – her mother was even talking of leaving Gerald's beloved Hampstead – and, though she had never thought of herself as sentimental, she found herself obsessed with her father's past and haunted by memories of him, memories so strong and overpowering, she felt his presence pressing down upon her. But going to Cornwall the following spring she began to recover from his death, and from writing his biography (which physically and emotionally drained her), and started to make notes for a novel.

This was to be *Jamaica Inn*, her first big success, a novel she knew Gerald would have loved.

The Du Mauriers

Michael Holroyd

Daphne du Maurier published her family history, *The Du Mauriers*, in 1937 when she was aged thirty. She had already in her twenties written a remarkable biography of her father, the famous actor-manager Gerald du Maurier, and four novels, the last of which, *Jamaica Inn*, was a spectacular success.

But if her literary career seemed effortless and happy, her childhood and adolescence had been unusually complex. Her mother was an actress and had met her husband during a production of J. M. Barrie's comedy *The Admirable Crichton*. Barrie seems to have been Gerald du Maurier's favourite dramatist – St John Ervine calculated that 'his tally of Barrie pieces was eight, including *Peter Pan* (in which he "created" the parts of Captain Hook and Mr Darling)'. He was something of a Peter Pan himself, a man who would not grow up – at least not gracefully or with generosity. As the younger son and youngest child of a family of five, he was his mother's favourite and, made secure by her love, continued to feel happy during his schooldays at Harrow and confident of his success in the theatre. His nonchalant, easygoing style of acting, which concealed a fine technique, made it appear as if his great triumphs on stage came without any special exertion – indeed with the same inevitability as his daughter was to win her popularity as a novelist. 'He did not know what it was to wait at stage doors to interview managers,' she wrote of him, 'and to beg for parts in a new production.'

Everything began to change after his marriage. 'Muriel, I love you,' he wrote to his wife shortly after they married in 1903. 'It is a splendid thing that has happened to us both, dearest, and I hope the Great Spirit will bless us. It's by our truth, loyalty and devotion to each other that we shall accomplish a beautiful life . . . I seem to love you in all ways, as a child, as a boy, as a grown man.'

But the Great Spirit which blessed his first thirty-five years and granted him 'a beautiful life' was about to take away what he called his 'sweet sense of security'. The painful death from cancer of his brother-in-law Arthur Llewelyn-Davies in 1907, followed by his sister Sylvia's death three years later and, at the beginning of the First World War, those of his mother and his brother Guy, destabilised what had appeared to be Gerald's naturally buoyant and optimistic nature. The joker who was always such good company, the charmer who became everyone's favourite and who had been spared adult responsibilities was 'more than normally overwhelmed' by these tragedies. Daphne du Maurier's perceptive biographer Margaret Forster tells us also that he grew dissatisfied with his acting career, became subject to a strange 'moodiness' and eventually to periods of alcoholic depression which he inflicted on his wife. 'Mo', as she was called, 'worked hard at ensuring Gerald's "boredom" was kept at bay,' Margaret Forster writes.

> [She] gave Gerald what he needed: stability, adoration, the comforts of a well-run home. But as he became more dissatisfied with himself Gerald began to grow restless . . . What Mo could not respond to was the mercurial side of Gerald's character, the side of him which was quick, a touch wicked, even a little crazy . . . She was the centre of Gerald's life, but increasingly he liked to travel away from it.

She also gave him three daughters, but not the son for whom he longed to carry on the name and history of the du Mauriers.

Daphne, the middle sister, was born on 12 May 1907. During her early years she worshipped her father. He was funny, companionable, attentive – almost like another child. In temperament they were very similar. But he could not conceal his wish that she had been born a boy, and so, to please him, she imagined herself to be one – and he encouraged this. 'My tender one,' he wrote to her,

> Who seems to live in Kingdoms all her own
> In realms of joy
> Where heroes young and old
> In climates hot and cold
> Do deeds of daring and much fame
> And she knows she could do the same
> If only she'd been born a boy.
> And sometimes in the silence of the night
> I wake and think perhaps my darling's right
> And that she should have been,
> And, if I'd had my way,
> She would have been, a boy.

The onset of menstruation put an abrupt halt to Daphne's fantasies of being a boy. But the more she observed and experienced adult sexuality, the more bewildered and unhappy she grew. Though her father complained that he could not get to sleep without Muriel beside him, he had no difficulty in going to bed with a series of young actresses. Why did her mother put up with such philandering? Daphne could not understand it. But mother and daughter had never been close, largely because Gerald came so awkwardly between them.

Daphne was educated by governesses at home and then, at the age of eighteen, sent to a school outside Paris to complete her education. Here she formed an emotional attachment with one of the teachers. 'She has a fatal attraction . . . and now I'm coiled in the net,' Daphne wrote. '. . . She pops up to the bedroom at odd moments . . . it gives one an extraordinary thrill.' So perhaps, she reasoned, she really was a boy after all. 'I like women much better than men,' she confessed. But the knowledge that she was partly lesbian – or had 'Venetian tendencies' as she described it – further complicated her emotional life because she knew how much her father abhorred the 'filth' of homosexuality.

Daphne's flirtations with men, and her first, rather lukewarm *affaire* with the actor-manager Beerbohm Tree's illegitimate son, the future film director Carol Reed, provoked many scenes of possessive jealousy and anger from her father. Gerald seemed increasingly dependent: sometimes clinging to her, at other times accusing her of blatant immorality – to all of which was added her mother's disapproval for causing him such misery.

It was to find emotional and financial independence that Daphne took up writing. Her first short stories, apparently influenced by Katherine Mansfield and Guy de Maupassant, but nearer in mood, as Margaret Forster suggests, to Somerset Maugham, were bleak exposés of the hypocrisy and unhappiness of sexual relations between men and women. But though she would intermittently return to the contemporary world in her fiction and explore problems she herself experienced, her main strength as a novelist arose from the longing she felt to be someone other than herself and her need to escape the problems of contemporary life. Her passionate interest in other people, and the intensity of her desire to travel into their lives, gave her novels their extraordinary narrative power and a pervasive atmosphere that held her there, and holds the reader too.

These thrilling adventure stories and engrossing family sagas provided the entertaining fantasies and sense of security that were so desperately needed in an age of devastating world wars. The spirit of the age was with her and she was to lead a flourishing revival in romantic fiction. Her own needs and those of the country seemed to coincide, and she achieved a similar feat of popular escapism to that of her father, whose natural style of acting had led many audiences to think of highly dissimilar roles as being merely aspects of himself. Gerald believed that Daphne was furthering the du Maurier destiny by following the example of his father, George du Maurier, the famous author of *Trilby*. For this reason he supported her writing career even though it was to make her an independent woman.

More surprising was his approval of his daughter's husband, 'Tommy' Browning, whom she met in the spring of 1932 and married that summer. He looked like someone who might have stepped from one of her romances: a tall, athletic Old Etonian and 'the best-looking thing I have ever seen'. A much-decorated officer in the Grenadier Guards, Browning had a commanding air of authority which reassured Daphne that he would never become emotionally dependent on her like her father, and which also impressed Gerald himself as being beyond bullying.

Gerald was to die suddenly, following an operation, in April 1934. Daphne did not go to his funeral partly because, in her grief, she did not wish to admit he was dead. Almost immediately afterwards she began writing his biography, *Gerald: A Portrait*, bringing him back to life on the page. It is an extraordinary book, part biography and part autobiography, though written in the style of a novel. It gives a vivid evocation of her father's charm and engaging humour and, though not charting all his philandering escapades, it conveys something of the more difficult aspects of his character and their effect on her ('I wish I were your brother instead of your father'). The book was written at top speed, completed within four months and published before the end of the year.

The Du Mauriers, published three years later, is a companion volume going further back in time. It was written under unusually vexing circumstances. Her husband, now in command of the second battalion, the Grenadier Guards, had been posted to

Egypt where Daphne and their daughter Tess, with her nanny, accompanied him. While he busied himself happily with troop manoeuvres in the desert, his family settled down in the heat and dust of Alexandria. Daphne hated her life there. She hated the natives who were all 'dirty', often blind or covered with sores, and who 'don't speak English'; and she hated the English themselves who filled their empty days with gossip and cocktail parties.

'I never realised I liked England so much,' Daphne wrote. It was to England, and also to France, in more glamorous times, that she escaped in *The Du Mauriers*. She cut herself off from everyone and sat sweating over her typewriter in temperatures of 100°F, 'writing it like *Gerald*, so that it reads like a novel', though fearing that it might develop into 'a sort of Forsyte Saga'. By September 1936 it was finished. 'I feel it is something of a *tour de force* to have written it in an Egyptian summer,' she wrote to her publisher, Victor Gollancz. Such was her success at immersing herself in nineteenth-century Europe and obliterating contemporary Egypt from her mind while re-creating the lives of her great-great grandmother, mistress of the Duke of York, and of her own grandfather, the sensational novelist and artist George du Maurier, that it was only after she had dispatched the book to England that she became aware she was pregnant.

Gerald: A Portrait and *The Du Mauriers* belong to a vintage period of Daphne du Maurier's writing, a period that produced two of her best-loved novels: her Gothic thriller *Jamaica Inn* and the melodramatic novel of suspense, *Rebecca*. *Gerald: A Portrait* was composed in the imaginative genre of biography made fashionable by *Ariel*, André Maurois's life of Shelley. But *The Du Mauriers* goes further than this. Though there are a few biographical bones to be seen lying around, they have been exhumed and reassembled not by any systematic research or pretence of scholarship, but by pure dramatic instinct. The story is full of terrible events – prison, penury, a missing husband here, a court case there – all arranged as romantic comedy and marvellous entertainment (it would make a fine basis for a musical). The pain of life has been eradicated. Daphne du Maurier describes her great-grandfather, the mercurial Louis-Mathurin's fruitless search for an astronomical 'invention [that] will change the face of the world'. In this engaging book, his great-granddaughter has come up with a fictional equivalent of that magical device.

By the 1960s, following the publication of George D. Painter's *Marcel Proust* and Richard Ellmann's *James Joyce*, Daphne du Maurier's inventive essays in biography appeared terminally dated. But today, when Peter Ackroyd, Julia Blackburn, Andrew Motion and others are experimenting with hybrids of fiction and non-fiction, her two volumes of family biography find a new place in the history of the genre, reminding us of the need we all have in our lives for the consolations of romance and adventure.

The Infernal World of Branwell Brontë

Justine Picardie

The Infernal World of Branwell Brontë has always been the least
successful of Daphne du Maurier's books in commercial terms;
yet it remains as fascinating as the best of her work. When it
came out in 1960, her publisher, Victor Gollancz, printed eight
thousand copies – far less than was usual for his bestselling author;
and though it received several good reviews (including one from
Muriel Spark in the *Daily Telegraph*), the biography did not sell
well, perhaps because it was so different to her more popular
novels and family memoirs. This failure continued to be a source
of disappointment to du Maurier: in a letter to her friend, Oriel
Malet, written in October 1962, she referred to the painfulness
of seeing a book that 'just gets wiped off and forgotten, no matter
how good the reviews. I don't think I had any bad reviews for
my Branwell, but right from the start I know old V.G. was bored
by the thought of it, and he never made any effort to push it
after it was published.'

That her carefully researched biography had been intended
to rescue Branwell Brontë from obscurity made its lack of sales
all the more maddening. As du Maurier writes in her Preface,
she had sought to bring 'some measure of understanding for a
figure long maligned, neglected and despised' – and yet her
mission to rehabilitate Branwell, the reprobate brother labelled
as the drunken flop of the Brontë family, was itself thwarted.

Failure, of course, is an intriguing subject; not least for du
Maurier herself. By the time she embarked upon her Branwell

project, she was a famous author – *Rebecca* had not stopped selling since its instant success upon publication in 1938 – yet she was not immune to insecurities. In a letter to the Brontë scholar, J. A. Symington, who helped her with her research, she expressed her fears at being out-done by another writer, Winifred Gérin, who turned out also to be working on a Branwell biography at the same time as du Maurier. 'My novels are what is known as popular and sell very well,' she wrote to Symington, soon after she heard the news of the Gérin book, 'but I am *not* a critic's favourite, indeed I am generally dismissed with a sneer as a best-seller and not reviewed at all, so . . . I would come off second-best, I have no illusions to that.'

It was not the first time that she had felt herself to have been relegated as second-best: unkind critics had already deemed *Rebecca* an inferior *Jane Eyre*; which must have been galling, given how much she admired the Brontës, having been a passionate reader of their novels since childhood. Oriel Malet reveals in her book, *Letters from Menabilly*, that she and Daphne talked endlessly about the Brontës – and about their imaginary worlds of child-hood:

. . . the source of the Brontës' imagination, and their doom, for in adult life they were unable to break free from them. Charlotte sought refuge in the Angrian Chronicles when-ever life became too much for her, and suffered agonies of guilt in consequence. Emily, untroubled by conscience, immersed herself in Gondal, the country of her mind, until inspiration failed her, and she died. 'Gondal' became our codeword for all make-believe and pretence, whether conscious or not.

When du Maurier was asked to write the introduction to a new edition of *Wuthering Heights* in 1954, she used it as an oppor-tunity to visit Haworth, and asked Oriel Malet to accompany her and her younger daughter Flavia on the trip. The three of them spent time exploring the Brontë Parsonage, and went for long walks across the moors; and as Malet writes in *Letters from Menabilly*, du Maurier 'was becoming increasingly intrigued by Branwell (the son, predictably, interesting her more than the daughters).'

It was an astute observation: for du Maurier had always been more absorbed in her son, Kits, than her two daughters (despite the fact that she became closer to the girls as they grew up, and was adored by both of them). After the trip to Haworth, she read all of the Brontë juvenilia, and became convinced that Branwell had not received the credit he was due, from Mrs Gaskell's first, enduring biography of Charlotte Brontë, and thereafter. To that end, she wrote to J. A. Symington, one of the two editors of the juvenilia (and much else besides), saying that she was 'fascinated by Branwell and I cannot understand why Brontë research has neglected him'. Symington responded enthusiastically and du Maurier decided to embark on a serious, scholarly study of Branwell – a book that would be quite unlike any she had written before; a work, perhaps, that she hoped would be taken seriously by previously dismissive literary critics.

Margaret Forster's insightful biography of Daphne du Maurier makes it clear how important this project was:

> [it] gave her the opportunity to test herself in a way she had, in fact, always wanted to do. There was a good deal of the scholar *manqué* in Daphne, in spite of her frequent claims to have a butterfly mind. As it was, she was prepared to teach herself by trial and error . . .

And there were other reasons, too, for her fascination with Branwell. She had embarked on her research not long after her husband, Sir Frederick Browning – known to his family as Tommy – had suffered a nervous breakdown, in July 1957, a collapse exacerbated by exhaustion and alcohol consumption. By the beginning of 1958, as Margaret Forster writes, Daphne herself was also 'a little unbalanced'. Some of her fears concerned Tommy's position – he was a distinguished military commander who went on to work for the Duke of Edinburgh at Buckingham Palace:

> She began imagining that all kinds of plots were surrounding her – that Tommy was being spied on by Russians who were out to get the Royal Family, and other, similar delusions. Half the time she laughed at herself, knowing that she was being absurd, but then she would suddenly decide her fantasises were rooted in reality, and become agitated.

Her fears extended to Oriel Malet, by then living in Paris: 'She rang me several times, warning me not to go out at night alone, and to avoid all public places, such as the metro . . .'

Thus du Maurier was to write with perceptive sympathy of Branwell's breakdowns, of 'the waves of depression that engulfed him' and 'the shock to his own pride' when he, 'the brilliant versatile genius of the family', was unable to sell his paintings or publish his books. But she was also able to empathise with Charlotte's distress and irritation at her brother's slump, made worse by his drinking (du Maurier, after all, had by then nick-named her husband 'Moper'). She quotes one of Charlotte's letters at length, written to a close friend when Branwell had come home in disgrace after losing his job as a tutor, and distracting his sister from her manuscript of *The Professor*:

> It was very forced work to address him. I might have spared myself the trouble, as he took no notice, and made no reply; he was stupefied. My fears were not in vain. Emily

tells me that he got a sovereign from Papa while I have been away, under the pretence of paying a pressing debt; he went immediately and changed it at a public-house, and has employed it as was to be expected. She concluded her account by saying he was 'a hopeless being'; it is too true. In his present state it is scarcely possible to stay in the same room where he is. What the future has in store, I do not know.

Du Maurier clearly identified with Charlotte's feelings of disillusionment and frustration: as is apparent in her letter to Symington, explaining why she had been unable to spend more time looking at manuscripts in the Brontë Parsonage Museum, because of Tommy's ill health. 'I have been in constant attendance on my husband,' she wrote, 'I feel rather like Charlotte Brontë when nursing the Rev. Brontë and finding it difficult to get on with *Villette*.' And she imagined Winifred Gérin, meanwhile, speeding ahead with her biography, unimpeded by moping men.

Nevertheless, towards the end of 1959, with Tommy well enough to be left, at last, she returned to Haworth, and hunted through manuscripts and church records. Du Maurier's investigations there contributed to the novel idea, expressed in her book, that Branwell had been dismissed as a tutor from the Robinson family not, as has been commonly held, because of an affair with Mrs Robinson, but some gross impropriety with her son Edmund, Branwell's pupil. ('It is possible that, left alone at Thorp Green with Edmund, and free from the constraining presence of his employer, he had attempted in some way to lead Edmund astray . . .') Subsequent Brontë scholars have pointed out that this has more to do with du Maurier's imaginative reworking of history than any factual evidence; and it would have made an intriguing fictional plot. But as it was, she seemed to be losing interest in her idea of Branwell as an unrecognised

genius; certainly by Chapter Thirteen, when she quoted the
opening lines of his poem, 'Real Rest', written when he returned
home to the Parsonage in disgrace ('I see a corpse upon the
waters lie, / With eyes turned, swelled and sightless, to the sky, /
And arms outstretched to move, as wave on wave / Upbears it
in its boundless billowy grave . . .'). The remaining lines of this
poem, she then declared, 'are better left unquoted. Fantasy and
laudanum were rapidly destroying what creative powers were still
within him.'

For all that, du Maurier's own sustained efforts and creative
powers ensured that she beat her rival to the finishing post: *The
Infernal World of Branwell Brontë* came out eight months before
Gérin's book. But by then, du Maurier was already feeling
oppressed by another rival writer: in October 1960, just before
publication, she wrote to Oriel Malet, 'I see Nancy Mitford has
written a book called *Don't Tell Alfred*, and I bet it gets rave
notices. It comes out the same week as poor *Branwell*, who will
be chucked.'

Poor Branwell; poor Daphne. To be truthful, although I would
recommend her biography of him as essential reading to any du
Maurier fan, it is not the easiest of her work – weighed down,
occasionally, by her anxious diligence, and also by her own
increasing exasperation with Branwell's failure to live up to his
original promise. At the same time, she seemed almost to admit
to the impossibility of ever knowing the real truth of another's
life; least of all her Branwell. As she wrote in a letter to Oriel
Malet, in December 1959, it was hard to get people in Haworth
to talk about the facts of the past, when they so easily wandered
into the irrelevant events of the present:

> If you ask me, nobody there really knows anything any
> more. And Miss G[érin] can sit in their cottages til she's
> blue in the face, she will only hear the old Gaskell stories
> repeated over and over again, and embroidered. Imagine a

person a hundred years hence, going down to Polkerris, and asking . . . about me – I mean, what *would* they say?

Yet her biography had served its purpose, in that Branwell came vividly alive within it; and in doing so, du Maurier seemed able to write her way out of her despair, to see a future for herself and for her husband. Tommy recovered, and their marriage was ended only by his death in 1965. She lived on for many years, until 1989, and though she did not go back to Haworth, she returned often to the Brontës, and to Gondal, the sustaining landscape of the imagination.

Close to the end of her life, when she had finally stopped writing, and needed nursing at home, one of those who cared for her was a woman named Margaret Robertson, who came from Yorkshire. Robertson discovered that the Brontës were one of the few remaining topics of conversation that would spark du Maurier into animation; indeed, she would happily talk about their novels, while denying writing some of her own. The nurse, who had some psychiatric training, came to the conclusion that 'Daphne acted towards her writing past as though it were a person who had died – she was bereaved and the grief of her loss was too terrible to talk about . . .' Talking about the Brontës, however, was the best therapy; and in that, Daphne du Maurier remained entirely true to herself.

Golden Lads: A Study of Anthony Bacon, Francis, and Their Friends

Lisa Jardine

On 5 November 1972, Daphne du Maurier wrote to her much younger writer friend Oriel Malet from her home in Kilmarth: 'I am now happily settled in, I hope, for winter, surrounded by heavy-going books about Bacon, and trying to make notes. Whether or not I *really* get down to doing him, I don't know.'

A highly successful novelist, du Maurier was also an accomplished biographer – she had written a biography of her father, the actor-manager Gerald du Maurier, in 1934, a family biography, *The Du Mauriers* in 1937, and *The Infernal World of Branwell Brontë* in 1960. A year after publishing *The Winding Stair*, in 1977, she went on to write an autobiography of her early life up to her marriage – *Growing Pains*, or *Myself When Young*, as is now published. So it was a period when she seemed very much in the mood for the genre. As she approached her seventies, du Maurier embarked upon what was to become a pair of studies of the lives of Sir Francis Bacon and his brother Anthony. *Golden Lads*, the first of these, tackled the joint biography of the two brothers; *The Winding Stair* focused closely on the life of Francis, and revealed her underlying motive for being interested in the brothers at all – one or other of them, in her view, was the real author of Shakespeare's plays.

The problem was, du Maurier confessed to Oriel Malet, that whereas she was used to working comfortably at home with the books she could take out of the London Library, source materials for a serious scholary book on Francis Bacon, using primary materials, were less conveniently available. 'So much of interest about him seems to be hidden away in the British Museum or Lambeth Palace.'[1]

A person of considerable means by this stage in her life, du Maurier solved the problem of the dispersed and difficult-to-access materials by hiring Mrs St George Saunders and a team of fellow independent scholars to transcribe more than three hundred letters from the collections at the British Library, Lambeth Palace Library, and in the Folger Shakespeare Library in Washington in the United States.

Within weeks of her researchers beginning their work, however, du Maurier's own curiosity was thoroughly aroused: 'am getting more interested in Anthony than in Francis, even, he was so *in* with Essex, and with secret spies in France, and apparently spoke perfect French, which is always menacing.' In fact a good deal of the research du Maurier assembled on Anthony Bacon was entirely new; no previous biographer had teased out so much concerning the often murky career of Sir Francis Bacon's elder brother.

Her researchers found documents disclosing that Anthony had travelled around France for twelve years, collecting intelligence for the Elizabethan administration. In late September 1973, du Maurier decided to follow the Anthony Bacon trail herself. Chauffeured by her son Christian (Kits) Browning, she drove to the South of France.

> Our tour was as follows. From Bordeaux to Agen, and went from there to Montauban ... I wished in retrospect that we had stayed longer in that part, because we could have done 'Navarre', and all that Gascon part that Henry IV came from, and I bet it was at Pau that Anthony Bacon went, where he stayed with him. But *tant pis*. We went north instead, to the Loire.

At Montauban, du Maurier's team's assiduous exploration of the archives turned up a Bacon family secret: records in the *Archives Départementales* containing a charge of sodomy made against Anthony Bacon, probably during the summer of 1586. He narrowly escaped punishment, but, as du Maurier suggests, the fear of details of the case reaching England coloured the remainder of his political life.

In February 1975, du Maurier wrote to Malet describing the effort she was now devoting to gaining a closer understanding of the younger of her two subjects:

> All I have done these past weeks is to read through various translations from the Latin – unfinished works of Francis Bacon! Difficult to concentrate when one's mind is not at top peak, but golly, talk about Deep Thoughts! Montaigne is easy and chatty in comparison. But apparently, F[rancis]'s Latin stuff was thought very highly of in Europe, France, Italy etc., and that's why he wrote so much in Latin, so that his Deep Thoughts could be widely read. It's no good my trying to write about him, unless I can somehow explain his Thoughts! Scholars, of course, know – but not my sort of reader![2]

The last sentence here might suggest that du Maurier was intending to write her books on the Bacons in as racy a style, and to be as much page-turners as her bestselling fictional works. The Bacon books were to be for '[her] sort of reader'. Perhaps that was indeed what she had in mind – particularly if she could have found firm evidence of either brother's involvement in Shakespeare's creative process. In fact, the end product of her strenuous researches, and her long poring over Bacon's unfinished works, was a pair of remarkably conventional scholarly biographies.

Golden Lads: A Study of Anthony Bacon, Francis, and Their Friends (1975) and *The Winding Stair: Francis Bacon, His Rise and Fall*

(1976) remain useful volumes for anyone interested in Sir Francis Bacon and his elusive, ailing elder brother. The first takes the story to the final years of Elizabeth's reign, ending with Anthony's death in May 1601, and contains another original archival find by Mrs St George Saunders: the record of his burial in St Olave's Church in Hart Street, London. The second covers Francis Bacon's more glittering Jacobean career. It also revealed her underlying motive for being interested in the brothers at all. She was determined to stack up a compelling body of circumstantial evidence proving that either Anthony or Francis Bacon was closely involved in the writing of Shakespeare's plays.

It was because of this hidden agenda that the French connection of Anthony Bacon, when uncovered, had been particularly welcome, and why du Maurier now trekked down to Montauban to look at these particular records herself. Anthony, she wrote:

> stayed with Henry of Navarre before he became King, and as *Love's Labour's Lost* is all about the Court of Navarre, I get more interested than ever! Supposing brother Anthony was really the hidden Shakespeare person, and *not* Francis? I have got old Tudor maps of London, and am poring over them, to see what it was like in those days. Anthony lived in Bishopsgate, next to a theatre![3]

In *The Winding Stair* she went further and suggested that Anthony was one of the authors of 'Shakespeare's' sonnets:

> It must not be forgotten that Anthony Bacon ... was sending sonnets back to England from France as early as the mid-1580s; and as a close confidant of the Essex circle, devoted to Robert Devereux, he cannot be entirely dismissed, should the authorship of [Shakespeare's sonnets] have to be shared.[4]

Throughout *Golden Lads*, this suggestion runs just below the surface of the text: lines from Shakespeare are woven into her text, echoing passages she has found in the archival letters. Here, though, she merely hints at possible connections. In *The Winding Stair*, the question is tackled head on. There she asserts:

> Anthony Bacon was living in Bishopsgate, close to the Bull Inn where plays were performed, in 1594; William Shakespeare was living in the same parish, and acting with Richard Burbage and the Lord Chamberlain's Men. It was on December 28th of that year that *The Comedy of Errors* was performed at Gray's Inn. It is furthermore suggested that from this time forward both Anthony and Francis Bacon, and possibly others, were in collaboration with the actor–dramatist on some of the earlier plays, which were issued in quarto and printed, and that, after the Essex débâcle, Anthony's death and the start of the new reign, Francis Bacon continued this collaboration.[5]

Du Maurier's 'Bacon wrote Shakespeare' agenda is probably responsible for the neglect of these two serious and largely original books on the Bacon brothers. While *The Winding Stair* was in press, du Maurier entertained the academic establishment in the person of All Souls' don and popular historian A. L. Rowse. She reported to Oriel Malet that:

> A. L. Rowse came to lunch on Wednesday, and never stopped talking! Very complimentary over *Golden Lads*, but says he will poison me if I suggest in *Winding Stair* that Bacon had anything to do with the Shakespeare plays . . . (I didn't dare tell him what I have said about the Shakespeare plays in *Winding Stair*!).[6]

In public, Rowse declared how important du Maurier's researches had been: She actually did make a genuine contribution to sixteenth-century English history when she discovered [the Montauban] archive. It was a very remarkable achievement deserving wider recognition. She was very anxious that I should approve of the two books. She really worked at them; she didn't just rely on having good researchers.[7]

But scholars ever since have been as embarrassed as he was by a line of argument which condemned du Maurier's efforts to languish alongside those of other 'potty' Bacon scholars, most notoriously the early nineteenth-century scholar Delia Bacon.

We ought not, however, to consign *Golden Lads* to oblivion on this account. It is a landmark book on a much-neglected figure (the great Verulam's difficult elder brother), containing ground-breaking research on sixteenth-century archival materials. These revealed the extraordinary life of an Elizabethan intelligencer, who in his prime moved freely between intimacy with the great and the good at the court of Elizabeth I, the French king, Henri IV, and the renowned essayist Michel de Montaigne, in France. Here – just as du Maurier hoped – is a story pieced together out of scattered fragments of information and assiduous archival sleuthing, which remains a valuable starting point for further Bacon studies today.

It is also, at the end of the day, vintage du Maurier – a pageturner, and a thundering good read!

273

The Winding Stair: Francis Bacon, His Rise and Fall

Francis King

In 1934, at the age of twenty-seven, Daphne du Maurier published her first biography. Her recently dead actor father, with whom she had had an extremely close and, to some extent, psychologically disturbing relationship during her childhood and adolescence, was its subject. Son of George du Maurier, *Punch* artist and the author of *Trilby*, Gerald du Maurier was famous not for his assumption of any of the great classical roles but for the nonchalant elegance that he brought to contemporary drama. The biography provoked some of his friends and theatrical colleagues to disapproval for what they regarded as its undaughterly candour. But reviews and sales both immeasurably exceeded the young author's hopes and expectations and brought her to the attention of a far wider public than her previous three novels had succeeded in doing.

The circumstances in which, some forty years later, Daphne du Maurier came to write her last two biographical works, *The Winding Stair* and its predecessor *Golden Lads: A Study of Anthony Bacon, Francis, and Their Friends*, were sadly different. As Margaret Forster poignantly records in her fine biography of du Maurier, the robust, eager, energetic, highly ambitious woman of the early years had by then become increasingly despondent and reclusive.

Worst of all, the imagination that had once been so fertile and fervent in its plotting of such bestsellers as *Rebecca, Frenchman's*

Creek and *My Cousin Rachel*, now refused to yield up anything on which she could optimistically base another novel. The embarrassing and, to her, unexpected critical failure of her *Rule Britannia*, a satire based on the premise that Britain and the United States had been unified, must also have deterred her from embarking on further fiction – even though her fame ensured that that book nonetheless made her a satisfactorily large sum of money.

However, du Maurier felt confident that, even though she could no longer breathe life into invented situations, she still possessed the literary skill to do so into real ones. As both the Bacon books confirm, she was absolutely right in this belief. All the old ability incisively to delineate character, suspensefully to orchestrate incident and vividly to invoke atmosphere, are present in each.

One can only guess as to what impelled du Maurier, at this moment when the high tide in her life had suddenly begun to reverse itself, to write about Anthony and Francis Bacon and their friends. The novelist Robert Liddell, long resident in Greece, once told me that, on the occasion of a visit by her to Athens in the fifties, long before she had embarked on the Bacon project, he happened to mention that he had been rereading Francis Bacon's *Essays*. At once she had responded with an enthusiasm matching his own. She then told him that a governess of hers had urged her to read the *Essays* in her late teens, that she had done so most reluctantly, but had then at once been overwhelmed. Subsequently, as Margaret Forster records, a reading of James Spedding's monumental seven-volume *The Letters and the Life of Francis Bacon* deeply impressed her. Like other of Bacon's biographers, she was to rely heavily on it.

It may well be that du Maurier was also attracted to the subject by the rumours, current even in their lifetimes, that the two Bacon brothers had, as members of the intimate circle of Robert Devereux Earl of Essex, been involved in homosexual intrigues and even activities. Throughout her life, the subject of homosexuality fascinated du Maurier. Her unnaturally devoted father would often tell her that he wished that she had been born a boy. In her childhood and adolescence she even believed that she was a boy, trapped in the body of a girl – just as subsequently another writer, James (later Jan) Morris, believed that he was a woman trapped inside the body of a man.

When she was twenty-two du Maurier had had an affair, more passionate on his side than on hers, with the then apprentice but later famous film director Carol Reed, illegitimate son of the actor-manager Herbert Beerbohm Tree. This aroused the obsessive jealousy of her father. Subsequently she was a staunch wife to General 'Boy' Browning, a dapper, distinguished soldier. But nonetheless she was also repeatedly attracted to women. The most notable of these attachments, occurring in her fifties, was to the glamorous and worldly actress Gertrude Lawrence, for many years Noel Coward's closest female friend, co-star and muse. Lawrence's death at the early age of fifty-four totally devastated du Maurier. It could be said that it was after that bereavement that she began prematurely to give up on life and writing.

Unlike many authors of popular historical biographies, du Maurier resembled Antonia Fraser in being an indefatigable researcher. It is true that she employed others to help her in particularly onerous tasks, such as transcribing the letters of Lady Bacon, mother of Anthony and Francis; but nonetheless she wore herself out with her reading of boxes and boxes of arcane records and her travelling not merely around England but also to France. When the two books appeared, scholars generously praised her thoroughness and accuracy. It was she who first revealed to an English readership a surprise discovery, made in the departmental archives of Tarn-et-Garonne the year before the first of the books, *Golden Lads*, appeared. This showed that during a sojourn in France Anthony Bacon had been accused of sodomy, then a capital crime.

After A. L. Rowse had read the copy of *The Winding Stair* presented to him by du Maurier, who was both a neighbour and a friend, he remarked favourably on it to the publisher Charles Monteith. But then he added, 'The only trouble is that these woman biographers always fall in love with their subjects.' If by this he meant that du Maurier had not been stringent enough when dealing with the less attractive aspects of Bacon's character and life – his notorious extravagance, his deviousness, his consuming ambition, his disloyalty in acting for the prosecution at the arraignment for treason of his former friend and patron Essex at Westminster Hall, his unprincipled skill in shinning up the greasy pole of preferment – there was some degree of truth in the comment. But the fact that she was 'in love' with her protagonist had the great advantage that it enabled her to show for him the same kind of empathy that she had already shown in such abundance for even minor characters in her novels. Bacon was certainly a deeply flawed man; but he was also unique for his time in the depth of his erudition and the range and daring of his thought. Du Maurier is triumphant in conveying that uniqueness.

Macaulay wrote primly of Bacon that he was 'a man whose principles were not strict and whose spirit was not high'. Lytton Strachey wrote of him that, 'The detachment of speculation, the intensity of personal pride, and the uneasiness of nervous sensibility, the urgency of ambition, the opulence of superb taste – these qualities, blending, twisting, flashing together, gave to his secret spirit the subtle and glittering superficies of a serpent.' Perhaps du Maurier does not fully convey the serpentine danger and cunning of this all too fallible man; but what she does perfectly convey is the brilliance and glamour of his genius.

Since the publication of her two biographies, Baconians have often claimed du Maurier as one of themselves. But although she produces a lot of evidence that might, if favourably interpreted, be regarded as supporting the attribution of Shakespeare's plays to her hero, she never ventures further than the proposition that the two Bacon brothers and other noblemen with literary talent may have at various times acted as minor collaborators. As she saw it, this would have merely entailed providing Shakespeare with now a few lines, now a situation, now a character, and now perhaps even a sonnet.

Nonetheless, everything that du Maurier writes about this nobleman of formidable intellectual powers, potent imagination, wide culture, and a supreme gift for a memorable phrase, indicates that the sole authorship of such stupendous works of literature is something of which he might well have been capable.

Myself When Young

Helen Taylor

Daphne du Maurier has enjoyed a chequered reputation. As late as 2000, American critic Nina Auerbach bemoaned the fact that *Rebecca* was the only one of Daphne du Maurier's novels in print. Railing against the injustice of the writer's label as escapist women's romance writer, Auerbach nevertheless admitted to guilt at reading this often critically trashed writer ('I never should read Daphne du Maurier, but I regularly do') and then asserted that she reads her not for 'escape' but 'because she's a complex, powerful, unique writer, so unorthodox that no critical tradition, from formalism to feminism, can digest her'. A casual look at literary companions and biographical dictionaries bears out the uneasy way the critical establishment has long regarded this complex writer. When she died, the outpouring obituaries and tributes saw her insistently as 'the world's most popular romantic novelist' – this despite a distinguished track record as biographer, short-story writer, writer of historical and speculative fiction, and travelogue. In recent years, however, this bestselling writer – dismissed (in Mary Eagleton's words) as 'mere bedtime reading for middle England' – has been paid serious attention, and is being reread with new eyes.

Daphne du Maurier herself deplored her label as 'romantic' writer (a term, as she knew, invariably used pejoratively to denote a certain class of women's writing). In 1953, she wrote sardonically to her publisher Victor Gollancz craving a notice saying

279

'"Miss du Maurier has succeeded in writing a dull, heavy book all about a forgotten investigation in the House of Commons"; it might then attract the attention of a new class of reader'. Her essay, 'Romantic Love' (*The Rebecca Notebook*) began with the provocative sentence, 'There is no such thing as romantic love' – though she went on to define it, in medieval fashion, as the product of forbidden passions. It is well known that she regarded *Rebecca*, not as romance, but as a 'study in jealousy'. Alison Light argues that du Maurier 'wrote romances for readers who imagined they were above that sort of thing, and whose unhappy endings both prolonged the passion and provided a cynical comment on the impossibility of romantic love', while Auerbach says the achievement of the writer's 'romances' 'is to infuse with menace the lives women are supposed to want'. (It is perhaps appropriate that du Maurier's family used the term 'menace' to denote sexual attractiveness.) Many recent scholars have discussed her work in terms of the Gothic, the exploration of split subjectivity, and the Freudian uncanny.

This is the first volume of an autobiography that was never completed. Written as a memoir to celebrate the author's seventieth birthday, it was written out of depression and a fictional writing block, with considerable reluctance. Du Maurier's biographer, Margaret Forster, quotes a letter written by her subject to Michael Thornton: 'Few people really want to be frank about themselves or their ex-lovers and this is where one is bound to have a lot of glossing over'. In the cold winter of 1975–76, the reclusive writer was wrapped up in wool socks and fur-lined boots in her rented Cornish home, Kilmarth, weary of fans writing to her ecstatically about two novels written three decades earlier, *Rebecca* (1938) and *Frenchman's Creek* (1941). Repeatedly they asked why Maxim de Winter's second wife had no name, and begged for endorsement of their own romantic novels and/or sequels, while she was fretting at the lack of a new fiction project to keep her occupied. For some time she had been reading through (and was occasionally shocked by!) the diaries she wrote between the ages of thirteen and twenty-five, with a view to preparing a short memoir – but this was in far from gently nostalgic mood. She had become afraid her good memory was failing her; two of her children were in countries she regarded as dangerous (El Salvador and Libya); and she was hearing of Richard Attenborough's plans to direct a film version of Cornelius Ryan's *A Bridge Too Far* which indicted senior military men (including her late husband, Major Browning) for the disastrous Battle of Arnhem. Browning had been dead only two years and, feeling very protective about his reputation, she engaged in a bad-tempered correspondence with Attenborough; his minor script concessions were of little comfort. Forster claims it is astonishing the memoir has a light tone conveying none of these various anguishes.

The original title of this autobiography of a writer's early years, however, gestured to the brittle mood of its writer and the strains which emerge in its elliptical and often tantalisingly brief narrative. *Growing Pains: The Shaping of a Writer* signals the first twenty-four years of a life of experiment, frustration, complex relationships within the family and beyond, false starts, and irritations with a social round that left the young Daphne yearning for solitude and peace. Despite colourful accounts of a varied and privileged childhood, there is a bemused or impatient reflection on the organisation of family and social life, some exasperation with the world that would not leave her be, and a cruel carelessness about the depiction of character (including her closest family members) which may well have come from that winter's discontents by the inadequate Kilmarth fireside. It is somewhat ironic that (according to editor Sheila Hodges) du Maurier's American publishers, Doubleday, disliked the original title as to them it suggested the 'pains' of adolescence and especially menstruation.

Daphne du Maurier came from a literary and theatrical family, her grandfather the celebrated Victorian *Punch* cartoonist and author of *Peter Ibbetson* and *Trilby* (the origin of Svengali), her father the famous actor, theatre manager-producer and fulcrum of the London theatre set. Enjoying a relatively privileged childhood in London, she enjoyed – or endured – expensive holidays, French finishing school, and a family life that embraced some of Britain's best-known artistic and social figures (she even danced with the Prince of Wales!). Beginning to write in her early twenties, with her first novel, *The Loving Spirit*, published in 1931, she fell in love with the family's second home in Cornwall, and gradually removed herself permanently to that county which became the focus of her writing and a lifelong passion. Her reputation was first established with a brutally frank biography of her father (exposing his sexual and other frailties), while it was secured by the phenomenal international success of *Rebecca*. During a long writing career, she published fifteen novels, many short stories and articles, two plays and seven non-fiction works. Several of her novels and stories have been made into critically acclaimed screen and TV films (most notably, Alfred Hitchcock's *Rebecca*, 1940, and Nicolas Roeg's *Don't Look Now*, 1973). In 1932, she married Major Frederick (Tommy) Browning, and had three children. She was made a DBE in 1969, and died in Fowey on 19 April, 1989.

The Author's Note prefacing *Myself When Young* (the sanitised, less resonant title for the second and subsequent editions) is defensive and self-deprecatory: 'All autobiography is self-indulgent,' she writes, going on to claim that her short-term memory is fading in favour of long-term memory of childhood and adolescence. She justifies the 'self-indulgence' of the volume by suggesting this will answer the questions of those who wish to know what made her 'choose writing as a career'. How interesting that she uses the word 'career'; women of her generation and class were still too ready to see writing as an obsession or private hobby (even if they were deadly serious about it), but for du Maurier it was both a path she had chosen early on – writing consistently through her lifetime and taking a great interest in financial deals, film rights, critical reviews and so on – and also a job that paid the (large) family bills. Major Browning never earned enough to keep the family in the expensive style to which it became accustomed, and from the outset of their marriage she took on the role of breadwinner. Everyone knew this, but the dependence of the family was usually kept discreetly hidden; a telling anecdote in the memoir of du Maurier's daughter, Flavia Leng, describes her leaving home for boarding school and being given ten shillings pocket money by her father 'which I had seen him borrow from Bing [Daphne] that morning'.

Daphne du Maurier is best known as a novelist and short-story writer, but her reputation was made first as a biographer, initially of her father (*Gerald: A Portrait*) and then, in *The Du Mauriers*, of her nineteenth-century relations, including her grandfather, George. This penchant for biography has been followed to a limited extent by other members of her family. Her older sister Angela (who wrote eleven books, including nine novels) published two volumes of autobiography, the first of which, *It's Only the Sister* (1951), owes its title and much of its literary interest to the younger du Maurier. Angela was staying at a fashionable hotel in 1946, and was approached by a gushing woman (who had seen her name in the register) thanking her profusely for all she had done for her nephew. When informed this was not Daphne, the woman exclaimed to her husband, 'It's ONLY the SISTER!'. In 1994, Flavia published a biography of her mother, picking up the story where *Myself When Young* leaves off – the marriage to Tommy Browning and subsequent family life. The biography concludes with a celebration of the scattering of her mother's ashes over the Cornish cliffs, and a belief that she has joined her dead husband in a boat sailing them into infinity. Flavia also celebrates the return of Christian (Kits)

Browning, his wife Olive (Hacker) and four children, to live in Cornwall at Ferryside, the home bought originally by Gerald and containing for all of them the 'loving spirit' of four generations of the family and, in Flavia's terms, 'bring[ing] back once more that sense of belonging, a continuation which has been lacking for all of them since my mother died.' Christian has also written of his mother and recorded the family history through photographs and film. Ferryside is now a lively centre of du Maurier activity and knowledge – especially since the founding of the Daphne du Maurier Festival in 1997, four years after the Browning family's move back to the Bodinnick house that greets ferry passengers from Fowey. The house's *Jane Slade* figurehead conjures up for Festival-goers and residents alike the literary heritage of this corner of Restormel Council's 'Du Maurier Country'.

The Festival, held annually in May – when south Cornwall is at its best with bluebells, wild garlic and those first warm breezes and scents of summer – has brought the writer back to the attention of her adopted county, and attracted international readers to celebrate and reflect on her work and legacy. There are walking tours to Polridmouth Cove (of the *Rebecca* shipwreck scene fame), Gribben Head (the nearest one may approach the inspiration for Manderley, Menabilly), and the Black Head Walk of *The House on the Strand*. Teas are served in the Readymoney Cove house where Daphne first settled in Fowey with her young family, and visitors may go to Charlestown where Carlton Television filmed its adaptation of *Frenchman's Creek*, or to the bleak Bodmin Moor's Jamaica Inn. And, while scholars argue against a dismissal of du Maurier as 'merely' romantic novelist, it has to be admitted that the places associated with her life and work are some of the lushest, most romantic landscapes in the West Country, regularly attracting readers who have been drawn by du Maurier's enchanting evocations of Cornwall's varied natural beauties.

A passionate and observant solitary walker, Daphne was fonder of her own company than anyone else's (except, perhaps, that of her beloved dogs), and was always ill at ease in the intensely sociable atmosphere inherent in her father's theatrical lifestyle. Nonetheless, she became fascinated by the abstract notions of family, generation and continuity – themes that pervade her fiction and the several volumes of biography. Family portraits, parish graveyard visits to family graves, George du Maurier's *Punch* illustrations filling the bookcases, all brought home to the young girl a sense of 'family interest, family pride' which connected her with Gerald and the paternal line of the du Mauriers – the French name she wore with pride. Only seven when the First World War broke out, she was conscious early on of the precariousness of life. Air raids were a feature of life in London, and her Uncle Guy and cousin George were both killed in the war, while another cousin suddenly drowned. The imaginative child described her terror when Gerald – to whom she was always intensely close – went up to watch a daylight raid from the roof. 'Don't go . . . Don't ever leave me,' she cried, to general amazement. This early sense of imminent loss is echoed (almost to the same words) in her 1971 short story, 'A Border-line Case,' as well as in two novels, *The Loving Spirit* and *The Parasites* (1949). The possible, then real loss of parents, brought home to her the importance of lineage, continuity and routine ('routes' as she calls it), especially when all proved precarious and fragile even as she established herself as family chronicler.

Gerald du Maurier represented a line of creative and historically significant men whom Daphne began to place in her own narrative history. Visiting Milton, the grand house, converted during the War into a Red Cross hospital for soldiers, she gazes at a portrait of Thomas Wentworth, Earl of Strafford, executed in 1641, and sees: 'history, in his Van Dyck portrait, and this was history too, the stretchers taking the wounded men upstairs'. Unimpressed by the place in history accorded to women, she crossed gender lines and explored her own 'disembodied spirit' through fictional conflicts of gender, creativity and subjectivity.

The epiphanic moment about 'history' took shape within Milton, and such houses bear considerable significance in du Maurier's world view. She once proposed to her publisher a book centred on various houses she had known and loved, though nothing came of it. Of the autobiography's six chapters, three have titles of specific places: '24, Cumberland Terrace' and 'Cannon Hall', the family's two London homes, and 'Paris'. Chapter Five, 'Between Two Worlds', evokes the struggle the writer felt between a passionate attachment to Fowey, Cornwall – the location of the newly-acquired family home, Swiss Cottage (renamed Ferryside) and Menabilly, the 'sleeping beauty of the fairy tale' awaiting Daphne to come and awaken her – and parental pressures to return to Hampstead. Of the photographs originally included, a great many are of houses. As Alison Light points out, a rootless family on both sides – immigrants, cosmopolitan and metropolitan – the du Maurier family were restless and constantly mobile; they travelled, moved house, took holidays all over Europe, and bought a second home in Cornwall to escape London's pressures. Daphne travelled less and less as she became a writer and an independent figure (unless under duress with Tommy's early army career), and she had a profound need to burrow into her adopted home, Menabilly. Unlike the rest of her family, she did not jump on the train to Paddington to escape Cornwall's cold and rainy winters; she had put down roots far from theatrical and literary London and that suited her well.

Light argues that the narratives, though dwelling obsessively in 'unstable, unbounded places,' in the end reinforce 'a belief in the succour of four walls'. Not the four walls of a cosy domesticity, however; Daphne herself, like most of her heroines, had no time or talent for housework. Houses for her contained the past as well as individual identities and imagined selves, and life is lived through continuities (spectres and ghosts) in domestic and intimate spaces. She sees Gerald at Wyndham's Theatre, 'his personality . . . embedded in those walls'; there are the 'crouching figures by [the]window' that Godmother Billy conjures for her; and there is the Bluebeard's chamber of horrors in the house on the Strand, not to mention the constant presence of the dead Rebecca in Manderley's rooms. Although it is unlikely du Maurier knew Charlotte Perkins Gilman's Gothic tale of post-partum female imprisonment and madness, *The Yellow Wallpaper*, in which the paper itself embodies female desire and frustration, her description of traces within the homes of generations of families echoes Gilman's Gothic feminist fable. Daphne too imagines, 'embedded in their walls, one with the dust and cobwebs, one with the overlay of fresh wallpaper and paint, the imprint of what-has-been, the suffering, the joy. We are all ghosts of yesterday . . .'

As I have suggested about Daphne du Maurier Festival-goers, for many readers the romance within the novels – and indeed her autobiographical writings – derives from du Maurier's intense relationship with Cornwall. This combined a love of dramatic scenery, solitary walks through woods to secluded coves, and the smells of tar, rope and tidal water which to a London-born girl suggested new freedoms, 'to write, to walk, to wander, freedom to climb hills, to pull a boat, to be alone'. Sheila Hodges quotes a letter from Daphne in which she reflected, 'Fowey must have been the saving of me, and but for the grace of God, or Fowey, I would have become the all-time hippy!' She tends to represent Cornwall elegiacally, either in her appropriately titled *Vanishing Cornwall* (1967) and polemical challenge to governments to invest in the county's industrial revival, or in her protests against all attempts to make significant changes in local places; she joined the Cornish Nationalist Party and was wont to share her husband's term, 'honks' for the working-class people, including tourists, who might spoil her idyll.

From earliest childhood, Daphne reacted powerfully to where she was. She found safe places – like her nursery, or houses where she felt joyously at home – such as the grand house she visited as a child, Milton, near Peterborough, for which she felt the 'recognition . . . and love' that reappeared later in *Rebecca*'s Manderley. Escape from claustrophobic spaces, seeking out unattainable or mysterious locations, and yearning to be elsewhere are all central to this writer's concerns.

In *Myself When Young*, Daphne escapes from a group of ladies in hats who are cooing over her baby sister, Jeanne, in the Cumberland Terrace drawing room, and flees to the nursery window where she gazes over the rooftops to a red-painted house she pretends she owns and inhabits alone. Later in life, she was to trespass in the grounds of the empty, hidden-away house, Menabilly, which she went on to make her own (in life as in fiction) – albeit on a long lease that was terminated, bearing out Daphne's conviction that true romance is the unattainable. Adventure, secretive journeys and private bolt holes, such as the Dona St Columb of *Frenchman's Creek* or Rebecca's boathouse, are for Daphne temporary solutions to the problems of feeling out of kilter and joint with one's family, position and indeed age. And, as with many writers seeking an 'elsewhere' to feel at home, she found companionship in books and the possibilities they offered. Dissatisfaction and a yearning to escape characterise her autobiographical and fictional writing, thus satisfying in women readers what Auerbach describes as our 'insatiable desire to be somebody else, somewhere else'.

Daphne's uncertainty about her mother Muriel's feelings and real nature stands in interesting contrast with her certainty about her father, paradoxically because as an actor he was always pretending to be someone else. Her mother, who 'might have been the Snow Queen in disguise,' alarmed her; she concludes that 'evil women were more terrible than evil men'. From an early age, she identified with male heroes – Pilgrim (of *Pilgrim's*

Progress), David (versus Goliath), and Jim Hawkins or Long John Silver, from *Treasure Island* – playing heroic masculine roles in childhood games with her sister Angela (who was the Wendy to her Peter Pan).

The gender confusion, bisexual feelings ('Venetian tendencies,' as she called them), and impatience with feminine roles and responsibilities which characterise the adult writer, are all prefigured here. Margaret Forster's biography startled the world with its revelations of a complex bisexual history, her recurrent theme being the writer's attempt to deal, in life as in fiction, with 'the boy in the box' she identified early on within herself. For a woman of her generation, a boy's/man's life looked enviable; experiment and adventure were encouraged, physical restrictions seemed minimal, and there was none of the shame and mess of menstruation and girly clothing (Daphne moved into long trousers long before many of her contemporaries and remained there most of her life). Several members of her family apparently shared her confusions, and in both her father and husband Daphne had to come to terms with an emotional fragility, associated usually with femininity, as they performed an exaggerated masculinity – Gerald the theatrical pin-up, Tommy the army Major, then General – which manifested its many pressures through bouts of depression, emotional breakdown and alcoholism.

Daphne performed her own masculine self as a strong and wayward woman, enlisting other marginal or eccentric figures such as director Carol Reed, actress Gertrude Lawrence, and her married cousin, Geoffrey, to participate in the drama. She invented a character for herself, Eric Avon, a sterling masculine captain of cricket at Rugby, a figure she claims went underground to re-emerge as the male narrator of five of her novels, including *My Cousin Rachel* and *The House on the Strand*. 'Acting was in my blood,' she reminds the reader, and Eric was part of a dramatic role she was only too happy to play. She identified closely with male mentors, from her dead grandfather George to A. L. Rowse and Sir Arthur Quiller-Couch, a Fowey neighbour whose unfinished manuscript she completed (*Castle Dor*, 1962). The uncertainty Daphne felt about her mother's affection, coupled with her intense closeness to Gerald, left the girl ambivalent about femininity altogether. It was through a bohemian experimental sexual and social life in Paris, albeit conducted within a girls' school, that she began to identify with her French writer grandfather and became intrigued by contradictory and conflicting gender roles. In her daughter Flavia's biography, the remote, emotionally undemonstrative mother-daughter relationship between the two older girls and their mother is compared constantly with the passionate and physically close bond with her beloved youngest male child, Christian. Masculinity is prized in her life and work, even if seen to grow on thin soil. Her personal anxieties about, indeed contempt for, the constraints and sheer dullness of orthodox femininity in the early to mid twentieth century pervade the fiction, and resonate for all readers who have shared such feelings. And for predominantly women readers, there is the great pleasure of recognising the fact that her key literary influences are *women* writers who had shared du Maurier's profoundest concerns. The fiction begins in *The Loving Spirit* with a major homage to Emily Brontë, and her subsequent works owe a great debt to all the Brontë sisters and Katherine Mansfield.

One of the key ways du Maurier used earlier women's writing was to draw on romantic motifs and use romance themes in new ways. *Myself When Young* is a kind of autobiographical romance tracing the writer's development into creative freedom and independence. In her 1966 essay, 'Death and Widowhood', du Maurier refers to herself as 'a spinner of webs, a weaver of imaginary tales'. The partial memoir – from 'growing pains' to secretive pastoral wedding – is a *bildungsroman* with a Shakespearian comic conclusion. 'Reader, I married him,' is the end of this story: she felt unable to progress the story because too many characters were still alive, but of course to her readers the story ends with her complete literary works. The two love affairs at the heart of the narrative are the discovery of her 'house of secrets. My elusive Menabilly' (*The Rebecca Notebook*), the feminised house that belongs to the Rashleigh family and which she thus desires and tries in vain throughout her life to possess, and husband Tommy, in union with whom the story ends.

In the original manuscript submitted to Gollancz, the final sentences have an elegiac and stiffly formal tone: 'Adieu Daphne du Maurier, perhaps. But it was Mrs Browning and her soldier husband who started out from their boat Ygdrasil at Frenchman's Creek.' The writer probably decided to delete those two sentences at proof stage, concluding instead on a note of romantic optimism and assurance, with appropriate nautical metaphors: 'Then we were away, heading down-channel for the Helford River and Frenchman's Creek. We couldn't have chosen anything more beautiful.' Daphne du Maurier, who loved riding her boat down the Estuary to the sea, and who was continually trying to escape from mundane and difficult truths via the imagination, concludes her memoir with a supremely romantic adventure that both anticipates and helps mythify her achievement as a writer who has captured the public imagination.

Part 4

Daphne du Maurier in Adaptation

Hitchcock's *Rebecca*: A Woman's Film?

Alison Light

It's not just that Hitchcock's *Rebecca* wasn't exactly Daphne du Maurier's; it wasn't entirely Hitchcock's either. Arriving in Hollywood in 1939, Hitchcock's first American feature was overshadowed by David O. Selznick, the producer who had bought him and who liked to run things his way. 'Selznick's *Rebecca*' (as the publicity had it, relegating the director to the position of a 'mentor' who had 'collaborated' with Selznick) was to be 'the most glamorous picture ever made'. Made in 1940, it was heralded as the successor to *Gone With the Wind*, the film which in fact absorbed nearly all Selznick's energies during the actual shooting of *Rebecca*, though he reserved the last edit to himself and laid in the corny Franz Waxman score.

But it was the feminine angle of *Rebecca* that caused ructions. Or rather which Selznick defended in injured tones, rejecting as 'distorted and vulgarised' Hitchcock's first treatment of the novel, and insisting that the picture respect 'the little feminine things which are so recognisable and which make every woman say, "I know just how she feels. I know just what she's going through."' And this meant sticking to the story.

Selznick was renowned for his filming of literary classics (*Little Lord Fauntleroy*, *The Prisoner of Zenda*). He revered the capacity of film to bring books and their characters to life. The promotion of *Rebecca* concentrated on book tie-ins. From lending-library stands in cinema foyers to illustrated bookmarks, advance screening for 'book experts' and 'thorough school coverage', the literariness, and thereby the borrowed cultural cachet, of the film was enhanced. Tributes to 'the importance of the du Maurier family in English letters and the stage' mingled with shameless exhortations to the English distributors to 'cash in on the appeal of Your Famous Bestseller'. A letter competition invited local girls to discuss such nervous topics as 'Should A Girl Marry Outside Her Social Class?' or 'Would You Marry A Man You Knew Little About?' (though not, it should be noted, 'Why Marry A Man Old Enough To Be Your Father?').

There was every kind of tension between Selznick and Hitchcock. Hitchcock was impatient with the idea of movie-making as 'picturisation'. But he also in later years disowned the film as catering too much for the female audience Selznick clearly had in mind. 'It's not a Hitchcock picture,' he told François Truffaut. 'It's a novelette really. The story is old-fashioned; there was a whole school of feminine literature at the period, and though I'm not against it, the fact is that the story is lacking in humour.' (Two of the scenes which Selznick had cut from the script were of vomiting: hearty male jokes, presumably.) The taint of the novelettish lingered: 'Boots library in its level of appeal,' sneered Lindsay Anderson in 1972, with public-school hauteur and far more cultural snobbery than 'Hitch', who wanted to make films that could be both experimental and popular.

Slavishness to the literary and, even worse, to the woman's novel of the 1930s, was compounded by the kind of romantic glamorisation of settings and of actors that offended Hitchcock's more democratic sensibilities and documentary leanings. Where Selznick was drawn to the past, the gorgeous and the patrician, Hitchcock wrote articles in the thirties championing 'the only genuine life and drama' in Britain, that of 'ordinary everyday citizens'. He proclaimed himself a believer in the 'little man', loathing 'dress shirts, cocktails, and Oxford accents', the bottled-up stiff breeding of the English upper classes and the stagey actors who mimicked them. Like Laurence Olivier playing Maxim de Winter, du Maurier's suave but tormented hero.

It is easy to see *Rebecca* as a transitional, settling-in kind of film: Hitchcock's debut in Hollywood, his compromise with the producer-director system, his trial run of the superior resources that the American film industry had to offer. In the *auteur* theory, which charts the director's progress as the inevitable development of his genius (followed usually by the sad decline of the old man: enter his young disciples), *Rebecca* is an 'immature' film which nevertheless shows 'the Master' emerging from his apprenticeship. In their now classic account of Hitchcock, Eric Rohmer and Claude Chabrol did their best to blame du Maurier for any of the film's faults, curiously arguing that while Hitchcock absolutely faithfully adapted the 'gossipy and somewhat affected novel', he turned it into something quite different – a 'modern and disquieting' thriller.

Did they read the book? Fans of du Maurier's original might well argue that far from Hitchcock saving her novel, *Rebecca* provided him with the kind of material that brought out his strengths. *Rebecca* was in fact a long way from the Edwardian novelette or the standard fare of interwar romance, which is why it survived when so many titles faded into oblivion. (Who now reads Berta Ruck?) Transporting the gauche heroine to the aristocratic Manderley, the novel kicks off where most romances end, with life after marriage. None of du Maurier's novels close to the sound of wedding bells: rueful, violent, frequently gloomy, *Rebecca* is the most introspective of the lot. A post-romantic novel, it suggested that at the heart of every marriage is a crime.

More about hate than love, du Maurier insisted, *Rebecca* is above all a study in jealousy. The girl's first-person narration, her incessant imaginings about the dead Rebecca and her projections of her (and Rebecca's) life back and forth into past and future, crosses precisely that unstable psychological territory of fantasy and obsession, of guilty memory and fearful innocence, which were to become Hitchcock's hallmark. Herself a shy and lonely young wife, du Maurier wrote as the second Mrs de Winter. Her own romance with Frederick Browning, the strong, silent man who had swept her off her feet, was rapidly wearing thin. 'Tommy' or 'Boy' Browning, a war hero of the First World War, still suffered from nightmares and depressions: the family nickname for him became 'Moper' (though he became better known as one of the generals in the disastrous command of Arnhem through Dirk Bogarde's portrayal of him in Attenborough's *A Bridge Too Far*). Billeted abroad, Daphne dreaded regimental functions and found herself haunted by fears of her husband's passion for his ex-fiancée, Jan Ricardo, dark-haired, beautiful and exotic.

Part of the struggle over the film was between Selznick's love of the lavish, of expensive costumes and big houses, and Hitchcock's desire for surface realism and the carefully observed detail of the everyday. *Rebecca* begins as a love story and advances as a thriller. Manderley (like Tara in *Gone With the Wind*), with its loyal retainers and sumptuous breakfasts, represents a conservative longing; it bespeaks another kind of England (the sort that went down very well in Hollywood), frozen in the aspic of tradition. Manderley is the England Hitchcock must have felt well shot of, inhabited by stuffed shirts with cut-glass accents, as closed to him as to the nameless, and thereby average, girl. The film works hard to deglamorise it.

The first prospect of Manderley is not a view at all. Obscured in the pouring rain, it is reflected like a miniature paperweight model in the misty windscreen of the car (one of the many shots that seem to prefigure *Citizen Kane*, which came out the following year). We are never asked to marvel at sweeping shots of the grounds. Very little is made of the romance of Cornwall. The retinue of servants, who might be expected to stir up the viewers' envy and admiration, merely underline the girl's nervousness. Mrs Danvers, in particular, Rebecca's sinister housekeeper, appears suddenly and soundlessly, reminding us that servants make intimacy and ease impossible. In the film, as in the novel, Manderley, as Rebecca's home, is ultimately repudiated as excessive (like a good bourgeois, the girl is shocked by the leftovers), false and corrupt. It must be – and is – destroyed in the cleansing fire at the closure of both.

Hitchcock enjoys gently debunking the upper classes, making mild fun of the barmy upper-class relatives, using George Sanders, in a wonderfully camp performance (as Jack Favell), to expose their snobbery and complacency. The orphaned heroine may be Cinderella but she is also, in her shabby cardigans and sensible skirts, clutching her handbag, Miss Ordinary of 1938 (the kind of 'thoroughly nice girl' Hitchcock wrote so warmly of). Hitchcock brings the romance down to earth by means of contemporary idiom: 'toodle-oo,' 'right you are,' or the pipe-smoking Maxim, a brusque father-figure, telling his schoolgirl wife to stop biting her nails and eat up her breakfast: '"There's a good child."'

The topography of the Gothic – both its literal and emotional geography – is where Hitchcock really meets du Maurier. Combining the extravagant with psychological realism, it had room for Selznick too. The crenellated towers of remote Manderley, the long corridors down which the child-bride is compulsively drawn toward the secret atrocities of the hero-villain's past, the hint of deviant sexuality and the eroticism of death, *Rebecca* recasts many of those elements of the Gothic which had for centuries provided a pre-Freudian vocabulary for what we would call repressed desires. Hitchcock's camera works constantly to capture the vulnerability and insignificance of the girl dwarfed and isolated in draughty baronial halls or shrinking on oversize plush sofas alongside cabinets of treasures (Susan in Kane's Xanadu comes to mind again). As curiosity impels her – 'What was Rebecca really like?' – we watch her framed against vast oaken doors, reaching up like a prying child to turn the handle and enter the forbidden chamber, drawing back the curtains and veils in which Rebecca, and all she stands for, is shrouded. Alice in Wonderland (Joan Fontaine wears a velvet Alice band and Olivier calls her 'Alice', to reinforce the point) wandering in Bluebeard's Castle.

A home-movies scene, in which the anxious and insecure girl silently watches images of her own past happiness ('only four months ago,' so quickly does romance wither), is one of many brilliant improvisations for visualising the breakdown of her identity as she disappears into her fantasies of Rebecca. But unlike du Maurier, Hitchcock and Selznick, whatever their intentions, cannot really identify with the girl's point of view. The hindsight of the voice-over in the first five minutes is never resumed. They only give us half of the story of female identification and projection.

Joan Fontaine's tremulous expression in close-up always emphasises passive dissolution: what the film cannot show is her pleasure in imagining Rebecca, the active component of longing which could take the girl beyond her dullness, her orthodox femininity. The famous scene in Rebecca's bedroom, where Mrs Danvers seductively invites the girl to take Rebecca's place, shows Joan Fontaine's humiliation, disgust and nausea at being situated as voyeur. It conveys little of the voyeur's satisfactions. The novel, on the other hand, is as much *attracted* to Rebecca, her thrilling independence and sexual assertiveness, as repulsed by her: 'She had all the courage and spirit of a boy [. . .] She did what she liked, she lived as she liked. She had the strength of a little lion too.' Hitchcock and Selznick's script tries to limit this kind of damage: they don't want their female viewers believing that being Rebecca, and acting like a man, might be a great deal more fun than marriage to boring old Max.

Hostility Whitewashed

However loyal its makers thought they were being, the film is crucially unfaithful. Not least in its treatment of Olivier. Though he first appears as a remotely elegant romantic hero (in an immaculate suit, tie and trilby, brooding on a dizzying drop outside Monte Carlo), his mysterious dark moods are never quite sinister. Good-mannered, kind and quietly amused, he is hardly a hunted creature, the Maxim who (according to du Maurier) 'was not normal, not altogether sane'. And in the film version he turns out not to be a murderer at all, merely covering up the accidental death that Rebecca had brought on herself. (Du Maurier's Maxim, on the other hand, remorselessly insists, 'I'm glad I killed Rebecca. I shall never have any remorse for that, never, never.') It may have protected Olivier's image (just as Cary Grant's was in *Suspicion*), but this whitewashing is of a piece with the inability of the film to deal with female hostility toward men and marriage, the bedrock of du Maurier's novel, and the flipside too of her delight in Rebecca.

The masculine point of view runs away with the film, finally leaving the heroine literally behind as the men all go up to London to discover the truth about Rebecca. In the novel she takes on Rebecca-like confidence, managing the now wounded and helpless Max. (Hitchcock limits this to dressing Fontaine 'maturely' in a dark wool costume and putting her hair up.) Worst of all is the sentimental ending which leaves her a potential victim of the conflagration. And poor 'Danny', to boot, made more demented than devoted; the part is pure Grand Guignol. Not only responsible for the blaze but burnt to a cinder in it, she is the madwoman in the attic, proxy for Rebecca. This is the producer-directors' own kind of overkill, going one further than du Maurier in obliterating (they hope) all trace of errant or 'perverse' female desires. At least du Maurier involves Rebecca's incestuous cousin in the arson, and lets Mrs Danvers disappear.

Hitchcock liked his actresses to be docile and compliant, 'the kind of girl I can mould into the heroine of my imagination'. The latest 'discovery', twenty-three-year-old Joan Fontaine, got used to his well-known teasing, which bordered on erotic cruelty: 'Hitchcock kept me off balance, much to his own delight ... He would constantly tell me that no one thought I was very good except himself.' Of course 'the girl' couldn't actually be mousy and dull (though du Maurier's heroine really is): no amount of twin-sets and pearls, hunched shoulders or clumsiness can mar those idealising portrait shots where the breeze ruffles Fontaine's hair and she is radiant, wide-eyed and malleable. As a director who hated 'sex appeal', 'fake glamour' and 'the lady pose', Hitchcock had his own reasons to give Rebecca, the bold aristocrat with her see-through negligée and chiffon boudoir, a violent comeuppance. 'Modesty,' Frank Crawley, Maxim's aptly named agent, tells the girl in a pregnant moment, 'means more than all the wit and beauty in the world.'

So what seems like a woman's film turns out to be a man's after all. We might have guessed. Had we looked closely there was one stable point of view, following the path of the director, that might have led us through the film's apparent labyrinths. It is that of Jasper, the cocker spaniel, who is one paw ahead of the viewer. At first he signifies the lingering dominance of Rebecca: he leaves a room when the girl enters it; he sleeps like Cerberus at the entrance to Rebecca's apartments; he drags Mrs de Winter down to Rebecca's fateful beachhouse. But his allegiances shift and when we see him finally curled up at his new mistress's feet, we know Rebecca has been exorcised, and that we too must relinquish our attachment to her. Not only a marvellous part for a canine actor, Jasper is the film's unsung hero, since he is last seen, his head in the girl's lap, scenting danger in Mrs Danvers's ominously flickering candle. We must assume he saved the heroine. A pity he doesn't feature in the film's final clinch.

Du Maurier's ending is quite different. In fact it comes at the beginning of the novel, steeping it in retrospection. Beached up abroad in expat loneliness, the de Winters are a sad couple of relics, maundering about in hotels, reading *Country Life* and listening to the BBC World Service. They absolutely can't, whatever the film implies, start life afresh. 'We can never go back,' du Maurier keeps telling us. And yet in this circular novel, which ends up where it began, they do nothing else. On the final page the second Mrs de Winter is still imagining herself as Rebecca, only this time murdering Max.

Elegy For Lost Girlhood

It was in Alexandria, in stifling August heat, that du Maurier conjured up Rebecca's Cornwall, an artificial landscape redolent of a more glamorous past, but also of a bolder, more autonomous life, where she might even let out her 'Jack-in-the-box', as she called it, her desires for other women. The novel feels like a swan-song, an elegy for lost girlhood and a lament on the way marriage might move you from one state of anonymity to another. Her England is far more nostalgic than Hitchcock's, but then maybe she had more to lose. In fact she was thrilled and relieved by the film (unlike her reaction to Hitchcock's earlier travesty of her *Jamaica Inn*); despite the changes, she felt it had caught 'the atmosphere'.

For the film has its own central mournfulness, its pervasive sense of guilt. All the trouble starts because Maxim is a widower whose 'grief' can't be discussed; reticence is always muddled in the English middle classes with decency and respectability. Which is why it remains a trap. Despite its gleeful fire (and much of England was to go up in flames very soon), melancholy haunts Hitchcock's film like the mists around Manderley. Perhaps he too had a sense of the dangers of revealing oneself to one's partner, in what Angela Carter called 'the unguessable country of marriage'. Years later he wrote of his wife Alma, only half in jest, as 'The Woman Who Knows Too Much'.

303

Perhaps the English between the wars were especially stuck in mourning, traumatically reliving their memories, unable to let go of the past or make their peace with it. The Englishness of *Rebecca* lies not only in its overt references to the charismatic and intimidating power of class, but in its chafing against the so-called virtue of 'reserve'. It is one version of that model of a tight emotional economy, barely holding out against what it most dreads and desires, whose phobias and paranoias so fascinated Hitchcock. Though he shrugged off the paraphernalia of the Gothic and found more vernacular American subjects, he too returned obsessively to the pathology of repression.

Rebecca, coming back over and again, unscathed through water and fire, has given her audiences and critics a good run for their money. Reckless, decadent aristocrat: the woman who knew too much and the woman we longed to be; acting out lesbian desires, the female Oedipal drama or Hitchcock's tabooed femininity; the return of the repressed or just popular Freudianism itself; she is one of those larger-than-life figures who tempts us to inhabit her world and her feelings at the risk of losing our own. Just like going to the movies.

Du Maurier, Hitchcock and Holding an Audience

David Thomson

There's no doubt about the fondness that existed between Daphne du Maurier and Alfred Hitchcock – or between the writer and the movies as a whole. They were good to each other, and du Maurier's books inspired several more films than those made by Hitchcock. There was *Frenchman's Creek* (1944), with Joan Fontaine as Dona St Columb and Arturo De Cordova as her Frenchman; *My Cousin Rachel* (1952), with Olivia de Havilland and the young Richard Burton; and the story that inspired Nicolas Roeg's *Don't Look Now*. Throw in the Hitchcock trio – *Jamaica Inn*, *Rebecca* and *The Birds* – and you have a group where all but one picture did well at the box office, and du Maurier's sales bloomed all over the world.

Still, a serious writer needs to be wary of the movies – don't look for too many thanks, and keep away from the shooting if you're sensible, because writers' feelings are seldom spared. *Jamaica Inn*, the first du Maurier novel filmed, was significantly altered to make a star part for Charles Laughton. Far better that the author of *Frenchman's Creek* not hear the exasperation of Mitchell Leisen, who was obliged to direct the film. When asked whether his attention to colour, clothes and decor had lost sight of 'story values', he exploded: 'You tell me what the story values were in *Frenchman's Creek* and I'll answer that. She falls in love with a pirate, leaves her husband and comes back in time not to get caught. That's all. It's as dull as dishwater and it was a lousy picture. It was one of those things, either I did it or I got suspended and my agent didn't want me to take a suspension. I should have but I didn't.'

Well, you may say, that's what happens when a picture turns out badly. But then consider what Alfred Hitchcock had to say when François Truffaut asked him how many times he had read 'The Birds' as he pondered how to make that picture: 'What I do is to read a story only once, and if I like the basic idea, I just forget all about the book and start to create cinema. Today I would be unable to tell you the story of Daphne du Maurier's 'The Birds'. I read it only once, and very quickly at that. An author takes three or four years to write a fine novel; it's his whole life. Then other people take it over completely.'

Lovers of reading, and of Ms du Maurier, need not be alarmed. What we face here is the natural hostility, or trepidation, between novelists and those film-makers who elect to translate them to the screen. Once upon a time, many movie directors began as would-be novelists (I exclude Alfred Hitchcock from that company) and they failed. It wasn't that they couldn't write quite well for a few days at a time. It wasn't that they couldn't summon up good story material. Their problem was the stamina and the solitude, the way in which a writer of fiction for the page may nurse a world, an intrigue and a group of characters for a year, or much more, persevering in the loneliness. Film-making, by contrast, is communal and collaborative. You never know when an actor will improve a line or when the cameraman will suggest a movement you never thought of. But above all (and here Hitchcock was the leader of the pack), film-makers believe in 'visual storytelling' – in short they reckon that one packed moment on screen may deliver ten pages of a book.

And that's necessary, for novels are often three hundred pages or more, and the general working estimate is that, whereas a page of script equals a minute of screen time, a rich page from a novel sometimes requires twenty minutes in the movie. Indeed, when Hitchcock came to prepare *Rebecca* for the screen, he even worked it out that he was going to have to get into the 'back-story' (the events that have occurred before the book begins). He thought he was going to have to put Rebecca de Winter into the film! There's another valuable lesson that affects both narrative media: that until the last moment, the novelist or the film director is wrestling with problems. I daresay there was a time when Daphne du Maurier herself took it for granted that, if the book was called *Rebecca*, why, she had to be a living presence.

Then came the blessed moment when insight struck – of course not, she says, if Rebecca stays a ghost she can haunt the book; and if Rebecca is simply an atmosphere that explains why the second Mrs de Winter, the 'I' character is so intimidated, so threatened. Indeed, as Hitchcock might have reasoned: the 'I' character is just the eye that sees the whole thing!

You might then conclude, well, why should film-makers bother with books if they intend to tell every story visually? The answer is commerce. In the short history of the movies, producers have taken the prior success of a novel, a play or even a story very seriously. It helps them feel confident; it encourages them to believe that there is an audience primed for the film. In turn, that fosters the large fallacy: that there is a natural and true way of translating novels to the screen.

The point to hang on to is there in Hitchcock's rather brusque treatment of du Maurier's original version of 'The Birds' – 'if I like the basic idea'. Movie people have a simple test when it comes to possible projects. They may ask for a written synopsis, a treatment, or even a script. Yet, in truth, many movie people do not read easily, and film scripts – if you've tried it – are somewhere between prose and a blue-print. So film people say to a writer, 'Just tell me the story – in words, as if we were sitting at the same fireplace on a cold night. And if I'm hooked, if I want to know what happens next, if the hair starts to go up on the back of my neck, then we may be on to something.'

Alfred Hitchcock was very well disposed to Daphne du Maurier. For she was the daughter of Sir Gerald du Maurier, perhaps the leading actor-manager in the London of the early twentieth century, a handsome man, and a very accomplished actor in romance and melodrama. The two men had worked together on a picture called *Lord Camber's Ladies* (1932), produced by Hitchcock, and actually directed by Benn W. Levy, which starred du Maurier and Gertrude Lawrence. It proved to be more than a regular professional relationship, for Hitchcock and du Maurier discovered that they had a shared hobby: elaborate practical jokes. It has been said that if only, instead of *Lord Camber's Ladies*, we had the movie of these escapades – of bodies found in dressing-room cupboards; of immense emergency calls that required fools' errands; and the everyday booby-trapping of the prop in the picture.

So it was quite natural that Hitchcock should follow the emerging career of Gerald's daughter, Daphne (born in 1907), who was coming into her own by the mid 1930s. That's how he came to make the movie of *Jamaica Inn*, a project dominated by Charles Laughton's desire to play the villain, Sir Humphrey Pengallan, thus cancelling out the clergyman rogue from the book. Once more, Hitch was not flattering about the material: it was 'an absurd thing to undertake', he said, with a story that made no sense. But the film was a hit, and it is worth asking why. *Jamaica Inn* may have problems of logic or tidiness, but it has immense atmosphere, a wild setting (the Cornish coast) and a very strong clash between young and innocent characters and some who are older, darker and far more wicked. The story has a hook. We want to know what happens next.

Du Maurier wrote romances, and she liked to have innocent young heroines. But the romance often veers towards something more like horror – I note that in introducing *Jamaica Inn* in this series, Sarah Dunant said that the bond between the young woman and her towering uncle (the real relationship in du Maurier's book) is like that between Hannibal Lecter and Clarice Starling.

At some time during the work on *Jamaica Inn*, Hitchcock got an advance look at Daphne's next book – *Rebecca*. Did he read it himself, or did he get his very shrewd wife, Alma, to analyse it? Who knows? But the Hitchcocks were mad for the book, and Hitchcock tried to purchase the screen rights directly. Du Maurier was uncertain, for there was word that Hollywood – with much more money – was also fascinated by the book. David O. Selznick was bidding, the man famous for having paid $50,000 for the screen rights to Margaret Mitchell's *Gone With the Wind*. Hitchcock could not compete at that level. But Selznick was interested in picking up Hitchcock, too. The negotiations were very complicated, but they ended with the decision whereby Alfred Hitchcock would go to Hollywood where his first production would be *Rebecca*.

That is not the end of the story. Having arrived in Hollywood, Hitchcock was alarmed by the overbearing manner of Selznick, and was determined to stay independent. So he took the du Maurier novel and turned it into a Hitchcock scenario with a vengeance. In short, he delivered a script that made Selznick howl in complaint. 'But, Hitch, you've ruined the book!'

I do not mean to say that the Hitchcock scenario would not have worked. But Selznick had learned one thing on *Gone With the Wind*: if in doubt stay faithful to the book, for millions of readers are prepared to be upset if you make a foolish change. So, bit by bit, and with fierce comic battles, the producer dragged his director back to the du Maurier story. Hitch was hurt, and he took a little more umbrage when in the casting for 'I', Anne Baxter, Loretta Young, Margaret Sullavan and Vivien Leigh were all set aside in favour of a relative unknown, Joan Fontaine, who happened to have caught Selznick's fancy at that time.

To the end of his days, Hitchcock protested that Selznick had
interfered too much on *Rebecca*. But viewers of the film – for
over sixty years now – have had a hard time picking a fight.
They think Fontaine is perfect, and Olivier as Max. They feel
they know Manderley, the house, and they see Judith Anderson
as the incarnation of that great character, Mrs Danvers (one of
du Maurier's finest dark creations). Rebecca is nowhere, yet
everywhere. You want to know what happens next. And it won
the Oscar for Best Picture – which, after *Gone With the Wind*,
made two in a row for Selznick.

Hitchcock was set on a great Hollywood career. In the next
twenty years, he would make *Spellbound*, *Notorious*, *Strangers on
a Train*, *Rear Window*, *North by Northwest* and *Psycho* (his greatest
hit of all). At that point, he was at a peak where he could do
whatever he liked. And he remembered 'The Birds'. What had
hooked him about it? Well, this story may answer that. Once
determined to do *The Birds*, he looked around for a new screen-
writer, and his eye fell on James Kennaway who had just had a
great success adapting his own novel, *Tunes of Glory*. So Hitch
sent word to Kennaway: read the book, think it over and then
we'll meet and you are to tell me the story of our picture –
how we'll do it.

So Kennaway struggled with the short story about a Cornish
family and their response to a sudden, concerted and unexplained
onslaught by all the birds in creation. I think I have the answer,
said Kennaway. Yes? said Hitchcock. We film the story, Kennaway
began, entirely through the eyes of the family. We never see a
single bird. We hear them, but we only see and feel them as our
characters feel them!

Ah! sighed Hitchcock. Well, thank you very much, Mr
Kennaway, for your efforts. There will be a cheque in the mail.
That partnership was over. Hitchcock had other ideas: he would
switch the action from rural Cornwall to Marin County in
California; the characters would be educated, smart, self-aware.

But who cared why the birds attacked or what it meant or symbolised? Hitch just wanted to do every trick with real birds that the cinema was then capable of. He liked the idea because of the huge technical challenge it represented. He had – if you like – become a very artistic film director, not overly interested in why things happened. Whereas readers always treasure the story and its first grip; they judge a film by its ability to deliver that old thrill. I think they're right, and the best movies show how Daphne du Maurier could take ordinary nervousness and build it into . . . dread.

'Rebecca's Ghost': Horror, the Gothic and the du Maurier Film Adaptations

Mark Jancovich

Daphne du Maurier's fiction has been adapted repeatedly since the late 1930s. It has long been a standard of radio, with several versions of *Rebecca* alone during the 1940s,[1] and it has also been made into numerous works for television. This chapter will, however, concentrate on the film adaptations of her fiction, and particularly on the ways in which they have been understood in terms of genre. Although horror is often seen as a male genre today, the film adaptations of du Maurier's fiction have often been defined as such within the periods of their release, while still being associated with female audiences. However, while their status as women's films was directly related to their status as 'quality' productions,[2] horror became increasingly identified as a male genre and thus critically rejected the notions of 'quality' and 'good taste' associated with femininity, a rejection that has fundamentally rewritten the history of the genre so as to exclude female-centred horror. Du Maurier adaptations may be used to examine how distinctions between high and low culture are related to distinctions between genres, and the ways in which these are gendered. It is therefore salutary to examine reviews of these film adaptations in the *New York Times*, a key publication that represents mainstream orthodox judgements rather than those of the popular or the avant-garde.

Du Maurier's position in relation to both 'high' and 'low' culture has always been ambiguous, and her work is often seen as a curious hybrid that exists somewhere between popular and classic literature, a position that is clearly summed up by the *New York Times*'s term for her work, 'literate romance'.[3] However, this ambiguity is also a feature of the generic identity of her work, which has also been fluid. While the *New York Times* clearly relates her work with female-centred 'romance', on their original release the film adaptations were often classed as 'horror'. Of course, the association of these films with both 'romance' and 'horror' should not be a problem, except that many critics see them as inherently incompatible genres, associating romance and horror with very different gender audiences. While the romance has often been regarded as a distinctly feminine genre, horror has been claimed as masculine. These views may be seen both in the work of feminist critics, as part of a critique of horror, and also by the popular media.[4] However, contemporary horror writer Lisa Tuttle has complained about the ways this gender distinction has been used to privilege male writers and a male tradition, so as to marginalise women's production and consumption of the genre, and fundamentally to shape our understanding of horror and its history.[5]

It is therefore important to stress the ways in which du Maurier's fiction, and the film versions of these stories, draw on the Gothic novel, which was not only predominantly associated with female writers and readers, but is also generally acknowledged to be either a species of horror production or, at the very least, the soil from which the horror genre emerged. Furthermore, the first du Maurier adaptations appeared in the late 1930s and early 1940s, when the success of *Rebecca* (Alfred Hitchcock, 1940) was largely responsible for initiating a cycle of horror films that were directed at a female audience, and have been excluded from most contemporary treatments of horror. However, in 1944, the *New York Times* claimed that 'a new horror cycle is being launched on a far more ambitious level than the forerunning vampire, werewolf and Frankenstein chillers'.[6] Instead of the fantastic monsters associated with Universal Studios, these new horror films were described as 'fresh psychological efforts' that were 'bulging with screams in the night, supercharged criminal phenomena and esthetic murder' and, rather than low-budget efforts, were 'being dressed up in full Class "A" paraphernalia, including million dollar budgets and big name casts'. Most of the films that were listed as examples of this new wave of horror are rarely seen as 'horror' today. Most significantly, the new cycle was said to include such films as *Gaslight* (George Cukor, 1944), *Dark Waters* (André De Toth, 1944) and *Hangover Square* (John Brahm, 1945). These are usually seen as examples of the 'paranoid' woman's film or the gaslight melodrama, two production trends that were intimately related to one another and displayed clear debts to *Rebecca*, particularly in the situation of their gothic heroines and the potentially sadistic threat of their male leads.

Indeed, while critics today usually identify the films produced by Val Lewton at RKO as the only significant horror films made during the 1940s, critics at the time often dismissed these films as pretentious. They were seen as existing in a 'no-man's land' between the lively lowbrow fun offered by the Universal monster movies and the high-class women's horror represented by David Selznick, who had produced *Rebecca* and was associated with a series of 'Class "A"' horror productions that included *Jane Eyre* (Robert Stevenson, 1944, featuring Joan Fontaine) and *The Spiral Staircase* (Robert Siodmak, 1946). Indeed, Lewton had been hired by RKO due to his association with Selznick, for whom he had been script editor on both *Gone With the Wind* (Victor Fleming, 1939) and *Rebecca*. *Motion Picture Herald* even noted the similarity between the opening of *I Walked With a Zombie* (Jacques Tourneur, 1943) and *Rebecca*, in which the former provoked 'titters' from the audience due to its 'off screen narrative by a woman, à la Rebecca'.[7]

The late 1930s and the 1940s therefore represent the key moment of du Maurier adaptations. During that period, the three

314

main adaptations were made: *Jamaica Inn* (Alfred Hitchcock, 1939), *Rebecca* (1940) and *Frenchman's Creek* (Mitchell Leison, 1944). *My Cousin Rachel* (Henry Koster, 1952) may be seen as a rather late addition to this group, attempting as it does to reproduce the key features of this period, even starring Olivia de Havilland, Joan Fontaine's sister. At the time of their release, *Jamaica Inn* and *Frenchman's Creek* were largely identified as 'romances', with *Jamaica Inn* described as a film version of a 'romantic novel'[8] and *Frenchman's Creek* as a film that was 'loaded . . . with all the exciting conventions of romantic fiction'.[9] However, they are also clearly associated with the 'masculine' genres through claims that, in *Frenchman's Creek*, 'the action pops fast and horrendously' and *Jamaica Inn* is a 'melodrama'. While critics of the 1970s used the term 'melodrama' to refer to a motley series of weepies, family dramas and women's films, from the 1920s through the 1950s the term is used very differently. As Steve Neale argues: '[T]he mark of these films is not pathos, romance, and domesticity, but action, adventure, and thrills; not "feminine" genres and women's films but war films, adventure films, horror films, and thrillers, genres traditionally thought of as, if anything, "male".'[10]

However, the generic identity of *Rebecca* is far more directly associated with horror, and established the commercial viability of big-budget, female-centred horror films in the 1940s. For example, while Frank Nugent in the *New York Times* referred to it as 'an altogether brilliant film, haunting, suspenseful, handsome and handsomely played',[11] this comment balances two key features of the film. The 'haunting' reference suggests both the emotional impact of the film and also its generic associations with the ghost story. Similarly, the term 'suspenseful' associates it with horror, which was understood as a genre concerned with shock and suspense and also, as we will see later, with mystery. These two terms, however, are balanced with the two key markers of quality: the reference to the film as 'handsome' praises its high production values, while its performances are praised through the claim that it is 'handsomely played'.

The critics did not regard the horrific elements of the film as surprising; it was even claimed that the material 'demanded a film treatment evocative of a menacing mood'. The *New York Times* review therefore describes the film as one that abounds in familiar Gothic conventions. The house is haunted by 'Rebecca's ghost' and even contains its own 'Bluebeard room'. However, despite the highly conventional features of this 'macabre tale', both the 'Gothic manor' of Manderley and the 'demon-ridden countryside' within which it is located are said to contain 'real horrors'.

The reviews of *My Cousin Rachel* refer to it as a 'mystery' in 'the grand romantic style',[12] but the term 'mystery' has a specific meaning that is quite different from that which it carries today. In 1950, for example, Hollywood insider Leo Handel identified the key generic classifications used by the industry in the 1940s, in which mystery and horror were seen as virtually synonymous terms.[13] Indeed, the review of *My Cousin Rachel* begins with a description of the film's grim opening, in which 'waves are crashing wildly against the rock-ribbed Cornish coast' and 'a corpse is hanging from a gibbet at a crossroads on the windswept moors'. These images are then said to stand for the 'eerie and fateful mood that prevails' through the film. As a result, while the film is praised as a 'quality' production in which 'du Maurier's story . . . has been masterfully mounted and staged', it is also claimed that 'behind its serene and lustrous surface of walnut panelling, old silver and fabulous jewels, there seethes a delicious suggestion of refined passion, mysterious poisons and slow death'.

In this way, the late 1930s and the 1940s established a sense of the du Maurier film, which was significant to the second key moment of adaptation, when in 1963 Hitchcock directed *The Birds*. Not only did this follow the phenomenal success of *Psycho* (Alfred Hitchcock, 1960), strongly associating Hitchcock once again with the horror genre, but it was also made during another cycle of high-budget films that stressed their debts to the quality horror films of the 1940s. There were adaptations such as *The Innocents* (Jack Clayton, 1961, based on Henry James's *Turn of the Screw*) and *The Haunting* (Robert Wise, 1963, based on Shirley Jackson's *The Haunting of Hill House*), both of which are seen as central to the restrained horror tradition praised by critics such as Butler and Prawer.[14] This period also witnessed the production of a series of camp horror Gothics that followed the success of *Whatever Happened to Baby Jane?* (Robert Aldrich, 1962). However, it is not just the production values of these films that pay homage to the 1940s quality films but also their casts, which feature female stars from the earlier period, such as Deborah Kerr, Bette Davis, Joan Crawford and, once again, Olivia de Havilland. In short, these horror films identified themselves with the 1940s cycle precisely through a strong association between the classic woman's film and the horror film, in which the 'cat fights' of the former were presented as indistinguishable from the psychological torture of the second.

Reviews of Hitchcock's *The Birds* rarely relate it to these other trends, and concentrate almost exclusively on the film as a product of its director. The *New York Times*, for example, does not even discuss its status as a du Maurier adaptation but simply refers to it as 'a horror film' that is distinguished by a masterful build-up, in which, 'before we know it, [Hitchcock] is flying shockwaves of birds and the wild, mad, fantastic encounter with nature is on.'[15] Nonetheless, despite the 'unspeakable horror' that concerns the film, this quality remains 'latent' so that the film is one of 'shocks and chills' and 'melodramatic intent' in the classic manner of 1940s mysteries.

The final key moment is the 1970s, which also coincided with another horror cycle. Although this period is often associated with either the end of the classic era of the Hammer horror films, or with the *auteur* horror cinema of figures such as George

Romero, Tobe Hooper, Wes Craven, Larry Cohen and John Carpenter, it also produced a series of British cult films such as *The Wicker Man* (Robin Hardy, 1973) and *Don't Look Now* (Nicolas Roeg, 1973). These films drew on their Britishness to evoke a sense of respectability and quality and, in doing so, associated themselves with the restrained tradition discussed earlier. It is therefore significant that *Don't Look Now*, which now has classic status, is also a key du Maurier adaptation. However, at the time of its release the film had a much less certain reputation. For example, the *New York Times* saw it as 'a horror film', but one that ultimately fails because its 'dash and style' are 'not enough to disguise the emptiness of the screenplay';[16] while it has a 'shiny surface that reflects all sorts of colors and moods', it is no more than a soap bubble that 'doesn't [even] burst' but rather 'slowly collapses'. In other words, a supposed mismatch between style and substance is used to condemn the film.

If the early adaptations were praised as handsome quality productions, *Don't Look Now* was criticised precisely for its pretensions to quality, and attacked for its attempt to 'elevate' du Maurier's original story into 'something of the order of *Turn of the Screw*'. These criticisms are therefore related to the relationship between gender and genre in the evaluation of these films. While *Rebecca* was praised as 'handsome' and *My Cousin Rachel* was claimed to be 'masterfully mounted and staged', it is precisely such lavish productions and their suggestion of quality that were seen as inappropriate in *Don't Look Now*. By the 1970s, horror was largely associated with micro-budget films such as *Night of the Living Dead* (George Romero, 1968) and *The Texas Chainsaw Massacre* (Tobe Hooper, 1974) that were celebrated because their low-grade aesthetics associated them with the art cinema of the period. In such a context, there was a clear link between high-production values and the female audience, in which glossy, high-budget films were coupled with a banal, feminine, mass culture that was critically opposed to a heroic, masculine, avant-garde, and in which the avant-garde proved itself through an assault on supposedly feminine, conformist, middle-brow and legitimate culture.

As a result, this moment represents a fundamental reversal of the priorities of the late 1930s and the 1940s, so that a 'low-grade', masculine tradition of horror is privileged over a 'quality', feminine tradition, and a whole series of traditions are either marginalised within, or excluded from, the horror genre itself. It is therefore also significant that it was the late 1960s and early 1970s that saw the publication of a series of popular histories of the horror genre, which constitute some of the first serious attempts to engage critically with it.[17] As a result, with the sole exception of Alfred Hitchcock's *The Birds*, these histories routinely ignore the adaptations of Daphne du Maurier's fiction, and their particular significance to the 1940s horror. If the genre had a respectable reputation for reviewers in the 1940s, it was taken seriously only when it had been distanced from supposedly feminine 'good taste' and associated with the masculine transgressions of the avant-garde.

Daphne du Maurier and Alfred Hitchcock

Maria di Battista

Daphne du Maurier and Alfred Hitchcock: the coupling of these supreme fantasists of the macabre was not all that it seemed. Their union was contracted to produce that favoured child of modern popular culture – the 'movie version'. There were three of them: *Jamaica Inn*, *Rebecca*, and *The Birds*, all adaptations, some more faithful than others, of du Maurier's original stories about the evil lurking in the very places – an inn, a stately mansion, a country cottage – where we seek refuge from the dark. Two of these films are marvels of their kind, despite the fact that theirs was, in many respects, what the narrator of *Rebecca* might have called 'an alien marriage' (much like her own). Du Maurier's insistent emotionalism had modernised the Gothic without divesting it of its power to affright. The imperturbable Hitchcock sought out the demons waiting at the top of the stairs more out of curiosity than out of a psychological compulsion to confront them for what they were. He and du Maurier weren't exactly soulmates.

Because Hitchcock's art is so self-consciously modern, he is routinely proclaimed du Maurier's superior as a crafter of believable moral thrillers. In her early works, to which *Jamaica Inn* and *Rebecca* belong, du Maurier did indeed indulge a fondness for plot twists that often entangled stories in thickets of sensationalism. Her fiendish inventiveness was a gift from her grandfather, George du Maurier, the novelist who created a mythic figure new to modernity – Svengali, the demon-artist with hypnotic powers to control the mind and will of those in his thrall. There is a comic echo of Svengali's magnetism in the private language Daphne shared with her father and two sisters, in which 'being menaced'[1] was code for sexual attraction; a frightful menace was a very attractive person. Out of this family joke would one day emerge that magnificent figure of frightful menace, the irresistibly attractive wife-slayer, Maxim de Winter.

Hitchcock's ideas of menace (sexual and otherwise) generally took less fabulous, if equally dangerous, forms. He contributed to the critical condescension toward du Maurier's works by dismissing *Rebecca* as a 'novelette', an 'old-fashioned' story typical of 'a whole school of feminine literature'.[2] He thought the novel lacked humour (it did not) and fretted that his personal bogeymen – the 'plausibles', as he designated them in conversations with the filmmaker François Truffaut[3] – would detect the glaring flaws in du Maurier's plot, which unfolds with the remorseless illogic of a demented dream. Hitchcock preferred to construct his plots according to the cold, malign logic of the waking nightmare.

Yet reading du Maurier's fiction against Hitchcock's 'picturization', as the title card of *Rebecca* calls it, produces the distinct impression that it was du Maurier who had the clearer knowledge of moral danger, and that Hitchcock profited from having to confront that knowledge. Du Maurier's stories brought out the unironic romantic in Hitchcock by exposing him to her vision of evil as a power that can destroy, but also exalt those caught in its spell. Presented with du Maurier's fables of malevolence, Hitchcock's moral imagination was deprived of its central myth – that of the wrong man snatched from the midst of his daily routine and brutally thrust into an alien and inexplicably hostile world.[4] The myth of the wrong man allowed Hitchcock to ironise, at times laugh outright, at the misfortunes his films so ingeniously elaborate.

Du Maurier's narratives show up that myth as a psychological alibi; they give no quarter to the 'enlightened' modern notion that it is through blind chance that a man or woman find themselves in a world utterly mistaken about who they are or what they have done. In his 'du Maurier' films, Hitchcock was required to dramatise a female heroism that gave a new, and emotionally complex, meaning to what it feels like to be 'wrong' in the special Hitchcockian sense of that word. The heroines of *Jamaica Inn* and *Rebecca*, for example, are morally and temperamentally quite different, yet both are 'the wrong woman' for the world they inhabit, not by accident but by choice. Mary, the orphaned heroine of *Jamaica Inn*, seeks refuge in the last place that can provide it, and stays on even when she learns that its notorious reputation is deserved; no one believes more strongly that the second Mrs de Winter is utterly unsuited to be mistress of Manderley than she does herself, yet even when she suspects her husband no longer loves her, she offers to remain as an all-but paid 'companion' ministering to his wants. However beleaguered Hitchcock's other heroines might be, they are fundamentally the 'right' woman for the lives they pursue and the men they love (*Vertigo* is the exception that proves the rule). Du Maurier's heroines, in contrast, possess or gain a knowledge that would prove harder and harder for Hitchcock to dismiss as a view of experience peculiar to the airless, overheated interiors of 'female literature'. This is the knowledge that it is the ordinary, unremarkable self who is wrong or misplaced, and that there is another self, buried beneath the surfaces or subdued by the routines of 'normal' life, who is the right or true, if misguided, self.

This knowledge first declares itself in du Maurier's uncanny portrait of Aunt Patience in *Jamaica Inn*, her amazingly confident homage to Robert Louis Stevenson and the tradition of male adventure narratives. With a fiendish inventiveness, du Maurier modernised an anachronistic genre by making women and sexual enthralment central to her tale of land-pirates, or 'wreckers', who deliberately lure ships to the rocky shoals that will shipwreck them, slaughtering all survivors and confiscating their cargos. Aunt Patience's abject, yet undeniably tender, feeling for her husband, Joss, the landlord of Jamaica Inn and visible boss of the cut-throat band, is initially a puzzle to her niece, Mary. Why did Patience choose 'to live like a slattern with a brute and a drunkard', Mary wonders, when 'she might have been a farmer's wife at Gweek, with sons of her own, and a house and land, and all the little happy trivialities of a normal happy life: gossip with the neighbours, and church on Sundays, and driving into market once a week; fruit picking, and harvest time. Things she would have loved, things that had foundation'.[5] Things that have foundation, of course, possess little real, much less permanent, value for fantasists who are quite ready, even eager, to abandon the happy trivialities of a normal happy life, even if it leads to moral degradation. Du Maurier is such a fanta-sist, and her narratives are cautionary tales against her own imag-inative dispositions.

Mary's eventual decision to cast in her lot with rootless things without foundation (the novel's last page literally concludes with her following her lover despite, or perhaps because of, his promise of a hard and wild life 'with no biding anywhere') has no equiv-alent in Hitchcock's very loose filming of *Jamaica Inn*, in which the dark eroticism of du Maurier's tale of sexual subjection is dissipated by the gluttonous figure of Charles Laughton's Squire Pengallen. Pengallen is a villain invented for the film because du Maurier's villain, an albino clergyman whom Mary finds strangely attractive, would never play to mainstream audiences. Hitchcock was unhappy with the entire project, a Laughton vehicle that converted du Maurier's self-described tale of 'fatal fascination' (p.82) into a blustery elegy for a vanishing landed aristocracy and its magnificent, if corrupting, manners. But Hitchcock did catch, as if by contagion, du Maurier's strange tenderness for unions that endure despite degradation and madness. In the novel, Mary finds the slaughtered bodies of Aunt Patience and Joss, but in the film she witnesses their deaths – not, one suspects, as a lesson in the mortality that claims us all, but in the devotion that distinguishes the very few. Such rare devotion provides the only affecting note in the film's histrionic finale, in which Pengallen leaps to his death from a mainmast. Before he jumps he first hails himself – 'Make way for Pengallen!' – and then, off-screen, as if crying from beyond the grave, calls one last time for his faithful servant – 'Chadwick!' – whose distraught face is the last image of the film.

The mysterious bonds of servant and master, whether forged in marriage or through domestic service, display their more insidious power in the mad devotion of Mrs Danvers for her mistress, Rebecca. Overseen by David O. Selznick, who insisted on adhering as closely as possible to du Maurier's bestseller,[6] Hitchcock's film is uncharacteristically faithful to du Maurier's story in plot, character and dialogue; whole scenes, especially those involving the sublime Mrs Van Hopper, are virtually lifted from the novel. Truffaut suggested to Hitchcock that he might have discovered in the novel certain 'psychological ingredients' that would enrich many of his later films, particularly as those ingredients combine to bind victim and tormentor, often pictured as two faces, 'one dead-still, as if petrified by fear of the other'. Hitchcock's sympathy for du Maurier's tormented spirits is first reflected, however, in the image of the stricken face, the last shot of *Jamaica Inn* and the first human image we see in *Rebecca*. After the film's haunting prologue, showing us the ghostly grounds of Manderley as they appear to a dreaming, bodiless speaker, the camera suddenly cuts to a seascape. We are told it is in the south of France, but it looks more like Cornwall, so turbulent are its seas and desolate its coast. The camera tracks past the churning waters and ascends the cliffs until it discloses the silhouette of a man, perched on the edge of a precipice, entranced by the sight of the sea below, which seems to beckon him to destruction. Only the impertinent shout of a passerby – 'Stop!' – recalls him to less dangerous ground and, consequently, to himself. That transfixed gaze belongs to Maxim de Winter; the uncharacteristically intrusive voice to the nameless and utterly insignificant creature he will soon marry. It is she who calls him back to life – back, although neither of them knows it yet, to Manderley. After she departs, the camera cuts to the serene harbour of Monte Carlo, translating us to the human world where their love story can formally begin.

Maxim and the future Mrs de Winter do not meet so dramatically in the novel, but the scene captures the emotional intensity of du Maurier's meek narrator, who is as importunate as the most flamboyant neurotic (like Laughton's Pengallen). Her heroine descends from Charlotte Brontë's Jane Eyre and Lucy Snowe, female narrators whose self-effacing surface manner conceals an imperious, at times ferocious, imagination. The fact that the second Mrs de Winter never reveals her name does not contradict, but rather confirms, her narrative guile. Maxim remarks over their first luncheon that the narrator has a lovely and unusual name (as lovely and unusual as Daphne du Maurier, perhaps). Her reticence is not the sign of maidenly modesty, but of emotional cunning. The very indefiniteness of the narrator's past and identity is the truest representation of who she is. And who is she? She is a compulsive fantasiser, a novelist of her own life who craves for make-believe 'happiness', which her husband says he knows nothing about. Neither does she, but she pretends to him and to herself that she does.

Hitchcock is sympathetic to her claims on happiness and seems to validate them in his subtle reimagining of the conclusion to the 'broken Cupid' episode. The de Winters are settling down to watch home movies of their honeymoon when they are interrupted by news that a servant has been accused of stealing a valuable statue of Cupid. The ornament had actually been broken by the anxious bride as she was rummaging through Rebecca's desk, symbol of Rebecca's executive power over Manderley and the social world that worshipped her. The young bride confesses her fault and her pitiful attempts to conceal the shattered pieces. The ensuing conversation about her shyness and inexperience with great things (like family estates, like marriage itself) triggers one of Maxim's moody outbursts. Irritated and estranged, they return to the movie, which seems to project not just a different time, but a different state of their marriage: the state of being themselves, of being together. They clown before each other and the camera, and in the final sequence are for several moments united in the same frame, kissing and caressing each other's face. The movie within the movie is meant, of course, to call attention to the fact that we are watching *Rebecca* the film, not reading *Rebecca*, the novel. This fact is enhanced by the flickering light of the projector, which fitfully illuminates Maxim's glum face and his wife's confused and miserable one, casting shadows that blacken the transparent affection they once had for each other.

No such tender interlude inflects the emotional tempo of du Maurier's novel, which is dictated by the narrator's compulsion to imagine herself elsewhere and otherwise – to imagine herself, finally, as Rebecca herself. Rebecca may threaten, '*Je reviens*', but it is the narrator who insists on bringing her back to life, a project that makes her and Mrs Danvers allies as much as antagonists. Behind her timid and abject apologies, she is actively working to transport herself mentally out of the moment she inhabits, to 'picture', as she commonly says, what others are doing or saying or feeling. There is one exceptional moment in the novel when we in turn can momentarily picture the narrator as she might appear to others. It comes one morning at breakfast when Maxim abruptly asks: 'What the devil are you thinking about? . . . Do you know you were going through the most extraordinary antics instead of eating your fish?' She, of course, does not tell him what she was thinking, but she does tell us: 'I wondered what he would say if he really knew my thoughts, my heart, and my mind, and that for one second he had been the Maxim of another year, and I had been Rebecca.'[7] The narrator works tirelessly to extend that second, until it threatens to envelop both Maxim and herself in its absolute nullity.

In Hitchcock's version, this antic disposition and emotional cunning are softened and finally transformed by Joan Fontaine's physical mannerisms – her hunched shoulders, hurried walk (half childish scamper, half servile gait) and her open, guileless, expectant face. Hitchcock accentuates how ill-fitted she is physically to occupy Manderley, much less act as its mistress, by filming her huddled in doorways, hunched against walls, or sunk into over-stuffed and oversize chairs that leave her exposed and helpless before the dominating, ever-looming figure of Mrs Danvers. The only sequence in which she is shown commanding the centre of the screen, impervious to any rival, is her descent down the grand staircase, dressed like Rebecca for the Manderley Ball. Has any fantasist, however ingenuous, ever been lured into such an excruciating and grimly funny charade? How could Hitchcock think du Maurier had no sense of humour? Why, hers was as black as his own in conceiving for her heroine this most heartless of practical jokes.

This heartlessness is sublimated into an Olympian detachment in 'The Birds'. Du Maurier's magnificent tale hovers on the brink of a supernatural horror story. A similar mood of unnatural menace infuses Hitchcock's most visually precise, yet psychologically unhinged, film. (*Psycho* is a black-humour comedy compared to the pitiless terror unleashed in *The Birds*.) Hitchcock claimed to have read the story, which appeared in his 1959 anthology, *My Favorite Tales in Suspense*, too quickly to remember its details. It doesn't matter whether he did or not, for *The Birds* is not an adaptation. It constitutes a different sort of creative marvel, one that attests to the elective affinity between these two artists, so different in the medium and the manner of their work.

In 'The Birds', du Maurier fashioned a dark, poetic tale about the overrunning of the human world by the cold, dark, instinctual forces of nature. Her narrative is as relentless as the movements of birds compelled by 'a rhythm and ritual that brooked no delay'.[8] The disabled war veteran through whose consciousness we experience the increasingly violent and highly orchestrated attacks of the invading birds will eventually determine the rhythm of their assaults, but neither he nor the narrator presumes to understand what ritual is being enacted. The world is abandoned to movements that follow a pattern but disclose no meaning. Precision usurps the place of explanation. 'On December the third the wind changed overnight and it was winter.' The chilling accuracy of this opening sentence prepares us for the natural apocalypse to come.

Hitchcock, who was completely cavalier with the story, preserved its most important, and arguably least filmable, element – du Maurier's vision of how the end of the world might come, not with a bang or a whimper, but steadily, on extended wings. Hitchcock's apocalyptic imagination, however, demanded a ritual meaning, or it may be simply a ritual design, that du Maurier ascetically renounced in her telling. By his own account, *The Birds* has as its human centre 'a wealthy, shallow playgirl'[9] who undergoes an ordeal that elevates her into a figure of moral agony. No such agony – or accompanying transfiguration – dignifies du Maurier's tale. Her hero is the central human consciousness of the story, but his thinking has been reduced to a pure reflex. There are no lovebirds, no possessive mother, no dead father, no psychological 'ingredients' at all to suggest, as they do in the film, that the attack of the birds is in retribution for some outrage that the gods are now calling to account.

As happens in marriages, whether of persons or true minds, an exchange of qualities seems to have taken place, then, even if the partners were not visibly communicating at all. In *The Birds*, Hitchcock envisions Armageddon in a spectacular closing tableau, framed like an illustration to a bleak fairy tale: a vast army of birds amassed ready to take flight for one final assault.

Du Maurier's story ends with a lone man smoking his last cigarette as he watches an empty cigarette pack burn in the fire. Alfred Hitchcock has become the nervy sensationalist, Daphne du Maurier the cool ironist.

'Last Night I Dreamt I Read *Rebecca* Again': Reading, Watching and Engaging With *Rebecca* in Fiction and Film

Helen Hanson

No one, not even the author of an original work, can say with any degree of accuracy why a book has caught the fancy of the public; if it were this easy the author of the original could duplicate these elements and duplicate the success.

Memo from David O. Selznick to Alfred Hitchcock,
12 June 1939

I am addicted to *Rebecca* and read it at least twice each year. Somehow and for some unknown reason I have never been able to be attracted to Ms du Maurier's other novels. In *Rebecca* I am swept up from the opening line – 'Last night I dreamt . . .'

William, 21 September 2001, posting on the
Daphne du Maurier Guestbook,
http://www.dumaurier.org/guestbook.html

Daphne du Maurier's *Rebecca* (1938) has had a long-standing fascination for readers, viewers, critics, writers, playwrights, and adaptors, who continue to engage with book and film. Continuously in print since publication, *Rebecca* on page and screen has had an enduring ability to capture new readers and viewers, and to speak across boundaries. As an instance of the 'modern' Gothic romance revival of the late 1930s, it reaches back to literary antecedents such as the Brontës and is both old and new. The novel and its film and television versions have been very thoroughly debated by academic critics. *Rebecca* is widely studied on school and college syllabi, rendering it both classic and popular. A novel which is strongly evocative of Englishness, and of location, but with an international readership, *Rebecca* is transnational. Heard and viewed in its adapted versions on radio, stage, cinema and television, *Rebecca* has escaped the page to become a highly visible, money-making, multi-media text. As a story that is ambiguously ended, it has accrued sequels and parallel stories through the responses of other writers.[1]

Rebecca is, therefore, a highly provocative text. A story of secrets and revelation, of love and hate, of past and present, both offering and refusing romance, it is both questionable and questioning. Its powerful exploration of the ambiguous dynamics of desire, gender and identity is open to multiple interpretations, and the interpretive process draws readers and viewers themselves into that questioning process. *Rebecca*, then, is wonderfully, maddeningly, never done.

The purpose of this chapter is not so much to account for these fascinations and engagements, but rather to reflect upon the ways in which they have been articulated and to discern what has shaped them. So my questions are less, 'What is it in *Rebecca* that has caused these engagements?' (though this is an endlessly fascinating question), but rather, 'How do audiences use and talk about *Rebecca*?' and 'What might this reveal about reading as an activity in early twenty-first-century popular culture?'

Since the 1980s, critics working in the fields of cultural studies have shown an interest in the ways that real readers and viewers make meaning from popular fictions and films. Writings by Jacqueline Bobo, Stanley Fish, Janice Radway, Jackie Stacey and Helen Taylor have demonstrated how popular forms were appropriated and used by readers and viewers in ways which revealed their identities and social contexts.[2] The internet's increasingly central position in the contemporary media landscape has brought readers, viewers and fans of popular culture a visibility through sites where reader and viewer perspectives are posted. The personal postings on these sites, and dialogue with others, make clear a transformation in reading, its private, solitary status becoming public, shared and conditioned through interacting with an 'interpretive community' of other readers.[3] Media ethnographer Henry Jenkins suggests that books and films which encourage intense fan interactions and which can take on a cult status are texts containing elements of ambiguity, openness to interpretation, or excess. These allow readers or viewers to work with them, to assert their own interpretations, or to argue with others about the significance of these elements. In both novel and film form, *Rebecca* possesses these in spades, and debates about meanings recur in online discussions.

Part of the world wide web's image as a democratic, or even utopian, virtual space of communication exchange is due to the interactivity of many sites, and the trend towards eliciting interaction. Many sites invite web browsers to sign in and join the debate through guestbooks or guest logs. The BBC exploited this as part of two high-profile reading campaigns: The Big Read in 2003, and Women's Watershed Fiction, organised through Radio 4's *Woman's Hour* in 2004. Both were characterised by their focus on seeking out and publicising real readers' perspectives. Together with the desire to bring individual views into the public sphere, though, is the awareness that the limits of interactivity need to be carefully framed. The rules of 'netiquette' are usually to be found posted on interactive sites, while the BBC message boards include rules on moderation. The shaping of interactivity is evident where webmasters intervene into discussion strands, or withdraw material deemed 'inappropriate'.

Web discussions and negotiations about *Rebecca* as both novel and film are part of this new public engagement with reading, and they are suggestive of *Rebecca*'s status as a 'cult' text. One website in particular offers insights into *Rebecca*'s continuing

popularity, and into how different 'fan identities' are negotiated around *Rebecca* as text and du Maurier as author. This
site is the guestbook area of the du Maurier site
(www.dumaurier.org). Postings on the guestbook are interesting
in that they run back over a six-year period and show several
different moments of evolution. By far the most frequently
mentioned du Maurier text on the site is *Rebecca*, and many
contributions vividly relate either readers' first encounters with
the novel – often their reading for school or college assignments – or the route that led them to *Rebecca*, commonly
through recommendations of older readers, such as mothers or
friends: 'one of the best books I've ever read' (kiersti, 3 Nov
1999), and '*Rebecca* is one of the most engrossing books I've
ever read!! And the climax . . . it's tooo good !!. . .' (Shivani, 1
Nov 2000). Another reader enthuses:

> My Mum talked me into reading *Rebecca*, which she first read
> when she was 10. Yawn, Yawn, I thought, but I HAVE
> ABSOLUTELY LOVED IT I HAVEN'T BEEN ABLE TO PUT
> IT DOWN. I have shocked Mum and my friends by carrying
> it in my bag and reading it at the bus stops etc. I have almost
> finished *Rebecca* now but do not want it to end.
>
> Sarah, 21 Aug 2001.

And the Guestbook postings remind us that *Rebecca*'s appeal is
not limited to female readers:

> I just finished reading *Rebecca* today, this is a fantastic book, I am
> your average 18 year old guy, into trucks and stereos, etc., but I
> loved this book, every time I read I lost track of time and was
> totally involved in the story and the suspense and I had no idea
> how it would turn out. I would call it a masterpiece.
>
> Christopher, 18 May 2001.

Other readers write about *Rebecca* as their favourite book, and describe repeated readings: 'Daphne du Maurier has been my favorite author for years. *Rebecca* is my favorite book, and has been since high school' (Kirstee, 21 Oct, 1999). Movingly one reader relates the recent death of her mother, whose favourite book was *Rebecca*, and her sense of connection that rereading *Rebecca* offers:

> This is a special moment for me, a few weeks ago my dearest mother passed away and maybe she was the greatest lover of *Rebecca*. I am sure she read it 10 times over and over again, and now she is gone and left me alone, I will read it in her place, over and over again. A great book and a great author.
>
> Adelin, 1 May 2003

Encounters with *Rebecca*, and with the du Maurier site, allow the expression of readers' enthusiasms for the novel and its author, but postings are also expressive of readers' personal connections, to memories of reading, and its intensity, and of their connection to other readers.

The ambiguous elements of the novel frequently recur in discussions, particularly the 'unnamed' heroine, the fire at Manderley, and the story's ellipsis between Maxim and the second Mrs de Winter surviving the fire, and the opening of the novel. One reader argues that not naming the heroine positions her as an everywoman figure: '[T]he second Mrs de Winter has no name, and I believe that is intentional. She has no name, because she can be anyone. She can be you or me' (P.G., 17 Jul 2001). Others use the site to try to clarify the ambiguities of the novel, speculating: 'Who do you think started the fire? I bet it was Favell, or maybe not, how could he have made it there before Maxim?' (Maya, 27 Dec 2000). And wondering: '[H]ow many years have gone by at the beginning of the novel? . . . does anyone know if anyone dies in the fire? The servants for instance. I was also wondering how many years Maxim was married to Rebecca?' (Leah, 28 Oct 2000). The openness of the novel, then, allows readers to speculate about different forms of narrative outcome, to appropriate and work with it, and to share their speculations amongst a virtual community of self-identified du Maurier fans.

The site has a shifting and international community of readers, some of whom post only once or twice (such as students looking for information on du Maurier or *Rebecca* for school or college assignments), but others who find, and then join, the community through dialogue with more established members. The site as a whole holds information about the annual Daphne du Maurier Festival, held in Fowey, Cornwall, and is administered by Fowey residents. Several of the longest-established contributors are regular visitors to the Festival and to Fowey. The power of location is a strong thematic strand of many of the postings. Site members offer accounts of the Festival and their feelings of being in a location strongly associated with a favourite author: 'I recently visited Fowey and couldn't resist going to look at Ferryside by moonlight. The whole place was shrouded in mist and I could almost believe her spirit still lingered there' (Chantal, 18 Aug 2001). Manderley as a powerful literary (and filmic) location is underpinned by Cornwall, and the area around Fowey specifically, as a real location through its mediated and personal descriptions in the web's virtual space.

The du Maurier site is, then, strongly characterised by expressions of belonging to a community of du Maurier fans. However, this togetherness is not without its moments of dissent. While fan perspectives on du Maurier are frequently expressed in terms of personal meaning to readers, there are careful negotiations about discussions of 'personal' aspects of du Maurier's life, or interpretations of her work that explore issues of gender or sexuality. This is evident from a strand of discussion which begins on the Guestbook in April 2004, sparked through a contributor's comparison between du Maurier and Vita Sackville-West as authors, and parallels in their family relations and private lives. The discussion of these issues (usually about bisexuality) initially occurs in the public forum, but, with both contributors expressing concern about the appropriateness of the discussion for the du Maurier family, the contributors move their conversation to a one-to-one (private) email exchange. Evident within the public dialogue by these contributors is a protective impulse towards the author, and an interesting ambivalence towards literary biography: 'Biographers have books to sell, often about those who are no longer able to defend their reputations, so I am very wary of accepting such scribblings as gospel' (Sam, 11 April 2004). At the same time contributors are eager to defend the freedom of the guestbook:

> Most negative comments [received on the forum] seem to be around upsetting the family. I put it to all of you that I was only commenting on issues the family have put in the public arena by publishing autobiographies . . . Maybe I have misunderstood the remit of this guest book, I assumed it was for dialogue, comments, differing perspectives etc. Is it only for fans to say how wonderful everything du Maurier is? (and believe me when I say I am a huge fan of long standing).
>
> Jo, 7 May 2004

The circumspection that surrounds what can be said and what is perceived as private in this public forum is part of a negotiation within this fan community. A degree of consensus about propriety is part of belonging to the site, but this consensus is sometimes in tension with what individual fans wish to articulate about du Maurier as author, as persona and as object of discussion.

Rebecca's popularity has recently emerged into wider public view through the BBC reading campaigns already mentioned. The Big Read campaign was designed to find 'Britain's best-loved novel', and 'to get people talking about books' – in other words, to elicit reader opinions and debate. It featured celebrity 'book champions' putting a case for their favourite book on a series of programmes broadcast on BBC2 in the autumn of 2003. Television gardener, and writer, Alan Titchmarsh was the celebrity advocate for *Rebecca*. The Big Read was criticised by some for its populism.[4] However, other commentators praised 'its acknowledgement that, far from being a solitary activity, reading is most enjoyable when it is shared'.[5] The Big Read had a huge impact on book sales. The publishing industry's trade magazine, *The Bookseller*, reported that sales of *Rebecca* had quadrupled within the first four weeks of The Big Read's launch. On the final day of the campaign, the *Bookseller* listed *Rebecca* eighth within the top ten Big Read bestsellers. Three quarters of a million votes were logged throughout the Big Read campaign. In the final ranking, *Rebecca* was the nation's fourteenth favourite novel.

The 'Women's Watershed Fiction' campaign, which was featured on Radio 4's *Women's Hour*, asked listeners to nominate the novel 'which has spoken to you on a personal level'. The campaign was headed by Professor Lisa Jardine, and elicited readers' and listeners' interactions through broadcasting listener nominations and through featuring both celebrity nominations and those from regional book groups. 13,800 listeners voted in the campaign, and *Rebecca* was amongst the top-ten most popular titles.

While most internet sites focus on the novel, within them there are casual and frequent references to film and television versions of *Rebecca*. Postings to guestbook/discussion groups focus on the acting styles of the key characters, the locations in which film and TV versions are set (often with anecdotes of trips to Cornwall to see sites of filming), and the musical score and lighting. There is chat about the availability of video and DVD versions, notably the unobtainable 1978 BBC TV series, and knowledgeable references to other films. Hitchcock's 1940 film is compared with Welles's great classic that appeared a year later, *Citizen Kane* (1941), noting the similar final scenes (the burning 'R'), and with other memorable films of the same year – for example, Ford's *The Grapes of Wrath* and Chaplin's *The Great Dictator*. Most postings praise the film for its pace, acting and rightful place in Hollywood's Golden Age: 'Everything about this movie shines' (www.imdb.com, dragonfly, 20 September 1999). Several see it as Hitchcock at his finest: 'one of [his] best black-and-whites' (Arkaan, 2 August 1999); 'fresh in a dark and brilliant way . . . it is absolutely clear why it is an Oscar winning film' (Fairishadows, 12 October 2005). *Rebecca*'s ambition is admired: 'the best Gothic romance ever filmed' (ShootingShark, 14 August 2005); 'For Hitchcock and suspense buffs alike, this is a must see!' (moviebuf, 1 November 1998). A few key scenes are mentioned frequently – most notably, Mrs de Winter's visit to Rebecca's bedroom, and the confrontation by the powerful Judith Anderson as Mrs Danvers. Anderson, described in one posting as 'a little grandiose and over-the-top, but still a running characterisation, a steely-eyed witch who ranks right up there with the most enjoyable villains' (moonspinner, 3 November 2005), is recalled opening the drapes: '. . . she suddenly freezes the frame and dissolves to the next scene, epitomising the essence of the story – a place frozen in time, where nobody can move forward or shake themselves free of the past, and everything is stagnating' (Shooting Shark). The free DVD distributed in 2006 by *The Times* produced some critical comments on the 'rather dated' feel of a film with 'wooden' acting (jbo1, 20 March 2006), as well as the conclusion, altered by Hitchcock to make a 'proverbial happy "Hollywood" ending' (catatonic, 6 July 2006). The reissue of a new print by the British Film Institute produced many media reviews, and – as I write – is beginning to start fresh discussion online.

Fan discussions on the web are now a significant part of ways in which reading, viewing and interpretation of texts happen in contemporary literary culture. From students looking to the web to find information to complete assignments, through fans looking for more about their favourite authors and film directors, to reading campaigns such as those run by the BBC, there is a fascination with how others read and view, and a desire by many to complete or elaborate on their own experience through writing about it, accounting for it, comparing their personal experiences, investments, and interpretations with others. While *Rebecca*'s anonymous narrator states that 'we can never go back again, that much is certain', *Rebecca*'s readers and viewers return to Manderley 'again' through the virtual locations of the web. The text's provocative openness and thematic ambiguity prompt rereadings and multiple viewings of this work. Some readers move on to explore other of du Maurier's works and watch film and television versions, but, even so, it is their rereadings and repeated viewings of *Rebecca* that they offer to each other on the web.

Writing and reading about cultural consumption is part of a discussion about meaning that involves *Rebecca*, its readers and viewers alike. The digital disseminations of fan perspectives on du Maurier allow intense personal interaction with ideas of authorship, location and character to be articulated and archived in public, and these are part of a larger contemporary context in which conversations about reading and viewing are shared. Writing about her involvement in the Big Read, Bonnie Greer points out the current popularity of book clubs and reading groups, and relates her fascination in hearing the perspectives of the top books' celebrity advocates:

I was listening to strangers talk about what made them read a book, often over and over again, and how much they wanted others to know writing that had become a narrative for their own lives. It was utterly compelling, like eavesdropping on a conversation heard in a café, or on a bus . . .

And to this we could, of course, add 'on the web'. As Greer concludes: 'We are all readers now, and ultimately we are just as interested in what our mates have to say.'

Web Resources

The Daphne du Maurier Web Site: http://www.dumaurier.org
BBC The Big Read: http://www.bbc.co.uk/arts/bigread/
BBC Radio 4 Woman's Hour Watershed Fiction:
http://www.bbc.co.uk/radio4/womanshour/wwf_index.shtml

Drama in Daphne du Maurier:
Spirit and Letter

Michelene Wandor

Today is a Daphne du Maurier day. I began by reading the openings of *Rebecca*. The plural is apt. The novel, first published in 1938, was followed by du Maurier's own stage dramatisation of the novel. First performed in Manchester in 1940, it starred luminaries such as Celia Johnson as the second Mrs de Winter, and Margaret Rutherford as the forbidding Mrs Danvers. It was directed by George Devine, the man who was later one of the driving forces behind London's Royal Court Theatre pioneering of radical post-Second-World-War drama in the 1950s – emblematically heralded by John Osborne's *Look Back in Anger* in 1956.

The first scene of the version of the play I'm reading is set at Manderley, with the arrival of Mr and the young Mrs de Winter.[1] As was the custom with the 'well-made play', dating from earlier in the twentieth century (Harley Granville-Barker and others), the arrival of two of the main characters is set up by servants and relations, giving us information (exposition) about the back story: mention of Rebecca, the first wife, a teasing account of the youth of the new wife, a sense of suspicion and foreboding. This is a different point of departure (or arrival) from the novel, where the return to Manderley only happens in chapter seven, after we have followed the meeting, wooing and marriage of the de Winters in Monte Carlo.

However, this is not the only difference. Far more fundamental

341

is the change from the form of the novel to the form of the drama. The novel is narrated in the first person, a story told (in this case) by the woman at its centre. The play as genre, however, tells the story very differently. In the drama there is no over-arching first- or third-person narration, since each voice/persona/character speaks not only on behalf of him/herself, but also from 'within' him/herself – and literally so because each figure is always *in medias res*, within the action itself. In drama, all the significant moments happen in the present moment (and chronology) of the drama as it unfolds onstage.

Thus one of the elements so integral to du Maurier's fiction – atmosphere, the power of place, the co-presence of past and present, memories, superstitions, the unknown, all conveyed in the narrated prose passages in the novels – have a different relationship to the form and content both of *Rebecca* and of the two original plays that she later wrote.

The most obvious signal of this formal difference is in the fact that the novel, *Rebecca*, is set in other countries as well as England, in houses as well as the countryside. The play, *Rebecca*, is set entirely in the house, Manderley, with all the looming emotions contained within its walls and setting. Du Maurier undertook a rereading of her own work, in the interests of drama-tising it – literally changing its form, while still retaining all the key elements of the novel.

Du Maurier's family background in theatre very likely contributed to the poised stagecraft she undoubtedly possessed, both in the dramatisation of her own novel, and in her two orig-inal plays, *The Years Between* (first produced in 1944) and *September Tide* (first produced in 1948).[2]

The Years Between is set in 1942 and 1945. The eponymous years are significantly those in which Diana Wentworth, believing her husband Michael to have been killed in action, finds a new independence for herself. She becomes a successful MP, devel-oping a close and loving relationship with a male friend, Richard, as well as blurring some of the above-/below-stairs boundaries of their traditional country house. In a well-behaved Gothic twist to the plot, Michael returns, and the second half of the play becomes the site of a gender-role conflict, as we would now say: will Diana pursue independence and true love, or will she capitulate to the postwar demands of hearth and home?

In *September Tide* we see another postwar household; set on a Cornish estuary, the house belongs to Stella, a widow. Her daughter, Cherry, with wartime service experience, arrives back with Evan, her artist-husband of two weeks. Again, there is a local, reassuring male friend on the scene – Robert. Cherry and Evan live a life of bohemian freedom, and before we know it, traces of old, unfulfilled desires surface in Stella. She and Evan – within the proper moral terms of both Stella and the play – fall in love. Stella is briefly caught between the possibility of a taboo alliance with her own son-in-law, and a retreat into the safety of a loving (if dull) marriage with Robert. As with *The Years Between*, the play ends in a state of suspension; Stella seems to settle for perpetuating the past rather than launching into a new future.

Both plays cast the postwar dilemma through the situation of an older woman, and, in the younger generation characters, one can see the world of the 1950s and 1960s offering very different personal and professional lives to women and men. While Stella and Diana see the possibility of a new world for them as women (in terms of politics, art and sexuality), both are caught within the legacy of their own histories. There is a poignant proto-feminist theme here, as well as an interesting similarity with the plays of Enid Bagnold who wrote eight plays between 1943 and 1968, with her most successful, *The Chalk Garden*, running in the West End for over two years in the late 1950s. Bagnold also sets her plays in the houses of the upper-middle class, with the sea as evocative backdrop, and with intergenerational conflict played out, particularly between the women in the families.

Michelene Wandor

However, unlike Bagnold, du Maurier doesn't capitulate to prophetic or 'happy' endings. Her older heroines are on the cusp of history, with both the benefits and disadvantages which that position brings. Unlike the New Woman plays of the earlier twentieth century, she is not using the drama merely to make a polemical case (as happened in the suffragette agitprop pieces that have survived).[3] It is telling that while so many of du Maurier's novels are historical in their settings, the plays are fiercely contemporary and immediate. Perhaps this is a case of the immediacy of the dramatic form meeting the historical urgency of the content – rebuilding life in post-Second-World-War Britain.

This brings me to my own double relationship with du Maurier's novels. Drawn to them as a reader, with their gripping and sometimes dangerous representations of women (Rebecca, Rachel), and always eagerly caught up in the suspense of the pleasure of reading, I have also dramatised to date three of her works for BBC Radio 4: *Frenchman's Creek*, *The King's General* (both novels) and 'The Little Photographer' (a short story).

I have been using the term 'dramatisation', rather than the often-used term 'adaptation', and I have given some indication of the important formal, aesthetic and imaginative differences between the genres of novel and drama. 'Adaptation' should refer only to the process whereby a text originally written for one performance medium is made appropriate for a different performance medium. So, for example, I have 'adapted' George Bernard Shaw's *Arms and the Man* for the BBC World Service; the play had to be shortened to fit a sixty-minute slot. In the process, while retaining the integrity of the play in all major respects, I also had to tighten the fulsome conversational style of Shaw's period writing; the final tone was a meeting between past and present – a period play in modern conversational rhythms. The 'text' is both the same and different.

344

'Dramatising', however, is much more subtle and complex. Here the literary form is fundamentally altered – a textual revolution takes place as one genre is transformed into another. A novel, with all its conventions, becomes a play, in a dramatic rather than a narrative mode. It is often assumed that this means simply lifting dialogue from a novel and filling in some extra bits. But even where dialogue is fluent and neat, it can never just be lifted off the page. Dialogue in prose has different rhythms and inflections from dialogue in drama, where the imaginative text has no surrounding description, first- or third-person narrative.

The ability to dramatise a novel depends on two things: a) being a subtle and meticulously critical reader in the broadest sense, and b) knowing exactly what writing drama entails, and how its conventions are utterly different from those of prose fiction. At first (literally), one needs to be able to read carefully, critically, taking in the obvious and the apparently not so obvious, following the surface events of the text, and detecting the sub-textual, the gaps, the contradictions, the unwritten or under-written moments. One must engage with the rhythms and the style of the original, retaining as much as possible, while recasting and inventing new dialogue.

The second skill, the ability to write drama, means knowing that everything can only be presented and contained within the dramatic form, where dialogue is all. The single and singular narrative device of prose is a very different matter from the technically multi-voiced form of the drama, and the two skills must absolutely dovetail with one another. Stage directions may support the reading process, but they are never integral to the imaginative world which, in the end, stands or falls on the basis of its fundamental tropes in dialogue. The 'rewriting' of novel into play thus entails a transformative kind of rereading. The play resonates with its origins but is also something new. The novel remains, waiting to be read in its own right.

In the process of dramatising for radio, there are conventions which allow a surface fidelity to the novel. Du Maurier was a consummate adventure-yarn writer, so the story constantly pushes forwards; there are no tricky problems of chronology to iron out in order to make the narrative line clear. Even more freely than in film or television, any location is possible on radio. There is a huge collection of sounds available, and these can create any place, anywhere. In *Frenchman's Creek* there were sound effects evoking the sea, calm and stormy. Pirates and fights in *The King's General* arrive effortlessly in the digital editing. Cost is never an issue. For *Frenchman's Creek* the producer found some generic lute music to suggest period atmosphere.[4] It is always possible to have a voice-over, which gives the impression of being equivalent to the novel's narrative voice. This is a risky business since the 'voiced' narration in a radio play is always 'characterised' through tone, gender, accent and so on. The voice-over in drama is no more authorial than it is in the novel. I use voice-over sparingly, if at all. In the old cliché, drama 'shows' while narrative 'tells' and – for me – the dramatisation that is voice-over heavy doesn't make the full transition from one genre to another.

Certainly, du Maurier's novels have many features that make them exciting to dramatise: a combination of high historical romance and major historical events – wars, murder, crime, smuggling, terror, chases and swashbuckling. For me, with detailed syllable-by-syllable deconstructive reading, the pleasure always lies in taking apart and rebuilding the structure of the novels, observing spirit and letter, virtually writing in a combination of her style and mine as derived from hers. There is a real sense of a dialogue between the two writings, which happens in every dramatisation I do; a dialogue across genres, languages and time. Thus I have been able to dramatise even the most intractable of texts – for example, Henry James's short story, 'The Cage'. By comparison, du Maurier's narrative is clear and dynamic.

Daphne du Maurier was as accomplished a playwright as she was a novelist. Whatever her reasons, it was to fiction that she devoted most of her writing life, and she is best known and celebrated as a novelist. But we are very fortunate to have her plays, *The Years Between* and *September Tide*, which demonstrate that she could both move easily between genres and also engage imaginatively with some of the most important political issues of her day.

Part 5

A Rediscovered Short Story:
'And His Letters Grew Colder'

by Daphne du Maurier

And His Letters Grew Colder

Daphne du Maurier

Dear Mrs B:

Forgive me writing to you like this without the slightest introduction. The fact is, I know your brother out in China, and having successfully wangled six months' furlough, arriving in England a few days ago, I am seizing this opportunity to tell you how very pleased I should be if you would let me look you up sometime and give you news of Charlie. He is extremely fit, and sends you many messages, of course.

Please excuse me for blundering in upon you in this abrupt manner. I am,

Yours sincerely,

X.Y.Z.

June the fourth

Dear Mrs B:

I shall be delighted to come to your cocktail party on Friday. It is very charming of you to ask me.

Yours sincerely,

X.Y.Z.

June the seventh

Dear Mrs B:

I cannot let the day pass without telling you how much

351

I enjoyed your party yesterday, and the very great pleasure I had in meeting you. I must have appeared horribly gauche and awkward, for I am afraid three years in China have played the deuce with my manners and my conversation! You were so sweet and kind to me, and I am certain I babbled a great deal of incoherent nonsense.

It is a little bewildering to find oneself back in civilization, and in the company of a woman of your beauty and intelligence. Now I have said too much! Do you really mean I may come to see you again soon?
Yours very sincerely,
X.Y.Z.

June the tenth
Dear Mrs B:
I shall certainly accept your invitation to dine this evening. Will you excuse my poor bridge?
Yours,
X.Y.Z.

June the twelfth
Dear Mrs B:
I have taken you at your word and have secured a couple of seats for that revue you wanted to see. You won't break your promise about coming, will you? If you care about it, we might go on to supper somewhere afterwards and dance.
X.Y.Z.

June the fourteenth
Dear A,
Do you really mean I may call you A? And did you mean one or two other things you said last night? Whether you meant them or not, I want to thank you for a marvellous

evening. I was so happy, I don't believe I ever apologized for my atrocious dancing!

Thank you.

X

June the seventeenth

Dear A,

Sorry! I know I behaved like a bear on the telephone, but I was so wretchedly disappointed that you could not manage to come out, after all. Will you ever forgive me? Of course I understand. May I come round some time tomorrow?

X

June the nineteenth

I'm glad you put me off that evening, because if you hadn't rung me up to tell me so, and if I hadn't been rude over the telephone, then I should never have come round to see you this afternoon.

Why were you so wonderful to me? Perhaps you were merely taking pity on a poor dull dog arrived from the ends of the earth! I don't think ever in my life I have been able to talk to anyone as I have to you.

You made me feel as though things really are worth while; that there is more to look forward to in life than a dreary plantation surrounded by coolies. D'you know, I'll make a confession to you. Out in China I used to go to Charlie's place merely to look at the photograph of you that he had hanging over his desk.

In a way, I believe I idolized it; I could not believe that there really existed anyone so lovely. And then, when I came over here and knew I was going to meet you for the first time, I felt as nervous and shy as any schoolboy. I was so terrified that my photograph was going to be spoiled in some way.

When I saw you – well, I could go on for pages and
pages just describing how you looked and what I felt. But
what's the use? You would probably throw it unread into
the wastepaper basket, and who would blame you! No; I
shall do my best not to bore you in that way. You must be
sick and tired of all the men who tell you you are beautiful. Can we be friends, though – real friends?
X

June the twenty-second

My dear,

I explained myself badly on the telephone this morning.
I called round at once after you rang off, but your maid
told me you had already gone out. So I am writing this
note instead. You did not understand what I meant about
this evening. It's only that it's so marvellous talking to you
that I feel as though the hours were somehow wasted by
going to a theatre!

Yes, I agree; I am idiotic and unreasonable. Somehow, I
had imagined us dining somewhere quietly in Soho – and
then perhaps going back to your house. But of course I
will do anything you want.

Incidentally, I forgot to tell you that I am moving from
this hotel. The service is bad and there seems to be no
privacy. I'm thinking of taking a furnished apartment. But
we will talk about that this evening. You aren't angry with
me, are you?
X

June the twenty-third

A,

What am I to say? What can you think of me? I am so
desperately ashamed of myself. No; there is no excuse, of
course. I must have been mad ... I never went back to

354

the hotel after I left you. I've been walking about all night, miserable and out of my mind.

It is impossible for you to imagine my agony of reproach. I don't know if for one moment you can understand what it means for someone who has spent three lonely, uncivilized years, living like a savage among other savages, to find himself all at once treated as a human being by a lovely and adorable woman like yourself. It proved too much for me – too intoxicating.

Yes, I lost my head; I behaved as I should never dreamed it possible that I could behave. Can't you see how difficult you made it for me? No; how should you? You were gentle; you were wonderful; you were you. I am to blame entirely. I will do any mortal thing if only you will try to forget what I said.

I swear to you solemnly by all I hold most dear that I will never make love to you again. Never . . . never . . . We will start once more at the beginning. My dear, I want to be your friend: somebody you feel you can trust; someone with whom you can relax, with whom you need make no effort.

Words . . . words . . . How can I explain? A, is there a chance of my being forgiven? A word from you will rouse me from my present depths of desolation. I shall be waiting all day, in case. Forgive me.

X

June the twenty-fifth

When I heard your voice on the telephone, I trembled so that I could hardly answer! Absurd, isn't it?

But none of that matters now. The only thing that matters is that you have forgiven me, and we are friends again. It is all right, isn't it? We are friends, aren't we? Yes; let's drive into the country tomorrow to some little place miles from anywhere, and talk and talk. I have so much to tell you.

Bless you,

X

June the twenty-seventh

A, here are some flowers for you in memory of yesterday. I wonder if you have the remotest idea of what the day meant to me! You said you loved it too. Did you? I can't forget that little inn by the side of the water, and how we sat there dreaming.

I'm so glad the country appeals to you as it does to me. You know, we think alike in most things. In some ways, my dear, your brain is most extraordinarily like that of a man. You see straight; you don't muddle your ideas – and you have such a sense of values. And then on the other hand, you are perhaps the most feminine person imaginable.

I have taken the apartment I told you about. The sitting room wants only one thing now – your photograph. You promised me one days ago.

Yes, I'll call for you this evening at ten, and we'll go some place and dance. It will be perfect, of course. Wear your green dress, will you? I saw some beads exactly that colour. May I bring them for you?

X

July the first

A, darling, it's no good, I couldn't help myself. You looked so lovely. I'm not made of iron, but flesh and blood. What am I going to do about it?

I value your friendship more than anything in the world, but why aren't you old and ugly? It would be so much easier for me.

You like me a little bit, don't you? Or don't you? I don't know what I'm writing.

When am I going to see you?

X

                                        July the fifth

My darling, you made me so absurdly happy last night. I can't believe they are true – the things you said. You told me you liked orchids. Here are all the orchids I could find.

I'll rob every hothouse in England if you want me to. I'll do anything you want, give you anything you want – if only you'll let me see you every day.

I won't ask for much in return – just to be allowed to sit at your feet and worship. Nothing more than that.

You're lovely, lovely, lovely.

X

                                        July the seventh

I can't exist like this. I tell you it's impossible. You're driving me insane. You let me see you, and then you expect me to stand like a dummy without senses.

I've been at the telephone all day and have had no answer from you. Where were you and whom were you with?

Oh! Yes, laugh at me, I don't care. Of course, I agree I have no right to ask you questions. You are perfectly free. When you laugh like that I want to strangle you – and then I want to love you.

I must see you.

X

                                        July the eighth
                                        3 A.M.

Beloved,

   It's absurd to write to you, isn't it, after this evening?

The room is full of you still. I can't think of anything else.
I know now that I have been waiting all my life for this.
Sleep well. God bless you. Take care of yourself.
Do you love me?
X

                                        July the ninth
Sweet,
   Of course it's all right. Expecting you this afternoon
between five and six.
X

                                        July the tenth
My darling,
   No: come tomorrow. You must, you must! I can't wait
for you until Saturday, not after yesterday.
   Couldn't we possibly lunch somewhere first, and then
come back here afterwards?
Please! I love you so much.
X

                                        July the fifteenth
Beloved,
   Your maid answered the telephone this morning when
you were out, so I disguised my voice and gave another name.
   Couldn't we go out into the country? You remember
that little place we went to in June, by the water? Then
after luncheon we could stroll in those woods . . . They
look very lonely and deserted.
   Say yes, will you? Telephone me and we'll arrange to
meet somewhere. I had better not pick you up.
Your
X

July the nineteenth

What about four o'clock?

X

July the twentieth

My dearest,

I think we had better go to the other place, it's quieter. Besides, there are two entrances. What bad luck, your knowing the fellow who lives here in the same block! We'll have to be careful.

X

July the twenty-first

Angel,

Very well; I'll pick you up tomorrow outside your club. Leave the car parked outside with the hood up, and I'll sit inside and wait for you. I suggest we go to the country again. There's less chance of running across anyone.

By the way, I've found out that the fellow you know is out all day, doesn't get back until the evening, so we needn't worry about him when we're at the apartment.

I don't know how to wait until tomorrow.

You know that question you asked me? The answer is Yes – a thousand times!

You are *adorable*!

X

July the twenty-fifth

Yes, I know I was nervy and irritable today. You must forgive me. But seeing you as I do, at odd hours, makes me dissatisfied. I don't know. It's as though I wanted to be with you all the time. Couldn't we go away some-where, for the weekend? Some place where we could be by ourselves.

We would be very careful; no one need ever find out.
What do you think, my sweet?
Your
X

July the twenty-seventh

Angel,

But you are marvellous! What a brilliant idea! I should
never have thought of a sick friend in Devonshire! Yes; you
can rely on me to be discreet. I'll be at Paddington at a
quarter to eleven.
X

August the fifth

My beloved Sweet,

I haven't dared ring you up in case it should seem odd.
These few days with you have been so marvellous, so utterly
unspeakable. Darling, I don't know how I am going to go
on as we did before.

Those wretched, hurried meetings after the hours we
spent together. I'm so happy and so miserable. I'll wait at
the apartment all day in case you should come.
Your own
X

August the seventh

Yesterday was *heaven*. What time tomorrow? I think the
afternoons are safest.
X

August the twelfth

Dearest,

What about suggesting your idea and seeing how it is
taken? After all, if you are in the habit of going to Aix

every year for this cure, why should it look strange suddenly? You can say you are tired of Aix itself and have heard of a smaller place just as good but not nearly so expensive. That is sure to go well!

You see, sweet, I could go out there about the nineteenth and you could join me a few days later. I think that would be the wisest plan.

Anyway, there's no harm in trying, and you can tell me tomorrow what happened.

See you after seven.

X

August the fourteenth

My own,

To think that it will really come true – that we shall be together night and day for three weeks, perhaps a month. It's too wonderful, my precious; it's like a dream out of which one will be wakened suddenly.

Tell me you are happy, too. Hours and hours of each other, and nothing to separate us. I'm never going to stop loving you for one single instant.

Your very own,

X

August the twentieth

I'm just off, sweet. I'm so excited! Three days of agony until you follow me South – and then . . .

X

September the twenty-sixth

Darling,

I arrived back in town about two hours ago. I can scarcely believe we've been away a month. Sometimes it seems a day; sometimes it seems a year.

Thank you for your sweet letter, darling. When am I going to see you?

X

                        September the twenty-ninth

My darling,

It was lovely being with you all yesterday. It was almost as though we were down in the South again.

And the little inn by the river was just the same as ever, wasn't it?

Now, dearest, about our seeing each other. We must be terribly careful because if our names get coupled and people start talking, and it all came out about our being away together – well, you can imagine what would happen. We had better go very slowly at first. You do understand, don't you? It's all for your sake.

X

                                 October the fourth

Yes darling, come along if you like between six and seven, but do remember not to bring the car. Sorry about not having telephoned. I thought it safer.

X

                                 October the ninth

Dearest,

Wouldn't you rather do a theatre and dance afterwards than spend the evening here? I mean, there's always the chance of your being seen.

I've heard the new Wallace play is a thrill. What do you say? Let me know so that I can get seats.

X

October the twelfth

Sweetheart,

You mustn't be so unreasonable. You don't seem to understand what the consequences would be if we were found out. I've thought it all over very carefully from every angle, and it would be hopeless – quite hopeless. Life wouldn't be worth living for either of us.

You know I want to see you as much as you want to see me, but it's no use running into danger. You were in a difficult mood yesterday, and deliberately misunderstood every word I said. I don't mean to be hard, but you do see, don't you? Come for luncheon tomorrow and we'll talk over plans.

All love,

X

October the sixteenth

Sorry, darling, I was out when you telephoned, and didn't get back till late so couldn't ring you. Was your message for dinner on Thursday? I can't manage Thursday, darling. What about Friday afternoon? We might go to a picture.

Do remember to ring me up from your club and not from your house. Servants might be listening. Haven't you any sense of discretion? See you soon.

X

October the twenty-fourth

Darling,

Don't you realize it would be madness to go away for the week-end? Surely we've been over that question time and time again. We've only to take a wrong turn and the whole affair is broadcast to the world. To say we did so in July is no answer to the present argument.

363

It's absurd to say I'm different. I'm just the same as ever. I wish you wouldn't be so feminine and unreasonable. You don't see straight at all, darling.

By the way, the price they asked for that necklace was sheer robbery. Perhaps we can find something else. I'll ring you up at the end of the week.

X

October the twenty-ninth

Isn't it rather cold for the country? Let's have luncheon Saturday instead.

X

October the thirty-first

Here are some chrysanthemums for you. Of course I love you. But you mustn't behave in that absurd way again, darling, or I shall be very angry. I can't bear scenes. See you Monday.

X

November the fifth

Darling,

I'm afraid this week is very difficult. I've got loads of things that must be done. I might be able to snatch an hour on Thursday. Keep the afternoon free.

In haste,

X

November the ninth

My dear,

Why must you spoil everything? I was perfectly ready to enjoy our afternoon together, and you needs must cross-question me as though you expected every word I said to be a lie.

364

Sometimes I don't think you have ever understood me at all. What's to be the outcome of it? Is it always to be this incessant quarrelling whenever we meet? It looks that way, doesn't it?

And why this new thing of jealousy? It's ridiculous and nerve-wracking. Can't we be friends without all this nonsense?

X

November the thirteenth

All right. Wednesday at one. But don't come to the apartment. I'll meet you at the Savoy.

X

November the sixteenth

Just a line to say I can't manage tomorrow night, after all. So sorry not to let you know before. Will ring the club tomorrow.

X

November the eighteenth

A, dear,

I should be glad if you would cease spying on my movements. If I chose to spend the evening talking business with a friend it's my affair entirely. Remember this once and for all. Aren't you making yourself slightly ridiculous?

Yours,

X

November the twentieth

My dear A,

I received your extremely incoherent message on the telephone but scarcely know what it is all about. I accept your apologies, but need we go into that?

About seeing you – I can't definitely say when. I have so many things to see to. I will try to let you know.
X

                    November the twenty-fourth
Dear A,

How ridiculous you are! As if I should disguise my voice on the telephone. It was the servant who answered. I was out all day. No, I'm afraid I shan't be able to see you this evening. I'll let you know when I can.
X

                    November the twenty-seventh
Dear A,

Why not be frank with yourself and admit that it isn't because you have messages to send to Charles that you want to see me? I know only too well that it will mean another scene of reproach, more tears, more nerves.

I've had enough. Can't you realize that it's finished? I shan't be able to breathe until I get out of this over-civilized, oversexed country, back to the peace and security of my plantation.

Now you know the truth.
Good-by.
X

Telephone message sent December first to Mrs B:
'Mr X.Y.Z. sailed for China today.'

Further Reading and Filmography

Sunie Fletcher

(a) Daphne du Maurier Bibliography

Original dates of publication and publishers given.

FICTION

The Loving Spirit	1931	Heinemann
I'll Never Be Young Again	1932	Heinemann
The Progress of Julius (later *Julius*)	1933	Heinemann
Jamaica Inn	1936	Gollancz
Rebecca	1938	Gollancz
Come Wind, Come Weather	1940	Heinemann
Frenchman's Creek	1941	Gollancz
Hungry Hill	1943	Gollancz
Happy Christmas	1943	Todd
Nothing Hurts For Long and The Escort	1943	Todd
Spring Picture	1944	Todd
Leading Lady	1945	Todd
The King's General	1946	Gollancz
The Parasites	1949	Gollancz
My Cousin Rachel	1951	Gollancz
The Apple Tree (later *The Birds and Other Stories*)	1952	Gollancz
Mary Anne	1954	Gollancz
The Scapegoat	1957	Gollancz

Early Stories	1959	Bantam
The Breaking Point (later *The Blue Lenses*)	1959	Gollancz
Castle Dor (with Sir Arthur Quiller-Couch)	1962	Dent
The Glass-Blowers	1963	Gollancz
The Flight of the Falcon	1965	Gollancz
The House on the Strand	1969	Gollancz
Not After Midnight (later *Don't Look Now*)	1971	Gollancz
Rule Britannia	1972	Gollancz
Echoes From the Macabre	1976	Gollancz
The Rendezvous and Other Stories	1980	Gollancz
Classics of the Macabre	1987	Gollancz

PLAYS

Rebecca	1939	Gollancz
The Years Between	1946	Gollancz
September Tide	1949	Gollancz

NON-FICTION

Gerald: A Portrait	1934	Gollancz
The Du Mauriers	1937	Gollancz
The Young George du Maurier:		
A Selection of His Letters, 1860–1867 (ed.)	1951	Peter Davies
The Infernal World of Branwell Brontë	1960	Gollancz
Vanishing Cornwall	1967	Gollancz
Golden Lads: A Study of Anthony Bacon,		
Francis, and Their Friends	1975	Gollancz
The Winding Stair: Francis Bacon,		
His Rise and Fall	1976	Gollancz
Growing Pains: The Shaping of a Writer		
(later *Myself When Young*)	1977	Gollancz

The Rebecca Notebook and Other Memories	1981	Gollancz
Enchanted Cornwall	1989	Penguin

INTRODUCTIONS TO OTHER AUTHORS' WORKS

Austen, Jane, *Northanger Abbey*, introduction by Daphne du Maurier (London: Williams and Norgate, 1948).

Bottome, Phyllis, *Best Stories of Phyllis Bottome*, chosen, with a preface, by Daphne du Maurier (London: Faber & Faber, 1963).

Brontë, Emily, *Wuthering Heights*, introduction by Daphne du Maurier (London: Macdonald, 1955).

(b) Filmography: Selected film and television adaptations of works by Daphne du Maurier

Jamaica Inn (film, UK, 1939, Mayflower Pictures).
Dir. Alfred Hitchcock, starring Charles Laughton, Maureen O'Hara, Robert Newton.

Rebecca (film, USA, United Artists, 1940).
Dir. Alfred Hitchcock, starring Laurence Oliver, Joan Fontaine.

Frenchman's Creek (film, USA, Paramount, 1944).
Dir. Mitchell Leisen, starring Joan Fontaine, Basil Rathbone.

The Years Between (film, UK, Sydney Box, 1946).
Dir. Compton Bennett, starring Michael Redgrave, Valerie Hobson.

Rebecca (TV, UK, BBC, 1947).
Starring Michael Hordern, Dorothy Gordon.

Hungry Hill (film, UK, J. Arthur Rank/Two Cities, 1947).
Dir. Brian Desmond Hurst, starring Margaret Lockwood, Dennis Price, Jean Simmons.

My Cousin Rachel (film, USA, 20th Century Fox, 1952).
Dir. Henry Koster, starring Olivia de Havilland, Richard Burton.

The Scapegoat (film, UK, MGM, 1959).
Dir. Robert Hamer, starring Alec Guinness, Bette Davis.

Rebecca (TV, USA, NBC, 1962).
Starring James Mason, Joan Hackett.

The Birds (film, USA, Universal, 1963).
Dir. Alfred Hitchcock, starring Tippi Hedren, Rod Taylor, Jessica Tandy.

Don't Look Now (film, UK/Italy, Eldorado, 1973).
Dir. Nicolas Roeg, starring Julie Christie, Donald Sutherland.

Rebecca (TV, UK, BBC, 1979).
Dir. Simon Langton, starring Jeremy Brett, Joanna David.

My Cousin Rachel (TV, UK, BBC, 1983).
Dir. Brian Farnham, starring Geraldine Chaplin, Christopher Guard.

Jamaica Inn (TV, UK, HTV, 1985).
Dir. Lawrence Gordon Clark, starring Jane Seymour, Patrick McGoohan, Trevor Eve.

The Lifeforce Experiment [based on short story *The Breakthrough*] (TV, Canada/UK, Filmline/Lillian Gallo/Screen Partners, 1994).
Dir. Piers Haggard, starring Donald Sutherland, Mimi Kuzyk.

Rebecca (TV, UK/Germany, Carlton/Portman/ITV/TMG, 1997). Dir Jim O'Brien, starring Charles Dance, Emilia Fox, Diana Rigg, Faye Dunaway.

Frenchman's Creek (TV, UK, Carlton, 1998).
Dir. Ferdinand Fairfax, starring Tara Fitzgerald, Anthony Delon.

(c) Biographical Studies of Daphne du Maurier and Family

Cook, Judith, *Daphne: A Portrait of Daphne du Maurier* (London: Transworld, 1991).

du Maurier, Angela, *It's Only the Sister* (London: Peter Davies, 1951).

du Maurier, Daphne, *Gerald: A Portrait* (London: Gollancz, 1934).

du Maurier, Daphne, *The Du Mauriers* (London: Gollancz, 1937).

du Maurier, Daphne, *Growing Pains: The Shaping of a Writer* (London: Gollancz, 1977), reprinted as *Myself When Young* (London: Virago, 2004).

Forster, Margaret, *Daphne du Maurier* (London: Chatto & Windus, 1993).

Harding, James, *Gerald du Maurier: The Last Actor-Manager* (London: Hodder & Stoughton, 1989).

Leng, Flavia, *Daphne du Maurier: A Daughter's Memoir* (Edinburgh: Mainstream, 1994).

Malet, Oriel, ed., *Daphne du Maurier: Letters From Menabilly: Portrait of a Friendship* (London: Weidenfeld & Nicolson, 1992).

Ormond, Leonee, *George du Maurier* (London: Routledge & Kegan Paul, 1969).

Shallcross, Martyn, *Du Maurier Country* (Bodmin: Bossiney, 1987).

Shallcross, Martyn, *The Private World of Daphne du Maurier* (London: Robson, 1991, revised 1998).

Whiteley, Derek Pepys, *George du Maurier: His Life and Work* (London, Art and Technics, 1948).

(d) Selected Critical Studies of Daphne du Maurier

Abi-Ezzi, Nathalie, *The Double in the Fiction of R. L. Stevenson, Wilkie Collins and Daphne du Maurier* (New York: Peter Lang, 2003).

Armitt, Lucie, *Contemporary Women's Fiction and the Fantastic* (Basingstoke: Macmillan, 2000).

Auerbach, Nina, *Daphne du Maurier: Haunted Heiress* (Philadelphia: University of Pennsylvania Press, 1999).

Bromley, Roger, 'The gentry, bourgeois hegemony and popular fiction: *Rebecca* and *Rogue Male*', in Peter Humm, Paul Stigant and Peter Widdowson, eds., *Popular Fictions: Essays in Literature and History* (London: Methuen, 1986), pp.151–72.

Creed, Barbara, *The Monstrous Feminine: Film, Feminism, Psycho-analysis* (London: Routledge, 1993).

Denisoff, Denis, 'Where the Boys Are: Daphne du Maurier and the Masculine Art of Unremarkability', in *Sexual Visuality from Literature to Film, 1850–1950* (Basingstoke: Palgrave Macmillan, 2004).

Doane, Mary Ann, *The Desire to Desire: The Woman's Film of the 1940s* (Basingstoke: Macmillan, 1987).

Gallafent, Ed, 'Black Satin: Fantasy, Murder and the Couple in *Gaslight* and *Rebecca*', *Screen*, vol. 29, no. 3, 1988, pp.84–103.

Harbord, Janet, 'Between Identification and Desire: Rereading *Rebecca*', *Feminist Review*, no. 53, Summer 1996, pp.95–107.

Hollinger, Karen, 'The Female Oedipal Drama of *Rebecca* from Novel to Film', *Quarterly Review of Film and Video*, vol. 14, no. 4, 1993, pp.17–30.

Hopcraft, Arthur, *Rebecca: The Screenplay* (London: Chameleon, 1996).

Horner, Avril, and Sue Zlosnik, *Daphne du Maurier: Writing, Identity and the Gothic Imagination* (Basingstoke: Macmillan, 1998).

Horner, Avril and Sue Zlosnik, '"Extremely Valuable Property": The Marketing of *Rebecca*', in Judy Simons and Kate Fullbrook, eds., *Writing: A Woman's Business: Women, Writing and the Market Place* (Manchester: Manchester University Press, 1998), pp.48–65.

Horner, Avril, and Sue Zlosnik, 'Deaths in Venice: Daphne du Maurier's "Don't Look Now"', in Glennis Byron and David Punter, eds., *Spectral Readings: Towards a Gothic Georgraphy* (Basingstoke: Palgrave Macmillan, 1999), pp.219–32.

Horner, Avril, and Sue Zlosnik, 'Daphne du Maurier and the Gothic Tradition: Rebecca as Vamp(ire)', in Avril Horner and Angela Keane, eds., *Body Matters: Feminism, Textuality, Corporeality* (Manchester: Manchester University Press, 2000), pp.209–22, also reprinted in *Gothic Literature: A Gale Critical Companion Volume 2* (Thomson Gale, 2006), pp.284–90.

Izod, John, *The Films of Nicolas Roeg: Myth and Mind* (Basingstoke: Macmillan, 1992).

Kelly, Richard, *Daphne du Maurier* (Boston: Twayne, 1987).

Leff, Leonard, *Hitchcock and Selznick: The Rich and Strange Collaboration of Alfred Hitchcock and David O. Selznick in Hollywood* (New York: Weidenfeld and Nicolson, 1987).

Light, Alison, '"Returning to Manderley": Romance Fiction, Female Sexuality and Class', *Feminist Review*, no. 16, Summer, 1984, pp.7–25.

Light, Alison, *Forever England: Femininity, Literature and Conservatism between the Wars* (London: Routledge, 1991).

Meyers, Helene, *Femicidal Fears: Narratives of the Female Gothic Experience* (Albany: State University of New York Press, 2001).

Modleski, Tania, *Loving with a Vengeance: Mass Produced Fantasies for Women* (Hamden, Connecticut: Archon, 1982).

Modleski, Tania, *The Women Who Knew Too Much: Hitchcock and Feminist Theory* (London: Routledge, 1988).

Paglia, Camille, *The Birds* (London: British Film Institute, 1998).

Pirie, David, *A Heritage of Horror: The English Gothic Cinema 1946–1972* (London: Gordon Fraser, 1973).

Radway, Janice, *Reading the Romance: Women, Patriarchy and Popular Literature* (Chapel Hill and London: University of North Carolina Press, 1984).

Sanderson, Mark, *Don't Look Now* (London: British Film Institute, 1996).

Simons, Judy, 'Rewriting the Love Story: The Reader as Writer in Daphne du Maurier's *Rebecca*', in Lynne Pearce and Gina Wisker, eds., *Fatal Attractions: Rescripting Romance in Contemporary Literature and Film* (London: Pluto, 1998), pp.112–27

Stoneman, Patsy, *Brönte Transformations: The Cultural Dissemination of Jane Eyre and Wuthering Heights* (London: Prentice Hall/ Harvester Wheatsheaf, 1996).

Thomson, David, *Showman: The Life of David O. Selznick* (New York: Knopf, 1992).

Truffaut, François, *Hitchcock* (New York: Simon and Schuster, 1967).

Tuttle, Lisa, *Skin of the Soul* (London: Women's Press, 1990).

Vickers, Stanley and Diana King, *The du Maurier Companion* (Fowey: Fowey Rare Books/Alexander & Associates, 1997).

Westland, Ella, *Reading Daphne* (Truro: Truran Press, 2007).

Wheatley, Helen, 'Haunted Houses, Hidden Rooms: Women, Domesticity and the Female Gothic Adaptation on Television', in Jonathan Bignell and Stephen Lacey, eds., *Popular Television*

Drama (Manchester: Manchester University Press, 2005), pp.149–65.

White, Patricia, *Uninvited: Classical Hollywood Cinema and Lesbian Representability* (Bloomington: Indiana University Press, 2000).

Wisker, Gina, 'Don't Look Now! The Compulsions and Revelations of Daphne du Maurier's Horror Writing', in *Journal of Gender Studies*, 8, 1, March 1999, pp.19–33.

Wisker, Gina, 'Dangerous Borders: Daphne du Maurier's *Rebecca*: Shaking the Foundations of the Romance of Privilege, Partying and Place', in *Journal of Gender Studies*, 12, 2, 2003, pp.83–97.

Manuscripts

University of Exeter Library, EUL MS 144, 'Literary Papers of George du Maurier and Daphne du Maurier, *c*.1893–1981'.

University of Exeter Library, EUL MS 206, 'The du Maurier Papers, *c*. 1946–2002' including the papers of Sheila Hodges.

University of Exeter Library, EUL MS 207, 'The du Maurier Family Papers, 1816–1988'.

University of Exeter Library, 'Margaret Forster: Daphne du Maurier Research Papers'.

Cambridge University Library, GB 12 MS.Add.9395, 'Daphne du Maurier: Letters to Regis Bouis, 1957–1958'. (Correspondence concerning the author's French forebears, especially the Bussons.)

John Rylands University Library of Manchester, DEA1/1724–731 and DEA1/2/512–524, 'The Papers of Basil Dean'; also LPH Box 1, File 4 'The Papers of L. P. Hartley'. (Correspondence with Daphne du Maurier.)

The University of Warwick Modern Records Centre, Gollancz Papers, MSS 157, Correspondence between Daphne du Maurier and Victor Gollancz.

Acknowledgements

As is usual with a collectively produced book, there are too many people to credit by name; I am indebted to family, friends and colleagues for their support. Virago Press, especially Lennie Goodings and Jill Foulston made this possible. Donna Coonan, my editor, has been extremely meticulous and supportive. Daphne du Maurier's immediate family – Tessa and David Montgomery, Flavia Leng, and especially Kits and Hacker Browning – have offered unfailing help and charming hospitality over the many years I've known and worked with them. Staff at the Daphne du Maurier Festival and Literary Centre, notably Jonathan Aberdeen, made my research pure pleasure, and Bookends of Fowey's Ann and David Willmore helped in many ways (not least in discovering a forgotten story by Daphne du Maurier, reprinted here). The Browning family, Margaret Forster, Sheila Hodges, Sally Beauman and Maureen Freely all gave their time to be interviewed at length. My Research Assistant, Sunie Fletcher, cheerfully undertook editorial and bibliographical work. The School of English, University of Exeter, gave financial and other assistance, and its administrative staff (Ges Macdonald, Dawn Teed, Julia Davey and Sue Cocker), helped greatly in the preparation of this book. I am most grateful for the inspiration offered by the many Daphne du Maurier enthusiasts I've met over the years at the Du Maurier Festival and elsewhere, and particularly for the careful and informative questionnaires completed by contributors to my Festival session, 2005, 'What Daphne du Maurier means to me'. My final thanks go to all the contributors to this Companion, who have collaborated wonderfully, helped me in

378

innumerable ways, and whose writing pays a fitting tribute to this important writer.

Virago gratefully acknowledges the following for permission to reproduce copyright material:

Lisa Appignanesi: Introduction to *The Scapegoat*, published by Virago. Copyright © Lisa Appignanesi 2004.

Nina Auerbach: 'Tales of Awe and Arousal: Animals Invade'. Copyright © Nina Auerbach 2007.

Sally Beauman: Introduction to *Rebecca*, published by Virago. Copyright © Sally Beauman 2003; Introduction to *My Cousin Rachel*, published by Virago. Copyright © Sally Beauman 2003.

Nina Bawden: Introduction to *Castle Dor*, published by Virago. Copyright © Nina Bawden 2004.

Charlotte Berry and Jessica Gardner: 'Who I Am: Adventures in the du Maurier Family Archive'. Copyright © Charlotte Berry and Jessica Gardner 2007.

Celia Brayfield: Introduction to *The House on the Strand*, published by Virago. Copyright © Celia Brayfield 2003.

Christian Browning: Introduction to *Vanishing Cornwall*, published by Virago. Copyright © Christian Browning 2007.

Amanda Craig: Introduction to *The Flight of the Falcon*, published by Virago. Copyright © Amanda Craig 2005.

Michelle de Kretser: Introduction to *The Glass-Blowers*, published by Virago. Copyright © Michelle de Kretser 2004.

Maria di Battista: 'Daphne du Maurier and Alfred Hitchcock'. Copyright © Maria di Battista 2007.

Daphne du Maurier: 'And His Letters Grew Colder', Hearst International combined with *Cosmopolitan*, Sept 1931, vol. xci, no. 3. Copyright © The Estate of Daphne du Maurier 1931.

Sarah Dunant: Introduction to *Jamaica Inn*, published by Virago. Copyright © Sarah Dunant 2003.

Acknowledgements

Elaine Dundy: Introduction to *I'll Never Be Young Again*, published by Virago. Copyright © Elaine Dundy 2005.

Margaret Forster: Introduction to *Gerald: A Portrait*, published by Virago. Copyright © Margaret Forster 2004.

Antonia Fraser: 'Rebecca's Story', published in *Harpers & Queen*, November 1976. Copyright © Antonia Fraser 1976.

Helen Hanson: '"Last Night I Dreamt I Read *Rebecca* Again": Reading, Watching and Engaging with *Rebecca* in Fiction and Film'. Copyright © Helen Hanson 2007.

Melanie Heeley: 'Christianity Versus Paganism: Daphne du Maurier's Divided Mind'. Copyright © Melanie Heeley 2007.

Lisa Hilton: Introduction to *Mary Anne*, published by Virago. Copyright © Lisa Hilton 2003.

Sheila Hodges: 'Editing Daphne du Maurier', published in *Women's History Review*, Vol. 11, No. 2, 2002. Copyright © Sheila Hodges 2002.

Michael Holroyd: Introduction to *The Du Mauriers*, published by Virago. Copyright © Michael Holroyd 2004.

Avril Horner and Sue Zlosnik: 'Glimpses of the Dark Side'. Copyright © Avril Horner and Sue Zlosnik 2007.

Mark Jancovich: '"Rebecca's Ghost": Horror, the Gothic and the du Maurier Film Adaptations'. Copyright © Mark Jancovich 2007.

Lisa Jardine: Introduction to *Golden Lads: A Study of Anthony Bacon, Francis, and Their Friends*, published by Virago. Copyright © Lisa Jardine 2007.

Francis King: Introduction to *The Winding Stair: Francis Bacon, His Rise and Fall*, published by Virago. Copyright © Francis King 2006.

Alison Light: Introduction to *The Rebecca Notebook and Other Memories*, published by Virago. Copyright © Alison Light 2004; '*Rebecca*: A Woman's Film?' first appeared as 'Rebecca', *Sight and Sound*, Vol. 6, No. 5, May 1996. Copyright © Alison Light 1996.

Acknowledgements

Rebecca Munford: 'Spectres of Authorship: Daphne du Maurier's Gothic Legacy'. © Rebecca Munford 2007.

Julie Myerson: Introduction to *Frenchman's Creek*, published by Virago. Copyright © Julie Myerson 2003; Introduction to *Julius*, published by Virago. Copyright © Julie Myerson 2004; Introduction to *The Parasites*, published by Virago. Copyright © Julie Myerson 2005.

Justine Picardie: Introduction to *The King's General*, published by Virago. Copyright © Justine Picardie 2004; Introduction to *The Infernal World of Branwell Brontë*, published by Virago. Copyright © Justine Picardie 2006.

Michèle Roberts: Introduction to *The Loving Spirit*, published by Virago. Copyright © Michèle Roberts 2003.

David Thomson: 'Du Maurier, Hitchcock and Holding an Audience', published as the Introduction to *The Birds and Other Stories*, Virago. Copyright © David Thomson 2004.

Minette Walters: Introduction to *The Rendezvous and Other Stories*, published by Virago. Copyright © Minette Walters 2005.

Michelene Wandor: 'Drama in Daphne du Maurier: Spirit and Letter'. Copyright © Michelene Wandor 2007.

Ella Westland: 'The View from Kilmarth: Daphne du Maurier's Cornwall'. Copyright © Ella Westland 2007; Introduction to *Rule Britannia*, published by Virago. Copyright © Ella Westland 2004.

Notes on Contributors

Lisa Appignanesi was born in Poland, and grew up in Paris and Montreal before moving to Britain. A university lecturer, she was a founder member of Writers and Readers Publishing Cooperative and then deputy director of London's Institute of Contemporary Arts. She is currently deputy president of English PEN and also a member of PEN's Writers in Prison Committee. She is also a noted broadcaster, critic and cultural commentator. Her translation (together with John Berger) of Nella Bielski's *The Year is 42* was awarded the 2005 Scott Moncrieff Prize for Translation and her novel *The Memory Man* won the 2005 Holocaust Literature Award and was shortlisted for the Commonwealth Writers' Prize.

Nina Auerbach is the John Welsh Centennial Professor of History and Literature, University of Pennsylvania, USA. She has written many books about demure women who are tougher and knottier than they look, including: *Woman and the Demon: The Life of a Victorian Myth; Ellen Terry, Player in her Time*; and *Daphne du Maurier, Haunted Heiress*.

Sally Beauman was born in Devon and graduated from Girton College, Cambridge. As a journalist, she has worked for *New York* magazine and has written for the *New Yorker*. In England, she has worked for the *Daily Telegraph*, for *Vogue*, and was editor of *Queen* magazine. She has published two works of non-fiction, including *The Royal Shakespeare Company: A History of Ten Decades*. She is the author of seven acclaimed novels that have been bestsellers worldwide, including the authorised sequel to *Rebecca*, *Rebecca's Tale*.

Nina Bawden, CBE, is one of Britain's most distinguished and best-loved novelists, both for adults and children (*The Peppermint Pig* and *Carrie's War* being among her most famous books for young people). She has published over forty novels and an auto-biography, *In My Own Time*. In 2004 she received the S.T. Dupont Golden Pen Award for a Lifetime's Contribution to Literature. She lives in London.

Charlotte Berry has a background in Scandinavian Studies and English Language, particularly Old Norse, Old English and modern Scandinavian literature. Following a period in Denmark studying History and teaching English, she trained as an archivist at the University of Wales Aberystwyth. She then worked at West Glamorgan Archive Service where she catalogued antiquarian and family/estate archive collections and specialised in local history. In 2003, she joined The University of Exeter Library, where she is Archivist, Special Collections, responsible for curating literary archives.

Celia Brayfield is the author of nine novels, the latest of which, *Wild Weekend*, is a social comedy that transposes conflict of rural and urban values from the play *She Stoops to Conquer* to a Suffolk village in the near future. Her most recent non-fiction book is *Deep France*, an account of her year as a writer in a small village in the Bearn. Her early success with three international genre bestsellers led to the publication of *Bestseller*, a study of popular fiction writing. She heads the creative writing programme at Brunel University in London and also writes regularly for *The Times* and other publications. Currently she is working on a study of arts journalism and a historical novel set in sixteenth-century England. For more information, see her website, www.celiabrayfield.com.

Amanda Craig was brought up in Italy and Britain. Educated at Bedales and Clare College Cambridge, she worked in journalism before becoming a full-time novelist. She is the author of five novels, *Foreign Bodies, A Private Place, A Vicious Circle, In a Dark Wood* and *Love In Idleness*, and is currently at work on her new novel, *Night and Day*, forthcoming in 2007. She lives in London and contributes regularly to the *Daily Telegraph*, the *Independent on Sunday* and *The New Statesman*. She is also the children's book critic for *The Times*.

Michelle de Kretser was born in Sri Lanka and emigrated to Australia when she was fourteen. Having studied French at Melbourne University, she spent a year teaching in Montpellier before doing an MA in Paris. She has taught literature at Melbourne University and worked as an editor and a reviewer. Michelle de Kretser is the author of two critically acclaimed novels: *The Rose Grower* and *The Hamilton Case*, which has won several awards. She lives in Melbourne.

Maria di Battista is Professor of English and Comparative Literature at Princeton University, USA. Her books include: *Virginia Woolf: The Fables of Anon; First Love: The Affections of Modern Fiction*, and, as co-editor and contributor, *High and Low Moderns: British Literature and Culture 1889–1939*. Her most recent book is *Fast Talking Dames*. She has also written numerous articles on modern literature and film.

Sarah Dunant is an internationally bestselling author, who has become renowned for her historical novels set in Italy. She set her first, *The Birth of Venus*, in Florence and *The Company of the Courtesan* is set in Venice. Both books have been translated into over thirty languages and have received major international acclaim. Sarah Dunant has worked widely in television, radio and in print, and has written eight novels and edited two books of essays. She lives in London and Florence.

Elaine Dundy was born in New York. She worked as an actress in Paris and London, where she met her first husband, the *enfant terrible* of British theatre critics, Kenneth Tynan. Her first novel, *The Dud Avocado*, based on the year that she spent in Paris, was an immediate bestseller on both sides of the Atlantic. Two more novels and two plays followed. In 1964, divorced from Tynan, she returned to America where she wrote extensively for magazines. She is also the author of several biographies, including *Elvis and Gladys*, and an autobiography, *Life Itself!* Elaine Dundy lives in Los Angeles.

Sunie Fletcher left school at sixteen and worked in music journalism, radio and television. After six years at MTV Europe, where she was Senior Manager Talent Production, she read for a BA at Queen Mary, London, an MA at Birkbeck College, London, and a PhD at the University of Exeter. Her research interests include female aesthete writers of the late 19th and early 20th centuries, the novels of Dickens, and the links between Victorian fine art and literature. She teaches at the Universities of Exeter and Plymouth.

Margaret Forster was born in Carlisle and educated at Somerville College, Oxford, where she read History. She is an award-winning novelist and biographer. Her biographies include those of Elizabeth Barrett Browning (winner of the Heinemann Award) and Daphne du Maurier (winner of the Fawcett Society Book Prize). She wrote about her mother and grandmother in *Hidden Lives*, and the follow-up volume, *Precious Lives*, was awarded the J. R. Ackerley Prize. Margaret Forster's recent novels are: *Diary of an Ordinary Woman: A Novel*; *Is There Anything You Want?*; and *Keeping the World Away*. Margaret Forster lives in London and the Lake District.

Antonia Fraser was made CBE in 1999, and awarded the Norton Medlicott Medal by the Historical Association in 2000. Since 1969, Antonia Fraser has written many acclaimed historical works which have been international bestsellers, including *Marie Antoinette, Mary Queen of Scots* (James Tait Black Memorial Prize), *Cromwell: Our Chief of Men, The Six Wives of Henry VIII* and *The Gunpowder Plot:Terror and Faith in 1605* (St Louis Literary Award; CWA Non-Fiction Gold Dagger). She is married to the playwright Harold Pinter and lives in London.

Jessica Gardner is Head of Special Collections, University of Exeter Library, where the du Maurier family archives are held. She is co-author of *Modern Literary Papers in the University of Exeter Library*, and previously worked on the archives of *Stand* and *London Magazine* at the University of Leeds, where she took her doctorate in the School of English.

Helen Hanson is Lecturer in Film Studies, University of Exeter. Her publications include: *Hollywood's Gothic Heroines*; 'Sound Affects: Post-Production Sound, Soundscapes and Sound Design in Hollywood's Studio Era,' *Sound Journal*; 'Sounds of the City: the Sonic Fabric of Film Noir,' in Peter Franklin and Robyn Stillwell, eds., *The Cambridge Companion to Film Music*; and 'From *Suspicion* (1941) to *Deceived* (1991): Gothic Continuities, Feminism and Postfeminism in the Neo-Gothic Film,' *Gothic Studies*.

Melanie Heeley regards the study of literature as her first love, though she began her academic career studying Physics at York University. She then worked in computing for fifteen years, studying English part-time, before returning to full-time education. She organises the Nottingham branch of the nationwide debating society, Café Scientifique and Culturel, and is currently studying for her PhD at the University of Loughborough, focusing on psychology, religion and politics in the life and work of Daphne du Maurier.

Lisa Hilton studied English at New College, Oxford and art history in Florence and Paris. She is the author of *Athenais: The Real Queen of France* and *Mistress Peachum's Pleasure*, and is currently working on her third biography. She is a regular contributor to the *Observer* and a reviewer for the *Sunday Telegraph*. Lisa Hilton presently lives in Milan.

Sheila Hodges edited all of Daphne du Maurier's work for nearly forty years, from 1943 to 1981. She joined the publishing firm of Victor Gollancz in 1936 in an editorial capacity, becoming Assistant Managing Director in 1943. She left in 1953, and worked as a freelance editor and reader for Gollancz and other publishers. Her books include histories of Gollancz and Dulwich College, as well as a biography of Lorenzo Da Ponte, the librettist of Mozart's three most famous operas. In addition, she has contributed to various music journals, including *The Music Review* and *Opera Quarterly*.

Michael Holroyd's biographies of Lytton Strachey, Augustus John and Bernard Shaw have established him as one of the most influential biographers of modern times. He is President of the Royal Society of Literature and has lectured around the world for the British Council and at literary festivals. He holds honorary degrees from the universities of Ulster, Sheffield, Warwick, East Anglia and the London School of Economics. He has also written two volumes of autobiography, *Basil Street Blues* and *Mosaic*. In 1989 Michael Holroyd was awarded the CBE for services to literature and in 2005 was awarded the David Cohen British Literature Prize.

Avril Horner is Professor of English at Kingston University, London. She has co-authored many articles and book chapters with Sue Zlosnik, with whom she wrote *Daphne du Maurier: Writing, Identity and the Gothic Imagination* and *Landscapes of Desire: Metaphors in Modern Women's Fiction*. Her most recent books are (with Sue Zlosnik) *Gothic and the Comic Turn* and an edited collection entitled *European Gothic: A Spirited Exchange, 1760–1960*. She is currently working with Janet Beer on *Edith Wharton: Sex, Satire and the Older Woman*, to be published in 2008.

Mark Jancovich is Professor of Film and Television Studies, University of East Anglia. He is the author of many books, including: *Horror, Rational Fears: American Horror in the 1950s*, and, with Lucy Faire and Sarah Stubbings, *The Place of the Audience: Cultural Geographies of Film Consumption*. He has also edited several collections, including *Horror, The Film Reader* and, with James Lyons, *Quality Popular Television: Cult TV, the Industry and Fans*. He is currently working on a study of horror in 1940s American cinema.

Lisa Jardine, **CBE**, is Director of the AHRB Research Centre for Editing Lives and Letters, and Centenary Professor of Renaissance Studies at Queen Mary, University of London. She is a Fellow of the Royal Historical Society, an Honorary Fellow of King's College and Jesus College, Cambridge, and holds honorary doctorates from the Universities of St Andrews and Sheffield Hallam. She writes and reviews for the major UK national newspapers and magazines, and has presented and appears regularly on arts, history and current affairs programmes for TV and radio. She was Chair of Judges for the 2002 Man Booker Prize, and has judged the 1996 Whitbread Prize, the 1999 Guardian First Book Award, the Orwell Prize, and was Chair of Judges for the 1997 Orange Prize. Lisa Jardine is married with three children. She lives in London.

Francis King was born in Switzerland and spent his childhood in India, where his father was a government official. While still an undergraduate at Oxford he published his first three novels. He then joined the British Council, working in Italy, Greece, Egypt, Finland and Japan, before he resigned to devote himself entirely to writing. For some years he was drama critic for the *Sunday Telegraph* and he reviews fiction regularly for the *Spectator*. He is a former winner of the Somerset Maugham Prize, of the Katherine Mansfield Prize and of the *Yorkshire Post* Novel of the Year Award.

Alison Light is a freelance writer and Visiting Professor in the Department of Cultural Studies, University of East London, where she has helped establish a research centre in history. A study of Daphne du Maurier formed part of her book, *Forever England: Literature, Femininity and Conservatism between the Wars*. She has edited for Penguin Classics Virginia Woolf's spoof biography, *Flush*, and is the author of *Mrs Woolf and the Servants*. She contributed the chapter on biography and autobiography since 1970 to *The Cambridge History of Twentieth Century English Literature* and contributes regularly to the *London Review of Books*.

Rebecca Munford is Lecturer in English, Cardiff University. She has written on twentieth-century women's writing, the Gothic and contemporary feminist theory and popular culture. She is the editor of *Revisiting Angela Carter: Texts, Contexts, Intertexts* and co-editor of *Third Wave Feminism: A Critical Exploration*. Forthcoming work includes the co-authored (with S. Gillis), *Feminism and Popular Culture: Readings in Post-Feminism* and *Decadent Daughters and Monstrous Mothers: Angela Carter and the European Gothic*.

Julie Myerson was born in Nottingham. She read English at Bristol University and has worked for the National Theatre and in publishing. Her novels include *Sleepwalking, The Touch, Me and the Fat Man, Laura Blundy, Something Might Happen* (which was long-listed for the Man Booker Prize) and *The Story of You*. Her works of non-fiction are *Home: The Story of Everyone Who Ever Lived in our House* and a memoir about PE at school – *Not a Games Person*. She also works as a journalist and contributes reviews and articles to newspapers, magazines and radio programmes.

Justine Picardie is the author of several books including *If the Spirit Moves You: Life and Love After Death, Wish I May*, and *My Mother's Wedding Dress*. She was formerly the features editor of *Vogue*, and is a columnist for *Harper's Bazaar* and the *Sunday Telegraph*. Her new book is a novel about Daphne du Maurier, to be published by Bloomsbury in 2007.

Michèle Roberts is half-French and half-English. She has written twelve novels, three collections of poetry, two of short stories and one of essays. Her novel, *Daughters of the House*, was shortlisted for the Booker Prize, 1992, and won the W.H. Smith Literary Award, 1993. She turned down an OBE in 2002, but is a *Chevalier dans l'Ordre des Arts et des Lettres*. She is Professor of Creative Writing, University of East Anglia.

David Thomson was born in London and educated at Dulwich College and the London School of Film Technique. He has lived in California since 1975. Thomson is widely regarded as the pre-eminent film-writer of his time, with a reputation that spans both sides of the Atlantic. His books include: the *New Biographical Dictionary of Film*; *The Whole Equation: A History of Hollywood*; *Rosebud: The Story of Orson Welles* and *In Nevada*.

Minette Walters is England's bestselling female crime writer. She was born in Hertfordshire and read French at Durham University. She is the author of eleven novels, two novellas, and a number of short stories. Her work, which has been published in more than thirty-five countries, has received several major awards, including the CWA John Creasey Award, the Edgar Allan Poe Award and two CWA Gold Daggers for Fiction. Minette Walters lives in Dorset.

Michelene Wandor is a playwright, poet, fiction writer and musician, as well as Royal Literary Fund Fellow, Birkbeck College, 2005–2007. In 1987, she was the first woman playwright to have had a drama on one of the National Theatre's main stages – *The Wandering Jew*; in the same year her adaptation of *The Belle of Amherst* won an International Emmy for Thames TV. She has written original radio plays and dramatisations (novels by Dostoyevsky, Jane Austen, George Eliot, Kipling, Sara Paretsky and Margaret Drabble), many nominated for awards, and written books on contemporary theatre. For BBC Radio 4, she has dramatised Daphne du Maurier's novels, *The King's General* and *Frenchman's Creek*, and short story, 'The Little Photographer'.

Ella Westland studied for her Harvard doctorate in her thirties and moved to Cornwall in 1989 as Lecturer in The University of Exeter's Department of Lifelong Learning. She was one of the founders of the annual Daphne du Maurier Festival, Fowey, and is the author of *Reader's Guide to Daphne du Maurier*. She has published on education, place, romantic fiction and Victorian culture, and is working on a book about Dickens and the sea. She lives on the south coast of Cornwall, and can look across the bay to Kilmarth and the Gribben from the cliffs nearby.

Sue Zlosnik is Professor of English at Manchester Metropolitan University. She has co-authored many articles and book chapters with Avril Horner, with whom she wrote *Daphne du Maurier: Writing, Identity and the Gothic Imagination* and *Landscapes* *of Desire: Metaphors in Modern Women's Fiction.* Her most recent book is (with Avril Horner) *Gothic and the Comic Turn.* In addition to editing an issue of *Gothic Studies* she has also recently published essays on Robert Louis Stevenson, George Meredith and J. R. R. Tolkien. An essay on the fiction of Patrick McGrath is forthcoming in an interdisciplinary collection entitled *Liminality.*

Notes and References

Introduction

[1] Margaret Forster, *Daphne du Maurier* (London: Chatto & Windus, 1993), p.416.

[2] Daphne du Maurier, *The Rebecca Notebook and Other Memories* (London: Virago, 2004), p.55.

[3] Correspondence between Daphne du Maurier and Victor Gollancz, Gollancz Papers, Modern Records Centre, University of Warwick; Oriel Malet, ed., *Daphne du Maurier: Letters from Menabilly: Portrait of a Friendship* (London: Weidenfeld & Nicolson, 1993).

[4] Tessa Montgomery, 'Daphne du Maurier – a daughter's memoir', unpublished lecture, 2005.

[5] Daphne du Maurier, *The Rebecca Notebook*, p.57.

[6] Oriel Malet, ed., *Daphne du Maurier*, pp. 3 and 173.

[7] Oriel Malet, ed., *Daphne du Maurier*, pp.59 and 106; *'Let's Pretend':The Make-Believe World of Daphne du Maurier*, Banner Pictures-Westward TV, 1977.

[8] Oriel Malet, ed., *Daphne du Maurier*, p.31.

[9] *Ibid.*, p.195.

[10] Margaret Forster, *Daphne du Maurier*, p.167; Oriel Malet, p.293.

[11] Oriel Malet, pp.263 and 59–60.

[12] This account from telephone conversation between Margaret Forster and Helen Taylor, 22 March 2006.

[13] Roger Bromley,'The gentry, bourgeois hegemony and popular fiction: *Rebecca* and *Rogue Male*' (1981), in Peter Humm, Paul Stigant and Peter Widdowson, eds., *Popular Fictions: Essays in Literature and History* (London: Methuen, 1986), pp.151–172;

Richard Kelly, *Daphne du Maurier* (Boston: G.K. Hall, 1987); Alison Light, *Forever England: Femininity, Literature and Conservatism Between the Wars* (London: Routledge, 1991); Avril Horner and Sue Zlosnik, *Daphne du Maurier: Writing, Identity and the Gothic Imagination* (Basingstoke: Macmillan, 1998); and Nina Auerbach, *Daphne du Maurier: Haunted Heiress* (Philadelphia: University of Pennsylvania Press, 2000).

14   Questionnaire and interview material in response to Helen Taylor, Daphne du Maurier Festival, May 2005.

15   Graham Busby and Zoë Hambly, 'Literary Tourism and the Daphne du Maurier Festival', Philip Payton, ed., *Cornish Studies, Second Series: Eight* (Exeter: University of Exeter Press, 2000), pp.197 and 201.

16   *Ibid.*, p.199.

17   Jonathan Aberdeen, Interview with Helen Taylor, Fowey, 12 May 2005.

18   Margaret Forster, *Daphne du Maurier*, p.42.

PART 1

Interview With Sheila Hodges, Daphne du Maurier's Editor, 1943–1981

1   Du Maurier dates the writing of the book as 1931, two years before publication in 1933, when she was twenty-six – Ed.

Editing Daphne du Maurier

1   Daphne du Maurier, *The Parasites* (London: Gollancz, 1949), p.31.

2   Margaret Forster, *Daphne du Maurier* (London: Chatto & Windus, 1993), p.273.

3   Daphne du Maurier to Sheila Hodges, 13 October 1974.

4   Daphne du Maurier, *Growing Pains* [later, *Myself When Young*] (London: Gollancz, 1977), p.40.

5   Daphne du Maurier, 'A Borderline Case', *Not After Midnight* (London: Gollancz, 1971), p.157.
6   Daphne du Maurier, *The Loving Spirit* (London: Heinemann, 1931, reprt. Pan Books, 1976), p.259.
7   Daphne du Maurier, *The King's General* (London: Gollancz, 1946), p.8.
8   Daphne du Maurier, *Mary Anne* (London: Gollancz, 1954), p.117.
9   Daphne du Maurier, *The House on the Strand* (London: Gollancz, 1969), p.96.
10   Daphne du Maurier, *Growing Pains*, p.157.
11   *The Daily Telegraph*, 20 April 1989.
12   Daphne du Maurier to Sheila Hodges, 24 June 1976. Houses were always very important to her, both the ones where she lived and those which she visited with her two sisters as a child.

   She sometimes changed her mind about the degree to which she had identified. Writing to me she gave *The Scapegoat* as an example in which she had done so, but in a letter written in 1956 to her friend, Oriel Malet, she said that so far as she could realise, the characters in this book were completely imaginary, while with *My Cousin Rachel* (1951) she identified to such a degree that she felt she was writing her autobiography. See Oriel Malet, *Daphne du Maurier: Letters from Menabilly* (London: Weidenfeld & Nicolson, 1993), p.80.
13   Daphne du Maurier to Foy Quiller-Couch, 3 June 1959.
14   Daphne du Maurier to Sheila Hodges, 2 April 1959.
15   Daphne du Maurier to Sheila Hodges, 16 July 1952.
16   Daphne du Maurier, *Growing Pains*, p.162.
17   *The Parasites*, 'The Birds', *The Progress of Julius*, *The Scapegoat*, *Mary Anne*, *The Apple Tree*, *The House on the Strand*.
18   Daphne du Maurier to Victor Gollancz, 30 November 1953.
19   Daphne du Maurier, *The Rebecca Notebook* (London: Gollancz, 1981), pp.162–63.

[20] Daphne du Maurier, *Growing Pains*, p.70.

[21] Daphne du Maurier, *The King's General*, p.233.

[22] A. L. Rowse, *Friends and Contemporaries* (London: Methuen, 1989), p.270.

[23] Daphne du Maurier to Leo Walmsley, 26 May 1933.

[24] Daphne du Maurier to Victor Gollancz, 22 January 1952.

[25] Daphne du Maurier to Foy Quiller-Couch, 3 June 1959.

[26] Daphne du Maurier, *Not After Midnight*, p.259.

[27] Daphne du Maurier, *The House on the Strand* (London: Gollancz, 1969).

[28] A. L. Rowse, *Friends and Contemporaries*, p.270.

[29] Daphne du Maurier, *The House on the Strand*, p.51.

[30] *Ibid.*, p.202.

[31] Daphne du Maurier to Sheila Hodges, 18 October 1968.

[32] Daphne du Maurier to Victor Gollancz, 29 December 1953.

[33] Daphne du Maurier to Sheila Hodges, 18 July 1969.

[34] Oriel Malet, *Daphne du Maurier*, pp.80–81.

[35] Daphne du Maurier to Sheila Hodges, 14 October 1978.

PART 2

Spectres of Authorship: Daphne du Maurier's Gothic Legacy

[1] Angela Carter, 'Charlotte Brontë: *Jane Eyre*' (1990), in *Expletives Deleted: Selected Writings* (London: Vintage, 1992), pp.161–72 (p.163).

[2] Alison Light, '"Returning to Manderley" – Romance Fiction, Female Sexuality and Class', *Feminist Review*, 16 (1984), pp.7–25 and Avril Horner and Sue Zlosnik, *Daphne du Maurier: Writing, Identity and the Gothic Imagination* (Basingstoke: Palgrave Macmillan, 1998), p.69.

[3] Nina Auerbach, *Daphne du Maurier: Haunted Heiress* (Philadelphia: University of Pennsylvania Press, 2002), p.119.

4   Horner and Zlosnik, p.2.

5   Horner and Zlosnik, pp.24–25.

6   For more on this, see Joanna Russ's description of the patterns of similitude characterising 'drugstore Gothics', most of which 'advertise themselves as "in the du Maurier tradition", "in the Gothic tradition of *Rebecca*", and so on'. Joanna Russ, 'Somebody's Trying to Kill Me and I Think It's My Husband: The Modern Gothic', in *The Female Gothic*, ed. Juliann E. Fleenor (Montreal: Eden Press, 1983), p.31.

7   Anne Williams, *Art of Darkness: A Poetics of Gothic* (Chicago: University of Chicago Press, 1995), p.101.

8   See Susanne Becker, *Gothic Forms of Feminine Fictions* (Manchester: Manchester University Press, 1999), p.151.

9   Margaret Atwood, *Lady Oracle* (London: Virago, 1982), p.34.

10   Avril Horner and Sue Zlosnik, 'Daphne du Maurier and Gothic Signatures: Rebecca as Vamp(ire)', in *Body Matters: Feminism, Textuality, Corporeality*, ed. Avril Horner and Angela Keane (Manchester: Manchester University Press, 2000), pp. 209–22 (p.215).

11   Ellen Moers, *Literary Women* (London: Women's Press, 1978), p.91.

12   Angela Carter, 'The Bloody Chamber', in *The Bloody Chamber and Other Stories* (London: Vintage, 1995), pp.7–41 (p.7).

13   Elaine Showalter, *A Literature of their Own: From Charlotte Brontë to Doris Lessing* [1977], rev. and expand. edn (London: Virago, 1999), p.329.

14   Daphne du Maurier, *Rebecca* (London: Virago, 2003), p.35.

15   Carter, 'The Bloody Chamber', p.24.

16   *Ibid.*, p.16.

17   *Ibid.*, p.10.

18   Daphne du Maurier, *Rebecca*, p.15.

19   Carter, 'The Bloody Chamber', p.8.

20   *Ibid.*, p.10.

21 Daphne du Maurier, *Rebecca*, pp.27–28.
22 Susanne Becker, *Gothic Forms of Feminine Fictions* (Manchester: Manchester University Press, 1999), p.68.

Rebecca's Afterlife: Sequels and Other Echoes

1   See Richard Kelly, *Daphne du Maurier* (Boston: Twayne, 1987), pp.23–4, and Margaret Forster, *Daphne du Maurier* (London: Chatto & Windus, 1993), pp.218–19; Elizabeth von Arnim, *Vera* (London: Macmillan, 1921 and Virago, 1988).

2   *Harper's & Queen*, November 1976, pp.84–88.

3   Forster, n.1, p.441.

4   Malcolm Kelsall makes the interesting point that *Rebecca*'s title is a 'cultural sign that this is a romance . . . the coupling of her name with Manderley places the novel in a long tradition of silver fork or Cinderella tales marked by titles such as *Marcella, Camilla, Pamela*', 'Manderley Revisited: *Rebecca* and the English Country House', *1992 Lectures and Memoirs* (Proceedings of the British Academy, Oxford University Press, 1992), p.304.

5   See Alison Light, *Forever England: Femininity, Literature and Conservatism Between the Wars* (London: Routledge, 1991), p.158, and Avril Horner and Sue Zlosnik, *Daphne du Maurier: Writing, Identity and the Gothic Imagination* (London: Macmillan, 1998).

6   Joanna Russ, 'Somebody's Trying to Kill Me and I Think It's My Husband: The Modern Gothic', *Journal of Popular Culture* 6, no.4 (Spring 1973), p.144.

7   Kari J. Winter, *Subjects of Slavery, Agents of Change: Women and Power in Gothic Novels and Slave Narratives, 1790–1865* (Athens and London: University of Georgia Press, 1992), p.146.

8   See Patsy Stoneman, *Brontë Transformations: The Cultural*

Dissemination of Jane Eyre *and* Wuthering Heights (London: Prentice Hall/Harvester Wheatsheaf, 1996).

9   Ken Follett, *The Key to Rebecca* (London: Hamish Hamilton, 1980), features a Second-World-War Nazi spy in Egypt, carrying a copy of the novel, which is used in order to send coded messages about British military planning. Follett chooses the novel as quintessentially English, and makes faint allusion to its theme of jealousy for a 'haunting' first wife. He may also have chosen this text because du Maurier began to write the novel in Egypt in the late 1930s. Stephen King's *Bag of Bones* (London: Hodder & Stoughton, 1998) features successful writer and new widower, Mike Noonan, suffering from writer's block, who uses the novel to signify the importance of beloved and haunted places, and also to conjure up the power of dream/nightmares in unstable minds. For one of three epigraphs, *Bag of Bones* takes a quotation from the first pages of the novel, and Noonan − quoting − says, 'If there is any more beautiful and haunting first line in English fiction, I've never read it,' p.41.

10 David Roach Pierson, *Jeanne de Winter at the Wars* (London: Minerva, 1996).

11 Susan Hill, *Mrs de Winter: The Sequel to Daphne du Maurier's* Rebecca (London: Sinclair-Stevenson, 1993); Sally Beauman, *Rebecca's Tale* (London: Little, Brown, 2001); Antonia Fraser, 'Rebecca's Story', *Harpers & Queen*, November 1976; Mary Wings, *Divine Victim* (London: The Women's Press, 1992); Maureen Freely, *The Other Rebecca* (London: Bloomsbury, 1996). Maggie O'Farrell, *My Lover's Lover* (London: Headline Review, 2002), pp.40−43.

12 Mary Wings, 'Rebecca Redux: Tears on a Lesbian Pillow', in Liz Gibbs, ed., *Daring to Dissent: Lesbian Culture from Margin to Mainstream* (London: Cassell, 1994), p.32.

13 Interview between Helen Taylor and Maureen Freely, Bath, March 1997.

PART 3

Who I Am: Adventures in the du Maurier Family Archive

1   The du Maurier family archive is held in the Special Collections of the University of Exeter Library, where the papers are known as EUL MS 144 and EUL MS 207.

2   The archive includes a mid-twentieth-century copy of a memorandum dated 25 May 1863, concerning the suppression of Mary Anne Clarke's letters and memoirs (reference EUL MS 144/1/10/3). Daphne du Maurier used the text of this document to reproduce the contract between Clarke and the Duke of York in *The Du Mauriers*. A few copies of her memoirs did, however, survive: see for instance Mary Anne Clarke, *Recollections of Mrs Mary Anne Clarke. A Secret History of Court and Cabinet*, [1816]. The National Archives, reference TS 11/120.

3   A research assistant working on her behalf did trace correspondence between Mary Anne Clarke and figures other than the Duke of York to Berkshire Record Office: see BRO D/EPb (Pleydell-Bouverie).

4   See EUL MS 207/2/12.

5   See EUL MS 144/1/9/3, 'Busson research file no. 1', typescript introduction to *The Glass-Blowers*.

6   See EUL MS 144/1/9/3, 'Busson research file no.1'.

7   See EUL MS 207/1/1, MS 207/2/13 and EUL MS 207/2/19.

8   See EUL MS 144/1/9/3, 'Busson research file no. 1', and 'Busson research file no. 2'.

9   See EUL MS 144/1/9/3, 'Busson research file no. 1', typescript introduction to *The Glass-Blowers*.

10 See EUL MS 144/1/9/3, 'Busson research file no. 1', typescript introduction to *The Glass-Blowers*.

11 See EUL MS 144/1/10/1.

12 Lisa Hilton, 'Introduction', *Mary Anne* (2004), p.x.

13 See EUL MS 207/6/25.

14 Michael Holroyd, 'Introduction', *The Du Mauriers* (2004), p.x.

15 See EUL MS 207/2/13.

16 See EUL MS 207/2/13.

17 See EUL MS 144/2 and EUL MS 207/2.

18 See EUL MS 207/2/15.

19 For instance, in *Gerald*, Daphne du Maurier reproduced the first item pasted into the albums, a telegram congratulating George du Maurier on the birth of his youngest child: 'Welcome big little stranger [.] health just drunk with all the honours . . .'. The reference for the albums is EUL MS 207/4/1–2.

20 The notebook is known as EUL MS 207/4/3.

21 National Portrait Gallery, accession reference AX45600–AX45645.

22 A large quantity of papers from the Llewelyn-Davies side of the du Maurier family were sold at auction at Sotheby's on 16 December 2004, as part of 'The archive of J. M. Barrie and "The Lost Boys"', Lots 269 to 295. This archive had been acquired from Andrew Birkin from Nico Llewelyn-Davies. Many of the papers from this private collection were used by Birkin in his publication, *J. M. Barrie and the Lost Boys* (London: Macdonald Futura, 1980).

23 Following the release of the film of *Rebecca*, an American author came forward to claim du Maurier had copied one of her books when she wrote *Rebecca*. The case came to court in 1947, and the 'Rebecca notebook', with its first sketch of the novel's plot and characters, was presented as evidence. The case was found in du Maurier's favour.

The View From Kilmarth: Daphne du Maurier's Cornwall

1 Daphne du Maurier, *Enchanted Cornwall*, ed. Piers Dudgeon (London: Michael Joseph, 1989), p.7.

2   Daphne du Maurier, *The House on the Strand*, first published 1969 (London: Virago, 2003), p.188. Further references are given as *HS*.

3   Daphne du Maurier, *Myself When Young*, first published 1977 (London: Virago, 2004), pp.102–103.

4   Angela du Maurier, *It's Only the Sister: An Autobiography*, first published 1951 (Mount Hawke, Cornwall: Truran, 2003), pp.140–142. Further references are given as *AM*.

5   Oriel Malet, ed., *Letters from Menabilly: Portrait of a Friendship* (London: Orion, 1994), p.131, 15/1/62. Further references are given as *LM*.

6   Daphne du Maurier, *The King's General*, first published 1946 (London: Virago, 2004), p.287.

7   Daphne du Maurier, *Rebecca*, first published 1938 (London: Virago, 2003), p.2.

8   *The 'Rebecca' Notebook and Other Memories*, first published 1981 (London: Virago, 2005), p.149. Further references are given as *RN*.

Christianity Versus Paganism: Daphne du Maurier's Divided Mind

1   Daphne du Maurier, 'Apostasis'. Victor Gollancz Papers, Modern Records Centre, University of Warwick, MSS.157/3/I/DM/14.i. The poem appears with a letter dated 23 November 1955 and was written shortly before. The word apostasis has its counterpart in Greek so it is fitting that it should be in Greek characters. Permission to include excerpts from the correspondence between Victor Gollancz and Daphne du Maurier, including the full text of the poem 'Apostasis', has been given by Livia Gollancz and Christian Browning.

2   Victor Gollancz, *From Darkness to Light – A Confession of Faith in the Form of an Anthology* (London: Victor Gollancz, 1956). Although the anthology is not stated by name in the letter that

accompanies the poem, from the date – 23 November 1955 – it would seem evident that this is the anthology in question.

3   Daphne du Maurier, from a letter to Victor Gollancz dated 23 November 1955. Victor Gollancz Papers, *op. cit.*, MSS. 157/3/I/DM/13. 'The Double' refers to the working title of her novel *The Scapegoat*.

4   George du Maurier, *Trilby* (London: Dent, 1978), p.216.

5   Daphne du Maurier, from a letter to Victor Gollancz dated 18 May 1953. Victor Gollancz Papers, *op. cit.*, MSS. 157/3/LI/MFT/1/47.i. Please bear in mind, however, that Gollancz's initial act of apostasis was a rebellion against the orthodox Judaism of his father – when he rebelled he turned to liberal Judaism and then to Christianity. As in the case of du Maurier, Gollancz's apostasis could not be described as a clean break with a tradition – and was never formalised. Gollancz never really forgot his Jewish background and continued to adhere to some of its laws. For an explanation of the ambiguities and complexities in Gollancz's political and religious views, and how these developed with time, see Ruth Edwards, *Victor Gollancz – A Biography* (London: Gollancz, 1987).

6   Daphne du Maurier, 'This I Believe', *The Rebecca Notebook – And Other Memories* (London: Pan, 1982), p.101.

7   Daphne du Maurier, from a letter to Victor Gollancz dated 31 March 1958. Victor Gollancz Papers, *op. cit.*, MSS.157/3/1/DM/21.

8   Daphne du Maurier, from a letter to Maureen Baker-Munton dated 4 July 1957, in Margaret Forster, *Daphne du Maurier* (London: Arrow, 1994), p.422. Reproduced with permission of Curtis Brown Group Ltd, London on behalf of the Estate of Daphne du Maurier. Copyright © Daphne du Maurier, 1957.

9   Daphne du Maurier, from a letter to Oriel Malet dated Whit Sunday, 1956, in Oriel Malet, ed., *Letters from Menabilly:*

Portrait of a Friendship (London: Orion, 1994), p.71.
10   Carl Jung, 'Mind and Earth', *Vol 10 The Collected Works of C. G. Jung – Civilization in Transition* (London: Routledge, 1974), p.29.
11   Daphne du Maurier, 'This I Believe', *op. cit.*, p.108.
12   Daphne du Maurier, *Jamaica Inn* (London: Virago, 2005), p.13.
13   Daphne du Maurier, 'Remembrance Day', Du Maurier Papers, Exeter University Library, EUL MS207/6/24. The paper on which this poem is printed states 'Reprinted from *The Observer* – November 10, 1946.' Permission to include the full text of the poem, 'Remembrance Day', has been given by Christian Browning.

The Scapegoat by Lisa Appignanesi
1   Margaret Atwood, *Negotiating with the Dead* (Cambridge: Cambridge University Press, 2002).

The Glass-Blowers by Michelle de Kretser
1   Margaret Forster, *Daphne du Maurier* (London: Arrow, 1994), p. 324

Tales of Awe and Arousal: Animals Invade
1   Daphne du Maurier, *Jamaica Inn* (New York: Avon Books, 1971), p. 263.
2   Daphne du Maurier, 'The Blue Lenses', *Echoes from the Macabre* (New York: Avon Books, 1978).
3   Daphne du Maurier, 'The Chamois', *Echoes from the Macabre* (New York: Avon Books, 1978).
4   Angela Carter, *The Bloody Chamber and Other Stories* (Middlesex: Penguin Books, 1981).

5   Daphne du Maurier, 'Not After Midnight', *Echoes from the Macabre* (New York: Avon Books, 1978).

6   Daphne du Maurier, 'Kiss Me Again, Stranger', *Echoes from the Macabre* (New York: Avon Books, 1978).

7   Margaret Forster discusses at length and in depth du Maurier's metamorphosis into 'the boy in the box' when she fell in love with women. See *Daphne du Maurier: The Secret Life of the Renowned Novelist* (New York: Doubleday, 1993), esp. pp.221–3 and 421–2.

Glimpses of the Dark Side

1   See du Maurier's letter to Maureen Baker-Munton, included as an appendix in Margaret Forster's *Daphne du Maurier* (London: Chatto & Windus, 1993), p.422 for the claim that the Old Man's jealousy was based on that of du Maurier's husband for their son, Kits Browning.

2   *The Apple Tree* was first published by Gollancz in 1952; the same collection was published by Penguin Books in 1963, Arrow in 1992 and Virago in 2004 as *The Birds and Other Stories*.

3   *The Breaking Point* was first published by Gollancz in 1959; the same collection was published by Penguin Books in 1970 as *The Blue Lenses and Other Stories*.

4   First published by Gollancz in 1971 in the collection *Not After Midnight and Other Stories*; the same collection was published by Penguin Books in 1973 as *Don't Look Now*.

5   Forster, p.437 and p.440.

6   Oriel Malet, ed., *Daphne du Maurier: Letters from Menabilly* (London: Weidenfield & Nicolson, 1993), p.194.

7   See Avril Horner and Sue Zlosnik, *Daphne du Maurier: Writing, Identity and the Gothic Imagination* (Basingstoke: Macmillan, 1998), Chapter 1 in particular, for a fuller discussion of how du Maurier perceived her creative imagination as a 'boy-in-the-box' and as a 'disembodied spirit'.

Golden Lads: A Study of Anthony Bacon, Francis, and Their Friends

1   Daphne du Maurier to Oriel Malet, 5 November 1972, Kilmarth. Oriel Malet ed., *Daphne Du Maurier: Letters from Menabilly: Portrait of a Friendship* (London: Weidenfeld & Nicolson, 1993), p.262. I am extremely grateful to Professor Alan Stewart for drawing this source to my attention, and for generously sharing his own preliminary researches on du Maurier's work on Anthony Bacon with me.

2   Du Maurier to Malet, 9 February 1975, Kilmarth. Malet, *Letters*, p.273.

3   Du Maurier to Malet, 22 November 1972, Kilmarth. Malet, *Letters*, p.262.

4   Du Maurier, *The Winding Stair* (London: Virago, 2006), p.68.

5   Du Maurier, *The Winding Stair*, pp.193–4.

6   Du Maurier to Malet, 9 January 1976, Kilmarth. Malet, *Letters*, p.276.

7   Judith Cook, *Daphne: A Portrait of Daphne Du Maurier* (London: Bantam Press, 1991), p.277.

PART 4

'Rebecca's Ghost': Horror, the Gothic and the du Maurier Film Adaptations

1   Barbara Klinger, 'Cinema's Shadow: Reconsidering Non-Theatrical Exhibition' in Richard Maltby, Melvyn Stokes and Robert C. Allen, ed., *Going to the Movies: The Social Experience of Hollywood Cinema* (Exeter: University of Exeter Press, forthcoming).

2   The use of the term 'quality' is not used here as a judgement on the films but rather as a description of the ways

in which the films were presented to their audiences as films that signified 'quality' through their production values and their status as literary adaptations.

[3] Bosley Crowther, '*My Cousin Rachel* Presented at the Rivoli', *New York Times*, 26 December 1952, p.20.

[4] See, for example, Barbara Creed, *The Monstrous Feminine: Film, Feminism, Psychoanalysis* (London: Routledge, 1993) and Clare Hansen, 'Stephen King: Powers of Horror', in Brian Docherty, ed., *American Horror Fiction: From Brockden Brown to Stephen King* (London: Macmillan, 1990).

[5] Lisa Tuttle, Introduction, in *Skin of the Soul* (London: Women's Press, 1990).

[6] Fred Stanley, 'Hollywood Shivers: The Studios are Busily Stirring Up a Grade A Witches Brew', *New York Times*, 28 May 1944, p.X3.

[7] *Motion Picture Herald*, 20 March 1943, p.1214.

[8] Frank S. Nugent, 'Jamaica Inn', *New York Times*, 12 October 1939, p.38.

[9] Bosley Crowther, '*Frenchman's Creek:* A Film of Romantic Adventure, with Joan Fontaine, Makes its Appearance at the Rivoli', *New York Times*, 21 September 1944, p.26.

[10] Stephen Neale, 'Melo Talk: On the Meaning and Use of the Term "Melodrama" in the American Trade Press', *Velvet Light Trap*, 32, 1993, p.69.

[11] Frank S. Nugent, 'Rebecca', *New York Times*, 29 March 1940, p.28.

[12] Bosley Crowther, '*My Cousin Rachel* Presented at the Rivoli', *New York Times*, 26 December 1952, p.20.

[13] Leo A. Handel, *Hollywood Looks at its Audience: A Report on Film Audience Research* (Urbana: University of Illinois Press, 1950). See also Mark Jancovich, 'The Meaning of Mystery: Genre, Marketing and the Universal Sherlock Holmes Series of the 1940s', *Film International*, 17, 2005, pp.34–45.

14   Ivan Butler, *Horror in the Cinema* (New York: Warner Paperback Library, 1970) and S. S. Prawer, *Caligari's Children: The Film as Tale of Terror* (New York: Oxford University Press, 1980). For a discussion of this tradition and the criticism on it, see Gregory Waller, 'Made-for-TV Horror Films', in Gregory Waller, ed., *American Horrors: Essays on the Modern American Horror Film* (Urbana: University of Illinois Press, 1987), pp.145–161.

15   Bosley Crowther, 'Screen: *The Birds*', *New York Times*, 1 April 1963, p.53.

16   Vincent Canby, 'Film: *Don't Look Now*, A Horror Tale', *New York Times*, 10 December 1973, p. 56.

17   Butler, *Horror in the Cinema* (1967); Carlos Clarens, *An Illustrated History of the Horror Film* (New York: Putnam, 1967); William K. Evenson, *Classics of the Horror Film: From the Silent Film to* The Exorcist (New York: Citadel, 1974); Alan Frank, *Horror Films* (London: Hamlyn, 1977); Denis Gifford, *A Pictorial History of the Horror Movies* (London: Hamlyn, 1973); and David Pirie, *A Heritage of Horror: The English Gothic Cinema 1946–1972* (London: Gordon Fraser, 1973).

Daphne du Maurier and Alfred Hitchcock

1   Recounted in Margaret Forster's indispensable biography, *Daphne du Maurier* (London: Chatto & Windus, 1993), p.8.

2   François Truffaut, *Hitchcock* (New York: Simon and Schuster, 1967), p.91.

3   Truffaut, *Hitchcock*, p.86.

4   The theme recurs throughout Hitchcock's work, most literally in the 1957 film starring Henry Fonda as *The Wrong Man*, most exuberantly in *North by Northwest* (1959).

5   Daphne du Maurier, *Jamaica Inn* (New York: Avon, 1991), p.74.

6   'We bought *Rebecca*, and we intend to make *Rebecca*'

summarised Selznick's attitude. See Donald Spoto's *The Dark Side of Genius: The Life of Alfred Hitchcock* (New York: Da Capo, 1999), p.213. David Thomson gives a subtle account of the 'uncommon trouble' Selznick had in his first collaboration with Hitchcock in *Showman: The Life of David O. Selznick* (New York: Knopf, 1992), pp.330–35.

7   Daphne du Maurier, *Rebecca* (London: Gollancz, 1938), p.200.

8   Daphne du Maurier, 'The Birds', in *The Apple Tree* (London: Gollancz, 1952), p.7.

9   Truffaut, *Hitchcock*, p.217.

'Last Night I Dreamt I Read *Rebecca* Again': Reading, Watching and Engaging With *Rebecca* in Fiction and Film

1   See, for instance, Nina Auerbach, *Daphne du Maurier: Haunted Heiress* (Philadelphia: University of Pennsylvania Press, 2000); Avril Horner and Sue Zlosnik, *Daphne du Maurier: Writing, Identity, and the Gothic Imagination* (London: Macmillan, 1998); Judy Simons, 'Rewriting the Love Story: the Reader as Writer in Daphne du Maurier's *Rebecca*', in Lynne Pearce and Gina Wisker, eds., *Fatal Attractions: Rescripting the Romance in Contemporary Literature and Film* (London: Pluto Press, 1998), pp.112–27; Patsy Stoneman, *Brontë Transformations: The Cultural Dissemination of* Jane Eyre *and* Wuthering Heights (London: Prentice-Hall/Harvester Wheatsheaf, 1996); Mary Ann Doane, *The Desire to Desire: The Woman's Film of the 1940s* (London: Macmillan, 1987); John Fletcher, 'Primal Scenes and the Female Gothic: *Rebecca* and *Gaslight*', *Screen*, 35, 4 (1995), 341–70; Ed Gallafent, 'Black Satin: Fantasy, Murder and the Couple in *Gaslight* and *Rebecca*', *Screen*, 29, 3 (1988), 84–103; Janet Harbord, 'Between Identification and Desire: Rereading *Rebecca*',

Feminist Review, 53 (Summer 1996), 95–107; Karen Hollinger, 'The Female Oedipal Drama of *Rebecca* from Novel to Film', *Quarterly Review of Film and Video*, 14, 4 (1993), 17–30; Alison Light, *Forever England: Femininity, Literature and Conservatism Between the Wars* (London: Routledge, 1991); Tania Modleski, *Loving with a Vengeance: Mass Produced Fantasies for Women* (London and New York: Methuen, 1984) and *The Women Who Knew Too Much: Hitchcock and Feminist Theory* (New York and London: Routledge, 1988); Helen Wheatley, 'Haunted Houses, Hidden Rooms: Women, Domesticity and the Female Gothic Adaptation on Television' in Jonathan Bignell and Stephen Lacey, eds., *Popular Television Drama* (Manchester: Manchester University Press, 2005), pp.149–65; Patricia White, *Uninvited: Classical Hollywood Cinema and Lesbian Representability* (Bloomington: Indiana University Press, 2000); Gina Wisker, 'Dangerous Borders: Daphne du Maurier's *Rebecca*: Shaking the Foundations of the Romance of Privilege, Partying and Place', *Journal of Gender Studies*, 12, 2 (2003), 83–97; Susan Hill, *Mrs de Winter* (London: Sinclair-Stevenson, 1993); Sally Beauman, *Rebecca's Tale* (London: Little, Brown, 2001).

[2] Jacqueline Bobo, 'The Color Purple: Black Women as Cultural Readers' in E. Deirdre Pribram ed., *Female Spectators: Looking at Film and Television* (London: Verso, 1988), pp.90–109; Stanley Fish, *Is There a Text in This Class?: The Authority of Interpretive Communities* (Cambridge, Mass and London: Harvard University Press, 1980); Janice Radway, *Reading the Romance: Women, Patriarchy and Popular Literature* (Chapel Hill and London: University of North Carolina Press, 1984); Jackie Stacey, *Stargazing: Hollywood Cinema and Female Spectatorship* (London: Routledge, 1994); Helen Taylor, *Scarlett's Women: 'Gone With the Wind' and its Female Fans* (New Brunswick:

Rutgers University Press, 1989) and 'Romantic Readers' in Helen Carr, ed., *From My Guy to Sci Fi: Genre and Women's Writing in the Postmodern World* (London: Pandora Press, 1989), pp.58–77.

3   Henry Jenkins, 'Reception theory and audience research: the mystery of the vampire's kiss' in Christine Gledhill and Linda Williams, eds., *Reinventing Film Studies* (London: Arnold, 2000), pp.167–169.

4   D. J. Taylor, 'Cultural Camouflage', *The Guardian*, 12 April 2003, http://books.guardian.co.uk/news/articles/0,,935289,00.html; Catherine Bennett, 'The Root of Britain's Culture Problem', *The Guardian*, 23 Oct 2003, http://www.guardian.co.uk/Columnists/Column/0,,1068850,00.html'.

5   Claire Armitstead, 'Read Again', *The Guardian*, 30 June 2003, http://arts.guardian.co.uk/features/story/0,,987770,00.html.

Drama in Daphne du Maurier: Spirit and Letter

1   Daphne du Maurier, *Rebecca*, 'adapted' by Clifford Williams for the production he directed in Bromley, 1990 (London: Samuel French, 1994).

2   Daphne du Maurier, *The Years Between* (New York: Doubleday, 1946); *September Tide* (London: Samuel French, 1949).

3   See Julie Holledge, *Innocent Flowers* (London: Virago, 1981).

4   *Frenchman's Creek* is available as a BBC Enterprises audio cassette (1990).

Index

Delphine du Maurier

Delphine du maurier

maurier

Delphine du maurier

Delphine du maurier

maurier

Delphine du maurier

Delphine du maurier

maurier

Delphine du maurier